The Powers of

# The Powers of Literacy:
## A Genre Approach to Teaching Writing

*Edited by*

Bill Cope and Mary Kalantzis

University of Pittsburgh Press

**UK** The Falmer Press, 4 John St, London WC1N 2ET
**USA** University of Pittsburgh Press, 127 North Bellefield Avenue, Pittsburgh, Pa.15260

First published in 1993 by The Falmer Press in the *Critical Perspectives on Literacy Series*, edited by Allan Luke

Library of Congress Catalog Card Number 93–60338

Library of Congress Cataloging in Publication Data are available on request

ISBN 0–8229–1179–5 (cl)
ISBN 0–8229–6104–0 (pbk)

Jacket design by Benedict Evans
Typeset in 9.5/11pt Bembo and Printed
by Graphicraft Typesetters Ltd, Hong Kong

# Contents

*Contents*

# Introduction

The series, Critical Perspectives on Literacy in Education, focuses on approaches to literacy education that directly address issues of access and equity in the fluid and uncertain cultural and economic conditions of the 1990s. These have included: James Gee's connection of sociolinguistic research on literacy with approaches to ideology and discourse, Carole Edelsky's development of an explicitly political orientation to American whole language pedagogy, David Buckingham's reappraisal of British television literacy and cultural studies curricula, Bill Green and contributors' poststructuralist agendas for the teaching of English, and Linda Christian-Smith and colleagues' explorations of feminist approaches to reading. As in these and other volumes in the series, *The Powers of Literacy* begins from the position that literacy education is central to how school systems and curricula produce power, identity and, ultimately, inequality. Any effective solution requires a reframing of teaching, textbooks and programs in ways that explicitly take up and rebuild the educational dynamics of culture and class, gender and colour.

Speaking of how dominant cultures and discourses work, Afro-American writer Audre Lorde (1990: 287) has commented that 'the master's tools will never dismantle the master's house.' The questions that her claim raises are at the heart of many current debates over pedagogy, literacy and social change. Her case is that particular knowledges and ways of knowing, writings and discourses — 'old blueprints of expectation and response' — are so deeply implicated in racism, patriarchy and dominant cultures that they cannot effectively be used to critique or displace those systems. These, she goes on to argue, 'must be altered at the same time as we alter the living conditions which are a result of those structures.'

The contributors to *The Powers of Literacy* take a contrasting approach to issues of writing, access and marginality. They begin from a shared insight that many working-class, migrant and Aboriginal children have been systematically barred from competence with those texts, knowledges and 'genres' that enable access to social and material resources. The culprits, they argue, are not limited to traditional pedagogies that disregard children's cultural and linguistic resources and set out to assimilate them into the fictions of mainstream culture. But the problem is also located in progressive 'process' and 'child-centred' approaches that appear to 'value differences but in so doing leave social relations of inequity fundamentally unquestioned.' Although the contributors to this volume engage in a vigorous and challenging debate about the emphases and consequences of 'genre' teaching, their shared goal is social and economic access via teaching which makes explicit how texts work.

Mary Kalantzis and Bill Cope began the Social Literacy Project over a decade ago, working with urban teachers and community members to develop social sciences curriculum for migrant and working-class students. The resultant curriculum materials provide students with sequenced instructional access to the powerful disciplinary knowledges, writing and research tools necessary for achievement in a school system where one's fate depends on the writing of formal year-end matriculation examinations. This approach has proven of continued value in several states and was recently applied to national adult literacy and numeracy programs.

In the 1980s this project was brought together with concurrent work by systemic linguists, previously introduced in this series by M.A.K. Halliday and James R. Martin's *Writing Science*. Then leading linguists and teachers — including Martin, Gunther Kress, Frances Christie and others in this volume — joined together to develop instructional approaches which focus principally on the teaching of expository writing. That work culminated in the influential Language and Education Research Network Project and the Disadvantaged Schools Project, which set out to implement 'genre approaches' to writing in Sydney schools.

*The Powers of Literacy* begins by setting these developments against the backdrop of international debates about literacy, equity and access. The volume builds from discussions of the instructional emphasis on 'genre' (as against, for instance, 'discourse' and 'register') and reappraisals of the significance of grammar, to specific curriculum planning cycles, examples of classroom implementation, instruction and assessment. Although the emphasis throughout is on writing, Anne Cranny-Francis provides an innovative application of conceptualisations of genre to literacy reading positions and practices.

In the 1980s Australian education has been the site of various curriculum developments and experiments supported by the Labor government's social justice policies. During that period educational progressivism has become a substantial force in Australian education, mainly via 'whole language' approaches in elementary schooling and 'personal growth' models in secondary English. As an alternative, Cope, Kalantzis and colleagues here offer a vision of a 'postprogressive' pedagogy, one which is intimately concerned with the achievement of minority and working-class children, girls and boys alike, through 'an explicit pedagogy for inclusion and access'.

*Allan Luke*
*James Cook University of North Queensland*

### Reference

LORDE, A. (1990) 'Age, Race, Class, and Sex: Women Redefining Difference', in R. FERGUSON, M. GEVER, T.T. MINH-HA and C. WEST (eds), *Out There: Marginalization and Contemporary Cultures*, New York and Cambridge, Mass., New Museum of Contemporary Art and MIT Press, pp. 281–8.

# Foreword

This book provides the first easy access for non-Australians to the ideas of an influential group of Australian educators about the teaching of writing. Its publication is important for several reasons.

Anyone teaching writing has what Linda Flower calls a 'situated theory'. That theory is based on some combination of our own previous experience, as teachers and/or writers, and what we learn from others — those who teach writing and those who analyse writing processes, practices and products. It should be that the more varied the new ideas we consider in formulating our situated theories, the better. Unfortunately, in the United States one set of ideas about teaching writing, often called 'process writing', has become so dominant — if not in classrooms, at least in professional journals and conferences — that it is hard even to conceive of alternatives.

Some language educators especially concerned about the continuing failures of language and cultural minority children, such as Lisa Delpit, have criticised process writing theories for being based on research in mainstream classrooms and only working well there. But it is easier to be sure about what we don't want to go back to (short-answer exercises and lessons on parts of speech) than to imagine what going forward, 'on beyond process' as some Australians refer to the needed next step, might include. It is here that this book can make a valuable contribution: it presents the ideas of a group of Australians, collectively called the 'genre group', offering new possibilities to be explored.

Being open to the ideas developed in the book may not be easy for some readers. I have met resistance to such openness in my course on the teaching of writing at Harvard. Since learning about the Australian genre work in 1991, I have shown my classes (most of them teachers) a demonstration video about that work made by the Disadvantaged Schools Program in Sydney (described in the historical essay that ends this book). It shows moments in a unit in which primary grade children are learning about and writing a report on mealworms. In the post-video discussion I realised how hard it was for these teachers to consider possible benefits of the explicit modelling of a generic form of 'reports' shown in the film. With the help of this book, I shall try again next year in a different way. I shall start with the chapter by Jim Martin — not because he is the theoretician of the group, but because he analyses a piece of 'writing that counts' from out-of-school life: a paper on 'Innovative Fisheries Management' presented to the Canadian

Wildlife Federation by one of its retiring directors. If we can agree that we should be helping students to develop the competences to write texts like this one on topics of personal interest and concern, then we can proceed more openly to consider his colleagues' ideas about how to do just that.

As the editors explain in their excellent overview chapters, those colleagues disagree, openly and vigorously, among themselves — about the linguistic purity or dynamic variation of generic forms, about the optimum classroom balance between immersion in text models and instruction in text features, and about how to combine the educational goals of socialisation and critique. The deliberate presentation, even highlighting, of these disagreements is itself a gift to sceptical readers. It should make it easier for us to take from these thoughtful colleagues new ideas for our own writing classrooms.

*Courtney B. Cazden*
*Harvard Graduate School of Education*

# Introduction: How a Genre Approach to Literacy Can Transform the Way Writing Is Taught

*Bill Cope and Mary Kalantzis*

A genre approach to literacy teaching involves being explicit about the way language works to make meaning. It means engaging students in the role of apprentice with the teacher in the role of expert on language system and function. It means an emphasis on content, on structure and on sequence in the steps that a learner goes through to become literate in a formal educational setting. It means a new role for textbooks in literacy learning. It means teaching grammar again.

At first sight, these generalisations about genre literacy teaching sound decidedly old-fashioned. In fact, in some respects they sound rather like one of the regular clarion calls we hear from the 'back to basics' movement. Nothing could be further from the truth. In its strongest, most creative and most exciting moments, genre literacy teaching represents a fundamentally new educational paradigm. It is based on an understanding of the nature of language quite different from that of traditional grammar. Not only does it move beyond traditional literacy pedagogies which stress formal correctness; it also goes beyond the process pedagogies which stress 'natural' learning through 'doing' writing. Genre literacy teaching is not liberal progressivism. Nor is it part of a movement 'back to basics'. Genre literacy is attempting to create a new pedagogical space.

This book documents an educational experiment that began in Sydney, Australia. Although the results of this experiment, we believe, are of international significance, the development of genre literacy needs to be explained in the first instance in terms of the politics and sociology of Australian education. In a nutshell, traditional curriculum was officially abandoned in Australia in the 1970s. There seemed to be very good educational reasons for this at the time — reasons that are still as strong today as they were then. Yet by the 1980s it was clear that the new progressivist curriculum was not producing the goods. It was not producing any noticeable improvement in patterns of educational attainment. In fact, all it seemed to do was make teachers' jobs harder. Despite the official paradigm shift, in practice many teachers found it more comfortable to stay with their old ways of teaching.

This is why the genre-based approach to literacy has been the subject of an extraordinary wave of interest in Australia, particularly over the last five years.

Teachers know a fresh approach is needed. And now that the genre-based approach to literacy has become well established in Australia, the interest is steadily spreading further afield — to North America, Britain, Scandinavia, Israel. Yet many people still have their reservations. The liberal progressivists claim that genre literacy entails a revival of transmission pedagogy. It seems to mean learning formal 'language facts' again. It is sometimes claimed that genre literacy teaching is founded on a pedagogy that will lead us back to the bad old days of authoritarian classrooms where some students found the authority congenial, and they succeeded, while other students found the authority uncongenial, and they failed. Conservative educators, on the other hand, are suspicious of the claims of genre literacy to be a strategy for equity in education, to give social groups historically marginalised in one way or another better access to social mobility through education. Is this a threat to standards, to the status of the Western canon with its great books, to the notion of elite curriculum for elite social and cultural responsibility?

If the debate around genre is a vibrant one — as the genre theorists line up against the external bastions of traditional or progressivist pedagogies — the debate within the genre school is at times even more heated. Among the proponents of genre as a matter of principle, differing views emerge on the nature of language and on viable or worthwhile pedagogy. The protagonists in the discussions within the genre school at various times label each other, according to their purported inclinations, traditional pedagogues or progressivist pedagogues. Nor do they all have the same theory of language informing their work, including even the definition of 'genre' itself. To be faithful to the intellectual dynamism in the debate, this book attempts to reflect the diversity in the argument about genre literacy teaching in Australia. As the idea of genre spreads, this is increasingly an international debate, too. Accordingly, we do not attempt to present a unified account of genre in literacy learning. The authors who have contributed to this volume only agree on the concept of genre in principle. They agree on the pedagogical project of genre literacy learning.

For all the authors of this book, genre is a category that describes the relation of the social purpose of text to language structure. It follows that in learning literacy, students need to analyse critically the different social purposes that inform patterns of regularity in language — the whys and the hows of textual conventionality, in other words. Beyond this the book deliberately sets out to represent a variety of different theories which attempt to describe what is in genre and how genre literacy pedagogy might be realised most effectively.

In the overall scheme of the book the purpose of this chapter is to introduce the basic principles of genre literacy teaching to educators. It discusses the educational dilemmas that genre literacy has set out to address. It also discusses the educational experiments that members of the genre school have mounted in an attempt to tackle these dilemmas, in which the concept of genre has frequently proved very helpful. The chapter then discusses some of the key debates within the genre school — moments of self-doubt, self-reflection and dissension which confirm our belief that this is a dynamic movement. It is a movement which, although based on some fundamental shared assumptions about language and education, has the positive potential to mean many things to many people and to enrich different people's educational practices and understandings in different ways. It is hoped that this book will have a similar effect.

### The Context: Why a New Approach to Literacy?

The question 'Why a new approach to literacy?' is the subject of Chapter 2. To answer it, we need to take two steps back. These are simultaneously historical steps and theoretical steps in the story of literacy pedagogy — crucial steps, nevertheless, if we are to put in context the essential problems the genre school set out to address. These two critical steps we will call traditional curriculum and progressivist curriculum.

Traditional curriculum, as much as the progressivist curriculum, is an invention of modernity. Yet ironically — even deceptively — traditional curriculum has pretensions to timelessness, as a curriculum which is based on the solidity of the classics. Traditional literacy teaching forged itself this link to the high culture of classical Greece and Rome by constructing what was ostensibly a universal 'traditional grammar' out of descriptions of Latin and Ancient Greek. Latin and Greek, in fact, were the main subjects in early modern education. Traditional grammar does, indeed, have some value in describing highly inflected and relatively regular languages like Latin or Greek. Applied to modern languages such as English, however, it simply does not work very well.

So why did traditional grammar become a critical element in literacy pedagogy from the beginnings of the Enlightenment in the sixteenth century right through the revolutionary universalisation of mass education in the nineteenth century and well beyond the decline of Latin and Greek as school subjects in the second half of the twentieth century? The answer to this question lies in the real modernity of traditional grammar. Traditional grammar is based on a uniquely modern logicoscientific culture and epistemology. It is based on the idea that the world can be described in terms of 'facts', rules and regularities epitomised in tables to conjugate verbs or decline nouns. Language, it seems, is something that can be meaningfully visualised in taxonomies and rationalised into tables arranged across the two-dimensional space of the textbook page. Nothing could be further from the classical pedagogy of historical reality in which grammar could never have been visualised in this way. In ancient Greece and Rome grammar was a social practice integrally related to dialectic or rhetoric and learnt in apprenticeship to masters of those arts.

The method in the apparent madness of traditional grammar was in teaching the epistemic culture and logic of modernity. Most immediately, it taught a certain way of transcribing reality. Yes, conservative educators are right: even learning Latin was not for its own sake; it was neither totally irrelevant nor completely mindless, as the progressivists would like us to believe. Teaching Latin the modern way, you also taught a certain sort of thinking. Applying traditional grammar to the teaching of English, the role of literacy learning acquired the same sort of social mission. By teaching parts of speech, by demanding standards of correctness, by being prescriptive about what were ostensibly language facts, teachers were teaching students respect, discipline, order. Transmission pedagogy and rote learning were the cultural artefacts of classrooms whose microenvironments anticipated the disciplined order of the modern world. This was the serious business of traditional grammar. This was its moral economy.

There was also its superficial business: don't split infinitives; say 'she did it' instead of 'she done it'; say 'isn't' instead of 'ain't'. Sometimes these sorts of rules were simply a waste of time, or even themselves embarrassingly 'incorrect' for many social contexts. There is a time and a place for many of the usages that traditional grammar deemed incorrect. Yet even in its most superficial moments of pedantry, traditional grammar had a social function, and that was to exclude, to mark as wrong and even to fail discourses that the school curriculum labelled incorrect — incorrect, that is, by the criteria of the self-appointed 'standard English' of the middle class. The logic of traditional curriculum was to serve up a universal 'standard', with pretensions to factualness and cultural universality, pass those who found the standard and its underlying cultural logic congenial, fail those who didn't, and then ascribe the consequent differences in social and educational outcome to individual 'ability' (Chapter 2).

Much the same generalisations can be made about that other element of traditional literacy curriculum: what is considered 'literary'; what deserves a place in the 'canon' and what might be considered a model of 'good' writing. In early modern curriculum the canon consisted of the classics of ancient Greece and Rome. With the rise of mass institutionalised education in vernacular languages, the canon was broadened to include modern 'classics', but under the pretence that there is a continuous Western tradition, superior to others. Again, the student's relation to the canon was to be one of uncomplaining ingestion, even if the canon bore a more familiar relation to the lived experience of some students than it did to others. If the canon did not 'work' for you, with all its gender, ethnic and class biases, you would probably fail (Cope and Kalantzis, 1992).

By the 1970s, many Australian educators were rejecting traditional literacy pedagogy, with its traditional grammar and literary canon. But the critique was from the point of view of a paradigm of progressivism that was emerging to official and institutional dominance in education. Belatedly perhaps, Australian progressivism as it flowered in the 1970s was founded on the critiques of traditional curriculum initiated by Dewey and Montessori at the turn of the twentieth century. The ensuing pedagogical revolution was nothing if not thorough, or at least it would seem to be that if one were to take the official proclamations of educational administrations at their word. Hardly a departmental syllabus remained that was not radically transformed by progressivist pedagogy. In literacy, for example, grammar and other aspects of the teaching of language through formal conventions were out — replaced by 'process writing' and 'whole language'. Nowhere in the world was the transformation in literacy pedagogy so radical, officially and on paper, if not always so thoroughly in classroom reality (NSW Department of School Education, 1987; Kalantzis and Cope, 1988b).

Following Dewey, students were now to be active learners, to learn by doing, to learn through practical experience rather than learn facts by rote. Learning was to be meaningful rather than formal. The most effective learning, it was assumed, would take place when it was relevant to the individual rather than institutionally imposed. Curriculum was to stress process over content. Textbooks which, in their nature, seemed to dictate content, were definitely out. Drawing directly on key American theorists — whose views enjoyed, incidentally, a much wider official and professional acceptance in Australia than they ever did in their homeland — a new pedagogical regime of 'whole language' and 'process writing' was based on an analogy drawn between the way children learn oral language and learn literacy at school (Graves, 1983; Goodman, 1986). Authentic resources, things that students wanted to read and write and which were of relevance and interest to their own lives, would be used instead of textbooks. The focus of the writing curriculum would no longer be on language in the abstract but on the meaning the child wanted to communicate.

Central to this literacy pedagogy was individual student motivation instead of the rule driven authoritarianism of traditional literacy teaching. The theory even went so far as to posit a concept of ownership; student texts were owned by their writers, and the teacher was no more than a resource assisting the student when called upon, a facilitator rather than the font of fixed knowledge about language, knowledge that had once been inscribed in the rules of school grammar. Student experience and communicative intent would now be brought to the fore rather than language facts and the rules of 'correct' speaking or writing. As there could be no 'proper language', there could also be no 'disadvantaged' student.

By the early 1990s, progressivist pedagogy has developed well beyond Dewey's avowed cultural and linguistic assimilationism and his notion that experiential literacy learning should always end with students learning standard English (Dewey, 1916). In fact, it has moved towards a relativistic theory of cultural and linguistic pluralism. This can be found in new institutional practices (principles of curriculum diversification and school or teacher-based curriculum), in the theories of literacy mentioned above, and, most recently, in 'postmodern' and 'poststructuralist' theories of education (Aronowitz and Giroux, 1991; Ellsworth, 1989). The key term in this latest version of progressivism is 'difference'. There is no superior Western canon any more, only different literary and cultural traditions. Just as there is no longer thought to be a singular, universal, canonical knowledge, there can be no fixed language facts, only language and dialect variation that is relative to different cultural needs and interests. The notion that there might be a 'standard' of correct English was only ever sheer prejudice, it is argued. Central to this new vision of literacy is the concept of student 'voice'. The teacher is no more than a facilitator who gives students space to voice their own interests in their own discourse. In some very revealing ways, the concept of voice is where the low theories of process writing and whole language meet the high theories of postmodernism and poststructuralism (Chapter 2).

In Australia the 'back to basics' people have shouted in protest at the way teaching has changed with the rise to official favour of progressivism, and the media have conveniently often heard their call. 'Confronted daily with glaring examples of poor spelling and grammar, the language purists are targeting "lefty-trendy" teaching methods, as well as a lack of funding, in their fight for reform. . . . Good news. Schools are swinging back to the old values: grammar is on the agenda again.' This indicates the tone of the cover story of *The Bulletin/ Newsweek* on 19 November 1991. In the United States the debate about 'political correctness' has led to a classical revivalism of sorts, in an attempt to meet the alleged onslaught of feminism, multiculturalism and the like — movements which supposedly threaten the educational place of the Western canon (Cope and Kalantzis, 1992). E.D. Hirsch is one of the more vocal members of this movement, and particularly influential in the debate about elementary and secondary schooling. By the end of elementary school, Hirsch spells out in his *First Dictionary of Cultural Literacy*, every student should know about Jekyll and Hyde, Julius Caesar, King Arthur and Rudyard Kipling, to take a random page from the list that makes up the 'Literature' section of the book. The 'English' section takes us squarely back to rules of correct usage: 'abbreviation, adjective, adverb, agreement. . . .' (Hirsch, 1988). Traditional curriculum, in other words, is very much alive and well, as is clearly evident in its vociferous protests against progressivism.

Far from being part of the 'back to basics' movement, genre literacy teaching objects equally strongly to both traditional and progressivist pedagogy. So, taking the progressivist critique of traditional curriculum as given, the task remains to analyse critically the principles and practice of progressivist pedagogy and show how it fails for a number of reasons. First, it should be exposed as culture bound, not open. The progressivist mould with its prescriptions for individual control, student-centred learning, student motivation, purposeful writing, individual ownership, the power of voice matches the moral temper and cultural aspirations of middle-class children from child-centred households. Second, its pedagogy of immersion 'naturally' favours students whose voice is closest to the literate culture of power in industrial society. Third, it is no more motivating than traditional curriculum, particularly for students who do not see the immediate point of learning literacy or even like school. Fourth, it simply reproduces educational inequities, given the inequities in the social value placed on 'different' voices in the world outside school. Fifth, far from elevating teachers to the role of professional, it reduces them to the role of manager. Sixth, progressivism often ends up fragmented, eclectic photocopier curriculum, where, to give content to the curriculum, the teacher brings in photocopies, often from old textbooks cast in the most traditional pedagogical mould. Seventh, and finally, the analogy of orality and literacy in the process writing and whole language approaches to literacy simply does not work. Orality and literacy could hardly be more different, not only in their discursive structures but in the different nature of the learning process that is involved. 'Natural' literacy learning is simply an inefficient use of time and resources. It leads to a pedagogy which encourages students to produce texts in a limited range of written genres, mostly personalised recounts. This is why the texts generated in the process writing classroom ('choose your own topic'; 'say what you feel like saying') often end up monotonous and repetitive. Worse, the most powerful written genres are those generically and grammatically most distant from orality — for example, scientific reports which attempt to objectify the world, or arguments which are especially designed to persuade.

From the point of view of the genre theorists, these are the theoretical reasons why the pedagogical regime of progressivism has failed in practice. Despite the revolutionary overturn of traditional pedagogy in Australian education systems, there is no evidence to suggest that the change brought about any improvement in opportunities for those students traditionally marginalised in school. This is why, practically, so many people have found genre literacy teaching such an attractive alternative. It is precisely why genre literacy is regarded with so much hostility by the protagonists of the progressivist as well as the traditional curriculum. In the fray, both these protagonists cast genre literacy teaching on the side of the enemy. The progressivists say the genre theorists, by teaching a new set of 'language facts', advocate a transmission pedagogy in the mould of the traditional curriculum. The traditionalists distrust the way the genre theorists lean towards a concern for cultural differences and insist that schools should attempt to achieve equitable outcomes. All these accusations are based on ignorance of what genre theorists are really saying, for, as this book will show, the objections of genre theorists to progressivism and to a revived traditional curriculum are, in fact, equally strong.

## Genre in Literacy Pedagogy

'Genre' is a term used in literacy pedagogy to connect the different forms text take with variations in social purpose. Texts are different because they do different things. So, any literacy pedagogy has to be concerned, not just with the formalities of how texts work, but also with the living social reality of texts-in-use. How a text works is a function of what it is for. Let's say an adolescent's interest is in fat wheels for cars. If they want to explain to someone how to fit fat wheels onto their car, they will tell them how to handle the wheels, what to do first to fit them on, what to do next and so on. If they want to discuss the advantages and disadvantages of fat wheels with their peers, they can raise various points for and against and assess the relative merits of the opposing views. If they want to argue with their parent why they want to buy fat wheels for their car, then their arguments will be arranged in such a way that they have the best chance of convincing (Kalantzis and Wignell, 1988). As text structures — grammatically in other words — these three oral texts will inevitably be very different from each other, and we can account for the differences in terms of the social purpose of each text. Explaining, discussing and arguing each involves the generation of a type of text structure peculiar to that social process. The reasons for the textual differences can be located in the social purpose of each text.

Genres are social processes. Texts are patterned in reasonably predictable ways according to patterns of social interaction in a particular culture. Social patterning and textual patterning meet as genres. Genres are textual interventions in society; and society itself would be nothing without language in all its patterned predictability. It follows that genres are not simply created by individuals in the moment of their utterance; to have meaning, they must be social. Individual speakers and writers act within a cultural context and with a knowledge of the different social effects of different types of oral and written text. Genres, moreover, give their users access to certain realms of social action and interaction, certain realms of social influence and power (Kress, 1989b, Ch. 1). In our commonsense understanding of lawyer's language, or academic language, or chess player's language, we know these are social realms from which a lot of people are excluded, and this pattern of social exclusion is marked linguistically. Learning new genres gives one the linguistic potential to join new realms of social activity and social power.

In the world outside schooling, the world of self-taught and self-inducted social mobility, immersion in the social practice of a genre is sometimes sufficient to 'pick up the language', so to speak, although there are obviously other institutional barriers that might still make this impossible or all but impossible. This is not to imply that language users need to be significantly aware of the linguistic 'how' of their activity, even if they are largely aware of the social 'why' of a particular discourse-in-use. You do not have to know about language to be able to use language. It is not necessary to know your linguistic 'hows' to be able to put text into social use and realise its potential 'whys'.

In school, however, there are two sorts of impulses that pull language away from this usual condition. The first is the social role yet inherent limitations of institutionalised schooling. School is the most significant of all sites of potential social mobility. Expressed in terms of language, schooling has the potential to induct students into a very broad range of genres with a broad range of potential social effectivities. However, it cannot do this by immersion alone, nor would that be an efficient use of resources. School is a rather peculiar place. Its mission is peculiar and so are the discursive forms which optimally carry that mission. It is at once a reflector of the outside world and discursively very different from the outside world. Because school needs to concentrate the outside world into the generalisations that constitute school knowledge, it is epistemologically and discursively quite different from most of everyday life in the outside world (Cazden, 1988).

So, as a site of cultural reproduction with an extremely broad charter, schooling is typically theoretical, concentrating knowledge into generalisations. When it comes to speaking about discourse itself — how language is used in school and in the outside world towards which school is oriented — schooling necessarily invokes a metalanguage, a language with which to make generalisations about language. This is just a matter of efficiency and a matter of school's peculiar relation to the world: of but not in the world. The argument of the genre theorists against the progressivists about the uniquely important place of metalanguage in schooling is 'let's not abandon the metalanguage, the grammar; education is the only social site where grammar as metalanguage is really important.' Against the traditionalists the genre theorists' argument is, 'let's always explain the meta-language in terms of social purpose; if the project of school is social access and part of that is access to genres of a variety of realms of social power, let's make that connection of structure and purpose explicit; let's keep grammar obviously relevant.'

The second reason why the 'hows' of language need to be brought to the fore in education is schooling's unique social mission to provide historically marginalised groups equitable access to as broad a range of social options as possible. This may include groups marginalised by reason of culture, or gender, or socio-economic background, or the social meaning ascribed to 'race'. Even in its most conservative moments, schooling in a democratic society boasts about creating equality of opportunity, and as educators we are duty bound to take this injunction at its word. However, for those outside the discourses and cultures of certain realms of power and access, acquiring these discourses requires explicit explanation: the ways in which the 'hows' of text structure produce the 'whys' of social effect. If you live with the 'hows' — if you have a seventh sense for how the 'hows' do their social job by virtue of having been brought up with those discourses — then they will come to you more or less 'naturally'. Students from historically marginalised groups, however, need explicit teaching more than students who seem destined for a comfortable ride into the genres and cultures of power.

This is genre literacy in principle. All the genre theorists agree on genre at this level of generality. Beyond this, however, there is no precise, common, understanding of the term. J.R. Martin (Chapters 5 and 6) claims it is possible to analyse language at a number of levels, where phonology/graphology realises grammar, realises semantics, realises register, realises genre, realises ideology (Martin, 1991b–c). Gunther Kress (Chapter 1) regards genre as a part of register, along with dialect, mode, plot and so on. Anne Cranny-Francis (Chapter 4) uses the term 'genre' in a way closer to the tools of the trade of literary criticism: to analyse text forms such as science fiction in order to account for the way in which feminist science fiction texts, for example, play the generic game but only in order to be subversive of its conventional textual features and social intent. Frances

Christie (Chapter 7) uses the term to analyse classroom discourse according to its patterns of predictability. Kalantzis and Cope (Chapters 2 and 3) want to force the concept to take on issues of cultural diversity and address general principles of pedagogy.

In a sense, the divergences are the essence of the vitality of the genre literacy movement. Sometimes they are just a matter of talking about different things. At other times they are matters of dispute with theoretical and practical implications. Whatever the differences, however, the genre theorists all believe that genre literacy leads to a third pedagogical direction, beyond traditional and progressivist curriculum. This third direction lies in the interstices of the debate, not in any one understanding of genre literacy at this point. From this perspective, the disputes are more interesting than any of the tentative answers.

In order to discuss some of the key disputes, however, we will first present the bare bones of just one view of genre — the J.R. Martin view. We present this view as a point of reference simply because, to date, it has had the broadest educational influence and is most commonly associated with genre literacy pedagogy, both by its critics and by its supporters. It was the Martin view of genre that was used in the LERN Project for the NSW Department of School Education, conducted by the Literacy and Education Research Network (LERN) — 'pushed' in some respects for the sake of consistency and getting the job done (Chapter 8 and the Bibliographical Essay). The following account is drawn from the publications that came out of that project (Macken *et al.*, 1989a–d).

J.R. Martin's own work started with a series of research projects that set out to analyse the textual demands of school literacy. Just what sorts of texts did schools expect students to generate? On what basis were some texts regarded as more successful than others? (Eggins, Wignell and Martin, 1987; Wignell, Martin and Eggins, 1987; Martin, 1986a, 1989, 1990b, 1991d, 1993). Among the genres identified as important to school literacy for the purposes of the LERN project were, to list six key examples, report, explanation, procedure, discussion, recount and narrative. To give some extremely synoptic content to just a few of these examples: reports are factual texts which describe the way things are, be these things natural phenomena, social phenomena or technical phenomena as humans interact with nature (their functions). They are frequently used in school in social studies and science (their educational context). As texts, they usually start with general classification which locates the phenomena, followed by successive elements contributing to a description, such as types, parts and their functions, qualities, uses or habits and so on (their schematic structure). The focus in reports is on generic participants, without temporal sequence and mostly using the simple present tense. Considerable use is made of 'being' and 'having' clauses (their lexico-grammatical features).

Procedures are factual texts designed to describe how something is accomplished through a sequence of actions or steps. They are more about processes than things (functions). In school they are frequently used in art, cookery and science, for example (educational context). Procedures mostly commence with a statement of goal, followed by an ordered series of steps (schematic structure). They usually centre on generalised human agents such as 'you' or 'the experimenter', use the simple present tense, link the steps in the procedure with temporal conjunctive relations such as 'then', 'now' or 'next', and mainly use material/action clauses (lexico-grammatical features). Recounts retell events for the purpose of informing or entertaining: diaries, personal letters, descriptions of events and so on (functions). In school, children's first writings are usually recounts, and the genre continues to have currency throughout schooling: for example, reporting on science experiments and some forms of 'creative' writing (educational context). Recounts characteristically begin with a contextualising orientation, followed by a series of events and often conclude with a reorientation (schematic structure). The focus in recounts is on individual participants, with the text sequenced temporally, often in the past tense (lexico-grammatical features).

Finally, narratives are texts that do not pretend to be factual, even though they might be closely linked to actual or vicarious experience. They set out to amuse, to entertain or to instruct (functions). In school, narratives are frequently expected in 'creative writing' (educational context). Narratives begin with an orientation which introduces and contextualises the participants. This may be followed by an evaluation which foreshadows the general direction of the story. The narrative develops via one or more complications. These then come to a resolution, and possibly a reorientation that returns to the scene that was set in the orientation and evaluation (schematic structure). Characteristic language features include specific individual participants, use of the past tense, temporal conjunctions and the use of material or action processes in the complication and resolution stages particularly, compared to relational and mental processes in the orientation and evaluation stages (lexico-grammatical features) (Macken *et al.*, 1989b).

The injunction to link social purpose to text structure leads to an understanding of language very different from that of traditional grammar. Starting with the question of purpose, analysis of the text proceeds by looking at the structure of the whole text. Only then does it account for the progress of the whole text in terms of what happens in sentences and clauses. Unlike traditional grammar which starts with words as 'parts of speech' and rarely gets further than dissecting clauses and sentences, genre analysis is concerned primarily with whole texts and their social functions. Sentence and clause analysis is only performed in order to explain the workings of the whole text and how it realises its social purpose.

How, then, is this linguistic conception of genre realised in classrooms? Research in implementing the Martin model of genre (Chapter 8 and the Bibliographical Essay) through the Disadvantaged Schools Program in Sydney came up with a teaching-learning cycle represented in the figure of a wheel. This cycle was also used in the LERN Project (see Figure 1).

The wheel is divided into three phases. In the first modelling phase students are exposed to a number of texts that exemplify the genre in question. If the subject was science and the topic was dolphins, for example, students might read texts on sea mammals from various sources. Generically, these texts are most likely to be reports. This could lead to a discussion of what the texts are for (functions), how the information in the reports is organised (schematic structure) and aspects of the way the text 'speaks' (lexico-grammatical features). Phase two involves joint negotiation of a class text. The first element in this stage is study of the field and the context of the genre: students observe, research, interview, discuss, take notes, draw diagrams and so on. This is followed by joint construction of a class text, in which students participate in the process of writing a report, guided by the teacher. The teacher acts as a scribe as the students contribute to a jointly constructed text which approximates the schematic structure of report genre and employs the key lexico-grammatical features of a report. In the third

Figure 1.   *The Martin/DSP 'Wheel' Model of Genre Literacy Pedagogy*

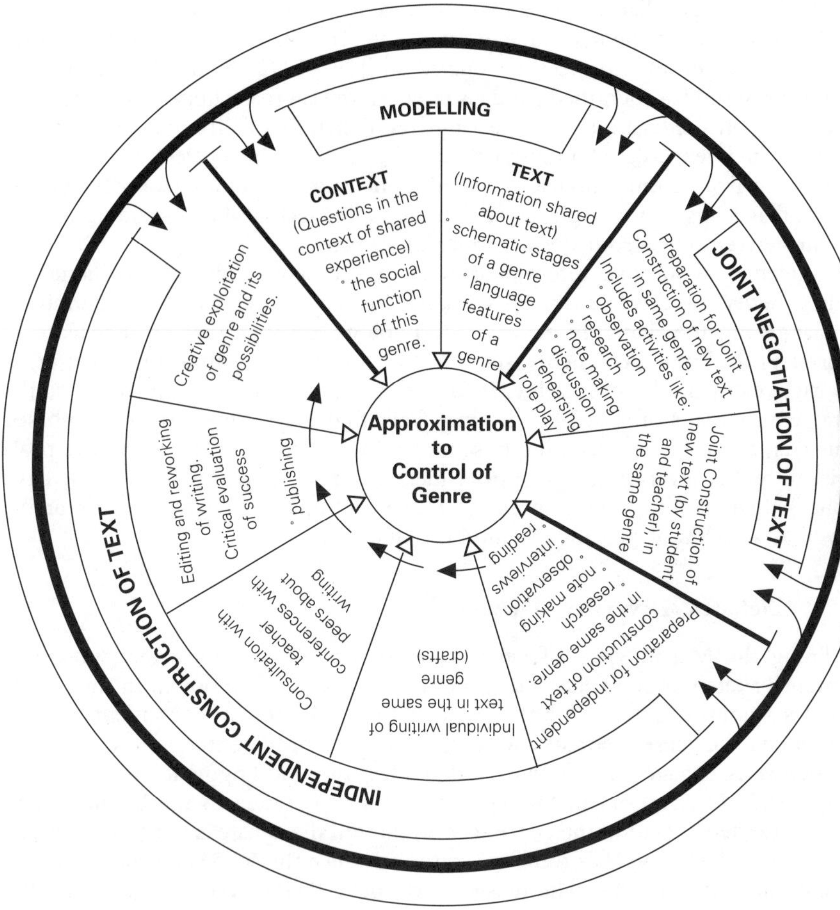

**MODELLING**

**CONTEXT**
(Questions in the context of shared experience)
· the social function of this genre.

**TEXT**
(Information shared about text)
· schematic stages of a genre
· language features of a genre

**JOINT NEGOTIATION OF TEXT**

Preparation for Joint Construction of new text in same genre. Includes activities like:
· observation
· research
· note making
· discussion
· rehearsing
· role play

Joint Construction of new text (by student and teacher), in the same genre

**Approximation to Control of Genre**

Preparation for independent construction of text in the same genre:
· research
· note making
· observation
· interviews
· reading

Individual writing of text in the same genre (drafts)

**INDEPENDENT CONSTRUCTION OF TEXT**

Consultation with teacher conferences with peers about writing

Editing and reworking of writing. Critical evaluation of success

· publishing

Creative exploitation of genre and its possibilities.

Source:   Macken *et al.* (1989b).

and final phase students independently construct their own reports: preparing with more work on the substantive field; drafting their own report; conferencing with peers and the teacher about their individual writing efforts; critically re-evaluating their texts as they edit for publication; and then, perhaps, creatively exploiting the genre to represent other fields. The cycle can then be repeated, working on progressively more sophisticated aspects of the report genre (Macken *et al.*, 1989b). The issue of text assessment and evaluation is also a critical part of genre theory (Chapter 9).

The process of developing a student's familiarity with a text is, on the one hand, linguistic, moving from orality to forms of literacy progressively more distant from the grammar of speech. On the other hand, the process is also epistemological. As students are inducted into the discourse and the field knowledge of school subjects, they move from commonsense to a kind of uncommonsense — the uncommonsense that carries technical and specialist knowledges which have their own peculiar ways of making meaning in the world.

In an analysis of the discourse of science in school and on worksites, another genre literacy research project conducted in 1991–1992 by the Disadvantaged Schools Program has identified parallels between the language demands of different stages of science education and the language demands of different occupational positions in science-based industries (see Figure 2). The project documents a progression from commonsense knowledge, from texts that are closer to speech, to texts that — by virtue of the increasing degree of technicality — end up further and further removed from the grammar of speech.

Students are moving into a workforce which, with industry restructuring, requires fewer and fewer unskilled workers. Moreover, the nature of technological change and the changing nature of technology are such that written texts — reports, procedures, arguments and the like — are becoming an increasingly important element of working life. If education is to remain relevant simply to the work requirements of students who may later find employment in science-based industries, and if literacy learning in school is to give students the discursive tools to rise to higher levels in the workplace hierarchy than they might otherwise have reached, then learning science needs to be viewed quite explicitly as a discursive as well as a technical process of cultural induction.

### Debates, Diversity, Dissent

Outlining the Martin view of genre literacy is to do no more than present a thumbnail sketch of one version of genre in practice at one moment in time. This provides a point of reference both to locate the main areas of agreement in principle among the genre theorists and to indicate some of the general lines of debate. The debate is engaged along two related axes: the one linguistic and the other pedagogical. The authors in this book represent the range of the linguistic and pedagogical debate within the genre school, though the debate is not foregrounded here because the purpose of the book is to introduce the scope and the principles of genre literacy teaching. The tensions are, nevertheless, critical to reading the book and to finding a version of genre that meets one's own pedagogical predispositions. To follow the debate in greater, and necessarily more technical, detail, the reader can use the historical and bibliographical material that forms the conclusion to this book (Bibliographical Essay and Bibliography).

Taking the linguistic element of the debate first, just what is this concept 'genre'? Here the debate within the genre school is mostly between adherents of the Martin line and those with a looser set of sympathies in the direction of the Kress view (Chapters 1 and 8). Kress expresses concern about Martin's apparent project of infinitely continuing to classify new genres as a result of educational practice. In basic terms, teachers keep stumbling over important 'new' texts which just don't seem to fit the generic descriptions. What if something is not quite a report, not quite a recount and not quite a procedure? The process of classification, he argues, seems at times to be heading in the direction of a new formalism, where the 'correct' way to write a report is presented to students in the form of generic models and exegeses of schematic structure.

Kress, by comparison, is less interested in classifying textual forms than he

*Figure 2. The Language of Science in School and Work*

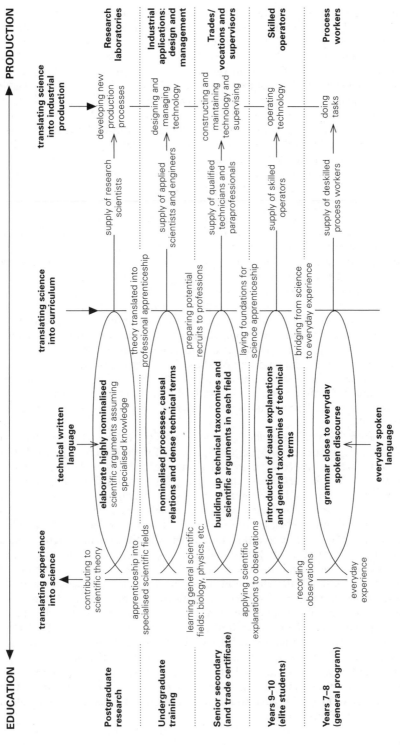

*Source: Rose, McInnes and Korner (1992).*

is in the generative capacities and potentials of using certain kinds of text for certain social purposes. In a sense then, Kress has remained closer to the origins of genre literacy in Halliday's systemic functional linguistics (Halliday, 1985a and the Bibliographical Essay). Even though Halliday does not use the concept of genre, Kress's use of the term remains close in spirit to Halliday's use of the concept 'register'. This is not to say that Kress's 'genre' is equivalent to Halliday's 'register'. Halliday's linguistic analysis pivots on register variation — the inter-relation of field, or what a text is about; tenor, which explains the interpersonal relations in the text; and mode, which demonstrates how the text interacts with the world. The important point for Halliday, however, is that register is not a basis for classifying texts into formal categories, but a tool for analysing texts in their infinite variety and subtle variations. This is closer to Kress's anti-formalist inclinations than to Martin's notion of genre.

A second linguistic difference is that Kress starts by describing the social relations between the participants before he begins to take apart a text. Martin, on the other hand, advocates 'a semiotic theory of the social' and starts with the text itself. By disentangling the layers of register, genre and ideology in text, Martin believes that the critically literate reader will be able to discover all they need to know about the social context of the text for the purposes of a semiotic analysis. Hasan, who follows Halliday's analysis of register — his theory of text in context — argues that this only collapses context into text — it collapses the social into language. She argues that it is impossible to construe the social entirely from the semiotic. To go beyond describing language in order to explain language, it is necessary to regard text and context as separate, while recognising that they are powerfully related. The tendency of Martin's approach to genre, argues Hasan, is to make it seem that text is a finished product to be described rather than a process to be explained. All too easily, this can lead to a structural formalism which does not reflect the fluid social and textual relations that characterise text in context (Hasan, 1992).

Turning now to the pedagogical element of the debate, some members of the genre school, while agreeing in principle that it is important to be explicit about text structure and its relation to social activity, argue that the formalistic tend-encies in the Martin version of genre in practice do not lead beyond progressivism, but towards the revival of a linear transmission pedagogy. In its practical mani-festations this version of genre pedagogy emerges as a very understandable re-action to the dominance of progressivism in Australia for almost two decades, and this is why it has been received so enthusiastically by so many teachers here. But from the point of view of Britain's education system, Kress fears this might fuel the slide to educational authoritarianism in the 1980s and early 1990s, taking schooling back to a time when students sat in rows in large classes, instructed by the teacher using the most didactic of transmission pedagogies. From where he stands, Kress calls for more openness about curriculum contents, and principles of generativeness in literacy curriculum instead of principles of modelling that lead to transmission of textual forms. Martin, on the other hand, argues that the only beneficiaries of open curriculum and active learning in the progressivist mould were middle-class students and that empowerment of marginalised students involves inducting them to the discourses of power. He also argues that the deconstructive process needed to understand the ways texts are manufactured and used is in itself empowering.

When it comes to the pedagogical details, Kalantzis and Cope have argued against the 'wheel' model. To them, modelling involves no less than telling students how they should write — a process which culminates in their achievement being marked in terms of how well they realise the predetermined generic structure. Despite the activity work around field early in the curriculum cycle — researching or discussing the substantive issues for a piece of writing in science, for example — in practice textual form is largely presented in an uncritical way at the modelling stage. The joint construction stage is then meant to help students internalise the form exemplified by the model so they can reproduce that form in so-called 'independent' construction. The cycle imagery, in other words, belies the fact that the underlying pedagogical process is linear. Not only is this a reincarnation of the transmission pedagogy but it also takes genres at their word and posits their powerfulness uncritically, solely on the grounds that they should be taught to groups of students historically marginalised by the school literacy. It also leaves out of the curriculum other texts that might be culturally important in students' lives.

To a certain extent, all genre theorists would agree that genre literacy should open students' educational and social options by giving them access to discourse of educational significance and social power (Chapter 3). However, standing alone, this view is one that tends to ignore the fact that many of the textual forms which constitute identifiable genres that have historically been relevant to school learning also represent a very particular set of cultural illusions, allusions and even delusions. Report is a genre that appears to be factual and voiceless. Far from it, reports carry powerful human agendas. Their neutrality is not just a part of their descriptive function. This is also a convenient pretence. Narrative is a genre that appears, if one takes its own textual devices at its word, to have its origins in individual creativity. Far from it, narratives are the products of social experience, and the reader of a narrative, as a cultured entity, is as much a part of the meaning making process as the ostensible author of the text being read. The reader is in a position even to disrupt narrative and read things into it which its author never intended. Report and narrative, in fact, might not be the best genres to be teaching, and certainly not uncritically.

To go back to the question of classification, one of the problems of the research base for some versions of genre literacy is the analysis of texts from traditional curriculum. Just because certain genres can be identified as those that have been required for success in school in the past does not mean that schools should redefine these as genres for success in the future. We need a new language curriculum and a new use of language in the curriculum, not just a better educational technology to reproduce the traditional genres of school literacy. In reality, fixed classifications of genre may even mean that teachers lose sight of where the real power lies. Those who are really innovative and really powerful are those who break conventions, not those who reproduce them. There is a generic moral in *The Jolly Postman* story by Janet and Allan Ahlberg.

Meeny, Miny, Mo and Co, Attorneys at Law

Dear Mr Wolf,

We are writing to you on behalf of our client, Miss Riding Hood, concerning her grandma. Miss Hood tells us that you are presently occupying her grandma's cottage and wearing her grandma's clothes without this lady's permission.

Please understand that if this harassment does not cease, we will call in the Official Woodcutter, and — if necessary — all the King's horses and all the King's men.

On a separate matter, we must inform you that The Three Little Pigs Ltd. are now firmly resolved to sue for damages. Your offer of shares in a turnip or apple-picking business is declined, and all this huffing and puffing will get you nowhere.

Yours sincerely

H. Meeny

This text succeeds because it disrupts genre distinctions and plays on cross references between texts. *The Jolly Postman* didn't sell a million copies because it fitted oh-so-well into a genre. On the contrary, it sold well because it broke generic conventions. Nor does it have one definable social meaning or social purpose. It works for children in different ways from adults — some of the jokes are really for adults — and that is another secret of the book's success. In response to this argument, those who want to classify and describe genres more definitively contend that this sort of play is only possible once you know certain fundamental genres. As genre theory evolves, however, it becomes obvious that more and more text is generically problematic. To describe this, we need to move beyond categorisations of the generic, towards using genre as an analytical tool for engaging with the multigeneric, intergeneric and heteroglossic texts of societies where differences of ethnicity and subculture and style are increasingly significant elements in daily interaction.

Indeed, the cultural or individual inclinations of a reader may violate genre distinctions, even when the text seems so straightforward as to prevent this from happening. Purpose, text and meaning are not always related in straightforward ways. Just as *The Jolly Postman* deliberately invites a reading that draws on the linguistic and cultural resources of the reader, so even apparently unambiguous genres can be disrupted by a reader's personal or cultural inclinations. To become 'good readers' and 'good writers', students should be encouraged to be critical and not just follow the generic line. The most powerful texts cross generic and cultural boundaries. We might gain new insights if we were to read a logicoscientific text on building a bridge as a story, for example, or a technical treatise on nuclear power as a moral homily.

Kalantzis and Cope also believe that schools must take the cultural and linguistic diversity of their social setting into account. In a sense, the worst practices of genre literacy not only tend towards a transmission pedagogy. They also resemble the cultural assimilationist model of education. These versions of genre literacy pedagogy seem to propose that there are certain genres of social power and it is the particular mission of school to deliver these to those groups marginal to the cultures and discourses of power. In an analogous situation, traditional curriculum simply failed students not attuned to middle-class English, the canon and the culture of literacy. It ascribed the subsequent 'results' to individual ability. In reaction, progressivism abandoned the cultural deficit model that seemed to underlie traditional curriculum, where students failed because they had a deficit measured in terms of the cultural and linguistic biases of the school. So, progressivism replaced the universalistic, homogenising pretensions of traditional pedagogy with curriculum diversification which set out to value difference, to grant self-esteem to students by valuing their own discourses, cultures, interests and aspirations. This notion of self-esteem, especially when handed down from middle-class liberals, was extremely patronising. In effect, it meant a live and let live approach to patterns of difference which, not coincidentally, matched patterns of educational and social outcome. This is the reason why genre literacy attempts to refocus on the discourses of power.

But to hand down discourses of power once again, with all their cultural and ideological loadings — reports that pretend to be voiceless, and narratives that pretend to express individual literary creativity are both very peculiar middle-class conceits — is in its own way just as patronising. It assumes again that the discourses of power are intrinsically more worthwhile than other discourses. This is an approach that has the potential yet again to fail students for reasons not intrinsic to the functional potentiality of their texts. It is inconceivable in this model, moreover, that transmission should take place in the other direction — from marginalised discourse to the discourses of power. Clearly, genre literacy could develop a tendency to restore a hidden curriculum whose linguistic and pedagogical presuppositions amount to a reconstituted cultural deficit model.

This outline of the debate within the genre school expresses worst fears about potential worst practice. Theoretically, it reflects alleged tendencies of different linguistic and pedagogical versions of genre in the context of a continuing dialogue. It does not reflect the more carefully modulated and qualified theoretical positions of each of the protagonists. The reason the debate is presented here in this form is because it is this that makes the genre movement interesting. As an unfinished project, both theoretically and practically, it remains open to such different interpretations and different uses.

## Genre in Principle

It cannot be stressed enough that there are important things about which all members of the genre school can agree. Even the fact that its members are concerned enough to argue along these axes of linguistics and pedagogy indicates a common frame of reference where it is possible to agree upon genre-in-principle. This reflects a great deal of respect for alternative views of genre, even if they are not the ones to which any particular member of the genre school might subscribe. We will conclude with some principles drawn from what we consider to be the best practice of genre literacy. In the flux of the debate within the genre school, these principles more or less fall out of the interstices between the various positions.

The most important point here is that genre-in-principle is pedagogically innovatory for a number of reasons. First, the pedagogy behind genre literacy in its most powerful moments establishes a dialogue between the culture and the discourse of institutionalised schooling, and the cultures and discourses of students. Unlike this, traditional curriculum attempts to transmit fixed cultural and linguistic contents through curriculum but fails those who do not find a comfortable home in the culture of schooling; while progressivist curriculum, despite its pretence to openness, operates with a set of cultural and linguistic presuppositions that are loaded in less explicit ways to favour a certain sort of middle-class culture and discourse. Second, genre literacy in its most powerful moments uses cultural and linguistic difference as a resource for access. In comparison, traditional curriculum sets out to assimilate students, to teach them cultural and linguistic uniformity in the interests of constructs like 'national unity' and 'failing' those who along the way do not meet up to these singular expectations; while progressivist curriculum values differences but in so doing leaves social relations of inequity fundamentally unquestioned. Third, genre literacy sets out to reinstate the teacher as professional, as expert on language whose status in the learning process is authoritative but not authoritarian. The bias of traditional pedagogy, on the other hand, tends to draw it towards a textual, classroom and cultural authoritarianism. The tendency of progressivism is to reduce the teacher to the role of facilitator and manager in the name of student-centred learning which relativises all discourses. Fourth, the pedagogy that underlies genre literacy uses explicit curriculum scaffolds to support both the systematic unfolding of the fundamental structure of a discipline and the recursive patterns that characterise classroom experience. Contrast this with traditional curriculum, which rigidly structures the knowledge it values as universal into dictatorial syllabuses, dogmatic textbooks and didactic teaching practices; and progressivism, which favours unstructured experience, 'natural' immersion and an eclectic pastiche of curriculum content. Fifth, and finally, in the pedagogy of genre literacy students move backwards and forwards, through alternate processes of induction and deduction, between language and metalanguage, activity and received knowledge, experience and theory. This transcends the limitations of traditional curriculum, which puts a premium on deductive reasoning by positing received epistemological truths as the point of departure, and progressivism, which puts a premium on inductive reasoning based on experience.

Insofar as curriculum is a dialogue between the culture of schooling and the cultures of students, the relation between students' discourses and the discourses of educational access has to be one of genuine give and take. In one sense, it is a pedagogical commonsense that students' starting points and curriculum starting points coincide in effective teaching. But more than this, even as curriculum progresses, it is not simply a matter of transmitting 'better' discourses, such as certain genres that have proved historically central to educational success. Curriculum should lend consciousness across cultural and linguistic boundaries without trying to erase these boundaries. It should give students new ways of meaning for unfamiliar social settings, but never because these new ways of meaning and social settings are considered superior or because acquiring these skills requires the denial of domestic or communal ways of meaning. Lending consciousness does not require cultural and linguistic assimilation. The dialogue has to be multicultural and heteroglossic. However, this is not a multiculturalism of irreducible, relativist difference — the multiculturalism of progressivism. It is a multiculturalism of genuine dialogue that allows both sides of the conversation some sort of access to each other's cultural realms without either party attempting to exert cultural sovereignty over the other.

In this dialogue, difference is a potential resource for access. Students who come from historically marginalised cultures have a unique resource for unpacking the hidden cultural agendas and linguistic wiles of discourses unfamiliar to them. To come back to our generic examples, they might be able more easily to see through reports, with their feigned voicelessness. Or they might be able to see through narratives that ostensibly flow from the pen of the creative individual author. They can do this because these sorts of texts immediately stand out as strange ways of speaking. For middle-class students, these genres may appear much more natural. Denaturalising texts like these, discussing the relation of textual form to social purpose, is potentially a more straightforward exercise for cultural and linguistic outsiders. Once they have come to grips with structure and purpose in genres of educational success and social power, cultural and linguistic outsiders stand a better chance of making meaning through the intergeneric play that characterises those texts that really grab people: for their originality, for their cogency, for their off-centred insightfulness.

For teachers working with minority students in economically depressed settings, all this might seem pie-in-the-sky, so idealistic that it is practically unachievable. In fact, the general approach to diversity is not so far-fetched. It is just a statement of commitment that underlies the best of genre literacy practices: that genre literacy need not mean a return to assimilationist transmission pedagogy. On the contrary, it can turn difference into a resource for access, a resource for creativity and a resource for cultural renewal. In this respect, students of the dominant group might benefit from an intergeneric, multicultural view of their own discourse. A genre literacy curriculum could be a site where the cultures and the discourses of the margins are also a subject for literacy curriculum, used not only to highlight by contrast the structures and purposes in the discourses of conventional school success and social power, but perhaps also to reshape these so that they are more potent, or more explicit, or more subtle. Through genre literacy, indeed, the discourses of the margins might be able to influence the discourses of the mainstream. Instead of one-way transmission, genre literacy might be able to foster the cross-fertilisation of discourses and the cross-cultural hybridity which is potentially an enormously creative asset in a society that recognises and values its diversity.

In this dialogue between the culture and discourse of school and the cultures and discourses of students, the teacher stands in an authoritative relation to students. As much as progressivism guilelessly tries to deny it, there is an inevitable asymmetry in the relation of students and teachers. No matter how much a teacher pretends to establish a relationship with students of learners-in-partnership, it is still the teacher who determines this teaching/learning style and remains the person who manages, facilitates, disciplines. The challenge is to minimise the management function — to do, in other words, what progressivism was unable to do. The solution of genre literacy to this dilemma is to attempt to displace as much as possible a discourse of authoritarian management with a substantive discourse that is authoritative in relation to curriculum contents. The teacher's authoritative position does not have to translate into disciplinary authoritarianism. Their authoritativeness is a relationship to knowledge. They are authorities in their discipline and their profession: language education.

To give the example of genre literacy, the teacher's authoritative position arises from three types of knowledge of grammar. The first is a substantive knowledge of the grammar of discourses of educational success. In this sense, history teachers and science teachers, insofar as their subjects are carried by the written word, need to know grammar just as much as English teachers: to be able to make explicit the way text structure serves a particular disciplinary and social purpose. Second, teachers need a knowledge of grammar as an heuristic for analysing the relation of text to social purpose. Beyond the fact that they need to know the grammars of the key texts of school literacy, it would be too much to expect them to have a substantive knowledge of the grammars of the range of possible discourses of their students. But they do need to know how grammar can be used as a tool for students and teachers to analyse and discuss the relations of text form to social purpose, and the intergeneric relation of the texts of different cultures.

The third authoritative role of the teacher is as an expert on pedagogy, an expert on what constitutes worthwhile learning and how language is best taught. In genre literacy, here again, grammar is crucial. But this time it is neither grammar as substantive knowledge nor grammar as a practical analytical heuristic. It is knowledge of the cognitive role of teaching students grammar for its own sake. 'Grammar' is a term that describes the relation of language to metalanguage; of text to generalisations about text; of experience to theory; of the concrete world of human discursive activity to abstractions which generalise about the regularities and irregularities in that world. This movement backwards and forwards between language and metalanguage involves, alternately, induction and deduction.

One of the world-historical peculiarities of the culture of industrialism is that, to get around socially, one has to be able to concentrate reality into generalisations: use scientific generalisations rather than describe empirical physical events, for example, or see social institutions at work and not just nameable individuals. Cognitively and linguistically, the forms of thought and metalanguage that doing grammar requires in school are just those that are required to negotiate with the social structures of industrial society (Chapter 3). So, the teacher as pedagogue is another sort of expert, an expert who knows that grammar is a tool for teasing students' consciousness from what Vygotsky characterised as complex thought to conceptual thought — a sociolinguistic peculiarity of the culture of industrialism (Vygotsky, 1962, 1978).

Finally, how does the authoritative role of the teacher displace authoritarianism and minimise managerial discourse in the classroom? The answer to this question lies in the notion of scaffolding (Cazden, 1988). A pedagogy for teaching grammar needs to be carefully orchestrated in educational practice. If students are to develop a metalanguage and the linguistic-cognitive skills for generalisation and abstraction that go with it, the teacher and the curriculum need carefully framed microstructures and macrostructures. One such microstructure was developed in the pedagogical research that was a part of the Social Literacy Project (Kalantzis and Cope, 1989a). This microstructure runs though the following steps, the move from one step to another being indicted here by a ^ mark: {focus question pointing to an area where significant generalisations might be made ^ input that presents text or empirical reality as problematic or contested ^ critical analysis of input ^ generalisation and theory making: working complexes progressively in the direction of pseudo concepts, concepts and theoretical discourse ^ relation of theory to individual and cultural experience ^ evaluation of whether the concept can be reapplied successfully to distant contexts, and, ultimately, whether it can be meaningfully defined in relation to other concepts}. Within this cycle, which may run for one lesson or extend over a number of lessons, students are always positioned as active learners, but active learners who need to move inductively/deductively between experience and generalisation (Chapter 3).

Then there are macrostructures, what Bruner calls the fundamental structure of subjects (Bruner, 1960). The generalisations need to be going somewhere, as they develop from complex thinking into conceptual thinking, and, as concepts, connect into theoretical knowledges. To speak specifically, a grammar curriculum needs to be sequenced across terms and years. It requires a sustained program where the theory itself builds up — knowledge about language — and, with it, students' cognitive-linguistic capacities.

Herein lies a new role for textbooks. Only carefully planned programs, sustained over long periods of time and founded on expert knowledge, can achieve goals this ambitious. This is too much to expect of individual teachers working in isolation even if they have the requisite knowledge of grammar. Apart from handing back to students a sense of the overall frame of the curriculum denied them by progressivism, textbooks are almost a logistical necessity. But they have to be very different from the textbooks of traditional curriculum, which tell facts and, at best, expect students to reason deductively from received generalisations — 'application' exercises and the like. New textbooks for a new pedagogy will have to remain faithful to certain of progressivism's insights, such as the power of active learning related to experience. Yet they will also need to have their own explicit recursive patterns which draw students beyond experience to generalisation, and back to experience. In this sense, they will need to speak in a new voice, a voice totally different from that of either traditional or progressivist curriculum.

These are the general directions of a new pedagogy that underlies the genre literacy movement in its most inspiring moments. In a sense, the genre literacy theorists would like to think that the pedagogy which grounds their work is not so much a radical new way, however much they eschew traditional and progressivist pedagogies. They would like to think it is what good teachers have always done. In its most general propositions about the nature of learning, the pedagogy of genre literacy tries to encapsulate the best of teacherly commonsense. It reflects the spirit in which the best teachers — as effective communicators — instinctively subverted the excesses of whatever the prevailing pedagogical regime.

*Chapter 1*

# Genre as Social Process

*Gunther Kress*

*The main outlines of genre literacy in theory and practice have been sketched in the Introduction, where both the points of agreement in principle within the school and the points of divergence which give the school an element of intellectual dynamism were explained. In this chapter Gunther Kress, Professor of English at the University of London, outlines his version of genre. For him, genre is a useful term for understanding what texts do and how they do it. He argues for a concept of genre in which grammar makes meanings of social and cultural significance. This sort of grammar, he says, needs to focus on function in texts and thus draw on social categories to explain texts. The notion of genre, as identified by Kress, is a device to analyse the conventionalised nature of linguistic interactions and the way in which language both reflects and constructs certain relations of power and authority. In educational terms, working with the genres of social influence, such as certain forms of writing, has the potential to extend students' linguistic and cultural options. Genre thus provides the powerful basis for a literacy pedagogy.*

*Kress goes on to discuss some aspects of the educational practice of genre as it has been developed by Martin and his colleagues (outlined in Chapters 5 and 6, and the first section of the Bibliographical Essay at the end of this book). Although Kress believes that the sequencing or 'staging' in texts so stressed by Martin is grammatically relevant, his conception of genre remains broader and more concerned with the realisation of relations of power. For this reason, he is less concerned with the staged structure than Martin. Notwithstanding the fact that genres reflect patterns of textual and social regularity, Kress prefers to see genre as a device to account for both stability and dynamic variation from text to text, rather than to classify or label them according to their formal features. Notwithstanding the importance of using genre literacy to expand students' linguistic, educational and social options, Kress is concerned that this could mean teaching the powerful genres of dominant social groups in an unreflective fashion. Genre literacy pedagogy, he maintains, has to work creatively with differences in power and cultural differences in a multicultural, heteroglossic context — issues which are taken up by Cope and Kalantzis in Chapters 2 and 3.*

*The Kress approach to critical linguistics is outlined in the Bibliographical Essay with which this book concludes. This is a starting point for readers who might wish to investigate further the background to Kress's understanding of genre to be found here in Chapter 1.*

Genre work in education is now well established and widely known, well beyond its origins in the Australian context. Nevertheless, it may be useful to give a brief characterisation of the broader thinking about language out of which it has arisen and in which it continues to be set. Broadly speaking, there are three approaches to thinking about language. One takes language as simply being there, and sees its task as that of setting out a formal account of its rules — that is, providing a grammar. This approach can be traced back first to Greek, and then to Roman grammars, which became the basis of the English (and generally the European) tradition of grammar teaching. It is the tradition some of us can still remember, as rather formal and sterile. It has left a legacy of ill-will and suspicion towards the teaching of grammar. It is also the tradition which has left us with the largest number and the best known of grammatical terms: noun, verb, subject, object, tense and so on.

A second approach sees language as a fundamentally psychological phenomenon. Here the assumption is that language is a uniquely human phenomenon, and is to be most plausibly explained on the basis of the structure of the human brain. In other words, language is as it is because of the kinds of brains which have produced language and still use and (re)produce it. This has been — and continues to be — the most influential view, and one which on the face of it promises much for an application in educational contexts. In this approach education is about the training of developing human brains — minds. A psychological approach might tell us much about mental development. Grammars within this theory tend to emphasise the structure, regularity, generality of forms and, in some cases their universality — arguing that all human languages are essentially the same. The structure, regularity and universality are assumed to be effects of the structure of the brain. This tradition has been particularly influential in second and other language teaching programs.

The third approach, the one adopted in genre theories, emphasises the cultural and social dimensions which enter into the formation and constitution of language and of texts. This approach does not necessarily deny the importance of psychological factors in language, but rather assumes that whatever is psychological is common to all human beings, and therefore to all cultures. In one sense, what is common is seen as less important and less interesting than those factors which make languages different, and specific to particular cultures. In educational terms this approach offers the possibility of understanding language-in-culture and language-in-society, to allow a focus on those factors which reveal matters of cultural and social significance, difference and relevance. Grammars, in this approach, are much more oriented towards meaning and function: what does this bit of language mean because of what it does?

Because of the major interest of genre work in meaning and function, the emphasis is, therefore, on an understanding of what language is doing and being made to do by people in specific situations in order to make particular meanings. The latter tells us about the social needs and the cultural values and meanings of its users. It connects with all the hurly-burly and messiness of life in the midst of social processes and cultural values and demands. Ultimately it connects equally with the pragmatic goals of politicians, business people and bureaucrats, as well as with the perhaps less pragmatic goals of those interested in an increasingly equitable, morally better society.

Thinking about language as a social phenomenon requires some considerable reorientation in relation to well established and commonsense notions of what language is. First and foremost, we need to rethink what the main focus of a theory of language is. Commonsense, folksy, notions of language are that it is 'made up' of sounds, words and sentences. Indeed, linguistic theorising through most of this century has reinforced this view. Grammar has either been about descriptions of parts of speech and the rules governing their form and combination, or, more recently, grammars have attempted to describe the structure of sentences.

In a social theory of language, however, the most important unit is the text — that is, the socially and contextually complete unit of language. For instance, in English-speaking (as of course in other) cultures, when two people meet briefly and casually, they will exchange greetings; will probably make a brief enquiry about each other's well-being, and perhaps that of near friends and relatives; and then will exchange some concluding and farewelling remarks. Something like this (to be spoken with a full Australian accent):

*Mike*: Oh, g'day John! How's things?

*John*: Hi, Mike, not too bad, not too bad. How's things with you? How's work?

*Mike*: Can't complain, can't complain, be going on holidays soon. By the way, how's Mary and the kids?

*John*: Good, real good actually. Well look, got to dash, good seeing you — catch up with you later.

*Mike*: Yeah, look, let's have a coffee soon.

*John*: OK, great; see you then.

*Mike*: Yeah, see you.

This exchange constitutes a text. Its origin is entirely social, as is its function. Its characteristics are specific to a particular cultural group, though in a more general form it is common to very many cultures. It is entirely conventional and re-cognisable, that is, it is a text with a recognisable and oft repeated structure, with a particular way of expressing (coding) social relationships — whether of famili-arity and solidarity as here, or of formality, distance and power difference as in other instances of this kind of text. The conventionalised aspect of this interaction is what we recognise as being generic, as making of this text a particular genre.

While these conventions have become entirely automatic and 'natural' to members of the social or cultural group who use them, there is in fact nothing natural about them. This becomes quickly apparent when we meet a member of a different culture and see him or her struggling with an unknown convention, or when we find ourselves out of our culture, not knowing 'how to behave', not knowing what the right thing to do might be.

Genre theory aims to bring some of these conventions into focus, show what kinds of social situations produce them, and what the meanings of those social situations are. In the example above, the meanings would be something like a wish to accord recognition to a familiar person, to indicate friendliness, to affirm existing solidarity and intimacy, and to ensure the continuation of this relationship in these terms. At the same time genre theory aims at creating a sufficient under-standing of grammar as a dynamic resource for making meaning, to enable teachers to understand their students' texts, as well as the texts which they would wish their students to be able to produce.

Two theoretical categories are, therefore, particularly important in this account: text and genre. A much more thorough account of these will be given throughout this book, but here I will briefly mention some other issues which are essential to a social account of language, and give just a thumbnail sketch of them. The first point is that in thinking about topics which we speak or write about, we need to consider how we talk or write about a topic. For instance, a scientific 'discovery' will be written about in very different ways in a popularising account, in a primary school text, in a scientific journal, or in an upper level secondary school text. This topic I deal with under the heading of discourse.

The second point concerns the differences between speech and writing. In thinking about language, we need to be quite precise about the distinction between the structures, forms and meanings of speech and the structures, forms and meanings of writing. Following from this, it will be clear that writing is much more, and something quite other than, the mere transcription of speech. That is, literacy is never simply a matter of transliteration from one medium (sound) to another (visual marks). So there needs to be discussion about the broader question of literacy, of what literacy is and what it makes possible — a discussion of literacy as a cultural technology. Genre theory has developed in the context of broad concerns with literacy. We need now to consider extending the applicability of genre work beyond the kinds of questions about literacy that have preoccupied us so far, and in the longer run even beyond concerns with literacy alone, to include a wider range of questions about language-in-society.

### Text as the Social Unit of Language

Consider this text. It is the front page of a local council election pamphlet which was distributed through letter boxes in a northern English town.

### Focus (Social and Liberal Democrats)

### Axe the Poll Tax

Household budgets continue to be squeezed by the excessive demands of the Poll Tax. Shirley Templeforth shares the widespread feeling of anger against this unjust tax and wants to see it replaced by a Local Income Tax, which would be fairer and cheaper:

FAIRER because it is related to ability to pay, CHEAPER because it costs less to collect.

But until it is scrapped, what can be done to bring the Poll Tax down?

Luneceaster City Council must play its part by cutting out waste and promoting greater efficiency, but it is responsible for only 10% of the bill, and so cannot have much impact on the total.

But the Government could help by restoring the £16 million it chopped from this year's grant.

The County Council could contribute by holding down the massive salary rises it gives to its chief officers and the generous perks that go to county councillors (meals subsidised by over £200,000 last year).

In Luneceaster, we need to look at all job vacancies, try to slim down the administration and take advantage of new technology. Do we really need to employ 37 people to count the cash from the city's car parks? Could this not be automated? Shirley Templeforth believes that greater efficiency could produce savings and keep the Poll Tax down.

### Consulting People First

First and foremost, any explanation of language has to start with the text as the relevant unit of analysis — not with the word and not with the sentence, but with the text. Beyond that, everything significant about this text can be explained by asking Who produced it? For whom was it produced? In what context, and under what constraints was it produced? In other words, my argument is that all aspects of this text have a social origin and can be explained in terms of the social context in which it was made. Any interesting explanation of a text must draw on social categories to give that explanation. Without them, nothing of great relevance can be said about any text.

There is a simple point about a social matter which immediately has far-reaching generic consequences. The piece of paper which came through the letter box was an A4 sheet in size. It had been folded in half to produce a four-page leaflet. The decision to use an A4 sheet may well have been due to the amount of money the candidate could afford to spend as this was a leaflet put out by a minority party in a council by-election. However, the decision to fold the piece of paper, rather than leaving it unfolded, was not made for financial but for generic reasons. To leave it unfolded would have made it into a typical local 'newsletter'. Folding it made it into something with four pages, more like a local 'newspaper' than a 'newsletter'.

Once this step had been taken, some generic conventions of the front page of a newspaper take over. The paper has to have a name, a 'masthead' and a 'logo'; there has to be a front-page story; and there have to be aspects of language of typical newspaper reports. Last, but by no means least, in this case the front-page story cannot go beyond the front page, so that the size of the piece of paper also determines how big this text will be. Newspaper stories are written by reporters, or that at least is the fiction, so we have here a 'reporter' reporting the candidate's views — her anger, her solutions. This generic convention allows Shirley Templeforth, who, after all, may have written this herself, to appear as the person about whom the report has been written. Had the publication been a 'newsletter', she would have had to speak to her readers herself, as the writer of a letter. She would have had to say things like: 'I think . . .'; 'I feel . . .'; 'I am angry. . . .' The objectivity of the report makes possible a certain distance and lends a different credence to the candidate's opinions. The generic conventions, in this case those of the 'tabloid' paper, also introduce a certain kind of language: words and phrases such as 'squeezed', 'excessive demands', 'scrapped', 'chopped from the grant' and 'massive rises'.

I don't wish to provide any detailed description of this text here. My point is that it is the text in its full social and cultural context which provides the relevant starting point for any useful speculation about the forms, uses and functions of language. A lot more could be said about this text from that point of view; for instance, why is there the sudden appearance of the personal 'we' in the last paragraph? Every text, and every aspect of a text, needs to be thought about in these terms. The texts produced by school children in the course of their passage through the education system, at any point at all, are no exception. This approach can provide a teacher with a new way of thinking about the writing produced by their students, no matter at what stage, or in what subject. It can also provide an interesting way of thinking about a teacher's demands and expectations of students.

### Kinds of Texts: Genre

In one way the most interesting point about the 'Focus' text is its vacillation between conformity to the generic conventions of a front-page newspaper report and deviations from those conventions. The explanation can be found in the social context of the production of the two kinds of text. A newspaper reporter operates, from the point of view of the writing of a text, in a stable, well known, well understood environment. There is the notion of news, which it is the reporter's task to report. Readers buy the newspaper because they think that they want to be informed. The reporter promises to inform the readers, without distortion or bias, fairly. The reporter is, or should be, detached from the event. All of this leads to a relative stability in the kind of text that is produced. We can recognise immediately that we are reading a front-page report from paper $X$, even if we see only a small part of it — provided, of course, that we know paper $X$.

The 'Focus' piece, by contrast, has no such stability. For one thing it has no clearly established readership. It has to create it. Given the heterogeneity of many electorates, that is a difficult task. Despite the overt appearance of a wish merely to report and inform, Shirley Templeforth wants to persuade. Hence the two slogans: 'Fairer . . . cheaper. . . .' She wants to cajole: 'what can be done . . .'; to bring readers on side: 'we need to . . .', 'Do we really need to . . .?' In other words, the relation with the audience is unstable; it is all over the place. This makes for the oddness of the text overall. But this also makes, by contrast, the point about generically strong texts. Because they are written in a situation of a stable social relation of writers and readers, they can have the appearance of being all of a piece. The stability and the repeatability of that social situation lead to texts with a similar stability, with a marked conventionality, which in the end makes the text seem simply natural and makes its constructedness unnoticeable.

This is the crux of the argument about the teaching of conventions of textual structures — the teaching of genres. In any society there are regularly recurring situations in which a number of people interact to perform or carry out certain tasks. Where these are accompanied by language, of whatever kind, the regularity of the situation will give rise to regularities in the texts which are produced in that situation — whether as here, as a political pamphlet masquerading mildly as a little newspaper; or in a science classroom in the writing up of the report of an experiment for the teacher; or in a primary classroom in the writing down of some recollection; or in any of the other generic forms which make up the inventory of a literate society. In our approach we would like to focus on making available at least the following:

- an understanding by teachers and students that texts are produced in order to do some specific social and cultural thing;
- an understanding by teachers and by children that all our speaking or writing is guided, to a greater or a lesser extent, by conventions of generic form, even where that takes the form of an attempt to break generic convention;
- an understanding by teachers and students that generic form is always the product of particular social relations between the people involved in the production of a text;
- an understanding that while generic conventions provide certain dimensions of constraint, generic form is never totally fixed, but is always in the process of change — for example, a job interview in 1992 is very different from a job interview in 1932;
- an understanding of the ways in which degrees and kinds of power and power difference enter into the production and maintenance of generic form;
- an understanding, in the context of what I have said above, of the possibilities for change, innovation and creativity — that is, the possibilities and means of altering generic form;
- an understanding by all teachers of the role which the functions, forms and structures (the grammar) of language play in the production of texts and their meanings;
- an understanding by students of the social role which the functions, forms and structures of language play in their own production of texts — an understanding sufficient for the task at hand.

## Genre and the Wider Socio-political Context

Work on genre in relation to literacy developed out of quite specific educational and political aims, namely to bring about greater possibilities of access to the resources and the technology of literacy, and, through greater access, to bring about some of the conditions for a redistribution of power in society. The question which has been at the forefront of considerations has been: what does someone need to know about literacy; what skills and knowledge would they need to have, in order to function fully and effectively in a literate, technologically developed society?

From the beginning, therefore, genre work has been both a pedagogical and a political project, a pedagogical project motivated by the political project of allowing greater, fairer, possibly equal access to the cultural and social resources and benefits of this kind of society. If one assumes that access to social, economic and cultural benefits has much to do with command of the highest level of literacy skills, then a quite revolutionary program might be built on the attempt to give

everyone access to literacy skills and knowledge in the fullest sense. The fundamental political aim has, therefore, always been that of access — on the assumption
that full access to, and control of, literacy is essential to full participation in all
aspects of social life.

It is an aim based on the assumption that freedom of choice in cultural, social,
political and ethical areas depends on access to the most powerful forms of writing,
the most powerful genres in one's own society. The program, therefore, is one
about extending options, widening the range of choices and possibilities, and
providing the freedom that comes from the possibility of choosing, rather than
leaving people locked into particular situations. This view of the political importance
of genre work has been shared by all those working in the framework of the so-
called genre school.

However, there is a need to keep refining and extending these aims. As the
educational project of real importance which it promises to become, genre work
needs to consider its activities in the context of two overriding questions for the
coming decades. First, there is the question of the possible productive forms that
multicultural societies can, or should, take. Second, there is the question of a
sustainable economic, social and cultural future, not just for Western technological
societies but for the whole world. Both these questions have profound effects for
any thinking both about the language (and not just the literacy) curriculum and
about appropriate pedagogies.

I will return to questions of pedagogy. My point about consideration of the
language curriculum, rather than merely a literacy curriculum, indicates the directions in which I believe genre work needs to be extended. If curriculum is seen
as more than the adding of knowledge or of skills to an otherwise unchanged
person — a kind of value-added view of education — that is, if curriculum is seen
as essentially a matter of design, a design for the characteristic cultural shape of
the future citizens of a society, then it is clear that literacy is an important part,
but only a part, of a larger curriculum concerned with language and its role in
education. In other words, the questions which genre work will need to encom-
pass will touch on every aspect of the language curriculum. If the curriculum in
its contents is to be able to deal with the questions of a multicultural, a pluricultural,
society, then concerns about literacy alone are simply not sufficient. The same
point applies to any thinking about how the curriculum can prepare productive,
innovative citizens capable of dealing with the problems of the coming decades.
At an abstract level the needs are the same: to produce a curriculum in which
linguistic plurality, diversity and difference are shown to be the inevitable conditions
of all societies, and that they constitute one of the most productive reservoirs and
resources for cultural (and consequently social, political, economic) innovation.
This would be in contrast to most language curricula (and, it has to be said,
linguistic theories) in use now, where the assumption of the single homogeneous
language system co-extensive with a society and a nation state prevails.

As a step towards such a curriculum I will indicate four central points. A
language curriculum appropriate for a multicultural society will primarily give
equal importance to considerations of oral language and its place in education and
in society. It will give central attention to the whole set of connections of culture,
society and language, codings of value systems, structuring and realisations of
systems of power, and to the possibilities of making meanings in language as
such, and in the languages of a specific plurilingual society in particular. It will

discuss the relations of the various languages in that society in the existing particular configurations of power, and make available means of analysing that structure, providing means of developing critiques and, via critiques, the possibilities of change. Lastly, it will pose as a central question for debate the relation between a language curriculum, society, and societal change in general, focal in which will be issues concerning possibilities of fundamental cultural, social, economic innovation.

Nevertheless, even in a book focusing on the literacy curriculum and on literacy pedagogy, some questions not currently central to the concerns of the 'genre school' will need to be given attention. The two major ones are consideration of the broad domain of literacy and not just of writing, and the question of an understanding of the range of genres and their projected social structures in all the languages of the society. If attention is not given to literacy as such — to all the considerations around reading as much as those around writing — then the producer-centred emphasis of mainstream linguistics will simply be reintroduced into genre work, with all its attendant problems. If attention is not given to the written genres of all the language groups in the society, then the possibilities of using the language or literacy curriculum as a means of developing the possibility of a multicultural society will be unused. Worse, the powerful genres of the dominant cultural group(s) will be taught in an unreflecting fashion as if they were a politically, socially and ideologically neutral set of forms, as a kind of universal commonsense.

## Pedagogies and Social Futures

In any consideration of a language or a literacy curriculum in the wider social and political context that I have indicated, the question of pedagogy has to be one central concern. If the aim is to produce citizens with particular abilities, knowledges and qualities, modes of learning are as important as kinds of content. The pedagogical approach which has been dominant in Australia and in the UK over the last two decades is progressivism, which has stressed process oriented methods. This has to be understood, both in the largest context of the continuing dominance throughout this century of various forms of (neo-)romanticism, of which poststructuralism is simply the most recent, and in the context of a reaction to the authoritarian, repressive decades following the Second World War, with Stalinism in the East and McCarthyism and the era of John Foster Dulles in the West. In the context of a reaction to that, process oriented pedagogies had a revolutionary potential and a liberating effect. At the same time this progressivism promised to produce citizens more able to adapt to what were seen, entirely correctly, as decades which would bring a period of rapid and unpredictable change.

Progressivism in that form was thus not simply some left-liberal subversive ideology, but was grounded in quite pragmatic social and economic goals. In the current reaction to its effects it is very easy — for both right and left — to overlook completely the positive effects which it achieved in terms of producing resilient young adults who have in so many ways proved to be extremely competent in coping with social and economic systems, which in their turn did not prove equally adaptable. It is unlikely that the products of the older authoritarian pedagogic systems would have proved as competent.

Given that there is now a relentless attempt on the part of reactionary forces to reimpose the older pedagogies, one needs to be wise in attempting to establish what kind of pedagogy will produce young adults who will need to find their way in an even more difficult set of social and economic circumstances in the next two or three decades. A simplistic choice between process or product (content) oriented pedagogies will not do. The skills, knowledges, habits and dispositions needed will be those of analysis and critique; understanding and acceptance of heterogeneity and difference; the ability to respond to social changes by producing the requisite linguistic forms, or conversely to affect social changes by productively using the resources of language to produce forms which aid the production of social change. A pedagogy which is satisfied to leave knowledge of forms — even where this is accompanied by explicit discussions of the social and cultural effects and effectiveness of forms — as a sufficient goal will fail in terms of these larger pedagogic and social aims. This is quite apart from the fact that a curriculum based on knowledge of form is always more disposed to be taught via a more authoritative and teacher-centred, rather than a less authoritative and child-centred, pedagogy.

The curriculum which I envisage includes knowledge of textual forms, but presents these as the product of stateable social factors. Hence the social factors provide the categories which produce linguistic form; the social factors are the generative categories out of which textual forms — genres — are produced. The curriculum, therefore, is based on a simultaneous presentation of social factors, and of possible forms of their linguistic realisation; and a developing understanding that textual forms — genres — are always the result of the realisation in linguistic form of a complex of social factors. This curriculum strongly shapes the pedagogy of the literacy curriculum. It starts with an acknowledgment of the teacher as a figure who has valuable and therefore valued knowledge, a figure whose authority derives from that knowledge. It situates the student as the person who will need to be, and become, linguistically productive in the face of relatively unstable future situations, and can be successful in that only out of a productive knowledge of relevant cultural and social factors, of their most common convergences in social situations, and of their linguistic production and realisation in specific textual forms, in genres.

In this chapter it is my intention simply to raise this issue as one of fundamental importance. No such pedagogy has as yet been developed, though an experiment approaching these aims has been started in the teaching materials developed in a project conducted for the NSW Department of School Education (Macken *et al.*, 1989a–c).

### Genre, Register and Text

The term 'genre' has a long history in literary studies, with a more recent intensive period of interest in screen studies, and in cultural studies particularly, through the 1970s and 1980s. Consequently the term comes with a considerable baggage of accumulated meaning. There is a problem in using such a term with a meaning which is relatively uncontrollable. In literary theory, the term has been used with relative stability to describe formal features of a text — epitaph, novel, sonnet, epic — although at times content has been used to provide a name epithalamion, nocturnal, alba. In screen studies, as in cultural studies, labels have described both form and content, and at times other factors, such as aspects of production. Usually the more prominent aspect of the text has provided the name. Hence 'film noir'; 'western' or 'spaghetti western' or 'psychological' or 'Vietnam western'; 'sci-fi'; 'romance'; or 'Hollywood musical'; and similarly with more popular print media.

In other words, a great complex of factors is condensed and compacted into the term — factors to do with the relations of producer and audience, modes of production and consumption, aesthetics, histories of form and so on. In genre theory as applied to education and literacy many of these factors have remained, though in a new mix, and embedded in a specific linguistic theory — Michael Halliday's systemic functional grammar. To complicate matters further, even the so-called genre school does not have a unified theoretical approach to the term. The best known and widely used approach, that developed by J.R. Martin and Joan Rothery, treats genre as a term which describes the whole complex of factors which needs to be described and understood about a text. In this approach the term 'genre' covers everything there is to know linguistically about text, which, in turn, can be accounted for by ideological context (see Chapter 6). In my own approach, which is to some extent reflected in work by other writers in Australia and which has some influence outside Australia, 'genre' is a term used to cover one aspect only of textual structuring. Both approaches focus on social structures and processes and their function in the production of a text. What I shall call the Martin/Rothery approach focuses most on the purposes of the participants who produced the text; on the task that they wished the text to perform. There is strong emphasis on the succession of stages in the text, which reflect the stages of the social task which the participants were performing.

Two types of textual form have been particularly influential in shaping this approach. Both have strongly marked sequential stages. One is the model of the 'service-encounter', following work done by Eija Ventola (Ventola, 1987). This describes the shopping encounter, from the first exchange between buyer and seller to their concluding exchange. Much like my invented greeting encounter above, such encounters have great regularity and predictability about the unfolding of successive stages in the encounter, so much so that one can readily produce algorithms or flowcharts to map out this sequential unfolding. The other model is that of narrative structure. Here the text is not a record of a direct interaction between the participants in the production of a text; rather a strongly marked, strongly conventionalised sequence which itself reflects or realises a more abstract cultural algorithm of initial equilibrium — disturbance of equilibrium — conflict or tension — resolution of conflict — re-establishment of new equilibrium. As in the service encounter, though in a much more abstract sense, the text performs a more abstract cultural task, in this case the assimilation and incorporation of some problematic event or factor into the larger classificational structures of the culture.

In the Martin/Rothery model this view of text is generalised descriptively to all kinds of texts, and a small set of types is established. The concern with the task being performed by the text can be followed through to smaller subsections of the text, to yield descriptions of the internal organisation of the stages. In a report, for instance, the stages can be identified, and then certain grammatical characteristics of the stages described. The tendency of this approach — more or less necessarily — is to attend to all aspects of structure in these terms, that is, in terms of the task that is being performed by or through the text. As a consequence, all aspects of the text become part of the generic description, and genre becomes that category which describes all there is to know and say about a text.

In my approach I have focused not on the task being performed by or with the text, but rather on the structural features of the specific social occasion in which the text has been produced and have seen these as giving rise to particular configurations of linguistic factors in the text which are realisations of, or reflect, these social relations and structures. For instance, in the greetings encounter above I have not, from the point of view of genre, been interested so much in the sequences in the text (which are clearly there), but more in the realisation of relations of power between, in this case, the producers of the text, and in the linguistic form which results, in terms of both grammatical detail and overall textual form. I have not been interested in the stages but rather, for instance, in discovering and describing who has the power to initiate turns and to complete them, and how relations of power are realised linguistically. In this approach 'genre' is a term for only a part of textual structuring, namely the part which has to do with the structuring effect on text of sets of complex social relations between consumers and producers of texts.

A brief example will show how the two approaches deal with the same text.

1   *Max*:    A couple of questions very easy to answer for a radio program we're doing the first of the questions is what would you say language is?

5   *Woman*:    Language well it's the dialogue that people speak within various countries.

     *Max*:    Fair enough and what would you say it's made out of?

     *Woman*:    [*8 second pause*]. It's made out of . . . [*puzzling intonation*]

     *Max*:    Hmmm.

10  *Woman*:    Well I don't know how you'd tell what it's made out of it's a person's expression I suppose is it?

     *Max*:    I haven't got the answers I've only got the questions (laughing)

     *Woman*:    [*simultaneously — small laugh*]

15  *Sid*:    That's not bad though.

     *Woman*:    Well it's an expression it would be a person's expression ,wouldn't it?

     *Sid*:    That's a good answer.

     *Max*:    Thank you very much.

The text has clearly marked stages: lines 1–2 represent the interview's opening; lines 2–18 represent the body of interview; and line 19 represents the conclusion. Within the body of interview, section substages can be described, each marked by the interviewer's question, the interviewee's response and the interviewer's conclusion. It is an instance of a kind of text which recurs over and over in contemporary Western societies — though it is important to point out that the interview in this form has a comparatively recent history, in that it differs from other question-answer genres such as interrogative and catechism, which have a much longer history. Its stages clearly have to do with specific social purposes, and, to that extent, the Martin/Rothery characterisation of genre as 'a staged goal-oriented social process' is perfectly apt.

While I would not ignore the sequencing which gives this text one of its characteristic features, I would prefer to begin with an attempt to describe the social relations between the participants in this interaction and the wider social structures which are exemplified here. In such an account there would be more emphasis on difference in degrees of power of the participants, as they seem to emerge here, and an attempt to understand how these are realised linguistically in the text. This would have to be set in the context of a more general social account of structurings of age, class, professionalism and gender. Hence I would be particularly interested in linguistic shifts such as those in lines 10–11: 'Well I don't know how you'd tell what it's made out of it's a person's expression I suppose is it', with its shift from the modality of certainty — 'it's a person's expression'; to the insecure 'I suppose'; to the confirmation seeking 'is it?'; or in lines 16–17: 'Well it's an expression it would be a person's expression wouldn't it?', where the shift in tense, so-called, from the modally certain 'it's an expression', to the modally uncertain 'it would be a person's expression', signals loss of confidence due either to a perceived difference in power, or to a calculation on the interviewee's part that on this occasion there is nothing to gain from challenging the interviewer.

This latter approach is particularly revealing in comparisons across instances of the same generic form. In another interview done on the same occasion, but this time involving middle-aged men, the interview's opening shows a revealing difference.

*Max*:   This is for a radio program that I'm doing John ah . . . um. . . .
Two questions that you can answer briefly the first is. . . .

Here the interviewer introduces himself as 'I', not as 'we'; he suggests that the questions need only brief answers rather than being 'very easy to answer'. Whatever the social motivations for the linguistic difference — differences or affinities in age, gender, familiarity — this approach does focus on the variabilities of social situation, hence variabilities in the performance of a generic form, and consequent variabilities in textual form. The emphasis on stages does not attend to this factor.

More recent work by Martin and his colleagues has increasingly focused on smaller-scale linguistic description within stages; though this remains within the framing context of the emphasis on stages. Quite clearly, the stages are a fact of textual and of social/cultural organisation, and hence cannot be overlooked in any approach to text. The question is how they are to be treated in theoretical accounts, and whether this makes a difference in any applications. There are a number of answers. In my approach, genre is one of several categories needed to provide an account of what a text is, or of what social factors go into the linguistic formation of the text. Other categories are, at the very least, questions of the social/linguistic organisation of content: discourse; the modes of speech and writing and their relative intermingling; the question of fundamental cultural textual types, such as narrative, report, dialogue, or perhaps even more fundamental distinctions of text types organised either temporally/sequentially or spatially/hierarchically. There is, for instance, the question of size which I touched on earlier, and other questions not at all touched on in linguistic accounts such as plot and character, which, despite their seemingly literary provenance, have quite pronounced effects on linguistic realisations. In the Martin/Rothery account these are all dealt with under

Figure 1. Elements of the Composition of Text

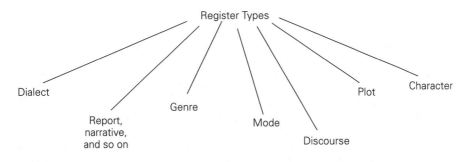

the label of genre, though differentiated at the level of the Hallidayan register categories of field, tenor and mode. For Martin/Rothery, 'genre' is the term which describes, in the end, significantly differing register types. For me, 'genre' is one term which, together with others, forms the complex which constitutes significantly different types of text; to which I am happy to give the label 'register'. Figure 1 provides a diagrammatic representation. It reveals at once that my account is quite underdeveloped theoretically in the sense that there are dependencies of many kinds between the categories which I need to include, to be described as they exist at a particular time in a particular society, and theorised in terms of larger social theories. For instance, certain genres will not co-occur with certain dialects; certain kinds of discourses do not co-occur with certain genres; genres are heavily interrelated with the modes of speech and writing. In *Social Semiotics* the term 'logonomic rules' was coined for the system of rules which governs this complex set of interrelations (Hodge and Kress, 1988). Nor are all the categories equal in terms of their effect in the formation of the text. In my view it is too early to move to a closing-off of the theoretical questions around the constitution of text. As far as application is concerned, I feel secure enough to suggest that teaching approaches can be developed involving the categories of genre, mode and discourse, such as, for example, narrative.

But does this theoretical difference matter? It does matter in a social and cultural account, as the two approaches imply differing social and cultural structures and processes. I also believe it matters in terms of education, which is where the theory is making its impact. The Martin/Rothery account necessarily tends towards a firmer view of generic structure, a greater tendency towards the reification of types, and an emphasis on the linguistic system as an inventory of types. With such a tendency goes a corresponding tendency pedagogically towards an emphasis on the matter of form, and a tendency towards authoritarian modes of transmission. My approach tends towards a more historical/fluid view of generic form, depending on the prior contingencies of social structurings; an emphasis on the generative force of social categories. With this goes a tendency towards production of text types out of an understanding of the generative social categories on the part of the student, and consequently less authoritarian modes of transmission on the part of the teacher. Given that in education modes of pedagogy have a fundamental role in the formation of the pupil-subject, I am certain that there are clear choices to be made which are amenable to rational, political, moral debate.

## Genres and Social Processes

The advance represented by work in the genre school consists of two equally important steps. One is to have put consideration of text at the centre of concerns with literacy; the other is to have put text squarely into the domain of the social and political. Both of the versions which I have discussed share this approach. Several consequences follow from this: these concern a view of individuals as social agents; a view of the social as inevitably heteroglossic (or multilingual); a need to examine the facts of multiculturalism for genre theory; and a constant concern for the fluctuating relations of the modes of speech and writing in specific texts.

Language always happens as text; and, as text, it inevitably occurs in a particular generic form. That generic form arises out of the action of social subjects in particular social situations. Consequently, the action of individuals as social subjects is at the centre of the production of text in generic form, and hence at the centre of the historical changes of particular languages. In a pluricultural or multicultural society the social histories of all individual members of that society will be histories of greater or lesser difference, producing social subjects who share significant social/cultural experiences, values, meanings and yet have significantly different experiences, values and meanings. In the production of any one text in any one social interaction there will be degrees of repetition (out of shared experience and knowledge) and degrees of difference.

Varying degrees of stability in social structures and in social relations lead to the relative stability of textual forms. Power may be thought to bear on certain textual forms to ensure relatively greater adherence to generic form; or groups may bring power to bear to resist the imposition of adherence to generic form. In any case the very facts of socially produced differences in the agents who make texts must always lead to differences of a greater or lesser extent. No one instance of a particular genre will ever exactly resemble any other instance of the same genre. History is a fact of generic as of all other linguistic forms.

In a theory which takes the heteroglossic and multilingual character of society for granted, socially produced linguistic change is a fact to be theorised, not to be denied. In many societies the conditions of heteroglossia now include the facts of multiculturalism, and hence of multilingualism. This complicates and intensifies the problems of genre theory, as each cultural group has its specific generic forms, developed out of the social structures characteristic of that group, and developed in its political history. So far little, if any, work has been done on this area, and on its implication for literacy-related work in genre theory. If the political and pedagogic project of genre theory is to succeed, this is an area of enquiry demanding urgent consideration. One cannot hope to have a strategy either for a productive multicultural society or, pedagogically, for producing citizen-subjects who will be able to function productively in such a society unless one has a clear sense of what possibilities are available in all the cultures of a multicultural society.

Last but by no means least, a social theory of genre will need to be closely attentive to the constantly shifting relations between language in the spoken and in the written mode, and its relations to shifts in power. This is so particularly if one wishes to add to the project of access the more ambitious project of social and linguistic reform: not merely giving all citizens an equal share in cultural capital, but entertaining at least the possibility of reforming the structures and the processes which exist wherever they are seen as limitations on human potentials.

*Chapter 2*

# Histories of Pedagogy, Cultures of Schooling

## Mary Kalantzis and Bill Cope

*In this chapter Kalantzis and Cope discuss the historical origins of the major educational paradigms already mentioned in the Introduction and in Chapter 1: traditional curriculum and progressivist curriculum. After discussing the origins of what they call the 'traditional curriculum of a classical canon' in early modern times and its role in the rise of mass, institutionalised education, they differentiate two versions of progressivism: Dewey's 'progressivist pedagogy of modernism and experience' and a more recent 'progressivist pedagogy of postmodernism and difference'.*

*This is more than a chronological presentation of successive educational paradigms. The important educational issues at stake today are connected in various ways to the key debates between adherents to these different approaches to education. The paradigms presented in this chapter are still very much alive and well and vying for our attention.*

*The chapter ends with a critique of the latest versions of progressivism, and what they mean for the practice of teaching literacy. This is a prelude to the following chapter which attempts to discuss some of the fundamental principles that would underlie a pedagogy which managed to move beyond the limitations of both progressivist and traditional curriculum.*

### A Tale of Two Classrooms

*Classroom One*: a Year 7 geography and commerce class at State High, a Sydney school in an old, traditionally working-class neighbourhood (Kalantzis, Cope and Noble, 1991). Since the late nineteenth century, this has been a first-stop suburb for wave after wave of immigrants — first the Irish, Scottish and English, then, after the Second World War, the Greeks, followed by the Lebanese and South and Central Americans, and now, since the end of the Vietnam War, the Vietnamese, Chinese, Cambodians, Laotians. The school is officially designated 'Disadvantaged'. Ninety-three per cent of its students come from families where English is not the main language of the household. This is why the Year 7 geography/commerce teacher has taken a three-week in-service training course called 'Multiculturalism in the Classroom', run by the New South Wales Department of Education.

*Classroom Two*: an English class at Ethnic Community College, seemingly another world away from State High, a distant civilisation in the cultures of schooling. Ethnic Community College is a private school for students of a single religious denomination and a single language background, a minority language in

Australia. But in other respects the social and even the literal distance from State High is not so great. A new and growing school of several hundred students, its constituency is one of the largest ethnic groups represented at State High. Some of the students at Ethnic Community College might have gone to State High had their parents not been able to pay the fees. Inside, however, the schools themselves could hardly be more different.

Neither of the lessons we will now describe illustrates the use of 'process writing' or 'grammar', two of the key slogans that are often used to mark off two of the camps in current debates about learning how to write. However, both are accounts of pedagogies which integrally involve written text. By illustrating the underlying cultures of schooling and their educational paradigms — both of which infuse every moment of the educational experience and which differ so dramatically — we can then discuss the specific case of literacy pedagogy. In other words, to tackle the issue of writing pedagogy, we need to go the the heart of the matter and not restrict ourselves to writing pedagogy as a subject in isolation. We must step back to re-examine educational assumptions at the deepest and broadest levels to explain how and why the cultures of schooling can differ so much, and how, as a consequence, the protagonists in the literacy debate so vehemently beg to differ.

*Classroom One.* To the Year 7 geography/commerce teacher at State High the multicultural classroom was a minefield to be crossed with special care if she was to cope with such widely differing levels of language proficiency. With this amount of diversity, the English language was a very practical priority and she had learnt a couple of language learning strategies at the in-service training course on multicultural education she had attended. One was an 'activities-based approach' in which the class divided into small work groups, which she now did much of the time. The other was to allow students to use whichever language they liked — English or their first language — to complete their work. If the students' English was not adequate to the task, they were encouraged to write in their first language. She believed that 'if you can get a kid to write something that they feel comfortable with and they write it well and they know they can do it in their own language, it gives them such a boost of confidence and self-esteem that they're prepared better to have a go when it comes to writing in English.'

Following are some snapshots of typical moments over three, one-hour lessons. 'Barter and Money' is the topic. To start, the desks are energetically rearranged for group work. Students are then allotted by the teacher to groups of four or five and told which of three alternative tasks they are to undertake: to write a play on barter; to prepare a poster suitable for a display at Sydney Airport explaining money in Australia; or to prepare a newspaper's classified advertisement section, showing items for sale.

The teacher starts to move from group to group. The students writing the play have never written one before, so the teacher suggests 'a complicated plot' — not just 'I'll swap this for that' but something they can 'create' and 'perform'. The classroom steps up to a loud hum. There is lots of pupil-pupil interaction, but almost all student interactions with the teacher are managerial in nature — instructions about what to do and what not to do. One group creating the classified advertisements have been given a page from a newspaper as a model or example of the kind of text anticipated. Unfortunately they get stuck on understanding the text in the example and go no further. Another group wonders why there would be a money poster at the airport. They have never seen one and wonder what it would look like.

One student leaves his group to write something for somebody in another group, in Arabic. The teacher has carefully divided the groups so that the language backgrounds of the students are mixed. Meanwhile, the group writing the play dissipates. A Vietnamese girl starts to read a book that had been set as homework by the English teacher. Another student wanders off to see what the other groups are doing. The most involved student in the play writing group writes out a script on her own.

Of the students in the money poster group, one laboriously colours a blue border. The others go off to the library to find information, only to return empty handed three-quarters of an hour later. So the teacher tells them that they will have to 'make it up'. A girl writes 'School Sux' on a piece of paper, puts it in someone else's bag, then changes her mind, takes it out and screws it up. A boy plays with a ball, and two others get started on a game that involves slapping hands loudly. The atmosphere is relaxed, the students seem to get on reasonably well with each other and there is no negative pressure placed upon students which might, for example, mean that their activity could be marked as unsuccessful or inadequate.

*Classroom Two.* Multiculturalism is not on the agenda at the Ethnic Community College where the focus of the curriculum is on 'the basics', such as 'writing without grammatical mistakes'. The school aims to promote academic rigour, the value of hard work, the significance of achievement, the importance of moral values, The Faith, and a sense of belonging to a community. Homework is set every night and lasts a minimum of two hours. Students receive a detention if it is not done.

Two straight lines of neatly uniformed students — the boys in one line and the girls in another — stand waiting outside the classroom for the Principal's Year 7 English class. When given the order, they file in to take their permanent places in the rows of single desks. This lesson consists of a continuous barrage of questions by the teacher, starting with a review of the contents of the last test. Students respond one by one. Onomatopoeia. Alliteration. Metaphor. 'Hands up!' The class is quiet, students never speaking unless questioned. There is virtually no pupil-initiated talk and no pupil-pupil talk.

Next, 'Do you remember we began to talk about a special type of poem in the last lesson? What was its name?' 'A Sonnet.' 'And what is a sonnet?' A girl stumbles towards a definition about rhyme and stress. Next, photocopies of a Shakespearean sonnet are handed out. A deluge of questions from the teacher follow with the goal of disentangling the meaning of the piece. Then, 'Identify the type of poem by the rhyming and stress scheme.' 'Mark the stressed and unstressed syllables on your sheet.' 'This is iambic pentameter.' 'Find a couplet.' The students are taking notes. After each question, he waits for most of the hands to go up. The discourse of the classroom is a kind of oral cloze. In command, relaxed, enjoying being a performer, he frequently jokes. Every now and then he targets a student whose hand is not raised. Then another sheet of poetry is handed out. Again, line by line, meaning is disentangled. Finally the class files out for lunch.

In the school playground the students crowd around the principal to discuss an upcoming barbecue, initiated by them as a way to raise money to fund their new school paper. He tells them that, since it was their idea, it was up to them to organise it, provide entertainment and organise the parents to bring food.

### History and Pedagogy

These vignettes show just how different the cultures of schooling can be, within the limits imposed by institutionalised education. It is remarkable that such differences should appear, even when the external conditions that come to bear upon the two schools are so similar. Each of the pedagogies in the vignettes — the first progressivist, the second traditional — is a cultural product. As such, each pedagogy is not immediately reducible to the school's social setting but represents a cultural choice on the part of the school and the teachers among several, major, historically evolved alternatives.

To understand this, we need to uncover the origins of such wildly variant cultures of schooling and account for their form and purpose — to undertake an exercise in historical recovery. For each approach is a perfectly explicable creature of the history of education. Each is wonderfully appropriate and faithful to historical experience, yet strangely inept and unsuccessful, too — as if limited precisely because it is a product of a very particular historical moment or a particular cultural context and perhaps not so readily generalisable to all other contexts. Then, with an historian's detachment, it is possible to see 'traditionalism' and 'progressivism' in a new light.

The fundamental epistemological and pedagogical orientation underlying the traditional classroom was virtually unquestioned for centuries. In the societies of Western Europe and their colonial offshoots this has been the main approach to pedagogy from the time of the rise of humanistic education during the Enlightenment. As the founding pedagogy of mass, institutionalised schooling in the nineteenth century, its dominance lasted well into the twentieth century. That so many classrooms worked upon so many millions of students in this way for so long, is testimony, surely, that this pedagogy must have been appropriate, for the time. Perhaps we might also have to concede an element of lasting appropriateness for the late twentieth century, in some cultural contexts at least, given that the second classroom is not just to be found as a relic in some anthropological museum. But the progressivist pedagogy, while newer, still has roots almost a century old. The vociferous academic and public contest between competing conceptions and practices of education has seen a lot of change; but beside the new, there stands living tradition. Just down the road from classroom one, newest of the new, is classroom two, bastion of tradition.

Taking an historian's view, we need to schematise and draw broad categories. The first pedagogy of institutionalised mass schooling we will call the traditional pedagogy of a classical canon, in which teaching the structure of Shakespearean sonnets must surely be a living example. Then emerges a progressivist pedagogy of modernism and experience. In recent decades we have witnessed the development, within the progressivist framework, of a pedagogy of postmodernism and difference which builds upon progressivism but also diverges from it insofar as it represents a very different worldview, elements of which are to be seen at work in the commerce lesson at State High.

## The Traditional Pedagogy of a Classical Canon

'Traditional' is a difficult word. It implies continuity with a distant, primordial past. It implies changelessness in the present. Despite its newness, traditional curriculum instils this sense of timelessness and continuity as its cultural content purports to teach a classical canon, ostensibly linked back through the 'classics' of ancient Greece and Rome to origins in a continuous Western culture. This classical canon typically lives on through the 'great books' of Western literature, the 'great men' of history and the religiosity of the Christian tradition. Its underlying epistemology assumes that there are fixed and constant 'facts' and moral and social 'truths' in the world. This conveys the impression of cultural fixity, making it ideologically, if not historically, traditional.

The sixteenth century French scholar Petrus Ramus 'invented' the modern textbook, one of the most distinctive icons of the traditional curriculum of a classical canon. His detailed expositions of knowledge shifted the educational centre of gravity away from the scholar-teacher and Socratic dialogue toward the universal text, with printed copies for each student. His textbooks — remarkably running to some 1100 editions and spreading across much of the intellectual world of early modern Europe — dealt with dialectic, logic, rhetoric, grammar and mathematics. Apart from being written in Latin — the *lingua franca* of intellectual life across Renaissance Europe — the Ramus texts were profoundly classicist in their contents. Rhetoric or dialectic, for example, were considered important because they were part of the cultural legacy of classical Greece and Rome. The learning of grammar was no more than learning the grammars of Latin and Greek. This is of enduring consequence to the form taken by traditional grammar even in the twentieth century, a grammar better suited to describe Latin and Classical Greek than modern vernacular languages.

This classicism was deceptive, however. For example, rhetoric and dialectic had become formalised, didactic texts instead of the practical skills they had been originally. Knowledge was now associated with the silent, visual world of the written text. The Ramus texts were very modern things, in other words, even though their subject matter referred way back into the past. Moreover, the formalising of knowledge into a text required a peculiar economy. A very specific logic was applied to the way information was arranged, a logic that proceeded, to use Ong's words, 'by cold-blooded definitions and divisions leading to still more definitions and more divisions, until every last particle of the subject had been dissected and disposed of' (Ong, 1982, 134–135). Knowledge was reconstituted through written language, carefully arranged in a spatial order and no longer founded on oral language and its sounds. Directives to the source of knowledge could now take the form of 'look at page seven, line three, the fourth word'. Unlike even the handwritten manuscript, to which students previously had only limited access, the Ramus texts were based on fixed and repeated relations — generalisable abstractly from student to student, faithfully reproducing the logic of the printer's form.

A very particular orientation to knowledge was also implied. The text portrayed the world 'objectively' such that there was no engagement outside itself. There appeared to be no difficulties with the knowledge requiring criticism. The contents seemed self-evident and self-contained. Knowledge was such that it could be printed in dichotomised outlines that showed how it was organised spatially, both in itself and in the mind (Ong, 1983, 307–314). Knowledge, in other words, appeared as objective and universal truth. The language of the text presented itself as voiceless and depersonalised.

The very possibility of such apparently universal objective knowledge was a product of new pressures towards standardisation and the rise of technocratic rationality, both cultural consequences of technological and social change. For example, with the spread of printing came a proliferation of grammar texts. Writing in the vernacular, previously primarily oral and variable languages, became more standard and uniform. Indeed, printers themselves were key figures in standard-ising the spelling and grammar of modern European languages (Graff, 1987, 117). The idea that there might be 'standard' or objectively 'correct' usage, in other words, was a new cultural phenomenon. All this added up to a unique cultural logic — a logic that was to form the initial basis of curriculum in modern schooling.

Here are two nineteenth century instances which illustrate the modern text-book form. The first is a mid-nineteenth century grammar school reader pub-lished in Philadelphia, consisting of eighty-five lessons, which selected prose or poetry from the 'great books' or used contemporary moral homilies. 'The reading lessons in this book contain just and moral sentiments', says the preface. Each lesson was introduced with pronunciation exercises. Reading aloud was seen to be a way of improving articulation, the principal purpose of the reader, and informed by a very rigid objective of 'correctness' and social exclusivity.

> The laborer acquires muscular strength and skill in the use of those limbs which are habitually and correctly exercised. The organs of speech are governed by the same law; and if we would secure a perfect enunciation, they must be exercised in the same manner. . . . [I]f children are required to utter correct sounds forcibly at the age when the organs of speech are most tractable, the habit of uttering words distinctively, and of pronouncing them correctly, will soon be formed. The voice should be early and frequently exercised upon the elementary sounds of the language . . . and classes of words containing sounds liable to perversion or suppression should be forcibly and accurately pronounced. . . . If the learner habitually mispronounce words, if he pervert or suppress impor-tant sounds, — as *prudunt for prudent*, or *boundin* for *bounding*, — his at-tention should be directed to the table of words containing sounds similar to those mispronounced, and the voice should be exercised upon it until the defect is remedied. (Swan, 1844, 3–5)

The second example is a history book published in Scotland in the late nine-teenth century — simply a voluminous list of facts about ancient Greece and Rome, listed by date. These were to be memorised with the aid of mnemonics, or sound association. One random fact about great literature, 174 pages into the book is '456 — Death of Aeschylus, the Father of Tragedy'. This was followed by a phrase that could be memorised, '*Aeschylus* the *illustrious poet*'. Taking the first consonant of each of the three key words, and referring back to a previously memorised table matching numbers with sounds, the date of the fact could be reconstructed: s = 4; l = 5; p = 6 (MacKay, 1869, 1, 174). The basic features of the pedagogy of a classical canon are all here in these two examples: a focus on great books and the Western tradition as originating in ancient Greece and Rome; a sense of the permanency and inviolability of 'facts' and moral truths; a pedagogy of memorisation and clearcut correctness; and a class exclusivism.

In traditional pedagogy, the textbook is complemented both by larger, institutional and systemic arrangements on the one hand and by the microdynamics of classroom culture on the other. Institutionally, mass schooling arose with powerful and rigid systems links between administration/governance, the syllabus, the textbook, the classroom and the examination. Through these, content is prescribed, presented and tested (Cope, 1987). The role of the teacher distinctively reflects this as well. Teacher talk exceeds student talk during instruction so chairs and desks are arranged in rows facing the blackboard. The teacher interacts with the whole class rather than groups and determines the use of classroom time (Cuban, 1984, 3).

Literacy learning in traditional curriculum meant memorising spelling lists; doing exercises in traditional grammar like filling in cloze gaps or simply rote learning grammatical rules; 'composition' marked according to its compliance with the conventions of 'standard' English; and testing 'correct' knowledge of spelling and grammar in formal examinations. Language learning became 'the art of speaking and writing in English correctly' based on prescribed, absolute standards in which grammar amounted to a set of facts, fixed, with no unresolved problems. The vernacular was not seen to be a legitimate part of language learning (Gleason, 1965, 7–8). Cuban quotes a 1914 report critical of the way high school English was being taught in Buffalo, New York: 'It is composed largely of such work as copying, composing, and correcting short illustrative sentences, selecting single types from constructions from sentences frequently too easy for the pupil, completing elliptical sentences, memorising terms and definitions, diagramming and parsing in a routine fashion' (Cuban, 1984, 29). The subject English also concerned itself with literature, particularly in the higher grades. Defined as the study of great books, literature stood both as a model of correct usage and as an exposition of moral values, inducting students into the sensibilities of the high culture of the Western world.

In the early nineteenth century this traditional curriculum developed a very particular, and very modern rationale. Mass education was an important cultural tool in the construction of industrial society. Objectivity, factualness and disciplined order were all new cultural requirements. Literacy learning was, as Graff says, used as an instrument to inculcate 'punctuality, respect, discipline, subordination . . . a medium for tutelage in values and morality'; something needed to create 'a controllable, docile and respectful workforce, willing and able to follow orders' (Graff, 1987, 262). At the heart of this new curriculum was the written text: formalistic, heavy handedly didactic, non-negotiable. The textbook was not just a metaphor for a new system of social order in which the written text took a place of unprecedented importance. It was also a crucial means of socialising children into that new society. The traditional curriculum thus represents an enormous break in human history, as societies, with the occasional and partial exception of some elites, had previously functioned through more fluid, intersubjective, oral texts with socialisation occurring informally.

At the end of the twentieth century the traditional curriculum of a classical canon is still alive and well. Although it no longer enjoys unrivalled hegemony, it remains a very powerful cultural force. In Australia we find the Ethnic Community College, just down the road from State High. In the United States, Cuban argues that American schools have changed less in the way they operate pedagogically over the past century than many would have us believe (Cuban, 1984, 2). If often only in a watered down form, the traditional curriculum of a classical canon lives on, suggesting that, unlike the stage coach which was irretrievably consigned to the dustbin of history by the railroad, traditional curriculum contains some workable and enduring insights into the nature of industrial society and mass, institutionalised schooling as an instrument of socialisation.

## The Progressivist Pedagogy of Modernism and Experience

A very new approach to schooling, one which might be described as a progressivist pedagogy of modernism and experience, emerged in the early twentieth century principally through the writings of John Dewey in the United States and Maria Montessori in Italy. Dewey's *School and Society*, founded on an ideology of movement, change and progress, opens with a chapter entitled 'The School and Social Progress'. To Dewey, progress in essence meant celebrating industrialism as the unqualified, unambiguous and unproblematic mastery of nature. The earth 'is the great field, the great mine, the great source of the energies of heat, light and electricity; the great scene of ocean, stream, mountain and plain, of all our agriculture and lumbering, all our manufacturing and distributing agencies.' By these means 'mankind has made its historical and political progress.' The earth is 'the home to whose humanizing and idealizing all his humanity returns' (Dewey, 1900a, 19).

Living as we do in another time when even the exponents of this sort of ideological modernism are guarded and defensive about the relationship of industrial society to nature, this view seems strangely limited, particularly for a scholar whose work has in other ways proved remarkably durable. Yet this modernist worldview had very important implications for early progressivist pedagogy. It gave curriculum a singular cultural purpose which could be traced to the confident culture of industrial progress. In a very immediate sense, this singular cultural intent was the reason for Dewey's concern that practical activities and experience be an integral part of schooling, instead of the bookish learning of traditional curriculum. At school, children should learn to be 'cooks, seamstresses, or carpenters'. Classrooms should be 'active centers of scientific insight into natural materials and processes, points of departure whence children shall be led into a realization of the historic development of man' (Dewey, 1900a, 19).

Progress, development, modernism, an activist relationship with the natural world, the risky experimentation and creativity that were at the heart of society driven by its own technological dynamism — these were values which could not, in Dewey's view, be taught by textbooks which were preoccupied with 'lore and wisdom handed down from the past'; which dictated fixed 'standards of proper conduct'; and which believed that 'the attitude of pupils must be one of docility, receptivity and obedience'. Progressivist education, in Dewey's conception, was a direct response to the inappropriateness of traditional curriculum which imposed knowledge from above and outside. 'To imposition from above is opposed expression and cultivation of individuality; to external discipline is opposed free activity; to learning from teachers, learning through experience; to acquisition of isolated skills and techniques by drill is opposed acquisition of them as a means of attaining ends which make direct vital appeal; to preparation for a more or less remote future is opposed making the most of the opportunities of present life; to static aims and materials is opposed acquaintance with a changing world' (Dewey, 1938, 3, 5–6).

He was also concerned that a traditional curriculum was one which 'imposes adult standards, subject matter and methods' simply because its contents were 'beyond the reach of the experience young learners already possess' (Dewey, 1938, 4). This pedagogy he considered to be nothing short of brutal, as it was virtually meaningless to its students. 'Textbooks and lectures give the results of other men's discoveries, and thus seem to provide a short cut to knowledge; but the outcome is just a meaningless reflecting back of symbols with no understanding of the facts themselves' (Dewey and Dewey, 1915, 14–15). The traditional classroom, moreover, was arranged for listening, thus teaching 'the dependency of one mind upon another' (Dewey, 1900a, 31–32).

Dewey expressed his alternative through the metaphor of organic growth. Don't interfere from an adult standpoint; 'give nature time to work'. This would mean a transformation of curricula and classrooms that would go to the root of the way knowledge is appropriated, even to the extent of questioning the status of facts. 'So, teachers, instead of having their classes read and then recite facts from the textbook, must change their methods. Facts present themselves to everyone in countless numbers, and it is not their naming that is useful, but the ability to understand them and see their relation and application to each other.' Instead of being a passive receiver of facts, in Dewey's progressivist pedagogy, the child would grow by assuming the role of questioner and experimenter (Dewey and Dewey, 1915, 6, 172).

Dewey's progressivism set out to remedy three evils in traditional curriculum. The first was the lack of organic connection with the child's life. Without such connections, knowledge and learning were purely formal and symbolic. Dewey did not deny that the symbol is important. He considered it to be a product of past reality and a tool for exploration. But he felt that it had to symbolise in an active and meaningful way. It had to have a meaning for the child. Facts, such as grammar, had to have an evident meaning and purpose. Otherwise they remained mere symbols, hieroglyphs, dead and barren. The second evil, as a consequence, was that traditional curriculum seemed to Dewey to give students no reasons to be motivated. 'An end which is the child's own carries him on to possess the means to its accomplishment.' Curriculum is most successful in conditions of equilibrium of 'mental demand and material supply.' Third, he argued that a typical method of traditional curriculum, simplification or making logical, removed the thought-provoking nature of a more problematic reality, a world which is much more messy than a simplifying curriculum and its textbooks might have us believe. And being presented with 'facts' and synthesis, the child is not made 'privy to the nature of generalisation'. Knowledge is presented only as the stuff of memory. 'The child gets the advantage neither of the adult logical formulation, nor of his own native competencies of apprehension and response' (Dewey, 1900b, 24–26). Quite profoundly, Dewey felt the traditional curriculum reflected the politics of an 'autocratic society' which he, as a liberal democrat, rejected. It was, he argued, a curriculum which cultivated 'the colorless, negative virtues of obedience and submission'. The responsibility for the conduct of a democratic society and government rested on its citizens, he argued, and this has implications for the micropolitics of the classroom. 'The function of the teacher must change from that of a cicerone and dictator to that of a watcher and helper' (Dewey and Dewey, 1915, 172, 297, 303, 304).

When it came to the specific question of literacy, Dewey's principles marked a dramatic break with traditional literacy teaching. He regarded language as social and purposeful rather than abstract and formal. The most effective language learning involved students 'having something to say rather than having to say something'. Language teaching, in other words, should be 'done in a *related* way, as the outgrowth of the child's social desire to recount his experiences and get in return the experiences of others' (original emphasis; Dewey, 1900a, 55–56). But while Dewey rejected the 'dry Gradgrind facts of a routine textbook type' (Dewey and Dewey, 1915, 129–131), he retained a singular cultural end to teaching — the 'correct' acquisition of the standard English which served a practical purpose in industrial society. This conception of language still made no concession to the fact that students' experiences of language outside school might be very different, be they native speakers of languages other than English or speakers of a non-standard dialect. There were new cultural assumptions at work here. Motivated student activity was a pedagogical tool in the interest of progress and modernity and these cultural assumptions were as powerfully singular as those of the traditional curriculum of a classical canon, even to the point of sharing some of the same objectives — correct grammar, for example — albeit objectives that were now to be achieved by a different means.

Cultural difference in general was still something that it was thought the school should erase. 'There is in a country like our own a variety of races, religious affiliations, economic divisions. Inside of the modern city, in spite of its nominal political unity, there are probably more communities, more differing customs, traditions, aspirations, and forms of government or control than existed in an entire continent in an earlier epoch.' Only through public schooling, Dewey argued, 'can the centrifugal forces set up by the juxtaposition of different groups within one and the same political unit be counteracted.' The curriculum itself was a critical instrument in creating a new cultural singularity. 'Common subject matter accustoms all to a unity of outlook upon a broader horizon than is visible to the members of any group while it is isolated' (Dewey, 1916, 21–22).

Progressivism was profoundly a cultural product, a product of an historic moment and not simply a series of universal insights into effective learning. There were some quite pragmatic social reasons why traditional curriculum was no longer considered appropriate in twentieth century education. Industrialism was, after all, 'a society where railroads and steamboats, newspapers and telegraph, have made the whole world neighbors.' 'The world has been so tremendously enlarged and complicated', not just by transport and communications, but by continual scientific discoveries. For Dewey, this only served to highlight further the increasing irrelevance of traditional pedagogy — the 'hopelessness of teaching with lists of facts' (Dewey and Dewey, 1915, 171–172).

Setting the new arguments on language education in this context, the ideology of progressivism represented a shift from what Cook-Gumperz calls a nineteenth century concern with literacy as a tool of social stability and a newly emerging twentieth century emphasis on literacy as a fundamental technology upon which modern societies are built (Cook-Gumperz, 1986, 16–44). By the late twentieth century there was yet another pedagogy, another major educational paradigm, with quite pragmatic social reasons to want to initiate change into educational debate and practice.

### The Progressivist Pedagogy of Postmodernism and Difference

While the progressivist pedagogy of postmodernism and difference has its roots in modernist progressivism and shares many of its most basic assumptions — about student activity, motivation and experience, for example — it diverges in some very important ways. Instead of the singular culture of industrial modernity, the new pedagogy emphasises difference, discontinuity, rupture and irreversible cultural and linguistic fragmentation.

This pedagogy is in fact founded in newly prevailing general senses of the world. In a deliberate counterpoint to the modernist doctrines, the postmodernists pronounce the end of history; the decadence of grand metanarratives, such as the world civilising mission of Western culture and industrial development; and the demise of progress, represented most potently by their newfound pessimism about the relationship of industrial society to nature. Melting pot and assimilationist ideas about cultural diversity are challenged by notions of cultural pluralism. Ideas that women should attain the same status, rights and roles as men are challenged by feminists revaluing women's culture — another line of cultural difference.

There is no doubt that, in cultural and historical terms, something very important is going on here, something which spreads far beyond the high culture of academe. In fact, a broader loss of universal meaning in the world is something which is daily felt in very real ways by millions of people, in the streets, in workplaces and in mass media. In Dewey's progressivism, homogenising modernity and progress were a singular cultural goal for the common curriculum of schooling. Postmodernists believe there can be no universal culture and no universal narrative — just multifarious readings or interpretations of the world, coming into play in contingent and fortuitous moments of intertextuality. For Dewey, the problem with traditional curriculum had been the meaningless, dislocated, formalistic character of the symbols it presented to students. He wanted these replaced with new symbols — a common experience of schooling in the melting pot that was industrial modernity. Now, for the postmodernists, symbols can have no consistent meaning. There are just readings, intertextualities, intersubjectivities. The world is a forest of signs unconnected by any overall ordering narrative. There is nothing upon which we might all be able to agree, or about which we might even be able to argue constructively with the aim of coming to some generalisable conclusion, except perhaps that we cannot agree or generalise.

There are two important aspects to postmodernist curriculum. The first is a radical individualism in which all knowledge is personal or relative to the individual's experience. Human beings, in Mayer's view, are active meaning makers. The world is no more and no less than what individuals construct by means of interpretations filtered through the prism of their own unique experiences (Mayer, 1990, 75–80). This extends Dewey's insights about individual motivation and experience by assuming that neither individual experience nor the knowledge that is subsequently constructed, can ever be universal. Rather, knowledge is a peculiar product of that experience. The second, connected consequence is relativism: that there can be no single and universal pedagogy. In different cultures students have different learning styles. Nor should schools impose cultures, discourses or learning styles on their students.

Traditional curriculum set out to transmit a social content. Modernist progressivism was concerned that all students be exposed to the the universal experience of constructing knowledge in a technologically and scientifically dynamic society. But with the premise that knowledge is individual or at most the product of localised cultural experience, now curriculum has simply to be relevant to that peculiar experience. The pedagogical and epistemological consequences of this view can be seen in the 'Media and Anti-racist Pedagogies' course taught by Elizabeth Ellsworth at the University of Wisconsin, Madison. Her aim, she writes in a paper on the experience of running the course, is to 'win semiotic space for marginalised discourses' in a university curriculum which, she argues, is dominated by 'the myths of the ideal rational person and the "universality" of propositions that have been oppressive to those who are not European, white, male, middle class, Christian, able-bodied, thin and heterosexual.' Her course allows other discourses, which are neither bound to this rationality nor inevitably subservient to its universalistic pretensions, a voice. Consistent with the philosophy of post-structuralism, the course cannot presume to do anything beyond giving students space to articulate views which are never more than partial, never more than representative of different interests and standpoints. As students necessarily bring experiences to class which others do not know and can never properly know, the teacher is a facilitator and definitely not a didact (Ellsworth, 1989, 302, 304). To teach any one discourse, such as a critical, rational discourse, is culturally laden and includes a presumption that other discourses are inferior.

C.A. Bowers, in a conservative variant of what is essentially the same pedagogy, has set out 'to formulate a theory of education for the post-modern era we are now entering.' He questions the idea that change is inherently progressive; that the individual is a source of freedom and rationality; and that learning scientific thought can lead to empowerment and self-direction. He complains that intersubjectivity is marginalised by instrumental rationality. He questions the validity of rationality as the basis of authority and the assumption that the individual is amenable to being shaped by environment. He claims that the deep, shared assumptions of liberal progressivists are at the bottom of the current crises of authority and social purpose — the ecological crisis, the loss of meaningful community life, nihilism. Instead, he proposes a conservative pedagogy based on a critique of 'dehumanising modernisation'. The individual is profoundly embedded, a bearer of tradition. Cultural conservatism is the struggle, on the part of minority groups, for example, against being colonised (Bowers, 1987, 2, 17, 26, 49, 51, 86, 90). Bowers' inclinations are in some obvious ways very different from Ellsworth's, a confessed conservative in contrast to a professed radical. But the similarities in what they are saying are much more interesting than their differences — the idea that students will speak from different experiences and traditions; the insistence that pedagogy must impose no cultural assumptions about what is legitimate knowledge; and the subsequent legitimation and nurturing of the different cultures of experience that students bring to the classroom.

Giroux, Aronowitz, McLaren, Macedo and perhaps Freire, theorists of critical pedagogy who rose to prominence in the 1980s, still retain some of the central concerns of modernism although they label themselves postmodernists with some justification. Aronowitz and Giroux point to the 'decay of master narratives' and 'metadiscourses'. They allow 'no privileged place to western culture'. Their intention is 'to legitimate subaltern discourses as equal'. They, too, focus on language and intersubjectivity. Language is 'a system of signs structured in the infinite play of difference' (Aronowitz and Giroux, 1991, 13–14, 18, 68, 75). Language positions the author or reader according to race, class and gender. As a consequence, the knowledge borne by language is contingent. Knowledge is no more than the expression of the context-related languages which organise perception and communication. McLaren interprets Freire and Macedo as being in sympathy with poststructuralism insofar as they regard truth and meaning to be contingent upon culture, language and history (McLaren, 1988, 213–234). Knowledge, in sum, is always a product of 'the partial, the local, the contingent' (Aronowitz and Giroux, 1991, 122).

Accordingly, in the postmodernist curriculum the primary task is to be relevant. Curriculum reform involves a struggle over textual authority, an authority that habitually presents itself as universal and which thus limits the possibility of students to mobilise their own voices (Aronowitz and Giroux, 1991, 15–16, 96). Knowledge is always a social construction, with social functions, representing interests, enforcing exclusion and institutionalising marginalisation. McLaren follows Foucault in arguing that truth is produced by regimes of power (McLaren, 1989, 169, 181). 'Voice' is a critical term for formulating an alternative pedagogy. Making a space for student voice 'entails replacing the authoritative discourse of imposition and recitation with a voice capable of speaking in one's own terms, a voice capable of listening, retelling, and challenging the very grounds of knowledge and power' (Giroux, 1988, 165).

However, these critical pedagogues come up with a vision for education that includes, rather uneasily, elements of structuralism and modernism. Voice is a product of 'the ways in which students produce meanings through the various subject positions that are available to them in the wider society' — hardly a poststructuralist account as here language and knowledge are clearly the product of social structures (Aronowitz and Giroux, 1991, 100). So too, the regimes of power that critical pedagogy sets out to counteract are not considered 'relative in the sense that all truths have equal effects'. Critical pedagogy, with a quite obvious aspiration to a certain kind of universality, is based on 'actions informed by a disposition to act truly and rightly', in the battle against pain and oppression, for example (McLaren, 1989, 181–182). In the same vein Giroux argues for a new ethics of education and in public life generally (Giroux, 1988, 39–41). Ellsworth undertakes an analysis of the critical theorists from the standpoint of what she regards to be a more consistent poststructuralism, arguing that the rules of reason, the assumptions about the rational person and the propositions of universal validity typically have as their counterpoints the irrational 'other', such as women, or 'exotic' cultures and discourses (Ellsworth, 1989, 301, 304). A pedagogy which doesn't dominate, in other words, must be rigorously non-universalistic. In their turn, Aronowitz and Giroux respond to Ellsworth, accusing her of separatism and a crippling form of political disengagement. The critical theorists nevertheless confirm some of Ellsworth's more general points when they explain how their pedagogy 'draws on the best' of both modernism and postmodernism (Aronowitz and Giroux, 1991, 59–60, 132).

While these are essentially epistemological questions, they also say something about the institutional arrangement of curriculum. Progressivism regards curriculum as an active thing which must be in the hands of students, and driven forward by their motivation. In its most radical variants this pedagogy advocates a radical devolution of curriculum control, and consequently, an inevitable diversification of its contents according to the variety of student experience and student interest (Cope, 1987). In a postmodern high school, say Aronowitz and Giroux, students and teachers have the final authority in making curriculum decisions. There are no requirements imposed from above. Students plan their own courses of study. Teachers may well try to persuade students, but in the last analysis it is up to the students. They might choose courses which are offered, but if these are not to their taste, they might choose independent study. Even within a class or a course different groups will be working on different things (Aronowitz and Giroux, 1991, 20–21).

Garth Boomer carries this sense of the openness of the ideal curriculum right through to the dynamics of classroom discourse.

> The teacher rarely tells the student what he thinks they ought to know. . . . He [also] recognises that the act of summary or 'closure' tends to have the effect of ending further thought. If a student has arrived at a particular conclusion, then little is gained by the teacher's restating it. If the student has not arrived at a conclusion, then it is presumptuous and dishonest for the teacher to contend that he has. . . . Lessons develop from the responses of students and not from a previously determined 'logical' structure. The only kind of lesson plan, or syllabus, that makes sense to [the good teacher] is one that tries to predict, account for, and deal with the authentic responses of learners to a particular problem. . . . We have discovered in our attempts to install inquiry environments in various schools that great strides can be made if the words 'teach' and 'teaching' are simply subtracted from the operational lexicon. (Boomer, 1982, 3)

This means there can be no preset curriculum. The teacher is like the parent of a small child learning oral language, needing the 'uncanny knack' of being one step ahead of their students. Given classroom constraints, in the nature of this sort of curriculum, students will much of the time need to communicate with each other in teacherless groups (Mayer, 1990, 124, 129–130).

While traditional curriculum is a pedagogy that transmits fixed social truths and modernist progressivism is a common pedagogy of enlightened authority, postmodernism is a pedagogy without closure, studiously open to difference. What does this mean for language teaching and learning? For a start, it will open up the repertoire of great books and the obsession with literature, finished writing and correct language. Students will learn 'to write, to make language live' (Murray, 1982, 14). No longer will subject English be fair game for the peddlers of formulaic interpretative notes and cribs because the products, rather than the processes of literary analysis, are rote learnt by students and tested by teachers. No longer will English be simply a medium for elitism and tracking, an icon marking as separate those deemed worthy to be the inheritors of high culture (Mayer, 1990, 22–24, 27–28).

Linguists also question the connotations of linguistic normalcy or superiority in the concept 'standard'. They see 'standard' English as simply a culturally specific dialect in a world of dialect differences where no one culture, language or dialect can be regarded as superior. Indeed, in a study of urban 'Black English Vernacular', Labov argues that 'standard', middle-class English is deficient in some important ways compared to that used by Black, male, adolescent teenagers. Middle-class English is cumbersome and verbose in describing central human subjects such as death. As found in the academic discourse and technical or scientific books, it is 'simultaneously overparticular and vague', lacking the logical clarity and even grammaticality of Black English Vernacular. Nor does it have the sophisticated resource of ritual insult needed to manage peer group relations in urban street cultures. These are just a few examples of the comparative power of the dialect of the boys Labov studied (Labov, 1972a, 213, 222, 352–353). To deny Black English Vernacular a legitimate place in school, then, is not only to condemn a cultural resource born of students' experience — demonstrably an effective, living, working, cultural tool. It is also to do a serious disservice to its speakers by incorrectly assuming that their language and background are cognitively and linguistically deficient. The problem for speakers of Black English Vernacular is not in their language but in the school's prejudiced view of their language.

Rigg and Kazemek even go so far as to question labels such as 'illiterate', arguing that 'before we label people as "illiterate" or "functionally incompetent", let us look at how individuals operate in a wide variety of specific situations with a wide variety of specific purposes. We don't have 23 million "functionally illiterate" adults. . . . We have an uncounted number of real people, each one using literacy in different ways' (Rigg and Kazemek, 1985, 7). So a person who gets a job through a network of oral contacts and who follows the signs in the street should be considered no less a person than someone else who reads job advertisements and has a written curriculum vitae.

The solution in postmodernist terms is for schools to view all dialects, indeed all ways of using language in society, as linguistically equal. Schools must 'reject negative, elitist, racist views of linguistic purity that would limit children to arbitrary "proper" language', says Goodman (Goodman, 1986, 25). Let's not fall into the trap of teaching a traditional grammar which condemns non-'standard' dialects, say Aronowitz and Giroux (Aronowitz and Giroux, 1991, 12–13). 'The successful usage of the students' cultural universe requires respect and legitimation of students' discourses, that is, their own linguistic codes, which are different but not inferior', say Freire and Macedo; 'in the case of Black Americans, for example, educators must respect Black English' (Freire and Macedo, 1987, 127). In political terms, a critical approach to literacy adds up to a 'pedagogy of voice', a narrative for agency, says Giroux. It is part of 'a moral and political project that links the production of meaning to the possibility for human agency, democratic community and transformative social action' (Giroux, 1988, 15–16).

In the regime of postmodernism, then, schools have to assume that there are no literary truths or universal, stable language facts. There is just language variation, with functions appropriate and relative to cultural experience. Indeed, it may well be that the issue of communication in general can be seen as no more than a series of contingent events, subject to the vagaries of intersubjectivity and intertextuality. There is no such thing as truth in text, so we can never claim that we know what such and such a text really means. In reading a text there is just intertextuality, the infinitely variable politics of reading and writing.

In practical terms many of the ideas of 'postmodern education' have been around a few years now. Although James Moffett's *Student-Centered Language Arts Curriculum* comes from the 1960s, here, too, purpose, communication, intertextuality are central. 'How can you teach style, rhetoric, logic and organization in a unit stripped of those authentic relationships to subject and audience that govern the decisions about word choice, sentence structure, paragraph structure and total continuity?' asks Moffett. Language is not mere formalism and conformity to conventions but a relationship of writer and reader. He rejects the 'particle approach' to language learning, and sequential development — in which the formal study of language moves from word to sentence to whole composition — because this is not how language or students actually work. 'Only in the largest context — the whole composition — can meaning, style, logic, rhetoric be usefully contemplated' (Moffett, 1968b, 4–5, 205–206). There is no grammar in Moffett's conception of ideal language learning, not even a place for linguistics, including Chomsky's then new transformational grammar. In its rigid formalism, any grammar ends up as 'arbitrary and therefore unwelcome knowledge'. If, as it is claimed, grammar helps develop deductive reasoning, this, Moffett feels, would be better achieved in mathematics than using the medium of something so messy and ambiguous as language (Moffett, 1968a, 14–15). In any event, 'good grammar' is a troublesome concept. It 'really means conformity to the particular grammar of standard dialect' (Moffett, 1968b, 156).

Nobody would claim that Moffett was a poststructuralist or a postmodernist. Nevertheless, he conceived language as fluid, contingent and culture laden and his many practical ideas about curriculum would today be supported by the most avowed postmodernist. In the same spirit, Goodman has argued in more recent years for a 'whole language' approach, claiming it is only when considered at this level that text remains functional and purposeful. As written and oral languages, he believes, have all the same basic characteristics, children should learn how to use written language at school in the 'natural' way young children learn oral language. Immersion, lots of doing reading and writing, and doing it for a reason that fits in with the child's own interests, experience and intentions, he claims, are the best ways to learn. A whole language curriculum, as a consequence, will draw on 'authentic resources' instead of textbooks; on student experience and communicative intentions rather than formal language facts to be ingested. A whole language approach, in other words, will be assiduously relevant. It will encourage students to use language for their own purposes. It will focus, not on language in the abstract, but on the meaning the child wants to communicate. It will respect the individuality of learners and their different life experiences. So, there are no disadvantaged students as far as whole language is concerned. By giving students a sense of control and ownership of their own language, in broader political terms, they will also get sense of their potential power as social actors (Goodman, 1986, 7, 9–10, 23, 33).

'Process writing' has the same general set of concerns and puts student interest and intent at its heart. Teacher set assignments, Murray says, inhibit what students have to say. 'The student finds his own subject. It is not the job of the teacher to legislate the student's truth. It is the responsibility of the student to explore his own world with his own language, to discover his own meaning. The teacher supports but does not direct this expedition to the student's own truth' (Murray, 1982, 16, 129). Children, says Graves, must choose their own topic in order to gain a sense of ownership — a critical, indeed almost clichéd word in the lexicon of process writing. From this starting point, 'the writing process has a driving force called voice.' The teacher is not there to impart knowledge but must wait to give help when it is needed as the child struggles for control. 'Teachers who have waited find that children give them the energy, the energy of control and ownership.' As a result, student-initiated topics and information are primary, not writing conventions. Writing in the classroom is conceived, not as a matter of learning and correctly applying conventions, but as a number of steps (the process, open to any contents): prewriting, drafting, conferencing, editing, publishing (Graves, 1983, 9, 21, 87–88, 227, 244). Writing is a solitary business. Students must find their own voices and listen to themselves as they write. They must find their own ways to truth. This is why creative writing can't be taught. It is a process of self-discovery wherein the student becomes a creative individual (Murray, 1982, 17, 65, 136).

What is the historical meaning of all this? Is it fair to paint a picture of an intellectual landscape with such broad brushstrokes? There are many, many niggling details, debates, points of disagreement and subtle but important differences that have had to be glossed over. But the overall shift is clear. This is no longer a world in which dogmatic canonical texts, cast in the mould of a Ramist textbook, seem to make much sense. It is no longer a world in which Dewey's assimilating, homogenising modernity seems to make as much sense as it once did, either. This is a world that is losing its faith in the one true mission of progress and development, or at best it is sheepishly defensive about it. It is a world where the West and its cultural canon is well on the way to losing its messianic race pretensions even though they still harbour an anachronistic sense of their own self-importance. It is a world of fragmentation, of cultural diversity, of multiple gender identities, of half a dozen different types of family, no one of which commands a majority adherence, of subcultures and styles and fads. It is a world where there are thousands upon thousands of specialist magazines speaking in specialist tongues and where there are some cities that have sixty television channels for aficionados of all sorts of peculiar discourses from pentecostalism to pornography. It is a world where a dozen or more languages might be spoken on one city block, while the television brings live coverage to that same block of what is happening at the ends of the earth. So, what else can be done but create a pedagogy which gives voice to each child's cultural proclivities and to the bewildering kaleidoscope of dialects and discourses? No wonder the poststructuralists despair at there ever being anything more than accidental moments of intertextuality.

## Histories of Pedagogy, Cultures of Schooling

Our opening vignettes are just two illustrations of the ways in which the cultures of schooling are themselves creatures of the history of pedagogy. The lesson on barter in the Year 7 commerce/geography class at State High is an instance of the progressivist pedagogy of postmodernism and difference — the fundamental cultural and epistemological move that is at the bottom of whole language and process writing — motivation, authenticity, voice, creativity, difference. We see the teacher using strategies which attempt to cater for cultural differences; to build upon student motivation; to grant self-esteem to different languages; to relax teacher control; to involve the students as active learners; and to reposition the teacher as an orchestrator of pedagogy-as-process rather than as the didactic transmitter of knowledge-as-content.

Permeating the culture of this classroom is not only a critique of a traditional curriculum which does none of these things, but also a critique of a society which is often racist, exclusionary, unjust and violent in response to cultural difference. To the credit of both this teacher, who was sufficiently concerned in the first place to go to the in-service training course on multicultural education, and to State High as an institution, there were very positive things in the atmosphere of this classroom. Certainly, given the socio-economic context, there was a remarkable calm here. The teacher viewed learning commerce as learning language, and the students certainly worked without fear of negative approbation for failing at their work. It is to her credit that the students were actively responsible for their own learning. It was not even such a bad thing that the Vietnamese girl could freely read her novel in preparation for another lesson when she felt she was not gaining so much from the commerce lesson.

Still, it is not too rash a generalisation to say that even after three lessons, the majority of the students in this class had produced not a word of text, and most had learnt next to nothing of the discourse of commerce. In cognitive terms, few students moved beyond procedural matters and empirical description to the analytical, critical and theoretical modes of thought that are so important and powerful if one is to disentangle and manipulate the world of industrialism (Kalantzis, Cope and Noble, 1991). Despite the obvious intentions of this pedagogy, most of the teacher talk bore little resemblance to the discourse of commerce, even when conceived narrowly as a school subject. Ironically, teacher talk was at best managerial, at worst authoritarian. And encouraging the use of languages other than English meant, for example, that part of the text became unintelligible to the other students in the work group. There were also difficulties with using the students' first language, simply because the discourse of commerce was alien to their repertoire, which was essentially domestic. This meant that students were inclined to use a barely coherent combination of first and second languages. The students, moreover, gained little idea of how to write in a group through this sequence of lessons. Nor did they get much of an idea, not even in the form of models, of how to write a play or create a money poster for Sydney Airport, for example.

The lesson in the Year 7 English class at Ethnic Community College displays all the features of the traditional curriculum of a classical canon: from the layout of the classroom; to student 'discipline'; to pedagogical formalism; to the elevation of the great works of the Western canon; to teacher dominated talk that requires student recitation. The pedagogy is defined through a critique of what is seen as 'lax', unrigorous, undisciplined public schools. Ethnicity here is something very much bound up in the migration process — a drive to succeed on the dominant society's own terms and indeed to do more than that, to do better. At the same time this is articulated through a sense that social success can be complemented by hanging on to the enduring, traditional, grounding, conserving qualities of the ethnic community. In this way the pedagogy at Ethnic Community College is just as much a product of the cultural diversity that has so profoundly influenced State High. Only this school has made a decision which puts it in the opposite camp in the battle that is educational politics.

The canon, the high culture of the West, is perceived to be a path to success at Ethnic Community College. This is very true in a literal sense if one looks at the content of the English examinations which determine university entrance. More profoundly, in cognitive terms, the students did move at times beyond empirical description to the analytical, critical and theoretical modes of thought with their significantly higher linguistic and cognitive demands. On the negative side, if the aim of education is either to teach socially relevant things or a critical understanding of the nature of a culturally diverse, industrial society, scanning sonnets is irrelevant nonsense. There is a sense that Ethnic Community High is doing little more than parrot the pretensions of high culture while imparting what Dewey called the 'dry Gradgrind facts of a routine textbook type' (Dewey and Dewey, 1915, 129–131). There is no attempt to allow students to generate their own knowledge or to give voice to their own experience in their own terms. Rather, the school sets out to instil intellectual docility by locating knowledge in a fixed, canonical position — so unlike the real contestation and continual flux that characterises knowledge in the world outside the school gates. As the profound sense of community here is a product of cultural homogeneity, not cultural diversity, how effectively will it prepare its students for life in a multicultural society?

These two pedagogies both epitomise our times — the first as responsive innovation, the second as reactive invocation of spirits past. Set side by side, they are evidence that our times are being shaken by profound cultural crisis. Both are brilliant and apt reflections of our times, each ingeniously appropriate and ingenuously inappropriate. So are these bad versions of good pedagogies or good versions of bad pedagogies? The current spate of classical revivalism, which claims that the West's cultural legacy is being neglected (Bennett, 1984); that students are leaving school still illiterate (Ravitch and Finn, 1988); and that great books and the classics are more true and more valuable than other texts (Bloom, 1987; Hirsch, 1988; D'Souza, 1991) are just some of the most visible and public pyrotechnics of pedagogical dissatisfaction. But, as pyrotechnics, they must not be simply accepted at face value. A return to traditionalism is clearly not the answer. Instead we must ask what lessons can we learn from this critical dialogue between pedagogies? Just as the debate has been defined through successive critiques, so any new educational synthesis will in turn have to be critical if real weaknesses as well as real strengths are to be uncovered. Only then can we move on from the achievements and understand the mistakes.

## The Failure of Progressivism

The new progressivism may see itself as culturally open and proclaim that it does not impose a singular worldview but it is in fact as culture-bound a creed as any, full of its own viewpoints and intolerances. The postmodernists are tolerant and open to difference, except differences that are not liberal and tolerant. Ellsworth may say that to teach a critical, rational discourse is culturally laden and includes a presumption that other discourses are inferior. She may claim to give space to other voices in her course. But just how real is her cultural agnosticism?

How easily, for example, can the new progressivism give voice to cultures which revere textual authority or which elevate teachers as the source of educational knowledge? If every culture or point of view is as good as the next, how does it handle cultures with hallowed traditions of sexism and racism? Who is most opinionated and most able to vocalise their 'voice' in the classroom? Arguably, the most vociferous are those most comfortable with the cultures of power and with the idea of expressing individual opinion. Finally, the tolerance and cultural relativism behind the idea of voice is also deceptive. Tolerance does not extend to cultures perceived to be intolerant, to certain attitudes to textual authority that are considered to be uncritical, or to learning styles that situate the teacher as an authority figure. Rather ironically, a teaching philosophy ostensibly open to cultural diversity is closed to cultural diversity in some serious ways.

Student-centred curriculum — uniquely a product of a culture whose child rearing practices are child-centred — is another central device of this progressivism. So is parent and community involvement. But this only obscures the real centre of gravity in curriculum control. Someone, after all, is doing the devolving. So what cultural principles lie behind their actions? And how effectively can a school promote community involvement, parent participation and multicultural curriculum if parents and community still regard the teacher as the expert, and believe school is not a site for the expression of diversity, but a place where a singular authoritative knowledge is imparted (Kalantzis, Cope and Gurney, 1991)? Does progressivism allow them a voice as well?

Lisa Delpit argues that progressivism's apparent anti-authoritarianism is a cultural hoax — a cultural product of a White liberalism which, underneath, is as authoritarian as any (Delpit, 1988, 280–298). Here veiled, rather than explicit commands are used to enforce adult authority. 'Would you like to do this next, Betty?' White children in American schools know that this means they are expected to do something but to Black children this means the White liberal teacher has abdicated authority, so the class reacts accordingly. The problem for Black students is misreading the cues of an alien discourse.

The cultural bias of progressivist curriculum unconsciously favours certain students. The process writing teacher, waiting while the child struggles for control and ownership (Graves, 1983, 9, 127), actually favours White, middle-class students. Consider the 'natural' advantage children from print immersed environments have in the process classroom. Their homes are full of newspapers, computers, books, letters. They already have an inkling of how a text works — its beginnings, middles and ends — and how text and image relate. They know what text does. In a very tangible way they can see the point of gaining for themselves the sort of control and ownership that comes with literacy. No amount of inner struggle, however, will tell students who do not come from such backgrounds what text is for and how it works. Writing is from a world outside their experience. These students need to be told the things that privileged students will be able to find out for themselves.

This same cultural bias also appears in the assumption that all students will intuitively discover things for themselves and that to be explicit about rules or assumptions will limit a student's freedom and autonomy. Clearly, in Lisa Delpit's words, 'if you are not already a participant in the culture of power, being told explicitly the rules of that culture makes acquiring power easier.' By way of example, she describes how a Black university student complained that his writing skills teacher 'was . . . a fool who couldn't teach and didn't want to try.' Process writing 'didn't teach anything. . . . We understand how to improvise, how to express ourselves creatively. When I'm in a classroom I'm not looking for that, I'm looking for structure, the more formal language.' His friend's Black teacher on the other hand 'was very good. She went through and explained and defined each part of the structure' (Delpit, 1988, 282, 284, 287).

In the traditional classroom there is an obvious system of exclusion at work. But the new exclusion in process curriculum is more pernicious because it pretends to want democratic openness. These cultural assumptions are imposed without negotiation precisely because they are hidden rather than explicit. Ironically, they cannot be opened to question and debate because to be explicit is to be didactic and to appear to impose. In this class you must choose your own topic, you must struggle for control and not expect to be taught formal conventions except incidentally to your own writing; you must draft, conference, redraft and so on. The Black student didn't want to learn that way.

Traditional curriculum creates very effective systems of motivation and reward, albeit on the basis of certain cultural assumptions. Students work hard to finish quickly, to get a better mark than last time, to beat other students in competition. There are institutionally generated, 'artificial' incentives which keep the wheels of even esoteric subjects turning. There are external motivations too: to get a good report, to please one's parents, to win a privileged place in the next stage of education, to get a good job and so on. Now, this pedagogy might favour the few and even 'fail' many students, but this may well be just right for a society where the success of a few is supposed to motivate the many to keep on trying. The motivation in progressivism, however, is based entirely on the individual's voice, the individual's sense of destiny. McLaren relates how a class in a Canadian urban ghetto school was asked to investigate something that was important to them. Perhaps they would choose something about their environment, the arms race or even poverty. But none of the students seemed to want to investigate anything (McLaren, 1989, 33).

Just as complacently as traditional curriculum, the new progressivism sits by while educational inequity — not getting a fair chance to use education as a means to social mobility — continues to be perpetrated. While traditional curriculum puts students who come from other cultural traditions or who speak other languages or dialects at a 'natural' disadvantage and all too easily labels them failures, progressivism's insistence that 'they are just different' does not really solve their problem either. To say that tests can no longer be failed and only 'relevant achievements' will be recorded, does not necessarily build self-esteem. Students in Australian schools who do English literature courses oriented towards external examinations and university entrance denigrate as 'Veggie English' those other school-based courses with names like 'Communication Skills'. All students know the courses are not simply equal by virtue of being different. How could students' curriculum 'choices' be as culturally and socially innocent as this? This is not a real choice, but a convenient ideology of choice. The students know that some knowledge, skills and discourses open more doors than others. The rationale of self-esteem is a charade if succeeding at 'Communication Skills' does not give you the same life chances as English literature (Cope and Kalantzis, 1990, 159–172). Refusing to test across a student cohort because this passes negative judgment on individual students does not mean that the school system of choice and diversity will not find other ways to make sure that students come out of school unequal (Kalantzis, Slade and Cope, 1990, 196–213).

In this sense, there is an element of dishonesty in some progressivist forms of assessment. Parents are often enraged to find out that their children are not going to make it into law or medicine at university, after the school has been telling them for years that they are doing so well in their subjects. Self-esteem turns out to be a trick if it simply reconstructs failure as choice. Far from being democratic, this is little more than a retreat into populism. Curriculum can never be just open process. It involves cultural contents too. The only difference is that the content here, much of the time, is an eclectic series of photocopies brought in by the teacher, not a formal rigid textbook.

The new progressivism also suffers an identity crisis of its own making when it defines knowledge and pedagogy as contingent, eclectic, incoherent, fragmented and decentred. Hirsch may be guilty of misrepresentation when he alleges that Dewey wanted information thrown out of the curriculum altogether (Hirsch, 1988, xv; Aronowitz and Giroux, 1988, 172–194). Still, his generalisation is an apt counterpoint to a newer progressivism which despairs at information overload; which gives up ever really knowing anything because what seem to be facts one day are disproved the next; and which considers knowledge to be all a matter of reading, perspective or opinion. If anyone is to be accused of promoting a pedagogy that mindlessly piles facts upon each other, facts with no immediately apparent order to them, it is progressivism. Its epistemological nihilism provides few guidelines with which to evaluate information or learn to synthesise knowledge. As Freire and Macedo put it, students need to learn how to link the pieces on 'the clothesline of information' (Freire and Macedo, 1987, 130).

The newest progressivisms do not help us understand the ways in which shared discourses and knowledge produce social effects — and some to greater social effect than others. We are in danger, argue Aronowitz and Giroux, of being trapped in particularistic theories that cannot explain larger social, political and global systems. We are left with no way of meaningfully reorganising society (Aronowitz and Giroux, 1988, 70, 79). Furthermore, as Christie argues, a progressivism which is founded on the proposition that there is nothing more relevant than a student's own experience fails to do more than reproduce the student's own commonsense — the everyday and the commonplace. It does not foster, for example, skills such as questioning and speculation (Christie, 1989a, 152–198).

Progressivist pedagogy in its latest guises also deskills the teacher although it claims to do just the opposite (Goodman, 1986, 28–29) simply because there are no longer any authoritative texts. In the process writing conference, for example, the student acts and the teacher reacts; the writer follows language, and the teacher follows the writer (Murray, 1982, 163). 'Everything is reversed. I have to give up the active, non-delegating, pushing, informing role for another kind of activity, the activity of waiting. Action in conferences is redefined as intelligent reaction. The child must lead, the teacher intelligently react' (Graves, 1983, 127). These pedagogical expectations are wildly unrealistic. In most classes it is simply impractical to cater to all learning styles, or even to get inside a student's unfamiliar learning style and scrutinise it carefully for its potential to secure social access. Nor is the process as innocent as this suggests. In fact, Pam Gilbert's study of process writing classes shows the teacher really occupies a strange place as reader and judge. Needless to say, student writing remains inevitably the peculiar product of school (Gilbert, 1989c, 164, 166).

Far from promoting professionalism, the pedagogy of process reduces teaching to a management technique. The teacher is no longer the expert, simply the manager and orchestrator of student activity. Rather ironically for a pedagogy which does not prescribe, progressivism is almost exclusively focused on telling students to do things — the steps in the process. Gone is the bound textbook with its transparent structure of chapters and exercises, where the students know where they have been in the curriculum and where they are going; where they can go back over work they find hard or go ahead if they are bored. Progressivism is the arbitrary dogmatism of instructions about process or, worse still, the photocopier curriculum: a barrage of teacher imposed sheets of paper, often from old textbooks. This adversely affects the nature and quality of student learning. The process writing teacher might get children to do lots of writing and, by degree, they might gradually do it better. But at the same time students might never acquire the tools to understand, other than in commonsense ways, how meaning is made through system in language nor how to analyse critically the social roles of different discourses. The process mode is one of pragmatic immersion. It is not analytical, distanced or theoretical in temper. Process writing is a procedural prescription of the steps students are to be told to take when they write, devoid of a theory of language to explain what writing is and how it works to make meaning.

An Aboriginal Australian parent once asked if his child could be taught the 'secret English' of officialdom (Martin, Wignell, Eggins and Rothery, 1988). It is time to acknowledge again that teachers might have some secrets about the relation of form and purpose in language, secrets that they, as professionals, have a duty to tell their students. The teacher who defers to difference is simply being patronising. To say that Aboriginal English is just as important a focus of energy at school as the 'secret English' that qualifies them as a teacher is clearly absurd. Ellsworth claims agnosticism regarding different voices and discourses but it was one particular discourse which made her a university professor. Labov, picking up on a term in Black English Vernacular, may call himself a linguistic 'lame' for not having the vibrant linguistic resources for the street life of young Black males in a US city but they do not earn the dollars Labov does as a purveyor of academic discourse. He is hardly 'lame' in broader social terms. Rigg and Kazemek also patronise those officially labeled illiterate by implying that they would not, if given the chance, choose to apply for the sorts of jobs advertised in newspapers that require a curriculum vitae.

Progressivism gives the deceptive impression that it is a 'natural' and 'authentic' pedagogy, in contrast to the 'artificiality' of the traditional curriculum. The textbooks of the traditional curriculum must be replaced with the real stuff of students' 'authentic' experiences and voices, a pedagogy in which students' knowledge and language develop naturally. But what does 'authentic' mean when there is culture in every curriculum? And how 'authentic' or 'natural' is writing itself? Historically, many human societies have never needed the written word, nor have they used the institution we call schooling as an instrument of socialisation. Even in contemporary society it seems that writing is a much more 'authentic' or 'natural' thing for some students than it is for others.

This pedagogy of naturalism glosses over important differences between written and spoken language. Donald Graves argues that 'writing and speaking are different but writing, without an understanding of its roots in speech, is nothing'; that 'the human voice underlies the entire writing process'; and that 'a professional . . . writer makes writing sound like speech' (Graves, 1983, 162). However, the fact that a professional writer can create a hybrid of oral and written language hardly proves the point that speech is like writing. The professional speech writer designs a text to be presented orally. A novelist or a playwright mimics speech in a text. In the context of an academic lecture, people speak in ways that are more characteristic of written than spoken language.

Despite these sorts of crossovers, borrowings and powerful hybridisations, the differences between oral and written language are enormous. Written language does different things, in different social contexts, for different social purposes and uses a very different linguistic technology than spoken language. The process theorists, however, elide these differences. Young children, they argue, learn oral language informally, by immersion in oral interaction, by their needs to make meaning, and because of their parents' informal but constant modelling and cajoling. For this reason, they claim, children will best learn written language informally as well — this time by immersion in print; by the need they feel to communicate using the written word; and by gradually refining their use of conventions through repeated exposure and use.

But learning to speak and learning literacy are simply not comparable processes. First, when children learn to write, they have already learnt to speak. They have the ability to name and to generalise. In other words, oral language gives them the tool which facilitates formal learning. Second, learning to write is a product of institutionalised schooling — a formal, public setting, with strictures to operate efficiently — a far cry from the informal situation in the household where the child first learns to speak. Hypothetically, it has been calculated that children are immersed in 18,200 hours of oral language in the first five years of their lives. This equals about twenty years of classroom time — hardly a feasible suggestion. At school, children learn that writing has many complex genre variations and a massive vocabulary accessible in its fullest scope only through dictionaries. If learning were just the slow accretion of facts picked up through immersion, if students had to learn generalisations solely by induction, then education would be a slow, inefficient and very much more expensive business.

Rather arbitrarily, progressivists assume that learning to speak happens naturally. In fact, all language learning and use are quintessentially human products. Brian Gray shows how, in oral interactions with small children, parents actually 'scaffold' language structures in frequently very explicit ways. Progressivism in schools, he argues, ends up playing a rather unproductive 'guess what's in my head' game, quite unlike the parent/child relationship in learning oral language (Gray, 1987). So, even the whole language/process writing ideal of oral language learning as a model for learning writing is no more than a figment of the progressivists' imagination.

Apart from this, there is a further ideological bias in the way emphasis on individual motivation and voice skews interest in the direction of certain genres. Mayer claims this is necessary in order to correct the 'antiwriting' of the traditional essay. Narratives, by contrast, express how we really think and feel and do not hide behind a smokescreen of objectivity. He exposes 'the slipperiness of knowledge' and 'the intertwining of knowledge with expression'. Language is a creative system, and thus there is 'no evidence that making language rules consciously enhances language performance' (Mayer, 1990, 100, 113–114, 237).

Certainly there is a problem in the way essays suggest an aura of truth and social neutrality. But factual writing is a more effective way of communicating scientific information than, for example, narratives. They are just as human, and carry just as much social and cultural baggage. Rather than dismiss factual genres as things which destroy creativity and expression, we need to analyse factual genres for the ways they work and the human interests that they always embody. 'Voiceless' genres — from the objectivity of the Ramus text, to the language of the technical manual, to the academic argument that studiously avoids using the first person — are some of the most powerful discourses of our times. Indeed, even some of the most powerful and effective narratives in the literary canon are apparently voiceless. It is not surprising, then, that the most common classroom products of process writing are not even narratives, but more distinctively-voiced personal recounts.

The new progressivism wants to assume that cultures, dialects and voices are relative and equal as it romantically equalises all languages, discourse and cultures. But, pulling back from an unqualified postmodernism, Aronowitz and Giroux point out that differences are never innocently pluralistic. They involve relationships of power too (Aronowitz and Giroux, 1988, 102–103). Thus, say Freire and Macedo, 'The legitimation of Black English as an educational tool does not . . . preclude the need to acquire proficiency in the linguistic code of the dominant group' (Freire and Macedo, 1987, 127). Process writing and whole language are part of the cultural and educational crisis of our time — instances of a progressivism which is historically the most recently evolved of the major educational paradigms. Its critics in the literacy debate talk about 'grammar', 'basics', 'cultural crisis', 'whole language' and 'process', but much of the time this is less than productive. To reinstate the traditional curriculum, as advocated by the 'back to basics' people, is not the answer. Nor is it helpful to accept the terms of the debate at face value or pronounce judgments about pedagogical truth on the basis of the ostensible 'results' of test scores. It is only when we can dispassionately and analytically understand the origins of these widely separated pedagogies that we can site them correctly.

When it comes to teaching 'Western culture', the progressivists are right about the arcane classicism of traditional curriculum and its cultural arrogance and blindspots. But progressivism does students a disservice if it does not help them know the hows and whys of the dominant culture and if its students do not come to understand critically something of the set of cultural relations with nature which happened by some historical accident to emerge in Western Europe over the last millenium. The story may well be uncongenial to many, and precisely this might be one very important reason to read the story, and read it critically.

Chapter 3

# The Power of Literacy and
# the Literacy of Power

*Bill Cope and Mary Kalantzis*

*Building on their historical analysis in Chapter 2, Cope and Kalantzis now go on to
outline another model of pedagogy, one that attempts to move beyond the limitations of both
traditional and progressivist pedagogy. This they call an explicit pedagogy for inclusion and
access.*

*They argue that in the teaching of genre literacy, one of the main points of departure
is the differences between oral and written language. This is quite the opposite of progressivism
which is based so strongly on the ideas of natural learning and the fundamental similarities
in the development of speech and writing epitomised in the notion of voice. On the contrary, they say, literacy does very different things from orality, in very different places and
in very different ways. There is, indeed, a cultural peculiarity to the distance between
orality and literacy, and that can be traced to the culture of industrialism. Rooted in literacy
are ways of thinking that are a cultural peculiarity of industrial society.*

*They proceed to argue that literacy is not a natural outgrowth from orality, which has
immediate consequences for pedagogy. It is the role of schooling to make the nature of
literacy explicit, particularly in order to provide historically marginalised groups of students
access to literate culture and literate ways of thinking. Yet at the same time, they say, there
are all sorts of hidden cultural assumptions in socially powerful discourses. Certain genres
of factual writing, for example, deliberately downplay the author's voice and thus pretend
greater objectivity than they actually have. Schools, in other words, would be doing their
students a disservice if they were to induct their students uncritically into the literacies of
power. Part of the process of developing a critical literacy also involves a recognition of the
diversity of students' cultural and linguistic backgrounds, and that effective teaching is a
dialogue between the culture and discourses of schooling and those of students.*

*In the light of its historical-cultural argument, the chapter then outlines some principles
for a reconstituted literacy curriculum. In this curriculum there would be a new role for
grammar: in the careful and systematic nurturing of a language to talk about language in
school. Grammar is necessary for two reasons. First, school is a very different site for
learning literacy from the site where orality is learnt. In contrast to the conditions in which
orality is learnt, grammar is a viable and efficient way of learning literacy and learning
about literacy. Second, one of the fundamental linguistic-cognitive missions of school is to
teach certain ways of thinking about the world and operating in the world. These centrally
involve abstraction and what Vygotsky calls conceptual thinking. Learning grammar as a
metalinguistic tool in learning literacy is a very effective way of achieving these linguistic-
cognitive ends.*

*The origins of the pedagogy outlined in this chapter, and its implications for a way of teaching grammar that does not take us back to traditional curriculum, are discussed in the Bibliographical Essay at the end of the book — on Kalantzis and Cope's Social Literacy curriculum project. The notion of teaching grammar and what grammar to teach are explored again by Martin and Rothery in Chapters 5 and 6.*

## An Explicit Pedagogy for Inclusion and Access

It is time not for a return to traditional curriculum but for rethinking the nature of pedagogy. It is time to start thinking about the dimensions of a reconstituted pedagogy — an explicit pedagogy for inclusion and access. This involves processes of historical recovery — of reconstituting and recombining elements of the three major historically evolved pedagogies more than it involves invention. As such, it is based on a critique of inherent difficulties in each of these pedagogies.

A rethought pedagogy will build on the insights of progressivism by using differential pedagogies, starting with students' differential experiences. Its objective will be a commonality which does not exclude difference or force homogenisation around singular cultural principles, and which does not restrict social access through a fragmented curriculum which leaves difference as difference. Clearly there are common linguistic, cognitive and cultural conditions for social access. Using differential, specialised pedagogies, these common ends should be the singular objectives of curriculum. An acceptance of enduring difference is an essential pedagogical precondition to achieving singular educational ends. However, this reconstituted pedagogy will need to shunt between increasingly important parochial differences and a supracommunity that is genuinely inclusive in what it privileges, its symbols and access to social goods.

A postprogressivist pedagogy will also need to move beyond moralism about discrimination. Diversity and its less than innocent social consequences need to be addressed both empirically and conceptually. Core curriculum can address historical issues of gender and culture. In literacy pedagogy the assumptions about language and language learning at the heart of the existing educational paradigms will have to be reformulated. As much as this involves critique of the paradigms, it will also entail reclaiming insights about the nature of learning, language and social context that have emerged. The paradigms, in other words, and even more so the vigorous debate that has gone on between them, are a positive and fruitful basis for rethinking pedagogy in general and literacy pedagogy in particular.

## Orality and Literacy

But what is literacy? How is it different from orality? What particular literacy needs do schools have to address at the end of the twentieth century? Is literacy becoming more or less important? The answers to these questions will determine the shape of literacy pedagogy in the start of the next century.

Contrary to the assumptions of process writing and whole language, oral and written discourses do very different things, in very different ways, in very different social contexts. Spoken and written languages each make distinct semantic connections as they call to mind prior or common knowledge as a communicative frame. In the case of orality, the speaker and the listener have the benefits of face-to-face communication, including the resources of intonation, gesture, immediate feedback and so on. In the case of literacy, however, it is knowledge of genre which provides a key clue to communicative intentions and audience expectations (Collins and Michaels, 1986). These fundamental differences have an impact right through to the respective grammars of speech and writing.

Speech, Kress shows, is arranged in 'information units', defined by their orientation to the topic. Writing, by contrast, has the sentence as its minimal textual unit. Although there are clauses in both written and oral language, the principle of their organisation differs considerably. Speech is dominated by sequences of clauses with intonation imposing structure in such a way that new knowledge is highlighted over shared knowledge. Speech operates under an additive principle of order. Writing, on the other hand, arranges clauses according to principles of hierarchy: coordinating, subordinating, embedding and weighting clauses according to the writer's assessment of the 'logic' of the topic. Written language operates under an integrative principle of order, dominated by strong forms of causality. So, for example, scientific writing uses metaphor and nominalisation as embedding strategies; it is impersonal in tone in part through use of the passive; and it has peculiar textual devices for maintaining order over a large text (Kress, 1989a, 1982). This summary only touches on a very complex and extensive linguistic argument. In terms of the commonsense of educational assessment, it is hardly surprising that a child who transcribes oral language at school — not that this is possible without at least some modification of its structures — will not do well simply because their work does not sound like 'good writing'.

This is not to say that the differences between writing and speaking are by any means absolute. Language would hardly be human if deliberate disruption of the most common sites for the grammatical structure of speech and writing was not itself a source of communicative effect. Contrast the personal letter that tries to sound like speech with the academic lecture which tries to sound like writing (Collins and Michaels, 1986, 209); or the fact that some written language is clearly closer to spoken language than others. But there can never be a complete crossover. In the range of written genres, for example, a personal diary may be relatively close to oral language, but its absent, anonymous addressee still makes it a genre unique to writing. Even though the personal diary involves 'talking to oneself', this is not the same thing as doing just that (Kress, 1982, 2).

Acknowledging this complexity does not mean that broad generalisations cannot be made about common social sites for speaking and writing. The social domain of speech is primarily the private sphere; that of writing is primarily public. This discursive pattern finds itself reflected even in cases of crossover between the typical grammar of written and oral modes. When power is disputed in the public sphere, speech will tend to display the features of the written mode — formality, distance and the like. The peculiarities of distinctively written genres thus have an important feedback into the structure and the social power of speech. Social power in the public sphere comes with the invasion of the syntax of speech by the syntax of writing (Kress, 1982, 175–176; 1989a, 3–5). In a similar vein to Kress, Ong distinguishes between primary orality — untouched by writing or print — and secondary orality — a 'more deliberate and self-conscious orality, based permanently on the use of writing and print' such as to be found on radio and television (Ong, 1982, 136). To understand the peculiarity of secondary orality, one has to refer to the effects of literacy.

Bernstein and Hasan have suggested the concept of code as a way of explaining the amount of social power that various discourses can exert (Hasan, 1973, 253–263). Bernstein's theories are particularly controversial as his schema, in its logic if not in many of its sociolinguistic details, parallels the contrast between the distinctive features of oral and written language. Schools fail students according to a predictable linguistic pattern, he argues, not simply through dialect prejudice or by marking simply on the basis of the superficial stylistics of middle-class speech and the niceties of conversation. Rather, some students fail because their domestic discourses embody different levels of explicitness and implicitness. He calls these differences linguistic codes (Bernstein, 1971, 1973, 1975).

Drawing on Durkheim's sociology, Bernstein contrasts two archetypical social settings. The first is one where the individual is less important than the community. Here discourse is characterised by a high frequency of exophoric reference or implicitness. In other words, the effective making of meaning, rather like oral language in general, is highly context dependent. The language of this type of community, such as to be found in a working-class cultural context, he calls restricted code. The second type of community regards differences as being of crucial importance. Here discourse is analytic and minimises exophoric reference by being relatively explicit. This is embodied in the complex division of labour found, for example, in the public life of middle-class professionals in an industrial society. Yet, although differences between individuals are seen to be of importance here, no situations can be precategorised totally. Society is fluid and social roles are not permanently ascribed to empirical individuals. This leads to the need for a language which Bernstein calls elaborated code. Every person in society has access to the discourse of the restricted code, but only the privileged have access to the elaborated code as well (Bernstein, 1971, 242–243).

There are some clear sociological parallels between the association of the public sphere with the distinctive grammar of writing and the realm of the private with the distinctive grammar of speaking; and Bernstein's elaborated and restricted codes. Furthermore, there are important linguistic parallels in the analytical temper and relative completeness-in-themselves of writing and elaborated codes, in contrast to speaking and restricted codes. Tannen's critique of Bernstein points to the complex crossovers between speaking and writing. She argues that 'autonomous or literate-based language is not necessarily elaborated, nor is oral-based or nonautonomous speech always restricted' (Tannen, 1982, 1–16). But this does not disprove the association of the distinctive features of writing with elaborated codes. Operating in oral language, elaborated codes are rather like a second language whose forms have been imported back into the first language of orality from the grammar of literacy.

Labov dismisses Bernstein, saying he is biased against working-class discourse and culture because he suggests that middle-class language is superior in every respect — more abstract, more flexible and more subtle (Labov, 1972a, 204). There is, indeed, a degree of judgmentalism in the two categories, but this should not obscure the fact that the two codes are seen as separate. Both work perfectly well in their respective realms. 'Restricted' code even does many things that an 'elaborated' code cannot. Still there is no point in denying that types of discourse, regardless of how well they do what they do in their native realms, lead to different social effects, effects which give some people greater access to power and privilege than others. So writing and speaking have distinctively different linguistic structures; and different ways of using language have different social effects. Literacy, and the types of transformation of oral language that come with literacy, open linguistic doors into certain realms of social action and social power. It follows that literacy teaching, if it is to provide students with equitable social access, needs to link the different social purposes of language in different contexts to predictable patterns of discourse.

These patterns of discourse and their genre variations give access to different degrees and kinds of social power. Insofar as social structures are relatively stable, genres persist over time and are the products of culture, context and history (Kress, 1989b, 9–21; Martin, 1991b). Furthermore, genres have specifiable linguistic characteristics which are not fully controlled or determined by individual writers or speakers. Societies driven by inequality are tension ridden, so genres are also the linguistic sites of non-communication, miscommunication, deliberate counter-cultural subversion and ironical play. Genres, in other words, are not simply the basis for social stability. They are also political media, both reflecting and creating social dynamism.

Genres are learnt by some form of copying. As small children copy words and syntax in order to make meaning, so adults write, not through a transparent medium which represents individual voice, but through generic structures which they have copied in order to make socially identifiable meaning. What they write is immediately framed by linguistic patterns and markers which point to the purpose of the text. Genres are conventional structures which have evolved as pragmatic schemes for making certain types of meaning and to achieve distinctive social goals, in specific settings, by particular linguistic means. The progressivists believe that language is the outpouring of creative individuality, but, as Pam Gilbert argues, this ignores the iterability of all our discourses. 'Originality' comes only by way of the derivative, the imitative, the parodic and the play of the self-consciously inauthentic (Gilbert, 1989c, 80).

There are some very important generic distinctions in the types of written texts children are frequently expected to produce in school, which are obscured both by traditional ideas about 'composition' (such as 'story' writing) and by the bias inherent in process writing towards 'creative' writing founded on individual 'voice'. For example, outside subject English, report is a genre which describes the social or natural world factually. Explanation is a genre that describes how social or natural things work. There are even important genre distinctions between the range of texts produced within the personalised texts that the progressivists privilege in subject English. Recount is a genre which retells events for the purpose of informing or entertaining. Narrative is generally a genre intended to deal with problematic actual and vicarious experience, leading to a crisis or turning point and its resolution (Macken *et al.*, 1989a). Relating these differences to larger sociolinguistic generalisations, the more 'advanced' and successful these genres seem to be, in the commonsense appraisal of teacher evaluations of 'good writing' or 'understanding of the topic', the further their writers have moved away from the characteristic linguistic features of speech.

Certainly there are complex crossovers — times when the distinctive features of orality are inscribed into literacy — when a narrative breaks into direct speech, for example. But even then, the processes for framing direct speech bear little resemblance to oral language. Some genres, even though they are still characteristically written, are closer to the distinctive features of speech than others. A written personal recount, for example, can have features characteristically closer to speech than other forms of writing. This, incidentally, is why process writing, so long as it maintains its ideological commitments to the voice of the creative individual and to the basic similarity of oral and written language, will rarely take students beyond recount.

When it comes to the issue of the social effect of different genres, those most powerful in industrial society are not the ones which are the closest to speech, but the most distant — the ostensibly objective, abstract, scientific report, for example, or the complex, extended, narrative. The narrative may have an oral feel to it — because it involves the complex structuring of direct speech — but this is deceptive. Generically it remains a long way from speech. Despite the progressivists' belief in the 'naturalness' of narrative, the broader the access to a variety of linguistic genres, the broader the social access.

## Conceptual Thinking in the Culture of Industrial Modernity

Vygotsky's historical psychology of language helps explain the cultural dynamics of literacy and the special connection of literacy and theoretical thinking in developing the cognitive and linguistic capacities appropriate to industrial society. In Vygotsky's work there is an account of both the life history of individual children (the ontogenetic development of language and cognition) and the larger social history of the succession of characteristically preindustrial cultures by industrial cultures (the phylogenetic development of thought and language). It is an account, moreover, that has implications for pedagogy in general and for the peculiar cognitive conditions and consequences of learning literate discourses.

In his account of the ontogenesis of language, Vygotsky starts with the word as 'the most basic unit in verbal thought', an elemental indicator of the relationship of thought to language. 'A word does not refer to a single object but to a group or to a class of objects. Each word is therefore already a generalization. Generalization is a verbal act of thought and reflects reality in quite another way than sensation and perception reflect it' (Vygotsky, 1962, 5). At different stages in a child's development, these processes of generalisation take very different forms. The first stage in a child's linguistic-cognitive development is characterised by undirected extension of the sign (the artificial word) to inherently unrelated objects linked subjectively and by chance in the child's perception. Language and thought are characterised by highly unstable, unorganised congeries, or 'heaps' — vague agglomerations of individual objects that have somehow coalesced into an image in the child's mind (Vygotsky, 1962, 59–60). In a second stage the child begins to think in what Vygotsky calls 'complexes', a crucial precursor to the following stage of conceptual thinking. These are processes of the syncretic agglomeration of things and the association of these with words. 'A complex does not rise above its elements as does a concept; it merges with the concrete elements that compose it.'

Vygotsky identifies five substeps in this second stage, representing types of complexes that more or less succeed one another in order of development. First, there are associative complexes, rather like giving a 'family' name to a group of individuals regularly linked in empirical experience. Second, things that differ are put into collections where they are associated by contrast rather than similarity. The connection in a collection complex is the participation of objects in the same practical operation. Third, chain complexes involve the successive linking of objects, such as coloured blocks of different shapes, but where the decisive attribute for linkage keeps changing. Chain complexes are inherently unstable, too, as the child adds more blocks to the group on the basis first of shape but later on the basis of colour. Fourth, a diffuse complex is also marked by fluidity of the attribute that unites adjacent elements, as a child successively adds elements, potentially ad infinitum: triangle > trapezoid > square > hexagon > semicircle > circle. Fifth is a pseudo concept, when a complex coincides with an adult concept. For example, complex association might lead to a perceptual bond which means a child puts a group of triangles together and links this to the adult concept of 'triangle'. The child, in other words, ends up with what is operationally a concept, but has used complex thought to get there.

In pedagogical terms the pseudo concept is tremendously important because it shows the way in which adult language of a generalising, theoretical nature is imported into the child's language even before they can use words conceptually or theoretically. 'Complexes corresponding to word meanings are not spontaneously developed by the child. The lines along which a complex develops are predetermined by the meaning a given word already has in the language of adults.' This coincidence of words and referents, Vygotsky points out, often means that forms of adult thought are incorrectly assumed to be present in children in embryonic form (Vygotsky, 1962, 61, 62–3, 65, 66, 67, 68). On the contrary, the reality of mutual adult-child intelligibility is despite a much more significant linguistic-cognitive gap than the mere commonality of words might lead the communicants to believe. Yet the coincidence works pedagogically. Children learn by having words put into their mouths, words that tease their perceptions into shape, words that gradually impose a culturally inherited meaning on the world, words that mould cognition through its various phases of thinking in complexes. Adult language supplies children with words whose full generalising import, and ultimately the possibility of an inter-concept theoretical discourse, are not realised until puberty.

After complexes, evidence of the third major stage in the development of thought and language is to be found in the use of words as fully fledged concepts. Conceptual thinking involves using words and language to abstract, to single out defining elements that categorise events or people or objects under a single word, to unite and separate, to analyse and synthesise. Initially, these take the form of potential concepts, at which point children can demonstrate that they know what a concept can do by translating it into concrete language. 'Even the most abstract concepts can be translated into the language of concrete action: "Reasonable means when I am hot and don't stand in a draft." ' In the first steps of conceptual thinking, 'the adolescent will form and use a concept quite correctly in a concrete situation but will find it strangely difficult to express that concept in words.' Underlining the inherent difficulty of concepts, the same discrepancy is equally to be found with difficult or problematic concepts in adult thought. The greatest difficulty is encountered when, having grasped the abstract concept, it has to be reapplied to a new concrete situation. 'The transition from the abstract to the concrete proves just as arduous for the youth as the earlier transition from the concrete to the abstract.' So, once people can think conceptually, knowledge proceeds by the interaction of the generalising propensities of conceptual language and empirical experience. 'When the process of complex formation is seen in all its complexity, it appears as a movement of thought . . . constantly alternating between two directions, from the particular to the general, and from the general to the particular' (Vygotsky, 1962, 78, 79, 80). Conceptual knowledge proceeds, in other words, via the dialectical interplay of induction and deduction, and of theory and experience.

Vygotsky's theory of the ontogenesis of thought and language has profound pedagogical implications for the critiques of both the traditional and the progressive curriculum. The direct teaching of concepts, the transmission of received generalisations in the fashion of traditional curriculum, he characterises as no more than 'empty verbalism'. Concepts cannot be taught by drilling. Instead, Vygotsky stresses the developmental role of play, learning by doing under the guidance of an adult, the negotiated nature of adult-child interaction, and the relationship of received generalisations to practical experiences. Yet, against the presuppositions of progressivism, Vygotsky believes that schooling has some unique functions that are decidedly unnatural and inauthentic compared to the child's everyday experiences outside school. 'The mind faces different problems when assimilating concepts at school and when left to its own devices. When we impart systematic knowledge to the child, we teach him many things that he cannot directly see or experience.' Commonsense operates in very different ways from the forms of language and thought founded on what Vygotsky calls 'scientific concepts'. Unlike commonsense language, thought founded upon scientific concepts 'is guided by the use of words as a means of actively centring attention, of abstracting certain traits, synthesizing them, and symbolizing them by a sign' (Vygotsky, 1962, 81, 82, 83, 86).

By this point it is clear that Vygotsky is assuming that words, as media of cultural categorisation, cannot be meaningfully considered in isolation. He is talking about concepts which increasingly define each other — a syntax of abstraction which needs to use some specific linguistic technologies in order to be theoretical. Taxonomies, for example, define concepts by contrast and relationship to each other. Cognitively, Vygotsky says, this sort of conceptual, theoretical thinking takes students onto another plane — that of 'reflective consciousness' or a 'new awareness when you are conscious of being conscious'. In the same way that the syntax of writing invades the syntax of speech (as Kress suggests) and literacy reconstructs primary orality as secondary orality (as Ong suggests), so too, for Vygotsky, the scientific concepts developed through the language of schooling are transfered to everyday concepts, changing their psychological structure from the top down (Vygotsky, 1962, 91, 92, 93). 'For the young child, to think means to recall; but for the adolescent, to recall means to think. Memory is so "logicalized" that remembering is reduced to establishing and finding logical relations' (Vygotsky, 1978, 51).

The parallel between literacy and schooled scientific concepts is not a matter of accidental coincidence. In Vygotsky's view, 'the development of writing does not repeat the developmental history of speaking.' Even the 'minimal development' of writing 'requires a high level of abstraction.' For example, the child must 'disengage himself from the sensory aspect of speech and replace words by images of words.' Writing 'requires deliberate analytical action.' The child must 'take cognisance of the sound structure of each word, dissect it, and reproduce it in alphabetical symbols.' The motives for writing, moreover, are far from 'authentic' or 'natural', even if these words are accepted as accurate descriptions of the ways in which children's oral language in their first years expresses their immediate needs and interests. Writing is 'more abstract, more intellectualised, further removed from immediate needs.' In fact, this detachment goes as deep as the discrepancy between thinking in the language of 'inner speech' (imported as a tool for thinking from the oral language learnt as a child) and the language of writing. 'Inner speech is almost entirely predicative because the situation, the subject of thought, is always known to the thinker. Written speech, on the contrary, must explain the situation fully in order to be intelligible.'

The change from maximally compact inner speech to maximally detailed written speech requires what might be called deliberate semantics — deliberate structuring of the web of meaning. Obviously, children start to write long before they have the cognitive capacity to employ the full resource of a 'deliberate semantics'. At its highest levels this resource includes planning and drafting. But the fact that writing instruction starts when the cognitive capacities upon which writing is ultimately based are only at a rudimentary stage of development is evidence for Vygotsky that cognitive capacity does not precede instruction, but 'unfolds in a continuous interaction with the contributions of instruction.' Accordingly, 'grammar is of paramount importance in the mental development of a child' because it cultivates the 'abstract, deliberate' forms of thinking through language that are peculiar to writing (Vygotsky, 1962, 98, 99, 100, 101, 144; Luria, 1981, 165–166).

Running in tandem with this ontogenetic argument is Vygotsky's phylogenetic argument about the history and cultures of thought and language. 'Primitive peoples also think in complexes, and consequently the word in their languages does not function as the carrier of a concept but as a "family name" for groups of concrete objects belonging together, not logically, but factually' (Vygotsky, 1962, 71–72). To test Vygotsky's ideas, Luria went to Uzbekistan in Soviet Central Asia in the early 1930s to compare the linguistic-cognitive processes of illiterate villagers (both male and female), semi-literate collective farm workers (both male and female) and women students from a teachers' school.

Luria gave his subjects a set of linguistic tests which revealed the complex thought of the illiterate villagers and the conceptual thought of the literate speakers of the same language. Asked to group sets of objects, the illiterate villagers would put together hammer-saw-log-hatchet on the basis of situational thinking (all things the villager needed in a particular task), in contrast to conceptual thinking which might isolate three of the items under the category 'tool'. Asked to define things — a process of abstracting the essential attributes, structure and operations of objects, such as a car or a tree — the illiterate villagers would mention concrete instances. 'The "meaning" of the word had acquired an "outgrowth" of graphic-functional connotations.' Asked to follow through syllogisms to conclusions outside their experience, the villagers were resistant. Abdulakhm, age thirty-seven, was presented the syllogism: 'Cotton can grow only where it is hot and dry. England is cold and wet. Can cotton grow there?' In response, he said he didn't know. 'I've only been in the Kashgar country; I don't know beyond that. . . .' And, to give a final example, asked to analyse their own personality, the villagers described concrete and material aspects of their lives, whereas the schooled town dwellers talked more in terms of general psychological features (Luria, 1976, 56, 89–91, 108, 147).

In their phylogenetic arguments Luria and Vygotsky use the complex/concept distinction as a marker of the cultures of words — the theoretical nature of words as concepts in the culture of modernity, as opposed to the aggregative, associative nature of 'primitive' thinking in complexes. Even the same words in the same language can have very different linguistic-cognitive import, depending upon the speaker's stage of historical 'development'. This parallel of ontogenesis and phylogenesis, however, is not without its problems for it assumes that adult 'primitive' thought is childlike, and that conceptual, scientific thinking is an inherently superior stage in the progressive improvement of humanity. These judgmental conclusions suggest that the linguistic-cognitive world of preindustrial peoples is one of truncated development. On the contrary, there is ample evidence that the thought processes of preindustrial, primarily oral cultures required just as much time to master and culminated in forms of adult thought which are incomparably more sophisticated than the complex thought of any child.

As Lévi-Strauss points out, when translated into human cultures and relationships with nature, the intellectual achievements of preindustrial peoples are no less remarkable than those of the society of scientific concepts (Lévi-Strauss, 1966), with its decidedly mixed ecological and social blessings. Moreover, there is still an important place in the world of modernity for thinking through complexes, just as the characteristic discourses of orality continue to perform specialised functions. Adults, as Vygotsky points out, still use complexes (Vygotsky, 1962, 75). Lateral thinking, stream of consciousness and other such strategies for 'creativity' employ the logic of complex thinking to generate new ideas at times when more scientific thought has reached apparent points of closure. Still, after expunging any crass comparative cultural judgment, these phylogenetic arguments can be useful. They show that the schooled thought and language of industrial modernity, overlaid by the linguistic-cognitive logic of literacy, operates in the world in very different ways from oral cultures.

### Postmodernism: The Savage Mind

It is pointless to deny that quite peculiar linguistic-cognitive skills are needed to live in industrial modernity. And literacy in its most powerful forms invokes culturally and requires pedagogically just this sort of conceptual and theoretical thought. Of course, this is not simplistically to sanctify the culture of modernity that the postmodernists and poststructuralists just as simplistically condemn under the slogan logocentrism — the intellectual and moral process of European Enlightenment, the seductive dream of conscious mastery that has brought enslavement and horror to humankind as often as it has freedom and happiness. It is to be more pragmatic than that. It is to say simply that it is necessary to get around in this historically unique context.

Postmodernism has discarded the cultural logic of literacy. The analytical is replaced by *bricolage*; a tightness that eschews redundancy is replaced by the infinite repetition of the simulacrum; the very possibility of distancing is replaced by the irreducible subjectivity of voice; and balance or neutrality in reference to a reality is replaced by the indeterminacy of the sign and the referential arbitrariness of language.

With more than a hint of irony, Lévi-Strauss' famous anthropological treatise *The Savage Mind* sets out to compare the 'mythical' approach to the natural world of hunter-gatherer and preindustrial farming peoples with modern 'scientific' approaches. There is a striking parallel between his contrast of the metaphorical *bricoleur* of the savage mind to the engineer of modern science and Vygotsky's contrast of thinking in complexes to thinking in scientific concepts. Preindustrial societies, Lévi-Strauss found, had the generative power to create their own technological wonders — such as the classification of nature; the subtle orchestration of nature to human ends; and extraordinary technological breakthroughs such as farming. But magic, he concluded, is not the same as science even though it requires the same sort of mental operations. The difference lies in their linguistic-cognitive modes of appropriating the world.

Lévi-Strauss likened mythical reflection to the *bricoleur*, the person who does odd jobs and who makes do with whatever is at hand — the do-it-yourself inventor who is capable of brilliant if unforeseen results on the intellectual plane. The metaphorical person of modernity, in contrast, is the engineer. 'The engineer questions the universe, while the *bricoleur* addresses himself to a collection of oddments left over from human endeavours.' The 'engineer is always trying to make his way out of and go beyond the constraints imposed by a particular state of civilization while the *bricoleur* by inclination or necessity, always stays within them.' While the modern mind employs historical thought — interstitial, unifying, relating objects to one another — the savage mind enacts its wonders upon the world through analogical thought, in which the sum of the parts can only add up to discontinuity (Lévi-Strauss, 1966, 13, 16–18, 19).

The postmodernists see themselves as *bricoleurs* and revel in the interplay of the irreducible discontinuities they see in the world. Unfortunately, this is hardly a way to get around in industrialism. Worse still, it represents the intellectual false modesty of a cultural elite. Postmodernist authors write texts that are often so tightly woven, clever, beautifully written and canonically referenced that they cannot be other than the products of the type of pedagogy and literacy that they so vehemently oppose. Postmodern culture is the intellectual, cultural and linguistic evidence of the ascendancy of what might be called, perhaps with less irony than Lévi-Strauss, a new savage mind. It denies the possibilities of conscious appropriation of the world, critical dialogue and, ultimately, meaningful human agency. It rests purely on pragmatism and intellectual defeatism as it sums up the cultural crisis of our times, but does not allow itself to do anything about it, ruling itself helpless in the face of the world of difference.

Unfortunately, all these differences are not simply innocent. Many are also the basis for social inequity. Despite the fashion of postmodernism, the metaphorical engineers of industrialism and their employees keep working away. And they have a lot to answer for. But they can only be brought to account in a dialogue that is first able to read their order, then read through their discourse to what lies beneath. What is needed is a more analytical and reflective temper which comes only with those forms of literacy furthest from orality.

## The Power of Literacy

The 'back to basics' protagonists prophesy Armageddon because schools are no longer teaching children to Read and wRite. To counter this, the progressivists argue that being able to write is not as relevant or important as it once was and claim that literacy itself does not improve cognition.

The evidence for the power of literacy is, indeed, mixed. Scribner and Cole's research on the West African Vai script shows that literate people do not necessarily have higher level cognitive capacities. Comparing the cognitive skills of Vai who could write in their first language with those who couldn't, they found no significant differences among those who had not been to school. There were differences, however, for those who had become literate in English through formal schooling. Formal schooling, and not literacy per se, they concluded, was a variable that affected cognition (Scribner and Cole, 1981).

Harvey Graff talks about the propagation of a 'literacy myth'. Literacy, he says, does not produce jobs, increase democratic participation, end poverty, reduce inequality or make people more suited to the labour force. In fact, Graff points to declining literacy requirements for higher level jobs and the deskilling of workers that comes with technological development, job routinisation and rationalisation (Graff, 1987, 255–261, 382–384, 390–391, 396, 398). Industrial societies are moving in a direction in which literacy is becoming less and less relevant rather than more and more important. The development and extension of information technologies, Lakoff argues, means that information processing and audiovisual technologies now embody the emotional closeness of the oral channel with its immediacy and its ready accessibility. This makes possible for orality to have the preservability, the historical accuracy, the immortality that now characterises print. 'It is hard to say why literacy *per se* should be crucial for survival in the future,' Lakoff concludes. Already, he says, the most innovative writers are developing a style for the non-literate age, evidenced in the extent to which they incorporate oral devices in written language (Lakoff, 1982, 239–60).

However, literacy means more than simply phonics and orthography. It is the mastery of a range of genres which use very different linguistic technologies from orality and for very different social purposes. For this reason literacy remains crucially important; and illiteracy should never be underestimated. We live in a society in which many people are truly illiterate in a social sense that goes well beyond being able to hear sounds in the words on the printed page and scribe the sounds of speech. If our society is moving towards orality, then this is at the expense of peculiarly literate ways of knowing the world, and this in itself is a cause for our concern.

Take, for example, the CNN's coverage of the 1991 Gulf War. The technology of live news gathering makes this linguistic move possible, maybe even necessary. The camera points in the direction of an incoming missile while the reporter glosses the image with words about what is happening and what it feels like to be there. Characteristic of oral genres, the spoken text is full of redundancy and dominated by sequence of events rather than analysis. The redundancy is not just in the reporter's words, but in the editor's work as well, as moments of action are replayed and replayed. The larger text, moreover, can have no beginning or end because it presupposes people tune in when they want to know what is going on and tune out as they reach the point when the screen is simply repeating itself to them. The video editor's redundancy is an essential part of the logistics of twenty-four hour news and seamless transmission.

Beyond the technological wonder of it all, there is a strange inefficiency to all the redundancy and a constant triviality to the details. Someone runs; someone else puts on a gas mask; the air raid sirens wail in the background. A few minutes later the piece is shown again. For the viewer, the sensation is rather like being one of the frightened geese Vygotsky used to illustrate the difference between unlanguaged animals who communicate no better than through the spread of affect, and humans who have the analytical and generalising tool that is language. 'A frightened goose suddenly aware of danger and rousing the whole flock with its cries does not tell the others what it has seen but rather contaminates them with its fear' (Vygotsky, 1962, 6). The live telecast achieves little more than to contaminate its viewers with fear, a fear that is all the more alarming because the event being reported, at least before the cycle of replays, is happening in real time. The broadcast is at once incredibly captivating and incredibly boring — boring for the redundancy and triviality and boring in the intellectual sense of being quite unable to satisfy a viewer who feels the need to understand the whys and the wherefores of war.

It is not television as a medium that is drawing us into these sorts of orality. Old style television newscasts were spoken from written language, with selected visuals. From the whole text down to the sentence-length utterance, live CNN is incomparably different from this. Starting at a particular time, conventional newscasts have a distinctive beginning/middle/end generic structure — headlines, followed by elaboration story after story, followed by repeat headlines. Within each story there is a discursive structure which tends to analysis, and which, rather than convey the feelings of the speaker, presents itself (both insightfully and deceptively) through the language of balance and objectivity. It is a text ordered into sentences, deliberately sequenced, coherent, tight but not redundant.

Conventional newscasts have by no means gone. Even on CNN, some reports are still read and the news headlines are closer to the old secondary orality of television. But there is no doubt that CNN and the technology of live news are changing the face of television. In a sense, CNN stands for the rise of a new public orality in which the peculiar discursive modes of literacy, still present even when the written word is read out by the newsreader, are finding a place in the lives of fewer and fewer people. What will this do for the range of genres people have at their disposal to appropriate and reappropriate the world?

There is no doubt that distinctively oral genres play an indispensable part in certain realms of life — for example, the domestic and the affective. This makes orality just as important to our lives as literate discourses. But, the more genres people have access to, both spoken and written, the broader the range of social things they will be able to know and do. Some social realms need the peculiar linguistic technologies available to literate discourses, not only so that people can read and write in those places, but so that they can listen and speak and, ultimately, think in and through each realm. To go back to the Gulf War example, how else other than through the linguistic technology of literacy can this be understood? Even to think in order to be able to speak analytically about it, the grammar of literate genres has to be imported back into orality.

Ong describes the powerful traditions of orality to be found in preindustrial cultures. Epic poetry, rhetoric and dialectic are just three intellectual and linguistic crafts that have receded in importance since the rise of print and industrialism. His characterisation of the differences between literate and oral cultures, however, describes just as well the distinctive uses and logics of orality and literacy in a society which uses both. Oral as compared to literate cultures, he says, are additive, rather than subordinative. They are aggregative, rather than analytic. They are redundant and copious, rather than linear and concise. They are conservative in the sense that what has been learnt over generations is constantly repeated, rather than being intellectually experimentative because things forgotten can be retrieved from written text. They are situational, rather than abstract; empathetic and participatory, rather than objectively distanced; and close to human lifeworld (like learning through apprenticeship), rather than operating through a distancing and denaturalising neutrality (like learning from a manual) (Ong, 1982, 37–49).

This is not to dismiss orality. Epic poetry, rhetoric and dialectic are marvellously sophisticated linguistic-cognitive technologies. And we still need to be able to think and feel in characteristically oral ways. Literacy has its own cultural blinkers, being permeated with a whole series of restrictive ideological agendas which frequently circumscribe its privileges to particular groups. It privileges the formal and ostensibly objective voice over the personal and direct voice, for example. Reading and writing, Ong also points out, are culturally and class loaded since they assume that their participants have individual space, the quiet and privacy which is possible only in certain types of household. The private ownership of the written word, moreover, which finds its highest representation in copyright law, goes hand in hand with the isolationist aesthetics of a romantic print culture, embodied in simplistic and less than helpful ideas such as originality and creativity (Ong, 1982, 130–132).

It is, nevertheless, possible to delineate the characteristic frames of mind of literacy and its realms of social use. Orality and literacy do different things in different ways, to particular ends which in each case are just as socially problematic as they are socially appropriate. The literate reading of the Gulf War, for example, has the potential to feign objectivity. But it also has the potential to see into social processes and see through the interest laden discourses vying for our moral and political attention even as they use the seemingly innocent medium of telling us about these social processes. It does this in a way that orality unmediated by literacy cannot. Literate discourses have the peculiar power to generate certain kinds of analysis and critique. They have the power to produce synthesis out of complexity. They involve logics which are subordinative, analytical, tight and minimally redundant, distant and distancing, and either genuinely attempting or beguilingly feigning balance and neutrality. In these logics there are both powerful resources for reading the world and deceptive ideological loadings that need to be read through in order to unravel the human interests served by texts. Literate discourses, in a nice twist, can give us access to metalinguistic tools with which to unpack the ideological baggage of literate discourse, the social and political loadings in literate text. The deceptively ideological and incisive modes in literate discourses are complementary elements in a single project: the power of literacy and the literacy of power.

### Theory and Experience; Grammar and Text

Claude arrived in Australia from a Lebanese village at the age of eleven. He was asked by his teacher to draw two pictures, one which expressed what life had been like for him in Lebanon, and one which showed something of his life in Australia. The first picture turned out to be a landscape drawing, in which all the relevant pieces of his social life fitted together: his house, the fields, his uncle's house, the church, the graveyard in which relatives had been buried. Life could be represented as a series of empirical individuals and places, located in relation to each other in the fashion of a landscape. When he came to draw life in Australia, however, Claude became confused. Indeed, despite encouragement, he simply couldn't and wouldn't finish the drawing. After several attempts, the drawing began to take the abstract form of something that resembled a map. Opposite his house was a car yard, although its presence meant little to him. Several blocks away were the school and the church. In between these places, represented more symbolically than realistically, were large stretches of blank space, indicating contiguous social space that was irrelevant to Claude. One of his relative's places was missing because it would have to be placed well off the piece of paper, and he wasn't exactly sure of the way there anyway (Kalantzis and Cope, 1981).

This moment of cultural anxiety in Claude's experience of school is not just a metaphor about social difference but also an example that illustrates the broader dimensions of the linguistic-cognitive bases for access. It would not have been enough for the teacher to respond romantically and give a multicultural voice to Claude's difference — to celebrate the village of his mind — to single out and appropriate the colourful and the traditional. Claude needed to learn to make different social maps if he was to understand the society he was now living in.

Industrial society needs to be conceived abstractly — spatially as maps and socially as relationships between groups: social classes, institutions, subcultures. Its social processes are not conceivable simply as relations of adjacent empirical individuals. Instead, they need to be conceived through linguistic-cognitive modes of abstraction and generalisation about relationships which are patterned through aggregating structures and institutions. It is just not possible for Claude to understand through forms of mapping, of social cognition, that worked in the village he had left behind. It is simply too large and too complex. Yet despite the sometimes overwhelming sensation of complexity and diversity, there are some culturally peculiar ways of mapping the social terrain of industrialism — of maintaining a kind of epistemological order. Instead of empirical/associative ways of constructing the world, industrial society requires ways which might be termed theoretical. The landscape/map distinction, which baffled Claude at first, is the basis for a sort of critical distance, for standing back from empirical details and making the kinds of generalisations that characterise the most socially effective linguistic and cognitive tools in industrial society.

Claude's difference need not be viewed as a cognitive deficit or disadvantage. In the same ways that the proponents of bilingual education argue that there are cognitive advantages in having two languages with which to construct the world — assisting children, for example, to make the distinction between symbol and reality — so, too, in a more general way the ability to stand back and see the cultural specificity of different ways of knowing the world and operating in the world can be used as a resource for the kind of theoretical thinking peculiarly needed to make sense of industrialism.

Pedagogies need to approach literacy theoretically — to teach grammar as a theory of language — because theory is the most appropriate way of deconstructing socially powerful discourses. It is a fundamental cognitive technology behind these discourses. And much of the time these genres are themselves theoretical. The report, for example, uses very particular linguistic technologies in typically theoretical ways to make meaning out of empirical complexity; analysis and synthesis. Scribner and Cole's research on Vai literacy shows that merely being literate does not have the same cognitive effects as formal, schooled literacy. Cognitively, schooled literacy goes beyond the immediate focus of learning the mechanics of literacy. This casts doubt on the cognitive and cultural unambitiousness of process writing, with its emphasis on the 'natural', immersion and voice. Instead, literacy should be used as a medium to develop a theoretical metalanguage and to use this metalanguage as an efficient way to develop literacy further.

Schooling, moreover, has to cover a staggering amount of intellectual ground with resources which are constantly being squeezed to the limit. Often, theory is simply a handy short cut. The synthesis inherent in theory is a way of concentrating reality, a way of positing rules and encapsulating patterns of regularity. This is a quicker way of heading towards an overall picture for a complex situation than, for example, accumulating and linking by the association of contingent empirical events. The deductive inclinations of a traditional curriculum which simply tells students the rules are pedagogically inefficient. Active learning is more effective. Yet the more recent progressivisms go to the other extreme. They leave all deduction incidental to student creativity. But without working deliberately with grammar — getting students to think theoretically about language — it will take a lot longer for the patterned natures of the discourses of schooled literacy to become evident, to infuse their way by osmosis into the students' commonsense.

It is doubtful whether any amount of mere doing will ever lead to a more distanced, critical, conscious mastery. Perhaps students might develop their own rules of thumb, and thus make up a grammar of sorts of their own (or a mathematics, or a science). But there is not time in school to recreate all the processes by which theory is made. The diversity of generic expectations both within and across the disciplines makes it impossible to master the range of genres even to be found in schooled literacy solely through inductive osmosis (Eggins, Wignell and Martin, 1987; Wignell, Martin and Eggins, 1987; Martin, 1990b, 70–117). Schools are sites for theory making. At its most efficient, pedagogy must use a dialectical interplay of induction with deduction — of testing received generalisations against experience in one moment and formulating tentative generalisations in another. This is not just to argue about what is pedagogically appropriate. It is to argue about what is needed for social access as well.

## Basic Principles of an Explicit Pedagogy for Inclusion and Access

**First Principle**. *Classroom discourse is a subtle dialogue between students' various linguistic and cultural backgrounds and the culture of schooling with its language of schooled* *literacy. Cultural and linguistic differences can become a positive resource for access. A reconstituted pedagogy will be inclusive by affirming difference as a resource for social and educational access.*

A reconstituted curriculum will need a more dialectical view of difference. Dialect differences must not be seen either as something to be overcome or something to celebrate. Schools should actively work towards a positive bidialectism or multidialectism (Gumperz, 1986, 50) — nurturing different dialects to do different things. Students and teachers, for example, work outwards from the language they know best — such as jointly analysing the structure of RAP songs and then Shakespeare's plays (Delpit, 1988, 288). Building on the insights of the latest progressivisms, an effective pedagogy needs to canonise the marginal; to make the exotic ordinary. RAP and Shakespeare are both as exotic as they are ordinary; and they both have the potential to be as excellent as they are ordinary. Starting with students' own discourses, a reconstituted pedagogy will negotiate with the dominant discourses before coming back to the discourses of difference so that difference is itself marshalled as a resource for social access.

A curriculum which makes the discourse of social power and influence one of its authoritative knowledges need not erase diversity. The discourse of schooled literacy should always only amount to one knowledge among the many that students learn in school, albeit a centrally important one. Indeed, diversity can become a resource for access, while access can be used as a resource to sharpen diversity. As much as they are disadvantaged, students from marginal cultural and linguistic backgrounds also have potentially advantaging linguistic and cognitive resources: the ability to see things from two points of view; the self-evident need to live and work with an immanent epistemology of pluralism; and a linguistic and cultural positioning that can be a cultural resource for learning those theoretical, distancing modes of language and thought needed for successful (compliant or resistant) negotiation in or with dominant social discourses. Schools, in other words, can productively marshall difference. Schools are a site for negotiating multiculturalism, multidialectism and multilingualism.

**Second Principle.** *In an explicit curriculum for inclusion and access, teachers and their disciplined knowledges must be in an authoritative, but not authoritarian, relation to students.*

There is an inevitable asymmetry in the relationship of teacher and student. This is not to support the arbitrary power enforced by a disciplining teacher in the traditional classroom. But it is a view that rejects the progressivist ideas of formally equalising teacher and student; relativising school and domestic discourses in the name of relevance; and trying to make schooling 'natural' and at one with the students' own lifeworlds. Authority does not reside in the person of the teacher but in a peculiarly schoolish task — to master certain, often distant and distancing, discourses of social access. The teacher is in a position of knowledge — a position of social authoritativeness.

Classroom discourse is inevitably schoolish in both form and content and is very different from the other discourses of a child's life. Hence its distancing and reflective modes are essentially unfamiliar. Because it is so different from the child's commonsense, the teacher must help recontextualise and construct contexts actively in the mind (Cazden, 1988, 116, 117, 134). All language is grounded in social borrowings, and recreativity and reinvention (Freire and Macedo, 1987, 132–133) are powerful tools for learning. When it comes to learning the genres of literacy, far from being a new and transparent technology for expression of a culturally stable 'voice', the child's culture is remade through the authoritative relation of the social conventions of language to the student.

**Third Principle**. *Lesson scaffolds need to be explicit, accessible to students and patterned in predictable ways. They need to be explicit both in managerial terms and in the sequencing of curriculum content, even if this means producing textbooks that realise new pedagogical principles.*

Pedagogy needs to provide a staged sequence with its own recursive pattern of predictability — to be regularised and made explicit. This predictability is crucial if students are to have some degree and control over their work and the autonomy to keep on going without more instructions from the teacher. Lessons need to move from the concrete (the bias of progressivist curriculum) to the abstract (the bias of traditional curriculum) and back to the concrete; from experience (progressivism) to the received generalisations of theory (traditionalism) and back to experience. They need to move from the feel of empirical reality with its immanent complexities (progressivism) to abstracting, distancing, synthesis (traditionalism) and then back to a reconceptualised empirical reality. They need to move backwards and forwards through induction (progressivism) and deduction (traditionalism). They need to move from familiar discourses and personal voice (progressivism) to knowing other voices (traditionalism) to a personal voice reconstituted socially. They need to move from disinterested analysis (traditionalism) to creativity (progressivism) via theory and critique. They need to move from an epistemological standpoint inside a single culture (traditionalism), to a disinterested, static and relativistic reading of cultural difference (progressivism), to an epistemological position with a capacity for cultural critique and open to conscious cultural recreation.

**Fourth Principle**. *Curriculum should be structured in explicit ways according to the fundamental structure of subjects.*

In macrodynamic terms, curriculum has disciplinary ends which are reflected in the overall discursive structure of a 'subject' — the steps taken to learn what will emerge as an academic discipline area between kindergarten and the time the children leave school. Genres themselves need to be sequenced into the fundamental structure of literacy and the process of learning to write at school. As becoming literate involves moving from the use of oral language to a metalanguage that conceives language in ways characteristic of complex thought, the fundamental structure of language learning must involve the systematic and carefully orchestrated development of a metalanguage of complexes until they develop into a practically useful and socially purposeful theory of language. Having worked through the necessary steps to grasp the fundamental structure of literacy, these concepts should be able to articulate the linguistic character and social purpose of both socially dominant and marginal discourses, and also account for the linguistic differences as social and cultural phenomena. Students who have grasped the fundamental structure of literacy will be able to denaturalise language and account for linguistic structure in terms of social purpose in the case of both dominant and less socially powerful or countercultural discourses.

**Fifth Principle**. *Schools are the products of human artifice. Immediate motivation lies in the schoolish task itself. Longer-term motivation will only come with the demonstrable capacity of the discipline and the school to provide social access without prejudice.*

Schooling is an unnatural thing — twenty or thirty children placed in one room with one adult 'teacher'. Historically, the school of industrial modernity is a phenomenon without precedent. Accordingly, schooling inevitably generates a distinctive culture of which traditional and progressivist curricula are but permutations. The culture of schooling, whatever its complexion, is actively constructed.

If schools are especially artificial in the sense of being removed from the harsh realities of material subsistence and having to perform the peculiar discursive operation of concentrating on the outside world at the same time as being so dissimilar to it, this artificiality — this distance — might well be something that it is in the best interests of students and teachers to defend and preserve. Institutionally, schooling allows the possibility of a certain cultural detachment, of academic freedom and of thinking critically. Discursively, the necessity of exophoric reference (being about the world but not immediately and reflexively of the world) has a deep cognitive and linguistic relevance in preparing students for making their way in industrialism — the necessity to think abstractly, theoretically, critically.

It's time to abandon the feigned agnosticism about the culture of schooling that comes with ideas of naturalism in curriculum generally and learning literacy in particular. The self-consciously artificial school deliberately provides access to realms outside students' own experience. It deliberately uses linguistic and cognitive modes that are strange in comparison to students' commonsense experience — by virtue of having to concentrate on an external, exophoric referent. Certainly students may not want to learn what they need to learn; and because schooling is artificial they may not see the point immediately. For this reason an explicit pedagogy for inclusion and access must create new sorts of motivation.

Being explicit about the short-term requirements in lesson scaffolds and the long-term fundamental structure of subjects will generate task orientations which are motivating just because they are tasks set and rewarded by schooling itself as a human and affirming social structure. In the first instance these tasks will not have to pretend to be anything more than the artifice of school — rather like playing sport or a board game. There does not have to be an immediately obvious, grander purpose to be able to enjoy playing the game. But it has to be a good game, a well thought through game, a challenging and rewarding game. The added bonus in schooling is that the game can be spelt out, even though it is not necessary that students see the point at every moment of their learning. A curriculum which stresses the social purposiveness of knowledge, like an approach to literacy which links genres to social purpose, will end up more manifestly relevant in providing students with the broadest possible range of social choices. This is in contrast to an ostensibly natural curriculum that reduces relevance to the always individually motivated voice of the student.

## Towards an Explicit Pedagogy for Inclusion and Access

| *The Traditional Curriculum of a Classical Canon* | *The Progressivist Pedagogy of Modernism and Experience* | *The Progressivist Pedagogy of Postmodernism and Difference* | *An Explicit Pedagogy for Inclusion and Access* |
|---|---|---|---|
| **EPISTEMOLOGICAL PRESUPPOSITIONS** | | | |
| • Founded on an epistemology of universal knowledge. Facts are the atoms of knowledge. Objective, true knowledge is learned by acquiring facts. The best and truest of knowledge is enshrined in the canon of Western culture. Deductive methods of reasoning predominate: for example, the move from the formal grammatical rule to its manifestations. | • Founded on an epistemology of universal ways of knowing rather than a universal content knowledge. The methods of science as the basis of knowledge. Truth is a practical thing — those things that work and that are useful. Inductive methods of reasoning predominate: for example, the move from the practical text to generalisation about a grammatical rule. | • Founded on an ideology of epistemological relativism. There are no universal, objective, truths. Despite this professed agnosticism, there are in reality some powerful epistemological assumptions and a consistent culture to postmodern curriculum: for example, that knowledge is a matter of individual voice or cultural positioning. Inductive methods of reasoning predominate, although there is a good deal of scepticism about even these — there is little more than empirical diversity or specific, contingent events in the world. For example, students would not even be strongly encouraged to think through grammatical rules inductively. | • Epistemology is a dialogue of dominant ways of knowing (the Western canon or logocentric science) and other marginal discourses such that both core and margins are transformed. Knowledge generation as a matter of negotiation between and across the cultural and discourse differences that characterise contemporary industrial society. Both inductive and deductive processes of reasoning are used: search for patterns with the aim of generalisation; and applying or testing received generalisations. For example, inviting students to make grammatical generalisations or to test received generalisations in relation to social meanings and discourses in context. |
| **PEDAGOGY** | | | |
| • A pedagogy of presented social content: explicit, didactic, formalistic and structured exposition of knowledge through textbooks; closed to non-canonical knowledge. | • A pedagogy of common, universal process: experiential; based on student activity; an open but singularly purposeful curriculum. | • A pedagogy which sets out to be relevant to particular and different cultures and learning styles. Curriculum is diversified according to student interest and needs. There is a reluctance to state | • A pedagogy that shunts backwards and forwards between: on the one hand, explicit exposition of the common cultural contents and social experience of industrial society, to |

| The Traditional Curriculum of a Classical Canon | The Progressivist Pedagogy of Modernism and Experience | The Progressivist Pedagogy of Postmodernism and Difference | An Explicit Pedagogy for Inclusion and Access |
|---|---|---|---|
| | | curriculum intentions explicitly for fear of irrelevance or cultural insensitivity. | allow social access and critique for all social groups; and, on the other hand, the experience of diversity, starting with student experience, the ethics and epistemology of pluralism. A culturally open yet socially purposeful pedagogy. |

**LANGUAGE LEARNING**

| | | | |
|---|---|---|---|
| • The language that is the object of schooling is described by traditional grammar and embodied in a classical literacy canon. | • The language that is the legitimate object of schooling is a standardised tool in the service of the singular social ends of modernity. | • Schools should view language as different dialects and discourses, all equal and relative to individual or culture. Communication is contingent reading and intertextuality with no truth or meaning. | • Deconstructing the languages and dialects of students is the object of all schooling; but equally, it is the role of schools to induct students into those discourses and genres that are the most powerful in society. |

**EDUCATION AS SOCIALISATION**

| | | | |
|---|---|---|---|
| • Education is a form of political socialisation which singularly prescribes fixed social truths. Hence it has the moral function of instilling respect for received truths, discipline and stable hierarchy. | • Education is a form of political socialisation which singularly prescribes a pedagogy of activity and experience because progress means there can be no empirical fixity in the world — the only continuity is in its technological and social dynamism. | • Education is a site to give voice to difference: a creed of cultural agnosticism, notwithstanding the actual and frequently unself-consciously singular culture of postmodern liberalism. | • Education is a site both for: learning practical strategies for access to and/or critique of the dominant structures of society; and for preparing students for a world of cultural diversity. |

**THE SOCIAL ENDS OF EDUCATION**

| | | | |
|---|---|---|---|
| • The social ends of education are either induction to the high culture of Western society or failure as a mechanism for | • The social end of education is assimilation to modernity. Schools are one of the most important sites for forging unity out of | • The social end of schooling is to promote cultural pluralism. Ideological postmodernism. | •The two primary purposes of education now needed to be: to provide students with the tools for social access via the |

| *The Traditional Curriculum of a Classical Canon* | *The Progressivist Pedagogy of Modernism and Experience* | *The Progressivist Pedagogy of Postmodernism and Difference* | *An Explicit Pedagogy for Inclusion and Access* |
|---|---|---|---|
| ascribing the effects of social destination to causes rooted in individual ability. Actual modernity but ideological traditionalism. | diversity — *e pluribus unum*. A self-professed, ideological modernism. | | core knowledges historically and culturally specific to industrial society; and to negotiate cultural diversity. The one purpose cannot be achieved without the other. |

HISTORY AND PEDAGOGY

| | | | |
|---|---|---|---|
| • The meaning of history is in the continuity of the Western tradition, beginning with its emergence in Greece and Rome several thousand years ago. | • The meaning of history is in the progress, modernity, the technical superiority of an open relationship with nature of industrial society. This meaning can oly be located in processes because social and technological facts are in constant self-transformation. | • There can be no meaning to history — just meanings to individuals according to their peculiar experiences. Maybe even, with the death of the subject, there is no meaning at all. | • History is a series of strucured relations of the dominant to the margins — manifest in social relations and discourses, for example. |

## Why We Should Teach Grammar: Cultural Diversity and Social Access

The progressivists are often right in their critique of traditional grammar, but this does not mean that we should throw out the concept entirely. For grammar need not be just a matter of rote learning rigid notions of correctness. In its most general sense grammar is understanding the ways linguistic technologies make meaning. It is a tool for uncovering the principles of order in language — how language works; who it works for; why it works. It can be used to cast a critical eye over the connections between the structures of language and their social effects. Grammar, in other words, has the capacity to locate language socially; to identify the linguistic characteristics of genre; and to link these to social purpose. Grammar as theory is a way of making sense of linguistic complexity. It is a way of describing linguistic regularities which are reasonably predictable according to social context or purpose.

Building on Halliday's systemic functional approach, a socially useful grammar needs to be functional rather than formal, with a semantic rather than a syntactic focus, and oriented to discourse rather than sentences and their particles — a flexible resource rather than a rigid set of rules (Halliday, 1985a). So-called 'standard' English might do some things for some people, while 'non-standard' dialects do other things for other people. But progressivists go beyond this. They pronounce all discourses equal just because they are all relative to their users' cultures and individual purposes in the world. Granted, a given code or discourse or genre might be quite good at what it does even though its linguistic structures are 'incorrect' by some formal and invariably prejudiced 'standard'. The street vernacular of Black male adolescents in the poorer neighbourhoods of US cities, for example, is an effective means of regulating street life which also embodies a critique of the world that excludes them. But it is not the academic discourse needed for succeeding in school subjects and for using education as a means to social mobility. Nor is it one through which its speakers are likely to be able to negotiate effectively with bureaucratic power structures. We do not live with the luxury of differences which just add life. Difference still makes a difference. It portends differential access to power, to symbols, to wealth.

What is needed is a twofold approach to grammar, locating patterns in language use relative to social function, respectfully and non-judgmentally; but simultaneously evaluating the social effects of discourse in terms of social mobility and social access. While schools should respect and value community discourses — as Labov points out, these are much more powerful than the word 'restricted' implies and effective teaching has to start from what students already know — they also have a responsibility to teach grammars outside the experience of their students.

For example, at the level of the whole text, the grammar of narrative classically runs {orientation ^ evaluation ^ complication(s) ^ resolution}. Inside the text, the distinctive purposes of narratives are realised through a focus on individualised participants, the ordering of events into temporal sequence and so on (Macken *et al.*, 1989c). The grammar of the report, on the other hand, typically runs {general classification ^ description of specific features}, and relates generic participants in a sequence which is not temporal, but which operates through analytical, taxonomic connections (Macken *et al.*, 1989b). The written genres of narrative and report are tremendously powerful, but they are genres that come less 'naturally' to students from cultural, linguistic socio-economic backgrounds other than the socially dominant one. These students especially need to be exposed to learning experiences in which they work their way through explicit analysis of generic features, critical appraisal of the social function of the genre, and then writing in the genre. This means that teachers have a lot more to do than simply make space for their students' voices.

An explicit pedagogy for inclusion and access is not the same as an enforced cultural assimilation which teaches the use of alien social tongues for social purposes. Learning the grammar of the written genres of power is not just a matter of internalising dominant discourses. It also provides the tools for discourse critique, for understanding the ideological loadings in language. Authors are products of their language as much as they are producers of language. It follows that their language frequently embodies ideologies which may or may not be conscious. Students could uncover the linguistic technologies used by affectedly depersonalised genres, such as reports. They could realise to what extent depersonalised language is an ideological illusion. Students might disentangle the myths of author and authorship in narrative, myths that are unconsciously reinforced by progressivist pedagogies of 'voice' and 'creative writing'. The appearance of a natural and innocent transparency to language, the commonsense impression that it is simply a conduit for what the author wants to say, obscures the cultural and ideological nature of textuality (Gilbert, 1989c, 77–78).

Indeed, far from being disadvantaged, students whose first languages are not derived from socially dominant discourses are in a uniquely advantageous position to deconstruct the grammar of dominant discourses simply because they are less influenced by the cultural assumptions of literate culture and the secondary orality that comes with it. They have a critical cultural and linguistic distance which means that the social purpose of the text immediately seems 'unnatural' yet they need to appropriate its grammar explicitly to be able to master the discourse for their own ends. This stands in contrast to the inherently unconscious, uncritical, implicit 'feel' for written language of students born into the discourses of power. Cultural difference can be marshalled as a positive resource for acquiring a literacy for social access, and particularly in attaining conscious and critical control of written language. Difference, in other words, does not have to be erased in an explicit curriculum that is aimed at inclusion and access. It can be reaffirmed by using it as a resource.

Thus an explicit pedagogy for inclusion and access does not involve unproblematically telling students how to use genres for prescribed social purposes. It operates with a degree of critical distance so that, simultaneous with analysing the linguistic technology of a genre, students relate the form of the text critically to its purpose — its culture and the human interests it involves. Grammar, in this broad sense, is a technique not just for reading but for reading through the cultural and political agendas in discourses. Grammar is a basis for making social and linguistic connections; for revealing the social and constructed nature of discourses which make ideologies seem natural. It is a way of making conscious the unconscious. Learning genres is just as much a process of unlearning their ideological effects, as it is one of mastering their technologies.

## Towards a Pedagogy for Teaching Grammar

Learning grammar, or using a metalanguage to learn about language, is therefore not just another technology for becoming literate. It cannot be simply compared with process writing or whole language on the basis of literacy outcomes, although it is clear that we have been arguing that progressivist writing pedagogies do not produce the goods. More than this, grammar is something that should be taught for its own sake, beyond the utilitarian objective of assisting students to learn how to write. Teaching grammar, in other words, can embody some fundamental linguistic-cognitive objectives that the progressivists have abandoned.

At this point we need to return to Vygotsky's generalisations about the forms of thought and language that are culturally specific to industrialised social settings. Adults' words in these sorts of social settings are conceptual. As children are inducted into the culture of industrialism, analogical, situational associations around words are gradually replaced by abstractions that are capable of generalisation and definition. Cognitively, this move is from complex to conceptual thought. It means, for example, that the child moves from knowing one's relatives and significant others as 'family', to an understanding of the concept of 'family' and being able to locate this concept into an understanding of the role of the family in society. The same word becomes able to represent 'family' in new ways, both linguistically and in terms of underlying cognitive structures. This sort of linguistic-cognitive transition is critically achieved through the formal institution of schooling. Pre-eminently, the role of school is to tease children's consciousness from thinking and speaking through complexes, to thinking and speaking through a syntax of abstraction that ties concepts into frameworks of meaning. This linguistic-cognitive process transforms everyday consciousness into a new psychological structure, logicalised so that to recall means to think in a particular way, to think by linking generalisations into a theoretical language.

This is precisely the linguistic-cognitive process involved in 'doing grammar': from knowing the real world referents and associations of a text (complex thought); to being able to understand that text as text operating grammatically in context and to generalise about its operations (conceptual thought). There is a cultural temper to a literacy pedagogy which includes a focus on grammar, and this is the cultural temper of industrialism. It is even a cultural temper directly analogous to the ways certain central genres of school literacy themselves operate. Reports, in science or social studies, for example, translate everyday language and understandings of the world into technical ones. They make meaning out of empirical complexity in some culturally peculiar linguistic and cognitive ways: by means of description of taxonomic relations; by means of classification; or by objectifying processes through the grammar of nominalisation. Even in subjects that do not purport to be about language, school involves induction to certain cultural styles of thinking, and this process of induction is carried by language. This is the same style of thinking through language that doing grammar promotes by getting students to think through language about language.

But making grammar a tool in the process of cultural-linguistic access does not also have to mean cultural and linguistic assimilation of those marginalised by the mainstream culture and discourse of industrialism — potentially a kind of linguistically based ethnocide. Grammar is certainly a resource for access, a resource for expanding one's repertoire of forms of speech and thought and so to broaden one's options for strategic social interventions. This does not mean that schools teaching grammar need to erase other-than-schoolish forms of thought and language. On the contrary, locating text in context is to say no more than 'you may wish to use this sort of text to do this, but this does not mean you have to.' It certainly does not mean that broadening one's discursive options has to be to the detriment of other valued ways of being and meaning in the world. Grammar, indeed, can be a resource for establishing critical distance. In the business of linking text structure to social purpose — how reports do their work, what sort of work they do, why they do it this way — grammar can raise critical questions about the text: how and why reports pretend to be voiceless, for example. In this task, students who intuitively feel that reports speak strangely, students who do not speak the discourses of power so comfortably, bring with them to school a unique resource for doing grammar, for doing it with an insightful eye to the often less than immediately obvious cultural and discursive agendas in texts.

So, how do we make grammar a focus of curriculum? How do we shape lessons so that they encourage students to make generalisations about language? These are questions that need practical answers expressed in terms of explicit curriculum scaffolds. Here we will give two levels of answer, drawn from the experimental pedagogical work of the Social Literacy Project (Kalantzis and Cope, 1989a). The first level involves the microstructure of lesson sequencing. The second involves curriculum macrostructure at the level of the fundamental structure of the discipline.

To deal with microstructure — the cycle of activities the students undertake over a lesson or several lessons in learning to do grammar, and to think and speak in the way doing grammar requires — the Social Literacy sequence involves six steps. First, a *focus question* orients students to a grammatical problem. Why do people use language in a particular way; and how do they do it? Second, in an *input* step, text is presented. The question raised as the grammatical focus will be directed to this text in the first instance. This text (or texts) could in part serve as a generic model. The text must be presented in such a way, however, that it is negotiable — not a text form to be copied 'in your own words', so to speak, but as the basis for students writing later in the microstructure in ways which genuinely match their own sense of the sort of text that would best say certain things. In the interplay of these first two steps, there has to be a clear relation of learning grammar to students' previous experience, both domestic and at school. The *focus question*, for example, might direct students towards a contrast between the presented text(s) and their own experience of language. In the *input* step the text itself needs to be selected according to criteria of readability and so on.

In a third *analysis* step, students analyse the presented text. What is in it? Who would write this sort of text? Why would they write it? How does it pass on its message? Cognitively, this step moves students from the analytical (the whats and the hows of the text) to the critical (the whys, the what fors and the how wells of the text). This questioning does not have to be teacher led. On the contrary, the more each student has to talk their way around these questions, the more effective the learning experience will be for them. This sort of analytical work is ideally undertaken in small groups.

This leads into the fourth *main ideas* step — both the most important and the least important step in the sequence. It is the most important step because in encapsulates the grammatical point of the exercise. It also gives a technical label to the problems that the students have already been working through in the third step of the sequence. This is a critical moment in the linguistic-cognitive movement from the realm of concrete experience of language to the abstract realm of knowledge about language; from language-in-use to a metalanguage which describes the usefulness of language by generalising about language structure and function. In cognitive terms this is exactly what the Social Literacy pedagogy is aimed at: learning to abstract by generalising from the particular. But in another sense this is also the least important point in the microsequence. As no more than a technicalised restatement of the generalisations students should have already been making in the third step of the sequence, it is one of the least potent moments of learning. It exists for the reason that curriculum should periodically state its agenda, its own provisional answers, in an explicit way. This step could be presented either as a definition on the textbook page or as a teacher cue to indicate the end of the third step: 'What we have just been noticing happening we call. . . .'

The first four steps in the Social Literacy sequence involve students in making knowledge inductively, moving from questions addressed to the particular (text) to questions addressed to the general (grammar). Step five, *application*, involves students working with knowledge deductively, applying their generalisations about grammar to the particularities of text generation. 'Use the ideas you have learnt about the way a certain kind of text does certain kinds of things to write your own text about. . . .' Within this step students progress from critical enquiry (research on a certain field, possibly encountering along the way more texts that are now generically more recognisable and thus easier to read) to creative production of text (drafting, conferencing, editing, publishing — the activity sequence of process writing).

In a concluding *evaluation* step, students and teachers reassess the learning process by returning to the focus question with which the teaching/learning cycle began. 'Can the grammatical generalisations, which we have just been using, work for us in other places or say other things?' Here the focus of evaluation for the teacher should not be whether the students can repeat the grammatical generalisation stated in the *main ideas*. Definitions and generalisations about language are very difficult to formulate, even for linguists. Besides, this would be to encourage rote learning of received grammatical generalisations which rather defeats the point in abandoning the 'rules' of traditional grammar and the transmission pedagogy of traditional curriculum. Students have achieved the goals of this grammar curriculum if they can use grammatical concepts to describe language in a meaningful way.

This is to speak of the microsequences of a grammar curriculum. However, these will only work if they are framed by macrosequences, the structure of the subject as it unfolds in curriculum. Here two general principles towards program formulation need to be mentioned. First, the synoptic *main ideas* steps need to be read across a sequence of cycles as a theoretical progression, as the grammatical concepts relate to each other and build on each other to form an increasingly more sophisticated theory of language. Second, the written genres that the curriculum handles need to be sequenced, so that student activity is focused in the first instance on those written genres closest to speech (such as recount) and gradually moves on to genres whose grammar is more distant from speech (such as report).

At the level of macrosequence there also needs to be a progression from working with texts that represent canonical genres to working with texts that are multigeneric and intergeneric. Genres should not be presented just as rules for writing and getting ahead in the world. Equally, knowing genres is a basis for ironical play, a device for poking fun at the world, a basis for creative energy that transgresses generic conventionality, and a way to stand out in the crowd by stretching the discursive rules. Genre literacy teaching has just as much potential to be a tool for the unruly as it has potential to promote textual uniformity and cultural conformity.

Especially when it treads into the realm of the multigeneric and the intergeneric, genre literacy becomes a critical literacy, a tool to evaluate how well a text manages to communicate, and a tool which does not bind speakers and writers to formulaic adherence to canonical genres. Indeed, many of the most powerful of texts do not lend themselves to be simply unpacked as the realisation of a predictable formula. Herein lies real creativity. In a society which makes the most of the creative potential inherent in its cultural and linguistic diversity, genre literacy teaching should not mean redoing model texts from the dominant culture 'in your own words', but using a knowledge of genre and grammar to find one's own voice, not within genres, but across, between and around genres.

# Chapter 4

# Gender and Genre: Feminist Subversion of Genre Fiction and Its Implications for Critical Literacy

*Anne Cranny-Francis*

*In this chapter Anne Cranny-Francis discusses the uses of the genre as a literary category, to describe literary conventionality. In the realm of literary criticism sometimes the term is used pejoratively, to indicate a supposed lack of originality; other times it is used as a positive, descriptive reference point. Cranny-Francis uses the word 'genre' as a means not only to classify literary texts according to their conventional forms but also as a critical category with which to understand how they function. Genres carry all sorts of ideological messages, eliding their conventionality and their social messages under generic mantles such as 'realism'. In a sense, she argues, texts whose genres are 'naturalised' and which attempt to make social and cultural relations seem 'natural' coerce their readers into particular ideological worldviews.*

*People who want to tell a different story, such as feminist writers who want to produce science fiction but without its hallmark sexism, are faced with the contradictory task of operating within generic conventions in order in part to subvert them. This, Cranny-Francis characterises as a difficult balance between retelling a familiar story and saying something new.*

*This view of genre — both as a tool of compliance and conventionality and as the basis for creativity and critique — is characteristic of the critical approach to literacy that underlies all the work of the genre school. Cranny-Francis concludes her chapter by drawing connections between her work and that of Martin. Although the substantive content each gives to the concept 'genre' is very different, their use of the term for the development of a critical literacy is fundamentally similar.*

Consider: Anyone can turn his hand to anything. This sounds very simple, but its psychological effects are incalculable. The fact that everyone between seventeen and thirty-five or so is liable to be . . . 'tied down to childbearing', implies that no one is quite so thoroughly 'tied down' here as women, elsewhere, are likely to be — psychologically or physically. Burden and privilege are shared out pretty equally; everybody has the same risk to run or choice to make. Therefore nobody here is quite so free as a free male anywhere else. . . .

Consider: There is no unconsenting sex, no rape. As with most mammals other than man, coitus can be performed only by mutual invitation and consent; otherwise it is not possible. Seduction certainly is possible, but it must have to be awfully well timed.

Consider: There is no division of humanity into strong and weak halves, protective/protected, dominant/submissive, owner/chattel, active/passive. In fact the whole tendency to dualism that pervades human thinking may be found to be lessened, or changed, on Winter.

The following must go into my finished Directives: When you meet a Gethenian you cannot and must not do what a bisexual naturally does, which is to cast him in the role of Man or Woman, while adopting towards him a corresponding role dependent on your expectations of the patterned or possible interactions between persons of the same or the opposite sex. Our entire pattern of socio-sexual interaction is nonexistent here. They cannot play the game. They do not see each other as men or women. This is almost impossible for our imagination to accept. What is the first question we ask about a newborn baby?. . .

The First Mobile, if one is sent, must be warned that unless he is very self-assured, or senile, his pride will suffer. A man wants his virility regarded, a woman wants her femininity appreciated, however indirect and subtle the indications of regard and appreciation. On Winter they will not exist. One is respected and judged only as a human being. It is an appalling experience. (LeGuin, 1981, 84–86)

These are some of the anthropological field notes available to Ambassador Genly Ai as he attempts to make contact with the inhabitants of the planet Gethen, or Winter as it is known to outsiders. The Gethenians have an unusual sexual morphology: they are sexually inactive for much of the time, except during the period they call *kemmer* when they develop primary sexual characteristics and become sexually active. An interesting feature of this *kemmer* period is that they cannot know beforehand whether they will develop male or female sex organs. As the field notes explain, this sexual morphology and its consequences (for example, any Gethenian can become pregnant) is fundamental to the nature of Gethenian society.

So Ursula LeGuin constructs one of her 'mind experiments', her 'what if' games, which leads to the fundamental deconstruction of aspects of contemporary society. For *The Left Hand of Darkness*, the book from which this passage is taken, is not just about a planet 'far far away'; it is also, crucially, about this planet and this (twentieth century Western) society. As human Ambassador Genly Ai struggles to deal with his Gethenian hosts, the prejudices and opinions, behaviours and attitudes of a patriarchal man and the society from which he comes are exposed and examined. LeGuin's science fiction novel is a site for the critical deconstruction of contemporary society and for the reconstruction of gender discourses and gender identities.

This chapter discusses the ways in which the reading and writing of feminist genre fiction, such as science fiction, offer a model of a critical methodology which can be used by teachers in the development of an empowering pedagogy, a critical literacy.

### Genre as a Critical Category

The first points to consider in relation to this aim are the choice of 'genre' fiction as a model and the meaning of the term 'genre' in this context. After all, all texts are generic; they are all constructed and read in relation to usually one dominant accepted literary (or non-literary) category. They may diverge from the conservative functioning of that genre, perhaps through a mixing of different genres in the one text, but they nevertheless can be identified and made meaning of by their relationship(s) with one or more genres. Here we might be talking of the realism of Henry James or the fantasy of Marion Zimmer Bradley, the modernism of James Joyce or Sara Paretsky's detective adventures of V.I. Warshawski, or the postmodern pyrotechnics of Calvino or Pynchon. It is important to address this notion of 'genre' because the critical, deconstructive practice developed by feminist readers and writers began in their analysis of this term as a pejorative and dismissive label for many kinds of writing.

The word 'genre' came to be a pejorative label for literature in the late eighteenth and early nineteenth century. Before this, during the period of the Enlightenment and earlier, 'generic' was a positive term; good fiction was fiction that followed and improved on its dominant generic predecessor(s). When the romantics turned rationalism on its head, there was a revaluation of the term and of the aesthetic which accompanied it as a classificatory label. For the romantics and after, great literature was non-generic. It was individual, creative, inspired. The terms 'generic' and 'creative' were seen as opposites, not as complementary, as they had been before romanticism. Of course, the interesting thing for us as scholars now is that it is very easy to identify a romantic poem (or a painting and so on). Consider this 'emotion recollected in tranquillity':

> I wandered lonely as a cloud
> That floats on high o'er vales and hills,
> When all at once I saw a crowd,
> A host, of golden daffodils . . .
> (Wordsworth, 1950, 91)

And this more *angst* ridden version:

> My heart aches, and a drowsy numbness pains
> My sense, as though of hemlock I had drunk,
> Or emptied some dull opiate to the drains
> One minute past, and Lethe-wards had sunk . . .
> (Keats, 1950, 240)

There is after all something conventional about romantic poetry (and painting) which identifies it as such; it is generic. Similarly the realist fiction of the late eighteenth and nineteenth century, which persisted also with this notion of non-generic 'creativity', is just as recognisable; all those wonderfully enjoyable and almost gossipy novels about life and human interactions by Jane Austen, George Eliot, Henry James, George Gissing, which were all about middle-class life and middle-class people and all ended happily ever after — at least for the 'good' characters. Both realism and romanticism are after all generic, just like their non-mainstream contemporaries such as science fiction, fantasy, detective fiction, utopian fiction, westerns, romance.

The difference between romanticism and realism and their openly generic contemporaries is that romanticism and realism conceal or elide their conventionality. That is, they elide the fact that they use a characteristic range of textual strategies which identifies the genres and also defines their social function or practice. In the early twentieth century modernist writers revealed this conventional practice of the realists by questioning why these individual and realistic realist novels all had a happy ending. In fact, the happy ending was revealed as a convention of the realist novel, a form of the novel which had been so often declared non-conventional, non-generic (in contrast to its 'low brow' contemporaries such as the gothic novel, melodrama, fantasy and science fiction).

The point is that all fiction (and all non-fiction) is generic, but some of it works to disguise its conventionality. The reasons for that elision, that disguise, particularly with a fiction which represents itself as mirroring reality, are fascinating and have much to do with the discursive practice of all literature — and ultimately of all texts. It is particularly useful to disguise construction if the ideology of a text is such as to produce a naturalised (or ideologically conservative) view of everyday social relations, the 'real'. If the conventions of a text are apparent (as in the so-called generic fictions), the naturalness of the discourses constructed and enacted may be questioned. The obvious architecture of the text may seem to be the product of a particular set of values, ideas and beliefs, realised in/as a set of conventions, rather than some sort of depoliticised, non-ideological reflection of 'what is' — which was what the realists claimed for their texts.

This notion of an apolitical text, a text which simply reflects the outside world, has been laid to rest quite convincingly over the last 100 years, yet it is often still evoked by writers and readers who want to claim 'universality' for their writing or reading. This 'universality' means that the text is read as producing a very sensitive and accurate version of 'what is'. It takes us directly back to the claims of nineteenth century realists whose texts were said to be constructed non-generically, but which were nevertheless clearly generic. The realists simply naturalised the conventions so that they seemed obvious or inevitable to readers, and so became effectively invisible. When the conventions became invisible, so did their social and ideological function.

Consider, for example, the ever-popular happy ending. What kind of social or ideological function might be tied up with the happy ending? And note that this meant something very specific; it meant heterosexual love and usually marriage — as in the fairytales. At the very least this convention tells the reader that individual success and happiness means heterosexual romance and marriage. So this convention is involved in the construction of the compulsory heterosexuality which typifies patriarchal discourse. In other words, the convention itself is a discursive practice which positions readers to accept patriarchal heterosexual marriage as the greatest achievement of the individual subject, and so to negotiate their own subjectivity in these terms. In most realist texts, however, this discursive function is not obvious and not talked about; rather it is represented as the 'natural' outcome of the 'realistic' relationships constructed in the book. It is only when that outcome starts to look doubtful that we even doubt this naturalised explanation. A challenging example occurs at the end of George Eliot's novel,

*Middlemarch*, where her heroine, Dorothea Brooke, ends up married to her ex-step-nephew, Will Ladislaw — a man who has already explained that it is difficult for men to live with women of intellect. In ending the novel this way, George Eliot provides the conventionally required heterosexual romance and marriage, but leaves many readers with severe doubts about its success — a subversive move by Eliot which exposes the 'unnaturalness' of the happy ending, and its discursive function. In most instances, however, the conventions of realism are used without this kind of apparent self-consciousness to produce texts which reproduce the discourses constitutive of late eighteenth and nineteenth century European society.

As noted earlier, however, this realist notion of a transparent, experientially verifiable textuality is also evident in evaluations of texts as 'universal', an evaluation which characteristically fails to deal with the strategic or generic nature of writing. This 'universality' is particularly vulnerable to the very simple question: 'universal' in whose eyes? Many feminist scholars in recent years have questioned the validity of declaring D.H. Lawrence's writings on sexuality and relationships 'universal'. Instead, his work has been seen as typifying values and attitudes to sexuality which are fundamentally patriarchal. In other words, these 'universal' texts — or readings of texts — enacted a set of values, attitudes and beliefs which could be precisely discursively located. Their ideological function is as part of the reconstruction of that set of discourses: to position readers as compliant subjects of those discourses and so to (re)produce the dominant social/ideological formation. Of course, not all texts — or all readings — are necessarily conservative; not all texts and readings work to (re)produce powerful social/discursive positionings. But the readings of texts which are identified as 'universal' usually do. The naming of those readings as 'universal' is in itself a conservative social/discursive practice, which works to establish a particular set of values, beliefs and attitudes as 'true', as 'universally accepted'.

One of the earliest attacks on this notion of universality, the successor to nineteenth century romanticism and realism, came from feminist critics and writers. For feminists these readings and the texts on which they focused were a very long way from 'universal'; they were partial and specific, and one of the areas in which that specificity was most apparent was their treatment of gender and sexuality: the sexist and masculinist discourse(s) they construct and the patriarchal ideology they enact. At the same time feminist writers were attempting to write texts which told their own specific story, not the patriarchal story told by these 'universal' texts and their (compliant) readings. But the texts kept getting in the way; that is, the textual conventions or strategies by which the texts construct their meaning subverted the attempt to tell a different story. Or, to put it another way, they defined the extent to which a different story could be told.

## Feminist Deconstructions of Genre

Feminist writers were looking for a way to tell a different tale, to construct a different discourse about gender relations, a different vision of femininity and masculinity, a subversive rewriting of gender discourses. As a result, feminist writers had to remake the genres in which they wrote. Genres which had been

constructed and continually reconstructed to enact patriarchal ideology — patriarchal ways of thinking and acting — had to be modified to enact a different,
feminist discourse.

Some feminist writers use realism to construct their different voice and so
had to change that genre radically. In the place of the conventional 'heterosexual
love' happy ending (for example, they married and lived happily ever after), they
substitute a woman renegotiating her subjectivity, not dependent on a traditional
heterosexual relationship to constitute her sense of self(worth). So the happy ending
might be a woman establishing a happy life in which she is able to explore her
own talents and capacities among a group of friends and without any intimate
relationship. Or it might be with an unconventional kind of intimate relationship.
Or it might be in a reconstructed kind of heterosexual relationship. Whichever
ending is used is a change to the genre as constituted in other contemporary texts.
For that reason many readers may feel disappointed by these texts; they may feel
cheated that they haven't got the 'happy ending' they expected. They might, as
a result, read that ending as demonstrating that the text — and its feminist discourse — is unsuccessful or unconvincing. In other words, their expectation of
a (patriarchal) happy ending may be so strong that they aren't able to accept the
feminist positioning enacted in the text. Changing the genre might mean that you
lose a few readers — but it may give a voice to others who might not otherwise
have the possibility of a voice.

The same problem to do with genre modification affects writers working
with texts which are openly conventional — the so-called genre fictions. But at
least here the conventions are up-front, as they are here:

I woke up feeling like death. Ironically appropriate, given what the day
held in store. White light poured in, even before I opened my eyes and a
variety of sounds, all too loud. Someone was pounding my brain like a
two year-old who's just discovered a hammer. In between blows I
managed to prise open the eyes. Close by the bed was a bottle of Jack
Daniels: empty. And an ash tray: full. Clothes were strewn all over the
place and through the french doors roared the sights and sounds of Sydney.
As I got out of bed I realised I wasn't the only one in it. There was a
good looking blond in there as well. I didn't recall issuing the invitation
but I must have. No-one gets into my room, let alone my bed, without
one.

. . . After a couple of unsuccessful attempts I managed to light the
gas under the coffee and, closing the stable door after the horse had
bolted, crammed a handful of vitamins down my throat.

The coffee revived me a little, a hot then cold shower even more.
The blond slept on, unperturbed by my rummaging through the clothes
on the floor looking for something suitable to wear. Thank God the
black suit was hanging in the wardrobe neatly pressed. The black shoes
were where I'd apparently left them the night before — one in the waste
paper bin and the other on the mantelpiece. I dressed and took a long
hard look at myself in the mirror. As long as I didn't start haemorrhaging
from the eyes things would be all right. I grabbed the dark glasses. Just
in case.

'Time to go sweetheart.' I whispered into the blond's aural orifice.

> Not a flicker of an eyelid or a murmur. Next time I shook him. 'C'mon
> mate, wake up. I've got to go to a funeral.' (Day, 1988, 1–2)

This is the beginning of Marele Day's novel, *The Life and Crimes of Harry Lavender*,
which introduces her female detective, Claudia Valentine. Day signals her modification to the genre of 'hard-boiled' detective fiction by confronting immediately
one of the prominent conventions of that genre: the sexual characterisation of
the private investigator (the 'private dick', as he revealingly came to be known).

Science fiction was one of the first of the genre fictions employed by the
women's movement as part of its political practice. One of the reasons for this
was precisely the non-realism of the genre, here using realism in its common
sense of 'picturing reality'. As Pamela Sargent explained in her Introduction to the
collection of women's SF, *Women of Wonder* (Sargent, 1978, 48), the non-realist
aspects of the genre gave women a chance to explore imaginatively different
cultures, different societies, different kinds of gendered identities. According to
Sargent, realism had the problem of being too much entangled with and constrained
by the everyday, by what readers would accept as 'realistic' (for example, the idea
that a woman could be more happy without an intimate relationship rather than
living in a patriarchal heterosexual relationship was unrealistic for some readers).
With an infinite number of universes before her, the feminist writer could play
any number of Ursula LeGuin's 'what if?' games. For example, what if I lived in
a non-patriarchal society? What would it be like? What would masculinity and
femininity be like in such a world? What would parenting be like? What kinds of
work might people do?

At the same time, these texts fulfilled a metatextual function; they not only
told a different story, a feminist story; they also showed that the story told by
conventional texts in that genre is also a specific story, told from a particular
perspective, a patriarchal one. They showed that conventional science fiction novels
did not tell stories of human 'endeavour'; rather they tell stories of patriarchal
masculine 'endeavour'. This point is made very clearly in Ursula LeGuin's novella, *The Word for World Is Forest*, and in a number of brilliant stories by the
writer James Tiptree Jr (Alice Sheldon). For example, in her story 'The Women
Men Don't See', Tiptree tells a story of human-alien encounter, a stock situation
in science fiction. It customarily involves earthmen driving away bug-eyed monsters (BEMs as they were known in the golden age of science fiction) who not
only want to invade earth, but also want to mate with earthwomen. This combination of xenophobia and rape fantasy is extraordinarily pervasive in science
fiction. In Tiptree's reconstruction this human-alien encounter involves a sexist
male character, the narrator, Fenton, and his travelling companion, Ruth Parsons,
about whom Fenton has had a series of rape fantasies of his own. However, he
is unable to carry out these fantasies, partly because he has injured himself and has
to be half-carried by Ruth Parsons. When the aliens are sighted, Fenton attempts
to shoot them — and significantly only succeeds in shooting Ruth Parsons. He
then tries to steal their technology, but is again unsuccessful. The story ends when
Ruth Parsons makes a deal with the aliens — anthropology students on a field trip
— to take her with them, in a reversal of the typical BEM story, leaving Fenton
to ponder: 'How could a woman choose to live among unknown monsters, to say
good-bye to her home, her world?' The answer to that question has already been
given when Fenton first remonstrates with Ruth Parsons: 'For god's sake, Ruth.

They're *aliens*', and she answers absently, 'I'm used to it' (Tiptree, 1975, 160). Not only does this story deal with the alienation of women in contemporary society, but through its reconstruction of the BEM narrative, it reveals the aggressive, competitive, masculinist nature of the traditional versions of this narrative — where men go out into space to subdue it to their will — another version of the last frontier, the tremendous space fuck, as Kurt Vonnegut called it (Vonnegut, 1976, 241). As Tiptree's story reveals, the more conventional science fiction stories enact the construction of a patriarchal masculine subjectivity, characterised by sexism, aggression, colonialism and racism. They are stories about the constitution of a particular kind of subjectivity, not about 'universal' human endeavour.

This discovery of the gendered specificity of science fiction had important ramifications for feminist writing in a variety of genres; it informed the feminist deconstruction of semiosis across a range of text types. The recognition that the majority of texts in our society — and the readings made of them — work to reconstruct patriarchal ideology enabled those attempting to fashion a non-patriarchal, feminist discourse to locate and identify some of the problems they were having with achieving a fictional realisation of that feminist voice. They discovered that the problems women had had in using these genres to tell their own story were not a function of their incapacity as writers; rather the genres in various ways worked against them. It then became a matter of deconstructing the genres, understanding how the genres functioned, where and how discourses were constructed in/by them. As part of that pursuit it became important to theorise the notion of readership, to understand what readers did or might do with texts as part of their construction of themselves as gendered subjects.

Over the last twenty years feminist writers and readers have constructed a profile of many popular fictional genres, both their textual practice and the political significances of those textual practices. With that knowledge they have constructed texts and readings of texts which are still recognisably generic but which, at the same time, challenge the genres used and manipulated, and in the process construct new meanings, new discursive positionings. In other words, these writers and readers achieved the position of textual awareness described by Pam Gilbert and Sandra Taylor in *Fashioning the Feminine* as involving 'an understanding of the socially constructed nature of language practices and the discursive nature of subjectivity' (Gilbert and Taylor, 1991, 106). That is, they worked with narrative fiction by identifying the specific ways in which particular fictions worked to (re)construct a particular social formation; or, looked at another way, the way that a particular social formation is enacted and reproduced in a specific fictional type (what Gilbert and Taylor call the the socially constructed nature of language practices). They added to that a materialist conception of subjectivity, whereby the individual reader is pictured as renegotiating or re-forming her/his individual identity as s/he negotiates (that is, reads and assimilates) the text.

It is important to note that Gilbert and Taylor offer that description of language practice and subjectivity in the context of a critique of 'process' writing pedagogy. 'Process' pedagogy, they argue, ignores the social construction of language and the material nature of subjectivity in favour of a realist notion of language practice and an idealist (liberal humanist) notion of subjectivity. Basically texts are seen by process pedagogy as transparent points of engagement for individual students who will use the exchange with the text as a way of constructing an individual voice. This notion of textual transparency is a relatively recent one, dating from the late eighteenth century. As discussed earlier, it has more to do with the rhetoric of particular writing practices (romanticism and realism) than with their actual textual strategies.

Certainly feminist writers discovered very early that texts are not transparent objects; they are highly coercive linguistic strategies, positioning readers in particular ways which have nothing to do with encouraging individuality and everything to do with reproducing a particular social formation. Relying on textual engagement alone, where that means engagement with the 'story', is like leaving voters to vote for the politician who makes the best promises without giving any thought to why those promises are being made. It is a naive attitude to textuality which fails to account for the functioning of texts as linguistic and discursive practices. Feminist writers and readers were not only very aware of the political or ideological function of specific genres, they were also very aware of the effect of those genres on readers. From this feminist perspective it was apparent that people were not able simply to challenge and reject or ignore texts that they did not agree with and so form their own opinions in reaction to texts; rather, the engagement with texts was and is extremely coercive, and is an integral part of the reader's construction of subjectivity. Texts work on readers, positioning them discursively in particular ways, and often use the naturalised discourses of their own society (patriarchal, bourgeois, ethnocentric discourses) to do so.

The individual voice which is most likely to develop in the course of a naive engagement with texts is a totally naturalised or ideologically conservative voice. The 'authority' which some educators claim students will feel as a result of their textual engagement may simply be a totally naturalised positioning within the culture; so that social might, dominant ideas and values and beliefs are on their side — coming out of their mouths. That is a way many individuals within a culture feel powerful, but it is not the aim of a critical literacy to construct or create that kind of empowerment. For feminist writers and readers this is a crucial issue. With a history of innovative, creative, powerful and misogynistic writers in every genre to contend with, feminists were and are extremely sensitive to the ways in which the fictional genres of their culture reproduce the patriarchal ideology of that culture.

Instead, they began to challenge and change these genres so that they could and did voice feminist discourse. However, it was not possible simply to go in and construct — out of nothing — a new voice; that divine conjuring trick simply does not, and by definition cannot, work with mortals. We are able to read and understand texts because we already have an understanding of how texts work, from all the other texts we've read. So feminist writers were faced with writing texts which were like what people had read before, but different enough to be able to construct a different voice. The Tiptree story discussed earlier achieved this balance, telling a recognisable BEM story, but turning it on its head to construct an unconventional and subversive feminist narrative. Another, more blatant, example is Judith Viorst's rewriting of the Cinderella story in a short poem entitled 'And Then the Prince Knelt Down and Tried to Put the Glass Slipper on Cinderella's Foot':

> I really didn't notice that he had a funny nose.
> And he certainly looked better all dressed up in fancy clothes.

He's not nearly as attractive as he seemed the other night.
So I think I'll just pretend that his glass slipper feels too tight.
(Viorst, 1976, 73)

Viorst's text works as a deconstruction of the familiar story, not as a replacement for it. It refers to the story but changes it to construct a different narrative and a different voice. With many texts the intertextual reference is not as blatant as this; that is, they do not retell a familiar story with familiar characters. Instead, they use and reconstruct the conventions associated with a particular genre and in the process call to mind a number of similar stories, as Tiptree has done. Nevertheless, Viorst's short poem is an example, perhaps an extreme example, of this reconstructive practice.

Feminist writers achieved this difficult balance between retelling a familiar kind of story and saying something new mostly by trial and error: an untheorised method of textual deconstruction. Role reversal was one of the early casualties of this project (Lefanu, 1988). Even with non-realist fiction it was found to be not possible to turn a patriarchal text into a feminist text simply by substituting a female for a male hero. That change does produce something different, but it seemed often to result in a female character behaving just as badly as most male characters in that same 'hero' role, which is not the kind of change that most feminists were looking for. However, it does reveal the nature of the hero role — so is part of the deconstruction of the genre.

Subsequently, feminist theorists have systematised these explorations of text and genre in a number of ways, using as basic principles those points made by Gilbert and Taylor about language and subjectivity. First, it is recognised that specific genres of writing have a conventional range of textual strategies which they employ in the construction of meaning. Those textual strategies are configured or interact in order to enact particular discourse(s). So, for example, the conquest of space which is so familiarly associated with science fiction is conventionally an occasion for the enactment of a number of aggressive discourses — colonialist and patriarchal.

How does a feminist writer go about constructing a space adventure? Interestingly, the answer is that her space adventure operates by metatextual reference to the more conventional texts; in other words, she has to take account of the discursive meanings of this conventional situation and confront them in her own writing — and in the process offer a different reading of the convention. The Tiptree story, 'The Women Men Don't See', operates in exactly this way. With science fiction the feminist deconstruction of the genre has dealt with such characteristic features of SF as the alien, technology, the nature of scientific knowledge and extrapolation — and in the process dealt with the construction in the SF text of discourses which are patriarchal, colonialist, militaristic, racist, scientist (Cranny-Francis, 1990a, 1990e).

Fantasy is another genre used by feminist writers, and in that genre the deconstructions have covered the 'sword and sorcery' fiction, fairytale and horror, in each case deconstructing, among other things, the patriarchal ideology fundamental to most texts written in these genres (Lefanu, 1988; Cranny-Francis, 1990a). The 'sword and sorcery' deconstructions include Marion Zimmer Bradley's *The Shattered Chain*, Elizabeth Lynn's *Chronicles of Tornor* and Barbara Hambly's *Dragonsbane*. In all of these novels the masculinist and often violently misogynistic discourses of the conventional texts in the genre are reconstructed as investigations of the nature of human relationships and of the social construction of femininity and masculinity. *Dragonsbane*, for example, deals with the adventures of a very reluctant dragon-killer, Lord John Aversin, who is persuaded to try to kill a very old dragon terrorising a local kingdom. But Sir John is so very unlike the proud, arrogant, chivalric knight that he meets constant derision from the people he is trying to help. And his partner, Jenny Waynest, a witch, is so unlike the ladies at court that she too is subject to ridicule and abuse. They eventually succeed together in driving the dragon away, but they do not kill him, believing the death of such a rare creature would be a tragedy. *Dragonsbane* confronts many aspects of familiar sword and sorcery tales — the patriarchal masculine hero, the passive princess/prize, the battle with evil — and reconstructs them all. Instead, we have a gentle, caring and nurturing hero, a wise and sensitive female hero, no princess/prize, a deconstruction of the nature of evil, and victory through a partnership between the active female character and the relatively passive male character. It also works very well as a story; is interesting and suspenseful and very charming.

Fairytale became the focus of a lot of feminist writing because of its perceived function of acculturating young girls into passive sexual and social roles in which their only value was their physical appearance (Lieberman, 1986; Cranny-Francis, 1990a). Writers such as Angela Carter and Tanith Lee constructed different versions of the tales in which the female roles were often changed so that they became active participants in their own fate, and in which they were conscious of their own social positioning. Angela Carter's collection of reconstructed fairytales is titled *The Bloody Chamber* and includes different tellings of Bluebeard, Red Riding Hood and Beauty and the Beast. Tanith Lee's collection, *Red as Blood, or Tales from the Sisters Grimmer*, retells Cinderella, Red Riding Hood, The Pied Piper of Hamelin among others. The purpose of these stories is not to replace the traditional tales, but to expose the ideology of those tales: the patriarchal discourses they enact and their construction of femininity. Carter tells two Red Riding Hood stories, for example, and in both her little girl is a very active character who deals very successfully with the wolf. In *The Werewolf* she reveals that Granny is the wolf and succeeds in having her killed and taking over her property. In the other, *The Company of Wolves*, she is an active sexual partner with the alluring wolf, who is also the hunter, and Red Riding Hood needs no help from anyone to get on with her mature adult, sexual life. For Tanith Lee it is Red Riding Hood who becomes the wolf, a trait handed down by her grandmother who became a werewolf in order to deal with the excessive brutality of her wife-beating husband. In each case the passivity and sexual repression of the female character in the Perrault and Grimm versions of the tale are deconstructed and the tales reworked to construct a feminist discourse.

There are also some versions of horror which work either by replacing the characteristically masculine aggressor of most horror texts with a feminine one or by deconstructing the pathology of the masculine aggressor, so that his behaviour is recognised as a version of the patriarchal masculine, rather than as an anti-social aberration. In the case of the feminine aggressor, the female vampire, for example, not only is there a deconstruction of sexist constructions of feminine monstrosity (often a function of female activity rather than passivity), but there is again a deconstruction, by contrast, of the more traditional masculine role (Cranny-Francis, 1990a, 1990c).

The related utopian and dystopian genres, which tell stories about either a very good place (utopia) or its opposite, a very bad place (dystopia), are reworked to present visions of society not dominated by patriarchal ideology, which often means also a change in the socio-economic base and in the ideologies of class and ethnicity which function in this utopian world. In traditional utopian and dystopian fashion they also offer detailed critiques of the author's and readers' own society (Lefanu, 1988; Cranny-Francis, 1990a, 1990d, 1991b). Marge Piercy's *Woman on the Edge of Time* combines both a utopian and a dystopian vision in her detailed critique of life in contemporary American society.

Detective fiction is another genre which has attracted a large feminist participation in recent years (Cranny-Francis, 1989b, 1990a). Women have always been heavily represented as writers of the genre (Agatha Christie, P.D. James, Ngaio Marsh, Ruth Rendell), but there have been very few female detectives. In the detective fiction which has had a socially critical edge, like the work of Raymond Chandler, there is often a sexist discourse operating — and corruption of all kinds is often figured in these books as feminine, in contrast with the honest masculinity of the detective-hero. The female detective cannot operate effectively with this representation of corruption since it would implicate her, so one characteristic textual strategy has to be changed to accommodate the change in sexual identity of the detective. There is a range of other textual conventions which also come under challenge from the femininity of the detective — such as the use of violence, the nature of interpersonal relationships and the nature of crime. So Marele Day's Claudia Valentine, Sarah Paretsky's V.I. Warshawski and Sue Grafton's Kinsey Millhone are convincingly feminine and convincingly professional — but they are also very different from their hard-boiled masculine colleagues.

Every genre of writing is susceptible to this kind of questioning. Textual strategies or conventions can be deconstructed and their discursive function analysed. Then different texts can be constructed which are based on that deconstruction; texts which tell a different story, enact a different voice, and which, in doing so, identify the voice most commonly heard in other texts of the genre.

### Analysing Fictional Genres: Pedagogical Implications

One way to locate the genre conventions and identify their discursive function is to trace changes in a particular genre historically. Since genres are socially constructed, examining how the textual realisation of genres change over time is one way of understanding the (discursive) role of specific aspects of those texts which identify them generically. This is not unlike the kind of sociocultural analysis that Jack Zipes performed on the Red Riding Hood story, tracing the changes in the tale and referring them to the kinds of society in which they were enacted. Zipes provides a transcript of an oral version of Red Riding Hood, taken in the 1880s, and compares this with a whole range of written versions, including the most famous versions by Perrault and the Brothers Grimm. The change in the gender discourse constructed in the tales is obvious at first reading (Zipes, 1983).

This kind of historical research and analysis is powerful because it simultaneously enables the deconstruction of genre conventions; that is, it also reveals the voice which conventionally is spoken in those genres — and so reveals very clearly the social/political/ideological function of literature. As Rachel Blau du Plessis says in her book, *Writing beyond the Ending*: 'Narrative in the most general terms is a version of, or special expression of, ideology' (du Plessis, 1985, x) — and with fictional texts (and many others besides) we are dealing almost always with narratives. As noted earlier, then, this is the kind of analysis which enabled the construction of a body of writing which is identifiably feminist. I would also suggest that it is fundamental to any kind of writing which constructs a different voice from the mainstream one, that is, a feminist or non-Anglocentric or working-class voice (see, for example, Ashcroft, Griffiths and Tiffin, 1989 on post-colonial writing).

This analysis of generic history is particularly important to readers and writers working with the materialist concept of subjectivity; that is, a conception of the individual subject as constantly re-formed and renegotiated in relation to the discourses (and so discursive positionings) encountered by the individual. Because it is recognised that texts are active social practices working to position readers in particular ways, and because readers are understood as constantly renegotiating their own identities in relation to every aspect of their experience (textual and otherwise), then it became obvious that textually naive reading and writing practices were likely to be counterproductive.

Pedagogically, this awareness of the elided coercive function of literature and of the fluid nature of human subjectivity means that a very sophisticated deconstructive reading and writing practice is necessary if we are to avoid simply reproducing compliant social subjects — even when we think that what we are doing is helping students to develop an individual voice. So, for example, in order to use elements of critical pedagogy outlined by writers such as Giroux which involve students in critical self-examination, it is necessary to combine that with a sophisticated understanding of textual practice and individual subjectivity. That is, it is necessary to provide students with a theory of subjectivity which they can use to explain and understand their current identity as well as providing them with a kind of utopian potential, the possibility of change. Subjectivity is commonly grounded in, and demonstrated in relation to, the influence of textual positioning on the individual. So students interact with texts — visual and verbal — and use them as a basis from which to explore particular ways of thinking and acting and feeling, different discourses. However, without a complex understanding of textual practice, of the meaning or significance of textual strategies and how those strategies position readers, it is unlikely that students will get beyond the kind of ideological compliance that is of such concern to those involved in developing critical pedagogy. In other words, the students may be articulate, may write fluently, but they may do so by being naturalised social subjects; their empowerment is a function of their willingness not to challenge dominant attitudes and values and beliefs. Worse, for students who are alienated by their textual positioning (for example, students who are from non-mainstream social positionings), the exercise in critical examination is likely to be disastrous. Their failure to engage with a mainstream and ideologically conservative text, a failure produced by the text's construction of their social/subjective positioning as powerless and valueless or simply its failure to engage with meaningful aspects of their own positioning, may result in feelings of personal inadequacy and defeat — feelings that teachers report with alarming frequency.

As noted earlier, the feminist writers of the 1960s and 1970s who were involved in the recent expansion of women's writing, particularly in the popular genres, faced and conquered this same problem; they too were constantly made to feel that they were the problem, not the genres they were working with (Russ, 1984). They succeeded by developing a critical awareness of textual strategy, a historical understanding of genre and so of the possibilities for change, and a conception of subjectivity which acknowledged the influence of textual negotiation or interaction on the individual.

It is necessary at this stage also to challenge the claims made by some educators that to do so will result in the reproduction of these students as compliant social subjects (female students become 'honorary' males, working-class students become middle-class and so on). In the first place, for these (socially marginalised) students to be compliant social subjects they should not be empowered in this way in the first place. Like the working-class boys of Paul Willis's study, they should 'choose' not to gain access to this voice or voices — a choice which signals the success of the educational ideology in which they are positioned (Willis, 1977). When students from non-mainstream positionings are given this access to powerful voice(s), they do not lose their own culture; they gain aspects of another; they have more than one voice. Of course, they are no longer the disempowered subjects that educators may love to cherish, no longer the subjects of middle-class paternalism. In the same way it is important to remove female students from their positioning simply as victims of a patriarchal culture. On the one hand, that positioning denies the kinds of power which patriarchy offers women — and it is surely unrealistic to think that women have lived with patriarchy for centuries without it offering them some kind of power. On the other hand, it simply reinforces the perception that the only positioning available to them is that of victim, a radically disempowering perspective.

In my own teaching practice I have found it necessary to examine very critically the ways that feminist knowledge is constructed. For example, I found that analysing texts which construct femininity in sexist terms is not empowering unless you have a room full of very articulate worked-out female students. At one institution I did have that and there was no problem in dealing with a range of material; the women in the room dealt with the material very well, and the men often took their cues from the women's deconstructions. But at another institution where the women were from a very different demographic profile, where they were not articulate and were in the process of battling with sexist attitudes to femininity in their own families and peer groups, dealing with explicitly sexist material in class was a disaster. The men in the class, who were from a similar positioning and were often very sexist themselves, found the experience enormously empowering, even when they attempted unsuccessfully to play the game I described above of separating their classroom voice from their political practice (arguably a classroom full of white middle-class boys would have been able to put up a much better appearance of concern over the victimisation of women — and I suspect that is what usually happened at the other institution I mentioned).

This classroom situation raised a whole complex of issues which are part of the construction of a critical pedagogy. First, it was interesting that, for example, offensively sexist pictures of women are often found in texts which deal with the objectification of women. The obvious response is that the pictures just illustrate the argument, but this does not allow for the different kinds of uses made of texts by different readers. Another way to approach this problem is by asking a question based on the critical awareness of textual practice developed by feminist writers — what is the function of the pictures in this text, and how do they position readers? When the text is apparently written to empower women, and yet it uses, as a textual strategy, illustrations which women find offensive and debilitating, what does that tell us about the text itself?

Deconstructing the text itself, rather than what it apparently 'says', is one of the most powerful tools available to teachers and students. Again note that what we are dealing with here is the need to engage with the social construction of language, verbal and visual, and with its effect on the reader; in the terms used by Gilbert and Taylor 'an understanding of the socially constructed nature of language practices and the discursive nature of subjectivity' (Gilbert and Taylor, 1991, 106). This analysis is not possible with a textually, and I would suggest politically, naive approach to reading and writing.

The other question it raised was the nature of the power the male students had or felt they had in this context. Clearly a lot of them felt very smug and happy in their role as social oppressors, and yet it was particularly apparent with this group that they were socially marginalised in other ways — because of class or ethnicity. Was this sexist power a way of feeling powerful not available to them in other contexts? Was the transparency of their response also a marker of the fact that they weren't positioned as powerful in other ways; that is, that they didn't control the discourse which would enable them to appear sympathetic and socially responsible, no matter what they privately felt, and no matter what their personal politics were? It seemed that we needed to develop ways of talking about the oppression of men under patriarchy, not to dilute our attempt to support women, but to challenge the smugness displayed by some of the men. If sexist discourse constructs women and femininity in these very limited terms, then what does it do to men? Do they have a greater range of options? And what are those options? Textual material can be very useful in exploring this problematic, but again only if it is used in a critically sophisticated sense; if the students can get beyond the story to the way the text is positioning them and the discourses it is constructing. Again one way to reach that stage of textual self-consciousness is to engage explicitly with the generic conventions (and their discursive meanings) constitutive of the texts we encounter.

## Teaching 'Feminine' Genres: The Case of Romance

Romance is one genre which is often raised in the context of teaching young women, a genre for which young women have a great fondness. By romance I mean the Mills and Boon and Harlequin type of popular romance and its teenage versions like Dolly fiction. This is a genre traditionally characterised by its granite-jawed, hard-bodied heroes who are all very wealthy and/or professionally successful; its young, fragile and inexperienced heroines; the rude intrusion of a dark-haired successful *femme fatale* who momentarily distracts the hero from his true fate which is love and marriage with the heroine.

The developing debate around romance is a very interesting one (Russ, 1973; Creed, 1984; Modleski, 1984; Radway, 1984, 1986; Ang, 1985; Thurston, 1987;

Gilbert, 1989a–b; Brown, 1990; Cranny-Francis, 1990a; Gilbert and Taylor, 1991). For a long time feminist writers simply rejected romance as a source of study or even as worth critical attention on the grounds that it simply reinforces the most subservient characterisations of women and femininity. Then another school of thought developed which argued that if so many women read romance it surely demands critical attention. Along the same lines came work which attempted to look at the reasons behind women's attraction to this genre, often from a psychological perspective. There was another school of thought which argued, along the same lines as Virginia Woolf had early this century, that romance was considered a degraded form of fiction mainly because its audience is mostly female. So simply rejecting the genre as worthless could be seen as participating in the characterisation of women and their interests as trivial. The recent work on tactical reading, inspired by the writing of Michel de Certau, has also been part of this debate, with questions being raised about the particular uses to which women put this romance reading (Certau, 1984). It was argued that, while the texts in themselves might not have a great deal to offer in an empowering sense, maybe women use them in ways which are not predicted by the texts and which are after all empowering for those women.

This essentially feminist debate about romance has recently become part of a different debate, about the nature of an empowering pedagogy for women. Many of the participants in this latter debate attempt to address directly the fact that so many girls and young women read romance. So instead of ignoring or devaluing this reading, they attempt to incorporate it into a program of reading and writing. For example, Gilbert and Taylor deal with romance at great length in *Fashioning the Feminine*. They recommend that girls should be encouraged to explore the romance in a hands-on way; examining its generic history, trying to write romance (and so deconstructing the conventions), looking at its marketing, and analysing its audience appeal. It is exactly the kind of exploration that is required by the critical literacy concept discussed earlier.

Another perspective might be added to Gilbert and Taylor's analysis of romance which would enhance the interrogation of this distinctively feminine genre, and this is to do with class. To explain its applicability to the analysis of a genre which seems to be so specifically focused on issues of sexuality and gender, consider Gilbert and Taylor's own descriptions of their research. They identify recurrent plot features, such as this: 'The novice [meaning here the heroine of the romance] may have to carve out her new romantic identity by inscribing her body romantically: she must be "made-over" in the way that teen magazines make-over the ordinary girl into the desirable, "feminine" girl. She may need a weight loss . . ., and will almost certainly need different clothing and make-up' (Gilbert and Taylor, 1991, 87). A few pages later they discuss the readership of romance, asking why it is that some girls come eventually to reject the stereotypes offered by the romance, while other girls remain positioned compliantly by the romance. They go on:

> Social class membership has not been a key factor in the studies by Willinsky and Hunniford, Lam or Christian-Smith, but it could be argued that the lived social and cultural experiences of girls as members of oppressed and disadvantaged groups may be significant in positioning some girls more readily to adopt romance ideology — and to accept

romance fiction — as the most promising method of resolving the contradictions of becoming feminine. For instance Taylor's work with an inner city group of Australian girls found that those who came from non-English speaking backgrounds were more attracted by romance fiction than were the other girls in the class. (Gilbert and Taylor, 1991, 95)

It is worth noting here that their own work on the Dolly fiction supports this kind of conclusion. When they asked a group of middle-class girls to read the Dolly books, the girls were very reluctant to do so, regarding the books as trash. The girls were also aware that boys their own age devalued this fiction, and were very against introducing the books into the mixed-sex classroom. Of course, it is very likely that the responses of these articulate middle-class girls were formed largely by their complex negotiation of the responses from parents and peers they were likely to attract for reading this fiction, and that they were engaging in the denigration of romance which is largely related to it being seen as feminine and therefore trivial. However, there is an important aspect of these texts which many of the analyses neglect, and which Gilbert and Taylor's work hints at but doesn't consolidate — and this is their function in relation to issues of class and ethnicity.

Romance novels do fetishise interpersonal relationships; they seem to be totally concerned with 'meeting the right man'. Yet the evidence suggests that it is middle-class girls who list meeting the right man as a priority, while working-class girls are more concerned with growing up and having children — with the man part of, but not necessarily the focus of, that scenario (Gilbert and Taylor, 1991, 17). Yet the middle-class girls for whom romance would seem to be the natural expression of desire don't read the genre with the same frequency as the working-class girls whose apparent focus of desire lies elsewhere (Gilbert and Taylor, 1991, 94). Perhaps this reading of the romance as focused on gender relations is not sufficiently complex; perhaps the genre has another social function of which the fetishisation of the interpersonal is one element, but not the whole story.

If the readership of the romance is considered, along with the aspirations of that readership, then it seems reasonable to suggest that somehow the girls are using the romance as part of a program to achieve, not a marriage with Mr Right, so much as a secure relationship with Mr Provider. Perhaps the romance is a variant of what Carolyn Steedman calls the 'goose girls can marry kings' fantasy (Steedman, 1986, 16). The fantasy is marriage to someone who is powerful within the society, because that marriage offers security and the chance to raise a family free of debilitating worries about money. The make-over routine identified by Gilbert and Taylor may also be part of this scenario whereby a woman from an oppressed and disadvantaged social group is able to fit in with the group surrounding these prized providers. In other words, the make-overs may be read as a way of achieving the same powerful positioning as that of the married heroine, or in the case of the teen romance, the successful teenager. The (socially marginalised) working-class and non-Anglo readers of romance know very well that goose girls, who are simply goose girls, no matter how beautiful, don't marry kings. They may be seduced by kings, but not married. Goose girls who want to marry kings have to be able to pass for queens; their repertoire of discourses, bodily inscribed as well as thought and talked, has to be more flexible than that of just a goose girl — or even that of just a queen. Maybe this is what the romance seems to offer, the blueprint for achieving this kind of social mobility. Perhaps this is not so important to middle-class girls who are (relatively) powerfully positioned within the culture, even if their gender positioning is in some situations problematic. Middle-class girls don't need to learn the lessons of these romances because in a sense they live those lessons in their own lives, via their middle-class positioning.

Not that romances aren't about gender relations; they are. But their gender discourse has to be read within the context of the discourses of class and ethnicity which these texts also enact. To read them as only about gender underestimates the complexity of their modelling of discursive positionings. It is interesting to note that girls from non-mainstream ethnic backgrounds are among the biggest consumers of romance and that they regularly report using romance as a liberatory practice in relation to their own expectations about the future (Gilbert and Taylor, 1991, 95).

Returning to the feminist work on genre fictions with which I started, it is significant that while feminists have presented revisions of a range of genres, so that there is a recognisable body of feminist SF, fantasy, utopian writing and detective fiction, there is no similar collection of feminist romance. Perhaps that is because the feminist deconstructions of romance have failed to address this social function of the genre, which is to describe the discursive nature of successful feminine positioning. In contemporary Western society, successful feminine positioning is a function of class and ethnicity as well as gender. It also occupies a very specific relationship to masculine positioning which is also neglected in most studies of the romance.

It is possible to see this function of the genre through a historical study of the genre, the kind I suggested earlier as a way of deconstructing all genres. This means analysing texts such as Samuel Richardson's *Pamela* and the Bronte sisters' great novels, *Jane Eyre* and *Wuthering Heights*. If romance texts are used in schools, against the advice of the middle-class girls interviewed by Gilbert and Taylor (and I mention that only because it does represent a particular class and ethnic positioning in relation to romance which should be acknowledged), then it is important that this kind of historical analysis be done and that these texts be treated with the same kind of critical respect that I have outlined above as essential to any empowering pedagogical practice.

Given that this is done and given that students have an understanding of the social construction of individual identity or subjectivity, then it is possible to use genres such as romance to develop the critical, deconstructive writing and reading practice which feminists have developed over the last twenty years or so, and which might be characterised as a subversive writing practice and a resistant reading practice. This feminist work has only been possible because of an understanding or conception of subjectivity which acknowledges the role of writing and reading in the formation or negotiation of individual consciousness and so of the political nature of the processes of reading and writing. This is allied with a detailed analysis of the genres being used, which relates textual strategy and discursive practice.

## Genre and Critical Literacy

In this context a critical pedagogy might be developed which draws on both the experience of the individual student and on some kind of textual interaction involving the student — for example, a particular reading or writing task. Then, using the deconstructive practice developed by feminist writers, students can explore the ways in which the texts they use position them as readers. They can explore the way texts function as discursive practices. They can explore their own positioning as a negotiative practice involving textual interaction as well as a range of everyday actions and behaviours, many of them constructed variously by the texts with which they come into contact. By using this set of practices to shift the emphasis of this interaction from the psychological subject to the social or psychosocial subject, students and teachers can avoid the lapse into anecdotal and naturalised discourses which can otherwise result from reading and writing practices. Students and teachers can also explore the institutional ideology within which they work, and deconstruct its positioning of them — often via the curriculum texts which are its prescribed classroom intervention. With this set of practices students may also become empowered resistant readers, refusing a naive compliance with the texts with which they come in contact and the institutional ideology by which they are positioned — particularly important, of course, in the case of the non-masculine, non-middle-class, non-Anglo students, since in terms of this educational ideology those students, like Willis's working-class boys, are positioned to fail (Willis, 1977). They can become subversive writers, reworking the genres in which they write to construct discourse(s) which powerfully articulate their own positioning within society and their knowledge of the relationship of that positioning to the narrow range of socially empowered positionings. They can develop a range of voices, rather than simply the one prescribed voice. This can give those students an access to knowledges and to power from which they are otherwise socially excluded. They can become empowered, and that will mean being both resistant to, and subversive of, their own positioning within the dominant culture.

> The child dreams that her dream
> is faster than light, because
> we promised her that's how death
> would come for her . . .

> She soars through the universe,
> leaving the cliffs where her family
> hangs; she will not be Andromeda,
> bound to a rock until the prince
> comes, but fly on her own
> from our stifling kitchens.

> The prince is a figment
> of our boring legend, he is
> the gravity her sleep-ship
> may escape from. Dressed
> in a red shift, she's always
> a world ahead of his weight.
> (Dorman, 1978, 55)

### Genre in Literary Criticism and Linguistics: Commonality and Difference

In this chapter I use the term 'genre' in a sense common in literary criticism. In the next chapter J.R. Martin uses it in a way familiar to functional linguists — as in the work of Hasan, Ventola, Martin and Swales. Because these uses are not identical, it seems that this might be a good point at which to reflect on the relationship between the two uses of and meanings of 'genre' and to question how they might be related.

At its most basic, 'genre' simply means a kind, a style. It is used in literary criticism in a number of ways to define the 'kind' or 'style' of literary texts. It is used to classify fictional texts into three broad categories: poetry, prose, drama. It is also used to subdivide those categories. So we might talk of different poetry genres: the sonnet, lyric, ode and ballad. We might discuss different prose genres: the novel, the short story, the novella, the prose poem. Drama, too, might be classified generically as tragedy, comedy, history play. Then again, we might further subclassify. We might discuss different kinds of sonnet: the Elizabethan or Shakespearean sonnet, the Petrarchan sonnet. With the novel we might talk about the realist novel, the modernist novel, or about science fiction, fantasy, detective fiction and romance.

'Genre' in each case is a way of classifying texts into kinds or types, because of perceived similarities — characteristics or conventions that these texts share. With some generic classifications these shared conventions or characteristics are, in the most obvious sense, formal. So Shakespearean sonnets are identifiable by their use of a structure which includes three quatrains and a couplet, in contrast to the Petrarchan sonnet which divides its fourteen lines into two quatrains and a sestet. With other generic classifications, however, these shared characteristics are, in the most obvious sense, semantic — to do with the field or subject area of the texts involved. So we might talk about science fiction and include in that classification science fiction novels, short stories, poetry, film, television and visual arts.

If 'genre' has this range of different meanings and classificatory procedures — by formal characteristics, by field — we might ask what is its value? Why is it so useful to educators, linguists and critics, as well as to publishers, film makers, booksellers, readers and viewers? The main reason is highlighted by the proviso added to each of the classificatory systems suggested above — in the most obvious sense. The interesting and useful thing about 'genre' is that it is never simply formal or semantic and it is not even simply textual. Todorov writes of Bakhtin's theory: 'Genre is a sociohistorical as well as a formal entity. Transformations in genre must be considered in relation to social changes' (Todorov, 1984, 80). In a similar vein Fredric Jameson writes: 'The strategic value of generic concepts . . . lies in the mediatory function of the notion of a genre, which allows the coordination of immanent formal analysis of the individual text with the twin diachronic perspective of the history of forms and the evolution of social life' (Jameson, 1981, 105). In other words, the concept of genre is useful because it enables a number of different but related perspectives on texts to be developed and coordinated. First, it enables the reader to place a text within the history of a particular kind or style, by reference to the characteristic generic features it exhibits ('the history of forms'). The reader is then able to assess the particular interest of that text; for example, how it conforms to or changes the genre(s) of which it is a part. So, for example, if a contemporary poet decided to write in the Shakespearean sonnet form, we might use the notion of 'genre' to explore what changes she/he has effected formally to the Shakespearean sonnet. Perhaps the poet has reproduced faithfully the formal conventions of the Shakespearean sonnet. We might then use our knowledge of genre to place the text in relation to other contemporary poetic genres, like performance poetry, for example, and ask how modern readers might respond to this sonnet. In other words, this formal reading of genre enables us to explore the intertextual relations within which the modern sonnet is embedded, relations which influence critically the meanings it produces for modern readers. Its rigid stanza form, rhyme and rhythm might, for example, lead us to doubt whether many contemporary readers would find it possible to relate to their everyday experiences. We might conjecture that it would seem dated or, if its language or concerns were modern, that it would read as a parody of some kind — perhaps as a comparison of the ordered, rigidly structured, predemocratic Elizabethan age with the fragmentation of the postmodern world. So we arrive, inevitably, at what Jameson calls 'the twin diachronic perspective' of genre, 'the evolution of social life'. Classifying texts generically irresistibly leads us to place them socially, to identify them as social practices.

Since genres (and, therefore, genre conventions) are acknowledged as social, as well as formal, categories, the reader is able to trace in genre conventions the textual realisation or instantiation of social practice, and to explore in the changes to or developments of genres, changes in the social life of which texts are a crucial part. Exploring the meanings produced by a modern, 'Elizabethan' sonnet leads us back to an analysis of how that poetic genre formally realised or instantiated the Elizabethan society of which it was a product (or at least how we, as modern readers, understand that relationship). We read that relationship largely by generic contrast or comparison. We know that a lot of contemporary poetry is written in blank verse, that is, without a formal rhyme pattern and with a subtle (but often rigid) rhythm. This combination of apparent freedom and elided control can be read as typical of, or as an instantiation of, the way power is practised institutionally in our society, where democratic freedom is based on a fairly rigid and intrusive state control which is, however, elided. For example, who feels that obeying traffic lights is an intrusion on individual liberty? It is, but we accommodate it as the price of safety, of continued freedom, if you like. We do not, in a sense, feel it; and, in another sense, we do not even 'know' it because we do not think of it that way.

In an Elizabethan sonnet, on the other hand, the institutional power of the state is formally realised in the controlled rhythm and rhyme scheme. Or perhaps it is more correct to say that it formally reproduced the affective realisation of institutional power; the way that it shapes what we understand of the upper-class Elizabethan consciousness (the class which produced and read these sonnets). The rigid order of the Elizabethan sonnet connotes the 'order' of that English mentality, its acceptance of a rigid class structure and of the power relations which proceed from that social class structuring. With more attention to its intertextual history and to its discursive realisation of the Elizabethan world, the sonnet might lead us to examine the elisions in the Elizabethan upper-class mind; elisions of a similar order, perhaps, to those which characterise the contemporary middle-class mind (the class for which much, but certainly not all, contemporary poetry is written).

That task would lead us to compare the Elizabethan sonnet with the Petrarchan sonnet, for example, and to question the differences in mentality instantiated in their different formal structures — which, in turn, will lead us back to the differences between the societies which produced them, as seen through the eyes/mind of the class for which they were written. Which takes us back, again, to Jameson's formulation of genre as enabling us to explore 'the evolution of social life'.

Exploring the writing and reading of a modern Elizabethan sonnet leads us inevitably to a recognition of the repressions and contradictions which characterise the middle-class postmodern consciousness, the interplay of institutional power and personal liberty which constitutes what we call 'democratic freedom'. So, writing an Elizabethan sonnet might be, for some readers (middle-class readers, mainly, those with the cultural capital to 'read' it), a radically deconstructive practice confronting those readers with their (unconscious) acceptance of state control, control which infiltrates their affective or emotional perception of experience. That the sonnet is almost invariably concerned with love highlights the fact that this control is experienced not only intellectually but affectively.

A fairly simple example — a meditation on the hypothetical production of a poem written to obey the generic constraints of the Elizabethan sonnet — leads us to a series of conjectures about what we understand of the Elizabethan consciousness, and to specify that this is a particular (that is, upper-class) consciousness. We are led to explore the power structures of the Elizabethan world and to acknowledge the class-based nature of reading and writing as a social practice. Furthermore, we might be led to recognise the fact that the canonical texts of English literature (as a discipline and social institution) instantiate this class bias. We are led also to specify, by contrast, the postmodern consciousness capable of performing this reading. That is, we are led to acknowledge that the literacy skills (cultural capital) required to produce the reading discussed here are confined to those with a high level of formal education — and that specifies them as, in most cases, middle-class. Which might lead us to question the class bias within our own literature and literary institutions. We were led also to recognise particular features of the (middle-class) postmodernist consciousness we examined, the combination of repressions and liberty which constitute its sense of freedom — and that discussion might go a great deal further. What other blindnesses, contradictions and aporia constitute this middle-class consciousness, particularly, for example, in the area of class relations, gender relations, ethnic differences? The modern Elizabethan sonnet leads us to a confrontation with contemporary society; with the discourses (of class, gender, ethnicity, generation) which define its dominant ideology, with the conditional nature of their dominance (they can be challenged — as they are by this subversive poem); with the class bias written into the texts which constitute our 'literature' and into our literary institutions; with the ways in which texts can function subversively — challenging the (unconscious) acceptance of middle-class dominance of literature and literary institutions (publishing, educational) by revealing that bias.

Genre is a category which enables the individual to construct critical texts; by manipulating genre conventions to produce texts which engender the kind of analysis discussed above. It also enables, therefore, the construction of a new, different consciousness; a consciousness which does not contain or embody the repressions discussed above — or, at least, does not unconsciously embody them. Once they become conscious, they will inevitably become a source of questioning, interrogation and further contradiction, which will produce a new, different social subject.

Genre is also a category which enables the individual to produce the kind of analysis I have conducted above. It enables one to move from a randomly chosen hypothetical example to a meditation on the nature of contemporary society and postmodern consciousness, in the process questioning also the nature of the institutions which produce and maintain the textual field, 'literature', to which the sonnet belongs. For example, the publishing industry: what class, gender, ethnic biases are incorporated in their output? And educational institutions: why are certain texts chosen as typical of a society when they were actually only typical of one class in a society? What effect has that had on the development of contemporary literature? Is the same selection process still happening? I can perform this kind of analysis because I have been trained in literary criticism and history (so that I know about 'genres') and because I work with the concept of 'genre' formulated by the linguist, Mikhail Bakhtin, earlier this century and developed by literary critics such as Fredric Jameson.

'Genre' is an organising category which enables the individual using it to place a text within the networks of textual, disciplinary and technological practices in which it operates. In this chapter I have used the complex concept of genre to place a number of feminist texts in relation to some of those networks. I was particularly interested in the ways that feminist science fiction, fantasy and detective fiction function within the networks of texts in which they are implicated: their intertextual relations. By examining the intertextual relationships of these texts I was able to understand their parodic and/or critical functions. That meant understanding not only the way in which they criticised and parodied the kinds of stories told in more conventional texts in these genres (like Judith Viorst's reworked fairytale), but also how their reworkings of the genres revealed the assumptions and biases implicit in the more conservative texts (Marele Day's opening paragraphs in *The Life and Crimes of Harry Lavender* exemplify this).

This analysis also allows me to value these texts, to see them as critical and parodic, not simply as bad texts. This is an important point in relation to the networks of disciplinary and technological practices of which they are a part. In disciplinary terms, for example (and here I am referring to the discipline of English literature or Literature), texts which experiment with genre often receive an initially poor reception. We are familiar with stories of famous artists who did not sell a picture in their lifetime but whose work, after their deaths, has rocketed in value. This is sometimes crudely attributed to its rarity, the fact that no more can be produced (an explanation which says much about the workings of a capitalist culture, but is ultimately unsatisfying). The reason for the apparent 'failure' of such artists in their own lifetime can be explained more cogently by the fact that they were involved in changing the genres in which they worked — changing them sometimes so radically that their audiences could not understand the work or appreciate it, so they did not buy it. Such artists often suffered also at the hands of non-comprehending critics who were unable to elucidate the artist's work for this audience. Their relationship to their own disciplinary field was one of exclusion; their art was considered bad art.

The technologies which might have brought their work to the public also worked against them. Gallery owners would not hang their work, with the result that they were excluded from the crucial signs of recognition which elevate a text to some kind of legitimacy. The publication history of Joanna Russ's *The Female Man* is a recent example of this same exclusion by a technological discourse — here that of the publishing industry. Though *The Female Man* is now celebrated as one of the most innovative science fiction texts of the last twenty years, it took Russ five years to find a publisher. The main reasons for this exclusion were not only the feminist story it tells (though this was a time of a great flowering of feminist writing, so an opportunistic publisher might have seized on her work with glee), but also and principally her use of postmodernist ideas about subjectivity in the construction of her characters. Her use of a composite main character, constituted by four separate characters, and her interpolation of other kinds of material (factual materials, conversation fragments, reminiscence) into the narrative was a major challenge to the orthodoxy of the traditional narrative in science fiction. Russ offered a fundamental challenge to the genre — not only in what she said, but also (therefore) in the way she said it — and many publishers were simply not prepared to take the risk of publishing her book. In other words, her relationship to the technological practices in which her work is embedded was a very difficult one, which originally meant that the public had no access to her text.

A concept of genre allows the critic or analyst to explore all of these complex relationships in which a text is involved, relationships which ultimately relate back to what a text means. This is because what a text says and how it says it cannot be separated; this is fundamental to our notion of genre. Because of this, genre provides the link between text and context; between the formal and semantic properties of texts; between the text and the intertextual, disciplinary and technological practices in which it is embedded.

In the chapter by J.R. Martin which follows, this concept of genre is once again fundamental. The difference between the approaches taken in these two chapters is that where my work deals principally with the discourses constructed in a text, working back into the text from this perspective, Martin's work proceeds from the grammar of a text up to the discourses constituted by those grammatical choices. In a sense this view of genre is elided by the description of genre as a 'staged, goal oriented social process', particularly if the 'social' is left out of the subsequent analysis. When Martin analyses the staging of a text, he is identifying the linguistic features which identify a text as belonging to one or another genre (or genres). This is a linguistic way of identifying the kind or style of text being addressed — an identification which then enables the linguist to place the text intertextually, and in relation to disciplinary and technological practices. In other words, it is an alternative and complementary means of enabling the same kind of analysis discussed above to take place.

Martin analyses a text about whaling management in his chapter. He identifies the grammatical features of this text in order to understand how the writer is attempting to position his listeners. In doing so, he places the text in relation to the genre, in fact genres, of which it is a member, assessing its effectiveness for the purpose for which it was written. This text is also innovative in its bridging between technical and non-technical language and explanation and its assemblage of several genres — producing a conjunction of scientific and management discourses — to construct a convincing and persuasive argument. It is not designed to confront readers (like the feminist texts discussed earlier), but instead to ease them comfortably into a position of agreement with the views of the writer.

The focus of Martin's attention in this analysis is the effectiveness of this text, and the social value of this effectiveness. He is concerned that this kind of effectiveness, or literacy, should be available to the greatest number of individuals possible within a society, to enable them to produce texts which articulate their needs and viewpoints. So he is concerned to develop ways of teaching this literacy to students from a variety of different cultural backgrounds, including those for whom no part of the production process can be taken for granted or left implicit. That is, he is concerned to develop explicit ways of talking about and teaching the variety of text types or styles or kinds — that is, genres — that students may need to employ throughout their adult life in order to be active, empowered social subjects.

Implicit in this demand for universal literacy is a recognition that genres are not only socially functional ways of talking about, reading and writing texts; they are also ways of manipulating the meaning-potential within a culture. That is, they can work to expand that meaning-potential. So when an individual from a culture which is usually marginalised in and by the dominant culture of a society uses a particular genre or genres to produce a text, that individual almost inevitably — because of her/his very 'difference' from the dominant culture — constructs a slightly different realisation of the genre(s). This involves not only a different formal or structural arrangement of the text, but a different configuration of the discourses instantiated in the text — because, as Jameson and Bakhtin point out, genre is both, and at the same time, a social and textual category.

A reader who is aware of these properties of genre is best positioned to read the 'difference' in this text; its resistances to mainstream culture and its articulation of a new and different viewpoint. In the educational context this will mean a reader/teacher/examiner is able to recognise the (formal and discursive) significance of student writing, and to assist students to develop greater literacy skills. Pam Gilbert cites the example of schoolgirls' resistant rewritings of fairytale as an example of this kind of textual innovation, making the point that it is only the teacher who is critically aware of the function of genre as a formal and discursive category who will understand the achievement of these girls in their stories. Otherwise the stories might be read simply as bad or incomplete retellings of the conventional tale.

The use of genre by literary theorists such as Jameson and by linguists such as Martin can therefore be seen as complementary. The literary theorist approaches the meaning potential in the text by working on the relationship between the discourses constructed in and by the text, the genre or genres of which it is a member and, where available, knowledge of particular readings already made of the text. Without a knowledge of grammar, however, the literary theorist cannot take account of grammatical choices made in the construction of a text. The linguist, on the other hand, is able to do this — to trace the perceived generic choices to grammatical choices made in the production of the text. From that basis the linguist is then able to relate those grammatical choices to the construction of particular discourses in a text — by relating them to the manipulations of genre(s) by writers and readers.

Underlying both literary and linguistic uses of genre, then, is the use of this concept as a categorising function by both writers and readers, which enables writers to address a specific audience and which enables readers to read unfamiliar texts and to make sense of them, aligned with an understanding that the conventions which produce those classifications have social and historical, not simply formal, significance or meaning. Employing different but complementary methodologies, literary critics and linguists use genre to deconstruct textual practice, to identify the discourses potentially constituted in and by a text, and to locate the different readings produced from that text. The use of genre by the literary theorist is perhaps most often used in the discussion of reading, while that of the linguist is most most often used in the discussion of writing — but reading and writing are, of course, intimately related.

Chapter 5

# A Contextual Theory of Language

## J.R. Martin

*In Chapter 5 Martin begins to outline another interpretation of genre, founded on Halliday's systemic functional linguistics. His main point is that a functional linguistics can be a very useful tool for teachers and students. He argues that the genre approach to literacy not only provides the basis for a language-based theory of learning but also encourages the teaching of a broader range of types of writing in school. Genre literacy, in sum, is an eminently consumable theory of language.*

*Martin centres his argument in this chapter on analysis of a text that deals with the issue of whaling. He starts by placing the text in the context of its situation — why it was written and what it was trying to say. Then, defining genre as a staged, goal oriented social process, he identifies the text as a combination of the report genre and historical recount. Taking just a few key aspects of the grammar, he goes on to explain the ways clauses work in a text of this kind. In the analysis he points to larger patterns of thematic prediction, the way in which the arrangement of information in clauses fits into the overall pattern of the text and contributes to its social purpose. Martin also describes the ways in which scientific text challenges commonsense understandings of the world embodied in our everyday language. The genres and grammar of scientific discourse, he argues, have the capacity to create new forms of knowledge through the language of technicality and abstraction. In this way, scientific discourse becomes able to say things that could not be said in commonsense language. It follows that people who are functionally illiterate in scientific discourse are excluded by texts like the one about whales, and excluded on grounds that are at least partly grammatical. The task of an educational linguistics, then, is to explain the grammar of this sort of writing and the way it is used.*

*Martin's argument about a consumable grammar develops further in Chapter 6, co-authored with Joan Rothery. Chapter 9 returns to many of the key grammatical concepts introduced by Martin in Chapter 5, as Macken and Slade discuss the question of evaluating student texts. Inevitably, these chapters are no more than introductions to the educational possibilities presented by functional linguistics and a genre approach to grammar. The concluding Bibliographical Essay locates the Martin approach to genre in the context of the genre literacy movement and indicates further readings.*

### Writing That Counts

In June 1989 the Canadian Wildlife Federation (CWF) met for their annual meeting in Halifax, Nova Scotia. On the last day of the meetings their program focused on innovative fisheries management, an important theme for an organisation concerned with promoting the sustained harvest of renewable resources such as fish and game. One of the Federation's retiring directors began the discussion with a short paper on 'Innovative Fisheries Management: International Whaling' (W.R. Martin, 1989, 1–4), the beginning sections of which are reproduced below (along with the headings scaffolding the remaining sections of the paper, which have not been reproduced). The paper is one of four presented, which were later published together as *Innovative Fisheries Management Initiatives* (Bielak, 1989c).

### Innovative Fisheries Management: International whaling

There is much to be learned from the evolution of international fisheries management that is applicable to the development of fisheries management in Canada. An interesting case is the management of whaling which I have had the opportunity to follow for a few decades. So, I have decided to focus on whaling as an example of innovative fisheries management, and summarize my perspective under the headings of whales, whaling, international management, the current scene, and some observations about its relevance to the development of Canadian fisheries management.

### Whales

There are many species of whales. They are conveniently divided into toothed and baleen categories. The toothed whales are found world-wide in great numbers. The largest is the Sperm whale, which grows to about the size of a boxcar. Other species familiar to Canadians are the Beluga or white whale, the Narwhal with its unicorn-like tusk, the Killer whale or Orca, the Pilot or Pothead whale, which is commonly stranded on beaches, the Spotted and Spinner Dolphins that create a problem for tuna seiners, and the Porpoises which we commonly see along our shores.

There are fewer species of the larger baleen whales, that filter krill and small fish through their baleen plates. The largest is the Blue whale which is seen frequently in the Gulf of St Lawrence. It reaches a length of 100 feet and a weight of 200 tons, equivalent to about 30 African elephants. The young are 25 feet long at birth and put on about 200 lbs. a day on their milk diet. Other species are: the Fins which at a length of 75 ft. blow spouts of 20 ft., the fast swimming Seis, the Grays so commonly seen on migrations along our Pacific coast between Baja California and the Bering Sea, the Bowheads of Alaskan waters, the Rights, so seriously threatened, the Humpbacks enjoyed by tourists in such places as Hawaii and Alaska, the smaller Bryde's whales, and the smallest Minke whales, which continue to be abundant worldwide.

As with the growing interest in birding, increasing numbers of whale watchers can distinguish the various species of whales.

### Whaling

For one thousand years, whales have been of commercial interest for meat, oil, meal and whalebone. About 1000 A.D., whaling started with the Basques using sailing vessels and row boats. They concentrated on the slow-moving Right whales. As whaling spread to other countries, whaling shifted to Humpbacks, Grays, Sperms and Bowheads. By 1500, they were whaling off Greenland; by the 1700s, off Atlantic America; and by the 1800s, in the south Pacific, Antarctic and Bering Sea. Early in this century, the Norwegians introduced explosive harpoons, fired from guns on catcher boats, and whaling shifted to the larger and faster baleen whales. The introduction of factory ships by Japan and the USSR intensified whaling still further.

The global picture, then, was a mining operation moving progressively with increasing efficiency to new species and new areas. Whaling reached a peak during the present century.

While this high-seas drama was unfolding, coastal, shore-based whaling developed around the world. In Canada, for example, it was native whaling for Belugas and Narwhal in the Arctic, and commercial whaling from northern Vancouver Island in the Pacific, and from Quebec, Nova Scotia and Newfoundland in the Atlantic.

## International Management
. . .

## The Current Scene
. . .

## Relevance to Canadian Fisheries Management
. . .

### Demand Management
. . .

### Management Processes
. . .

Information: . . .
Partnerships: . . .
Public participation: . . .
Jurisdiction: . . .
Perseverance: . . .

There are a number of observations that we could make about this piece of writing; and we will return to it several times. The main point to stress here is that it is a powerful piece of writing from a leading member of an influential environmental organisation. It is also part of a significant political process which will, over time, influence the lives of millions of Canadians and visitors to Canada for generations to come, be they fishermen or hunters, whale watchers or birders, bushwalkers or biologists. If you can't write like this, you can't be part of this process. If you can't read this text, you won't even know what is going on. Writing like this matters. What about linguistics?

## Linguistics That Counts

Just over twenty-five years ago Michael Halliday (1964) wrote a paper called 'Syntax and the Consumer' in which he tried to explain to a group of American linguists assembled in Washington, D.C. that the kind of linguistics you devise depends on what you're trying to do with it. In Australia, a decade or so later, the notion of a consumer oriented linguistics did take off — largely because Halliday came to New South Wales in 1976 to found the Department of Linguistics at the University of Sydney. In Sydney Halliday continued to develop a linguistics for consumers — a theory known as systemic functional linguistics. And he continued to pursue various educational initiatives: beginning work on the Curriculum Development Centre's Language Development Project; kicking off the first of a continuing series of Language in Education workshops in 1979; starting the first MA Applied Linguistics program in Australia; and generally creating a supportive environment in which educators and linguists could come together to address teaching and learning issues. It was in this context that genre-based initiatives in literacy pedagogy were born.

How does this relate to writing that counts? In two ways. First of all it has an impact on the kind of linguistics that literacy teachers choose to use. Literacy teachers need a linguistics that can say something useful about writing. Systemic functional linguistics has proven itself throughout Australia to be a linguistics of this kind, and we will introduce the theory in broad outlines below to show why this is so. Second, it has an impact on education itself in very significant ways. The reason for this is that consumable linguistics does not sit very comfortably with the ways in which many teachers go about teaching writing nor with the writing they choose to teach. It challenges both traditional and progressive approaches to literacy pedagogy, making different suggestions about teaching and learning founded on a language-based theory of learning. It also challenges the kinds of writing usually taught in schools, suggesting that there is more to writing than story writing and that a broader range of types of writing, reflecting the needs of both schools and the community, needs to be introduced.

## Linguistics in Action

The best way to illustrate a consumable theory of language is to show what it can do. To do this effectively, we need a model of both language and context, since what we are dealing with here is a theory of how language is used. Bev Derewianka (1990, 19) has developed a map, similar to the one in Figure 1, to model the relationships between language and the theory of context (Callaghan and Rothery, 1988, 34). The model puts text in the centre of the picture, situates the text in its context of situation (its register, that is, its field, tenor and mode), and situates the register in turn in its context of culture (the level of genre).

How does this model relate to the 'Innovative Fisheries Management' text above? Let's begin at the top of the model, with what is referred to as 'genre'. One of the first things we can note is that W.R. Martin's paper is divided into stages: it has a brief introduction, and then five main sections — the last section in turn has two subsections, and the second of these has five sub-subsections of its own. Every section except the introduction has a heading; and the paper also has a title,

*Figure 1.   A Model of Text in Context*

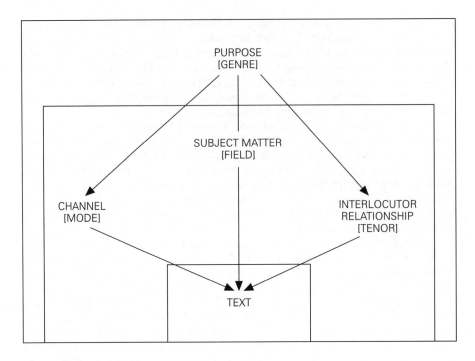

which like all the headings is in bold face. The different types of heading are distinguished in the formatting as follows:

| | |
|---|---|
| Title | large font, separate line; |
| Section headings | large font, separate underlined line; |
| Subsection headings | smaller font, separate line; |
| Sub-subsection headings | regular font, same line, colon following. |

The scaffolding these different kinds of heading provide for the paper is outlined below. They make the paper easier to read and to look things up in; they act as signposts, helping the reader find her or his way around.

**Innovative Fisheries Management: International Whaling**

. . .

**Whales**

. . .

**Whaling**

. . .

**International Management**

. . .

**The Current Scene**

. . .

**Relevance to Canadian Fisheries Management**

. . .

> **Demand Management**
>
> . . .
>
> **Management Processes**
>
> . . .
>
> > **Information:** . . .
> > **Partnerships:** . . .
> > **Public participation:** . . .
> > **Jurisdiction:** . . .
> > **Perseverance:** . . .

Why does the paper have stages? Why does it need signposts of this kind? The main reason is that W.R. Martin's message was a complicated one. The program chairperson summed it up as follows: 'Dr. Martin's presentation on international whaling gave us food for thought. Despite strong science which indicated a clear need for the protection of various whale species, the environmental movement was the key catalyst in focusing public attention on the issues, and this only after fifty years' (Bielak, 1989b, 27). It took W.R. Martin more than one section to get this message across. As he noted in his introduction, he found it important to include:

i.    some information about whales,
ii.   a short review of the history of whaling,
iii.  a review of the history of whaling management,
iv.   a description of the current scene, all as background to his comments on
v.    the relevance of whaling mis/management to Canadian fisheries management in general.

Essentially, W.R. Martin is summarising and making public his expertise in various aspects of his field in order to lend weight to his recommendations. Putting this in more technical terms with reference to Figure 1, W.R. Martin's paper has stages because in the context of culture in which it was written there was a considerable amount of semiotic manoeuvring to be done for him to achieve his goals.

What about genre? In fact, to do this work, W.R. Martin needed more than one genre. To put this another way, he assembled a big genre (technically a macro-genre) out of smaller ones. Let's look at just two of these: the report on whales and the historical recount on whaling (the first and second sections of the paper).

Martin, Christie and Rothery (1987) define genre as a staged, goal oriented social process. This means essentially that when looking at genres we are especially interested in the way they achieve their social purpose, which they usually do in more than one step. Two of the genres which were identified very early were report and recount (Martin, 1984; Martin, Christie and Rothery, 1987). Reports function as generic descriptions of classes of things — for example, dinosaurs, bears, planes, museums, television and so on. Recounts, on the other hand, focus on activities and relate an unproblematic series of events — for example, a trip to the zoo, what I did on the weekend, how my family ended up in Australia and so on. In later work it was noted that recounts could be generic too, focusing on sequences of activities undertaken by groups of people rather than individuals — for example, how the Irish came to Australia, how the Hunter Valley was settled, how the Aborigines lost their land and so on (Eggins, Wignell and Martin, 1987/1993). Because they are so common in history writing, these generic recounts can be referred to as historical recounts.

The section of W.R. Martin's paper entitled 'Whales' is an excellent example of one kind of report. It takes one biological family, cetaceans (one type of placental mammal), divides them into two groups, presents the species in each group and provides a descriptive comment on most of the species. The staging of this report is outlined below. The report begins with an introduction to the two categories of whale; it then introduces the toothed category and proceeds to present toothed whales; following that it introduces the baleen category and presents the baleen whales; and ends with a comment on the development of whale watching as an increasingly popular recreational activity. This final comment is particularly interesting in that it is not predicted by the canonical structure of the report genre. Rather it functions to adapt the genre to the social occasion for which it is employed, forming a kind of bridge between the technical biological classification of whales and the more generalised interests of Canadian Wildlife Federation members. It should be stressed that this adaptation illustrates one fundamental property of all semiotic systems, namely, the fact that they are dynamic open systems — for purposes of survival they have a built-in ability to adapt to their environment and so evolve.

## Whales

There are many species of whales. They are conveniently divided into toothed and baleen categories.

The toothed whales . . .

> the Sperm whale . . .
> the Beluga or white whale . . .
> the Narwhal . . .
> the Killer whale or Orca . . .
> the Pilot or Pothead whale . . .
> the Spotted and Spinner Dolphins . . .
> the Porpoises. . . .

There are fewer species of the larger baleen whales, that filter krill and small fish through their baleen plates.

> the Blue whale . . .
> the Fins . . .
> the fast swimming Seis
> the Grays . . .
> the Bowheads . . .
> the Rights . . .
> the Humpbacks . . .
> the smaller Bryde's whales
> the smallest Minke whales. . . .

As with the growing interest in birding, increasing numbers of whale watchers can distinguish the various species of whales.

The next section of W.R. Martin's paper, titled 'Whaling', is a good example of a historical recount. It focuses on the development of high-seas whaling from 1000 A.D. to the present and then comments on shore-based whaling, using Canada as an example. The staging of this historical recount is outlined below. It begins with an orientation, mapping out the piece of history about to be reconstructed. It then moves directly to the development of high-seas whaling, which it sums up as 'a mining operation moving progressively with increasing efficiency to new species and new areas.' The ideological implications of construing whaling as a mining operation (as opposed to, say, a harvest, a slaughter or murder) will not be pursued here (see, for discussion, Martin, 1986a). It then contrasts the development of high-seas whaling with shore-based operations, which it then breaks down into whaling by native peoples (the Inuit) and commercial whaling (grammatical themes have been highlighted for consideration below).

### Whaling

'For one thousand years', whales have been of commercial interest for meat, oil, meal and whalebone.

> 'About 1000 A.D.', whaling started with the Basques using sailing vessels and row boats. They concentrated on the slow-moving Right whales.

> 'As whaling spread to other countries', whaling shifted to Humpbacks, Grays, Sperms and Bowheads.

> 'By 1500', they were whaling off Greenland;

> 'by the 1700s', off Atlantic America;

> 'and by the 1800s', in the south Pacific, Antarctic and Bering Sea.

> 'Early in this century', the Norwegians introduced explosive harpoons, fired from guns on catcher boats, and whaling shifted to the larger and faster baleen whales.

> 'The introduction of factory ships by Japan and the USSR' intensified whaling still further.

'The global picture, then', was a mining operation moving progressively with increasing efficiency to new species and new areas. Whaling reached a peak during the present century.

'While this high-seas drama was unfolding', coastal, shore-based whaling developed around the world.

> 'In Canada, for example', it was native whaling for Belugas and Narwhal in the Arctic, and commercial whaling from northern Vancouver Island in the Pacific, and from Quebec, Nova Scotia and Newfoundland in the Atlantic.

*Table 1. Examples of Textual, Interpersonal and Topical Themes*

| | | David Griggs | served us a smorgasbord of ideas from out west. |
|---|---|---|---|
| | Maybe | that | is rubbing off in other areas. |
| However, | | we | have to note a possible down-side as well. |
| **Theme** | | | **Rheme** |
| textual | interpersonal | topical | |

## Genre and Functional Grammar

What about grammar? Why does grammar count? The basic answer to this is that texts are made up of grammar — or, turning this around, it is grammar that makes meaning into text. To illustrate this briefly, this section will concentrate on just one or two aspects of grammar, beginning with the system of *theme*.

*Theme* is the grammatical system that organises the clause in such a way that it fits into its environment (Halliday, 1985a; Matthiessen, 1990). For the clause, this environment is the text — just as for the text it is context as outlined above. So the question we are asking here has to do with the ways in which clauses are organised to construct the generic staging just outlined. How, in other words, do we know that the report and recount we're considering have the stages we've said they have? The answer lies in the grammar of the texts themselves.

In English the system of *theme* is realised through first position — as far as *theme* is concerned it is the things that come first in the clause that count. They represent what Halliday calls the speaker's angle on the message — the point of departure for the clause. There may be up to three different kinds of Themes in a clause. 'Topical Themes' are almost always present and draw attention to one aspect of what the clause is about. Often there are 'Textual Themes' as well, which help connect the clause to preceding ones. Sometimes there are 'Interpersonal Themes', which reflect the speaker's evaluation or attitude to the message. These kinds of Theme are illustrated in the following examples. The first clause begins with a Topical Theme (quotes); the second begins with a Textual Theme (underlined) followed by a Topical one; and the third starts off with an Interpersonal Theme (italics), followed again by a Topical one:

'David Griggs' served us a smorgasbord of ideas from out west.
However, 'we' have to note a possible down-side as well.
*Maybe* 'that' is rubbing off in other areas.

These different possibilities are summed up and exemplified again in Table 1. The part of the clause that is not theme is referred to by Halliday as Rheme.

As Peter Fries (1983) has pointed out, the pattern of Themes we find in a text is not random. Rather, it tends to be systematic, and constructs what he calls a text's method of development. This means that if we look at the pattern of Themes in the report and historical recount we are considering, we should find a pattern of Theme selection that both reflects and constructs the genres' staging. And this is exactly what we find.

In the whale report all of the eleven Themes are Topical Themes and all but three of these refer to whales. In the stage presenting the toothed whales, all three Themes refer to toothed whales; and in the stage presenting the baleen whales, two Themes refer to Baleen whales and two refer to Blue whales (one kind of baleen whale). The whale text, in other words, does just what Fries predicts: it organises its sentence beginnings so that they help construct the report's staging (the exception here is the marked Theme 'as with the growing interest in birding', introducing just that part of the report which adapts it to this particular occasion of use):

There
They [whales]
The toothed whales
The largest [toothed whale]
Other species [of toothed whale] . . .

There
The largest [baleen whale]
It [the Blue whale]
The young [of the Blue whale]
Other species [of baleen whale]

'As with growing interest in birding,'

Passive clauses play a significant role in getting this staging right. The passive is used to construct the first two whale Themes in the text: 'They *are* conveniently *divided* . . .' and 'The toothed whales *are found*. . . .' Contrast the active counterparts: 'We can divide whales . . .' and 'We find toothed whales . . .', which get the Theme wrong. This shows what utter nonsense it is to advise students to avoid the passive and vary sentence beginnings, as one often reads in composition handbooks or in syllabus documents such as *Writing K-12* (NSW Department of School Education, 1987), and how important it is to draw on functional linguistics when addressing literacy issues.

So far we have looked at sentence Themes. What about initial position in larger units? One obvious place to look is the beginning of paragraphs — for candidates for paragraph Theme (referred to as topic sentences in traditional composition teaching). The second paragraph of the whale report has a classic paragraph Theme of this kind. Its first sentence functions to introduce the topic of the paragraph as a whole, the baleen whales:

There are fewer species of the larger baleen whales, that filter krill and small fish through their baleen plates.

If we look back to the beginning of the first paragraph, the picture is more complicated. This paragraph begins not with the Theme of the paragraph but the Theme of the whole whale report:

*Figure 2.    Patterns of Thematic 'Prediction' in the Whale Report*

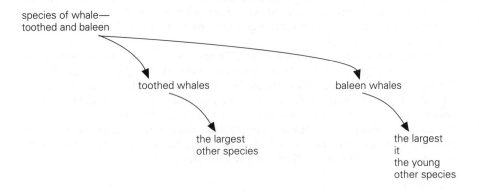

There are many species of whales. They are conveniently divided into toothed and baleen categories.

This is followed by something corresponding to the Theme of the second paragraph, introducing the toothed whales which are presented in the remainder of the paragraph:

The toothed whales are found worldwide in great numbers.

So we can see that paragraphing does not always match a text's staging (though it often does). In writing we often avoid paragraphs that are too short or too long, because they don't look right on the page (we value symmetry; but not always — the last paragraph of this report, for example, is only one sentence long, reflecting once again its 'special' nature). Since the Theme of the whale report as a whole was only two sentences long, it was apparently not felt to be worth a paragraph of its own. Themes for a genre as a whole and Themes for the genre's first stage are commonly combined in introductory paragraphs in this way.

In summary then, we can analyse the way in which texts look ahead and make predictions about they way they will develop. Headings do part of this work, as discussed above. In addition, the pattern of sentence Themes in a text is oriented to staging and reflects/constructs that text's method of development. Sentence Themes may be predicted by paragraph Themes, and paragraph Themes may in turn be predicted by text Themes for genres as a whole. This predictive patterning is outlined diagrammatically for the whale report in Figure 2.

If Fries (1983) is right about thematic prediction of this kind as a general pattern, then we should be able to find something similar in the whaling historical recount. A comparable pattern is certainly to be found. To interpret this pattern, we need first to introduce a further distinction between marked and unmarked topical themes. In declarative clauses (clauses which give information), the unmarked topical theme is the grammatical Subject. All of the Topical Themes in the whale report were unmarked Themes of this kind except the last one: 'As with the growing interest in birding.' This marked Theme precedes the Subject of the sentence, 'increasing numbers of whale-watchers', separating Theme and Subject and thereby giving the Theme special prominence. In the whale report this marked Theme was important to signal a break in the method of development predicted by the report's introduction: 'There are many species of whales.' Here's another example of a marked Theme (italics):

'And *even in successful schemes,*' we've seen refinements and adjust-ments. . . .

The unmarked way of organising information in this sentence would have been to make the Subject *we* Theme, with the phrase *even in successful schemes* coming later on:

'And we've seen refinements and adjustments even in successful schemes. . . .

In the whaling historical recount it is marked Themes which for the most part construct the text's method of development. In this text there are twelve Topical Themes, and eight of these are marked. Of these marked Themes, the first seven deal with the location of events in time and the last with location in space (*In Canada*). Again, Fries's predictions are borne out. The Topical Themes organise the text temporally, as it reviews the development of whaling throughout the centuries:

*'For one thousand years,'*
*'About 1000 A.D.,'*
They [the Basques]
*'As whaling spread to other countries,'*
*'By 1500,'*
and *'by the 1800s,'*
*'Early in this century,'*
The introduction of factory ships by Japan and the USSR

The global picture, then,
Whaling

*'While this high-seas drama was unfolding,'*
*In Canada,* for example,

Once again, if we look at the beginning of the historical recount, we can see that this method of development is predicted by a thematic sentence which appears to function simultaneously as a text Theme for the historical recount as a whole (including both high-seas and shore-based whaling) and simultaneously as a paragraph Theme for the development of high-seas whaling in the text's first stage:

For one thousand years, whales have been of commercial interest for meat, oil, meal and whale-bone.

The second stage of the recount has its own paragraph Theme, although the method of development it predicts is not elaborated, since the remainder of the paragraph is just a sentence long. This paragraph could easily have been elaborated, using location in space as its method of development, as follows: '*In Canada*, for example, there were three centres of shore-based whaling. *In the Arctic*, native peoples caught Belugas and Narwhal. *In the Pacific*, commercial whalers operated from northern Vancouver Island. And *in the Atlantic*, there was commercial whaling from Quebec, Nova Scotia and Newfoundland .

> While this high-seas drama was unfolding, coastal, shore-based whaling developed around the world.

So, like the whale report, the whaling recount looks forward, makes predictions about how it will develop, and then fulfils these expectations with a systematic, sentence by sentence pattern of Theme selection. Beyond this, the whaling recount does something the whale report does not do (and which reports in general tend not to do): it looks back! Let's look again at its middle paragraph:

> The global picture, then, was *a mining operation moving progressively with increasing efficiency to new species and new areas.* Whaling reached a peak during the present century.

This paragraph has the function of summing up the first stage of the recount. Essentially, it does this in a single nominal group: the history of high-seas whaling is distilled as *a mining operation moving progressively with increasing efficiency to new species and new areas.* Distillations of this kind are a very efficient way of encapsulating meaning, and critical to the argument W.R. Martin is developing. Keep in mind that what W.R. Martin is leading up to as he moves through these genres is a set of recommendations for innovative fisheries management based on lessons from whaling. The whaling recount is laying part of the foundation for his considered advice. By turning to the final stage of his paper we can see just how this works:

> In spite of *the whaling experience of mining whale resources* until innovative approaches could be applied to whaling management, we continue to mine our high seas fisheries resources.

At this point W.R. Martin is pointing out to the CWF that the same mistakes are being made with high-seas fisheries resources as have been made with whales. He draws his brief history of whaling into the argument with another nominal group: *the whaling experience of mining whale resources. . . .* This example focuses attention on the important role of summaries in decision-making processes: they distill the meanings it may have taken a genre or more to construct so that they can play their part in another decision-making genre. This is obviously a very important social process, and one that is made of language — it's grammar that makes the relevant meanings and it's grammar that distills them for mobilisation in related contexts. The consequences of not being able to participate in discursive processes of this kind are severe.

Unfortunately, there is no space here to consider in detail the special grammar

*Figure 3.   Relationships in the Grammar of Speaking and the Grammar of Writing*

| **Event** (cause) | **causal link** | **Event** (effect) |
|---|---|---|
| **[noun]**<br>the environmental movement<br>↑ ⌄<br>↓<br>environmentalists protested<br>**[verb]** | **[noun]**<br>was the key catalyst<br>↑ ⌄<br>↓<br>and so<br>**[conjunction]** | **[noun]**<br>in focusing public attention on the issue<br>↑ ⌄<br>↓<br>the public considered the issues<br>**[verb]** |

of distillation. Halliday (1985b) and Martin (1986b) point out that the grammar used for distilling meaning is the grammar of writing, not speaking, and that the general drift of this written grammar is in the direction of nouns — the world, people, places, things, what they are like, what they do, how they do it, how they feel about it, the lot, is construed as a collection of things. So when W.R. Martin is distilling his whaling recount, he constructs it as a thing ('a mining *operation*'), even though when he constructed his history it included a number of actions (namely, 'the Basques *using* sailing vessels and row-boats; the Norwegians *introduced* explosive harpoons, *fired* from guns on catcher boats') as well as actions which had already been processed as things (for example, the *introduction* of factory ships by Japan and the USSR).

To illustrate the grammar of distillation briefly, let's go back to Bielak's summary of W.R. Martin's paper and look at the following clause in more detail:

> . . . the environmental movement was the key catalyst in focusing public attention on the issues.

In this clause Bielak constructs meaning as a relationship of being — *was* — between two things — *the environmental movement* and *the key catalyst.* . . . One thing represents the other. But when we think about the piece of W.R. Martin's history that Bielak is reviewing here, we realise that there were more than things and relationships involved. There were people involved, and they did things. Using spoken grammar, we might well have construed this history as a happening: *the environmentalists protested and so the public considered the issues.* In this version, actions come out as verbs — *protested* and *considered* — not nouns — *movement* and *attention*; and the causal relation between events comes out as conjunctions — *and so* — rather than a verb and noun — *was* and *catalyst*. In the grammar of speaking, then, the history comes alive; whereas in the grammar of writing it is objectified as words. The grammatical relationships between these two constructions of what went on are outlined in Figure 3 (see also Halliday and Martin, 1993).

In Australia the job of teaching this special grammar of writing falls to the secondary schools. But by this point in their education, over ten per cent of Australians have failed to learn to read at a primary school level and are for all practical purposes out of the system. Of those that remain, only a small elite will learn enough of the grammar of writing to enter university where so much of the learning depends in one way or another on meaning making of this kind. So if we redefine literacy here as the ability to read and write powerful texts of the kind we have been examining, it may well be that a large majority of students are functionally illiterate. It follows that they cannot participate in decision-making processes such as the one which provided the social context for W.R. Martin's paper. They are excluded, on grammatical grounds; they have not learned to read and write.

### Where It Matters Most: A Summary

What makes this functional illiteracy even more serious is the fact that it excludes people from social processes at just those points where it matters most — at beginnings (where people might try and join in) and ends (where decisions are made). The reason for this is that predicting what will come and distilling the meanings that have already been made put tremendous pressure on the grammar of writing, pushing it even further in the direction of nouns. As far as looking ahead is concerned, note that even Bielak's 'chatty' introduction to the speakers on the program has to nominalise to present the topic of discussion: *Innovative Fisheries Management* (he does not say, using spoken grammar, that the speakers 'are going to talk to us about what people are doing in various parts of the country to stop people catching too many fish and to help fish reproduce better so that someday there are lots of them and we can catch more . . .'). W.R. Martin uses much more nominalisation than this to outline the plan of his paper (thereby excluding lots of readers right at the start); and he also uses nominalisation, as we have seen, to predict the pattern of Themes in his whaling recount. These key passages are reproduced below, with nominalisations in italics.

### Prediction: Levels of Theme:

> In the same spirit, the Fisheries Committee Chairman, Dr. Robert Martin, has, on behalf of the CWF, invited some very distinguished speakers from across Canada to tell you something about *innovative fisheries management* being practised in their neck of the woods. (Bielak's Introduction, 1989a, v)

> So, I have decided to focus on *whaling* as an *example of international innovative fisheries management*, and summarize my *perspective* under the *headings* of whales, *whaling, international management*, the *current scene*, and some *observations* about its *relevance* to the *development* of *Canadian fisheries management*. (W.R. Martin's Introduction to his paper, 1989, 1)

> For one thousand years, whales have been of *commercial interest* for meat, oil, meal and whale-bone. (W.R. Martin's introduction to his whaling recount, 1989, 1)

The grammar of distilling is, if anything, even more exclusive. W.R. Martin's distillation of his whaling recount and the use he makes of it in his recommendations are reproduced below, again with nominalisations in italics. Bielak's synthesis is much less 'chatty' than his introduction, precisely because it has the function of

Table 2.  *Outer Layers of Theme and News (Bielak, 1989c)*

| Layers of 'Theme' | Layers of 'News' |
|---|---|
| Table of Contents | [Biographies (of authors)] |
| Introduction (Bielak) | Program Chairman's Synthesis (Bielak) |
| W.R. Martin's Introduction | ['relevance to fisheries management'] |
| Grigg's Introduction | ['problems and future directions'] |
| Beamish's Introduction | Beamish's Summary |
| Cote's Introduction | Cote's Conclusion |

distilling news from all four of the papers presented. This critical contribution, which has some chance of playing a role in shaping Canada's fisheries management policies in years to come, would be quite inaccessible to functional illiterates.

### Distillation: Levels of News

The *global picture*, then, was a *mining operation* moving progressively with *increasing efficiency* to new species and new areas. (W.R. Martin's summary of his whaling recount, 1989, 1)

In spite of the *whaling experience of mining* whale *resources* until *innovative approaches* could be applied to *whaling management,* we continue to mine our high seas *fisheries resources.* (Martin's invocation of his whaling recount in his recommendations, 1989, 3)

Dr. Martin's *presentation* on *international whaling* gave us food for thought. Despite strong science which indicated a clear *need* for the *protection* of various whale species, the *environmental movement* was the key *catalyst* in focusing *public attention* on the *issues,* and this only after fifty years. (Bielak's Summary of Martin's paper in his Program Chairman's Synthesis, 1989b, 27)

There are two forces at work here. One is forward looking, encouraging writers to predict what they will say; the other is backward looking, encouraging writers to encapsulate their news. Both forces have a similar effect on the grammar: they encourage writers to nominalise in order to abstract their meanings as things. The outer layers of Theme and of News in the *Innovative Fisheries Management Initiatives* publication are summarised in Table 2. This summary does not, of course, include the inner layers of Theme and News structuring the various sections and subsections of the four main papers, such as those in W.R. Martin's report and historical recount considered above.

### Going further: Grammar and Register

As far as functional linguistics and writing are concerned, we are just scratching the surface. What exactly have we scratched? To answer this question, we need a more detailed map. The projection in Figure 4 will serve our purposes here (Martin and Matthiessen, 1990).

Figure 4. *Language and Context: An Alternative Projection*

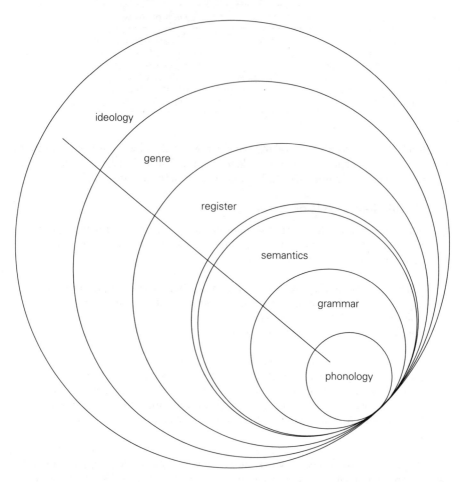

Basically, as far as the cartography of language and context in Figure 4 is concerned, our strategy has been to shunt between genre and one aspect of grammar, *theme*, looking in relative detail at the relationship between generic staging and first position in the clause. In the course of this shunting we have touched in passing on the phonology of writing (that is, graphology), noting the ways in which headings were formatted to highlight staging. We looked briefly at ideology, commenting on the way in which functional illiteracy restricts participation in decision-making processes which depend on the grammar of writing. Questions of register and (discourse) semantics we have to this point almost completely ignored.

By way of rounding off the discussion, let's look briefly at just one aspect of register — field. This will allow us to return to the level of ideology and qualify, in one important respect, the things we have said about functional illiteracy and

Figure 5. The Classification of Whales Constructed in W.R. Martin's Whale Report

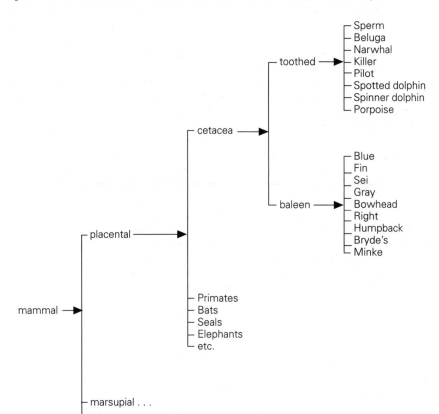

exclusion from social processes. W.R. Martin is a marine biologist by trade, who has spent about half his career doing basic research on 'groundfish', and the rest administering fisheries research programs at the federal level in Canada. It is not surprising that his whale report is a technical one. But what precisely do we mean by this? How can we be more specific about W.R. Martin's field? The best way to answer this question is to consider the taxonomy of whales which W.R. Martin constructs in his report, outlined in Figure 5.

Cetaceans are shown as one type of placental mammal in this figure, and the listing of other placental mammals is not exhaustive. If you look closely at this diagram, you will see that it makes use of specialised knowledge, not just in terms of naming the different whales, but also in terms of how they are related to each other. In addition, in one interesting respect W.R. Martin's classification defies commonsense. By a field-specific (systemic linguistics) convention, the diagram in Figure 5 is read from left to right, with the bigger classes to the left subclassified into smaller ones to their right. This contrasts with the alternative biology convention whereby bigger classes are placed at the top of the diagram and subclasses underneath. The two conventions mean the same thing. Technically, drawing on linguistics again, they are what are referred to as notational variants.

What is unusual is W.R. Martin's treatment of dolphins and porpoises as kinds of whale. This is uncommonsense. For the layperson, whales and dolphins are closely related as water mammals because they look and behave the same, and, for some people, by the same token, they are probably related as kinds of fish. Commonsense tells us that porpoises and dolphins have more in common with each other than they do with whales, which fall into a separate group. W.R. Martin, however, acting as a biologist, puts dolphins and porpoises together with Sperm, Beluga, Narwhal, Killer and Pilot whales in the category of toothed whale, and distinguishes them from baleen whales. Genetically, and in terms of eating habits, this makes good scientific sense. But it defies commonsense, which is based more on what we can see — size, shape, colour, movement and so on — than on teeth, baleen plates and genes, which we cannot directly see. Common and uncommonsense are different ways of constructing the world.

W.R. Martin is sensitive to this point. He is aware that most of his audience are non-scientists, and does his best to relate his scientific classification to their experience. This he accomplishes by describing each species of whale in commonsense terms. This strategy is outlined below, with descriptions in italics. In grammatical terms what W.R. Martin does is elaborate each of his nominal groups with additional descriptive material, which usually follows the name of the species.

> the Sperm whale, *which grows to about the size of a boxcar*
> the Beluga *or white whale,*
> the Narwhal *with its unicorn-like tusk,*
> the Killer whale *or Orca,*
> the Pilot or Pothead whale, *which is commonly stranded on beaches,*
> the Spotted and Spinner Dolphins *that create a problem for tuna seiners,*
> the Porpoises *which we commonly see along our shores*
> the Blue whale *which is seen frequently in the Gulf of St Lawrence. It reaches a length of 100 feet and a weight of 200 tons, equivalent to about 30 African elephants. The young are 25 feet long at birth and put on about 200 lbs. a day on their milk diet.*
> the Fins *which at a length of 75 ft. blow spouts of 20 ft.,*
> the *fast swimming* Seis,
> the Grays *so commonly seen on migrations along our Pacific coast between Baja California and the Bering Sea,*
> the Bowheads *of Alaskan waters,*
> the Rights, *so seriously threatened,*
> the Humpbacks *enjoyed by tourists in such places as Hawaii and Alaska,*
> the *smaller* Bryde's whales,
> and the *smallest* Minke whales, *which continue to be abundant worldwide*

Given his audience and social purpose, this for W.R. Martin is an effective compromise. He classifies whales as a biologist, sustaining his scientific expertise but running the risk of losing his audience. At the same time he describes each species in commonsense terms, relating them to the everyday experience of his listener/readers, and thereby including them.

It is also important to note in this context that presenting himself as a scientist is not the only reason W.R. Martin insists on a scientific classification. There is an important political consideration as well. Americans were among the first to propose a moratorium on whaling. At the same time scientists could charge that American native peoples and tuna seiners were responsible, and continued until very recently to be responsible, for killing more whales than commercial whaling nations — provided that porpoises and dolphins are counted as whales. Given the success of current moratoria on whaling, and the growing commercial threat to related cetaceans, we can be sure that dolphins at least would be much happier with the technical classification than the commonsense one.

The purpose of this short discussion of common and uncommonsense is to make the point that exclusion from social processes is not just a question of technicality. Technicality can exclude, and all of the scientists in Bielak (1989c) are capable of writing in ways that no-one but other scientists could understand. But technicality can be overcome. Scientists can talk to outsiders, and can do so very well, as Martin's paper illustrates. Technicality is a problem about which people are relatively aware. Political processes, such as decisions about fisheries management, bring together experts from many different disciplines. If they want to play a part in the decision-making process, then they have to learn to talk to each other. So they bring their technicality to consciousness and unpack it. However frustrating they find it at first, they do learn to adjust.

Alongside technicality, however, is the problem of abstraction — the problem of the specialised grammar of writing. This is much more difficult to bring to consciousness and act upon. The reason is in part functional, because abstraction is hard to get around. Decision-making benefits from having lots of people with complementary expertise involved. It suffers badly when there are either no experts around — as is sometimes the case with curriculum development — or just one — as in authoritarian regimes. But lots of experts means lots of writing and lots of talk which needs to be recorded in writing. This proliferation of meanings needs sorting out. People need to be warned what to expect, in order to know what to read or who to listen to; and they need summaries of what's been said, since they can't be everywhere at once, and can't remember everything they've read or heard. This puts tremendous pressure on processes of documentation — a problem which was solved a couple of millenia ago, independently in the Middle East and in China, through the invention of writing.

But the pressure of documentation did more than invent writing. It changed the grammar of written language as well. So when W.R. Martin and his colleagues come to predict and distill, they have a specialised grammar at hand to do the job — a grammar that has evolved over hundreds of years, with science at its cutting edge, to construct the world in different ways than talking does. It is a grammar that organises text, that summarises and abstracts, that encapsulates 'big' meanings for use elsewhere — a grammar for writing that nominalises rampantly and turns the universe into a set of interrelated things: a grammar that counts.

Non-specialists find this grammar hard to bring to consciousness and unpack, even in contexts where spoken grammar would be the better way to go. It takes a functional linguistics to explain the grammar of writing and the way it is used. Other approaches to language study, including traditional grammar, do not do the job. If you believe, as many educational linguists do, that you can't teach what you don't understand, then functional linguistics has a special role to play in literacy pedagogy. It is a role that is just beginning to be developed, as part of the evolution of the transdisciplinary field of educational linguistics in Australia and elsewhere. And it is a job for teacher-linguists, not just one for teachers and linguists working alongside each other with their complementary expertise.

Chapter 6

# Grammar: Making Meaning in Writing

*J.R. Martin and Joan Rothery*

*Building on Martin's argument in Chapter 5 about the educational usefulness of a functional linguistics, Martin and Rothery now discuss grammar at work. The chapter begins by contrasting three different types of grammar: traditional school grammar; Chomsky's formal grammar, which does not even claim to be applicable to educational contexts; and Halliday's functional grammar. It is, they argue, the latter — a grammar which explains system and structure in language by connecting text with its social purpose — that has the greatest potential as a resource for literacy teaching and learning. To illustrate the way grammar is a resource for meaning, Martin and Rothery explain the relation of field (what is going on in a text), tenor (who is taking part) and mode (the role language is playing). These three concepts, which together constitute register, help us account for the grammatical choices made in a particular text.*

*Applying these generalisations to the sorts of writing students encounter at school, the chapter goes on to examine the grammatical features of a report on bears. As was the case in Chapter 5, this example is presented not as the basis of a comprehensive account of those parts of functional linguistics that might be used to analyse texts used in school, but as an indication of the general ways in which functional linguistics can be used in teaching and learning literacy. Functional linguistics, Martin and Rothery conclude, is an adaptable and flexible resource, focused on meaning rather than syntax, and oriented to the text and its social purpose rather than to the sentence.*

*In Chapter 9 Macken and Slade further develop some of the key grammatical concepts introduced in this chapter, particularly the notions of field, tenor and mode. References to further readings on functional linguistics are to be found in the concluding Bibliographical Essay.*

To answer the question of whether or not grammar should be taught in school, we have first to consider what kind of grammar we are talking about and second what we want to use our grammar for. In this chapter we briefly survey the different kinds of grammars currently available and then demonstrate some of the ways in which one kind of grammar, functional grammar, can be used to understand the way in which meaning is constructed in text. Our basic point is that if a grammar is to prove useful in schools, then it must be a grammar that explains how language makes meaning, since making meaning is what teaching and learning is all about.

### Types of Grammar

Teachers who become interested in teaching grammar will find that there are a number of different kinds of grammar available. For educational purposes these can be usefully divided into three groups: traditional grammar, formal grammar and functional grammar. Traditional grammar is inherited from the Greeks and Romans. It was passed down through the centuries by way of helping scholars learn Greek and Latin and so gain access to the knowledge that was stored in ancient texts and in contemporary texts in Latin, which remained the language of international scholarship in Europe until the Renaissance.

During the Renaissance traditional grammar was applied to vernacular languages such as English as well and began to be used in schools, where it continued to be taught until 'progressive' education had a major impact on schools in the 1970s. Throughout this period traditional grammarians were concerned with establishing a 'standard' written language shared across speakers of different 'spoken' dialects. In eighteenth century England this was an important issue, since dialects were often so different that speakers from different parts of the country, or from different social classes for that matter, could not understand one another.

Until relatively recently, traditional grammar was closely allied with the study of rhetoric, also inherited from the Greeks (Christie, 1981, 1990a). For example, Plato's well known teacher, Socrates, belonged to a group of philosophers known as sophists who made their living in the marketplace teaching people (aspiring politicians, for instance) how to use language more effectively to achieve their goals. This tradition, as reflected in the teaching of composition, was also passed down through the centuries in schools until generally excised by progressivism a generation or so ago.

Currently, grammar and rhetoric (not to mention sophistry) have a bad name, but it is very important to understand why this is so. Christie (1981, 1990a) suggests that this is in large part because traditional grammar became disassociated from rhetoric in schools, and so lost its purpose; and once the purpose of teaching students to speak and write more effectively was removed, the grammar became trivialised as well. By the twentieth century traditional grammar teaching mainly involved learning the parts of speech, parsing words, analysing a small set of strange sounding sentences (that looked as if they has been translated, badly, from Latin or Greek) and correcting sentences by applying rules of usage. Most of these 'incorrect' sentences sounded fine when you spoke them aloud; but to make them look right in writing, you needed to change them into the dialect of white, middle-class people who originally come from around London in England (since they set the 'standard' for the whole of the traditional grammar-using English-speaking world). It is now very hard to imagine a grammar and rhetoric teacher being thrown in jail for what they teach. But this was exactly what happened to the sophist Socrates, who was jailed for subverting the youth of Athens and ended up poisoning himself with hemlock rather than recant.

Just as unlikely to be jailed for what they teach are formal linguists, who follow or are strongly influenced by the work of Noam Chomsky. Beginning in the 1950s, Chomsky created a revolution in formal linguistics by showing how the grammar of a language could be represented as a kind of algebra — an abstract list of rules like those used by mathematicians or logicians (Chomsky, 1965). Chomsky argued that these rules could be used to explore the limits of language, and that these limitations were neurological in origin. Unlike animals, Chomsky suggested, humans were born with an innate language faculty, and it was the job of formal linguistics to find out just what this faculty was. This enterprise excited the interest of linguists around the world and has preoccupied linguists for more than a generation.

Throughout this period functional linguists have pursued a range of complementary interests. In Australia, and elsewhere, they have been strongly influenced by the work of Michael Halliday, Professor Emeritus of Linguistics from the University of Sydney. Unlike formal linguists, these linguists have generally dedicated themselves to addressing practical concerns, including the kinds of problems that might be posed by language teachers. Unlike the Chomskyans, who are interested in the question of language and mind, functional linguists are more sociological in orientation — more concerned with relating language to society and with understanding how the ways in which language is used have shaped its structure. This has led functional linguists to develop semantically oriented grammars which show how people use language to make meaning in order to get on with their lives.

Before considering the 'syntactic' nuts and bolts of traditional, formal and functional grammar, let's sum up the three kinds of grammar considered here in terms of their social purposes and goals. Traditional grammar, as inherited from the Greeks, degenerated over the centuries to the point where its main goal was to teach children how to write and speak in the standard language of their community — to tell them what was right and wrong, where right was defined with respect to the writing of powerful middle-class speakers. We can gloss the social function of grammars of this kind as prescriptive. Formal grammar, culminating in the work of Chomsky, is a twentieth century development and aims to discover innate neurological limitations on the forms of possible grammars. We can gloss the social function of grammars of this kind as descriptive. Functional grammar, as represented in the work of Halliday, is an alternative twentieth century development and tries to explain the ways in which language is related to its social environment. Because of its engagement with the way in which people use language to live, we can refer to grammars of this kind as rhetorical. The following is a summary of types of grammar:

|  | **Goals** | **Social function** |
|---|---|---|
| **Traditional** | standard language | 'prescriptive' |
| **Formal** (Chomsky) | neurological limitations | 'descriptive' |
| **Functional** (Halliday) | ecological design | 'rhetorical' |

### Traditional Grammar

As noted above, traditional grammar teaching degenerated in schools to the point where it was reduced to learning the names of a few word classes ('parsing' the

*Figure 1.   Traditional Grammar's Model of an Independent Clause*

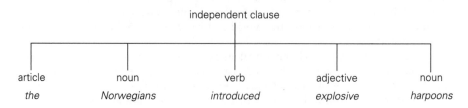

'parts of speech'), analysing a few textbook sentences, and learning how to correct a few other textbook sentences with so-called 'bad grammar'.

As far as knowledge about language is concerned, the main thing that traditional grammar set out to teach was the parts of speech, or what linguists would refer to as the names of word classes — noun, verb, adjective, adverb, preposition, conjunction and so on. These tended to be defined semantically — 'a *noun* is the name of a person, place or thing', 'a *verb* is an action word' and so on. Although helpful, definitions of this kind are fundamentally inadequate, as linguists are fond of pointing out (Huddleston, 1989). In a sentence such as 'There *was* lots of *commotion*', for example, the verb *was* is not an action word and the noun *commotion* is not the name of a person, place or thing.

Fuller grammars would include more exotic categories like gerunds and participles, and the names of different kinds of clause — coordinating and subordinating, indicative and imperative and so on. Sentence analysis might, in addition, involve picking out the subject of a sentence, along with its predicate and direct or indirect object (or complement, as objects were sometimes called). Gleason (1965) provides a very helpful review of school grammar in the American context, and for the Australian context Christie (1981, 1990a) and Huddleston (1989) are useful texts.

Sentence analysis in traditional grammar involved showing how clauses are made up of words. Where sentences included more than one clause, it might also be important to show how clauses combined. This theory of grammatical structure is exemplified in Figure 1.

Originally, traditional grammar functioned as a set of rules for correcting sentences. If, for example, a conjunction was defined as a word that joins clauses in a sentence, then you couldn't begin a sentence with a conjunction. The following sentence must be wrong (offending conjunction in italics below):

*So*, you can't begin a sentence with a conjunction.

But as traditional grammar degenerated in schools, often rules for correcting sentences were all that remained. These were designed to turn the spoken language of non-standard dialects into writing. From a social perspective what these rules amounted to was a set of prescriptions for white, middle-class, written English; the function of mass education was after all to civilise the working classes and debased colonials! A few examples of these rules are listed below:

A preposition is something you should never end a sentence *with*.
It is quite wrong *to* carelessly *split* infinitives.
*And* you should never begin a sentence with a conjunction.

In fact, one of the best known of contemporary split infinitives comes from the prologue to the well known television series, *Star Trek*: '. . . the Starship Enterprise, its five-year mission . . . *to boldly go* where no man has gone before. . . .'

As the examples themselves demonstrate, rules of this kind are made to be broken — not surprisingly, since they prescribe what people are supposed to do when they think about it rather than describe what people actually say. This means that traditional school grammar became not simply a grammar of etiquette but in addition a grammar of prejudice. It was a grammar that could be used to discriminate against people who spoke non-standard dialects or who wrote as they spoke. It is no accident that conservatives want to reinstitute a grammar of this kind.

Halliday (1979a, 185) makes the additional point that traditional school grammar was not only useless in helping people to use language more effectively, but was misleading about the nature of language: 'the grammar [was] not well suited to text analysis, but also grammatical analyses were presented as right or wrong. In fact, the analysis of language is a task of interpretation; there are often two, three or more possibilities, and the interest may lie precisely in the differences among them.' Halliday's first point perhaps needs amplification. Traditional grammar stopped at the sentence; it was not itself concerned with linguistic resources cohesion and text structure. Since most of the things people write are more than a sentence long, this was a severe limitation.

It is thus small wonder that both educators and linguists gave up on a grammar of this kind. It is rather worrying, however, that instead of replacing a useless grammar with a useful one, the study of grammar was simply eliminated from the curriculum. Faced with a generation of first year students or practising teachers who know nothing whatsoever about the grammar of their language, we have often felt that in spite of its limitations, traditional grammar was much better than no grammar at all.

### Formal Grammar

The formal grammarians are the most powerful group of linguists in the world today; even linguists who disagree with them often do so in a cringing way that defers to their work. For this reason alone their research and dominant institutional position must be taken very seriously. A useful, but highly technical introduction can be found in Radford (1981).

Like traditional grammar, formal grammar looks at classes, including classes of phrase as well as classes of word. More so than traditional grammar, formal grammar concentrates on structure — on the way in which these classes are combined. Remember that it is the limitations on combinations of classes that are of special interest to formal linguists. The way in which a modern formal grammarian might represent the structure of the example in Figure 1 is presented in Figure 2. Some of the labels are obviously derived from traditional grammar (N for noun, V for Verb, Adj for adjective and so on); there are also some new labels

*Figure 2. Formal Grammar's Representation of the Structure of a Clause*

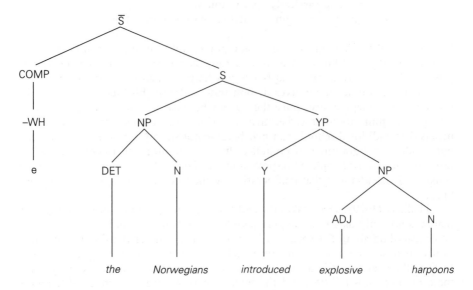

for groups of words (NP for noun phrase and VP for verb phrase). More significant is the presence of abstract labels like COMP, -WH and e which are not labels for anything we can see in the example itself (they are not realised by words).

These abstract labels are a very important part of a formal grammarian's descriptive apparatus because they are instrumental to the investigation of what cannot be said. The abstract labelling in Figure 2, for example, tells us that the clause in question begins with the kind of complement found in clauses which give information (-WH) rather than ask questions and which is not actually present in the wording of the clause (thus the e). Why, you might ask, is something represented which is not there? The answer is an indirect one. To reply, the formal grammarian would point to examples like the following:

He stated *that* the Norwegians introduced explosive harpoons.
He asked *whether* the Norwegians introduced explosive harpoons.

In this type of sentence the clause in question does, in fact, have a complement in first position (*that* and *whether*), and the complement does tell us whether the clause is giving (*that*) or demanding (*whether*) information. The abstract labelling in Figure 2 shows, in other words, the way in which the structure of the example clause on its own is like and unlike its structure when it is part of another clause.

What about rules? Again, like traditional grammar, formal grammar is concerned with rules. In a sense, because of concern with neurological limitations on possible grammars, the formal grammarian's rules are also prescriptive ones. But they don't prescribe what one should say, as in traditional grammar; rather they prescribe what is impossible to say. Consider the following sentences:

*That is* a Blue whale.
*That's* a Blue whale.

I wonder what *that is*?
*I wonder what *that's*?

In the first pair of sentences we can see that English provides us with an alternative. We can either treat the verb as a separate word (*that is*) or we can contract it with the subject of the sentence (*that's*). But if we look at the second pair of clauses, we see that this contraction is impossible. The asterisk in front of *I wonder what that's?* is the formal grammarian's sign that this sentence is not found in English. This means that we need a rule which blocks contraction under certain conditions. We can state this very informally as follows:

> You can't contract the first part of the verb unless it is followed by an noun, adjective or verb.

We can test the rule by adding nouns, verbs and adjectives after the verb we want to contract to see if it's right:

I wonder if *it's* an endangered species?    [noun following]
I wonder if *it's* endangered?    [adjective following]
I wonder if *it's* becoming extinct?    [verb following]

So far as we can see, it is. We are now on our way to finding out something about the limitations of human grammars. We've discovered something people can't say and have described it informally with a rule that makes it explicit just when they can't. If we keep working and find an abstract way of representing this rule that holds true for all human languages, then we're really onto something — something fundamental to humanity which makes us different from everything else. It is the quest for explanations of this kind that excites the imagination of formal grammarians. And, as Chomksy quite rightly explains, this enterprise has no practical relevance whatsoever to language teaching and learning in schools.

### Functional Grammar

Halliday became interested in linguistics when studying literature in secondary school. He thought it might be helpful for sorting out conflicting interpretations of literary texts. As it turned out, the first book he picked up was an American one — *Language* by Leonard Bloomfield which wasn't very helpful. But Halliday kept looking and eventually found that if he wanted a more useful model, he'd have to do some work developing it himself. Drawing on the work of his teachers in Great Britain, Firth in particular, and China, for example, Wang Li, he developed a linguistics which could do something — which could be applied to a range of problems faced by potential consumers of linguistics. This model is known as systemic functional linguistics.

Halliday (1979a, 186) contrasted his functional approach to grammar with traditional grammar, although he might just as well have been talking about formal grammar: 'It [traditional grammar] is formal; rigid; based on the notion of "rule"; syntactic in focus, and oriented towards the sentence. What is needed is a grammar that is functional; flexible; based on the notion of "resource"; semantic in focus, and oriented towards the text.' What kind of grammar is it that models language as a text oriented resource for meaning? (Note that Halliday uses the term 'text' to refer to a stretch of language that hangs together and is appropriate to its context.) Perhaps the first point we need to make about a meaning oriented grammar is that it has to take into account different kinds of meaning. We can look at these types of meaning in two ways: from the perspective of context or from the perspective of grammar.

Looked at from context, the different types of meaning reflect the register variables field, tenor and mode. Field refers to what is going on — the social activity in which language plays a part. Tenor looks at language as interaction — who is talking to whom and how they feel about it. Mode is concerned with the role language plays in channelling communication — with the degree of feedback encouraged and the amount of abstraction facilitated. These three contextual variables determine the register of a speech event.

Looked at from language, the different types of meaning organise the grammar and semantics of language into what Halliday calls metafunctions. Ideational meaning is concerned with making sense of the world — with constructing reality as configurations of people, places and things, what they do, who or what they do them to and where, when, how and why they do them. Interpersonal meaning is concerned with enabling interaction — with constructing social reality as exchanges of goods and services or information and the ways people evaluate these negotiations. Textual meaning is concerned with organising communication — with constructing symbolic reality as a wave of information (see the discussion of Theme and New below).

In systemic functional linguistics the organisation of context correlates with the organisation of grammar. This means that there is a strong association between the register variable field and ideational meaning, between tenor and interpersonal meaning and between mode and textual meaning. If we know something about a text's context, we can make predictions about its grammar; and conversely if we analyse a text's grammar, we can recover information about its context. It is this solidarity relationship between register variables and metafunctions that makes systemic functional linguistics such a valuable model for teachers. These important correlations can be summarised thus:

| **Organisation of context** [register] | **Organisation of grammar** [metafunction] |
|---|---|
| field: 'what is going on' | ideational meaning |
| tenor: 'who is taking part' | interpersonal meaning |
| mode: 'the role language is playing' | textual meaning |

Because they deal comprehensively with meaning, systemic functional grammars are very complex — much more complex than traditional school grammars and including many more labels than formal grammars (which are more concerned with rules). This is an obstacle for teachers and their students; functional grammars take time to learn. The pay-off is that once you have learned a functional grammar, it can do a lot of work. Because of this complexity, we can only hint at the kind of work a functional grammar does here, basing our work on Halliday (1985a) and Matthiessen (1990), which are grammars for linguists and their apprentices, not for teachers and their students in schools.

As a grammar of ideational meaning, one of the jobs a functional grammar does is to sort out the kinds of goings-on in the world. In broad outlines English does this by sorting out reality as action (what is happening outside our head), mental processing (what is 'happening' inside our head) and being (how things are related to each other). We can gloss these categories informally as doing, meaning and being and illustrate them as follows:

**Clause as 'representation'**
(ideational meaning)

[doing]      The young *put on* about 200 lbs a day . . .
[meaning]    We commonly *see* porpoises along our shores.
[being]      The largest *is* the sperm whale.

As a grammar of interpersonal meaning, part of the work of a functional grammar is to organise dialogue. In very general terms English does this by giving speakers the option of exchanging goods and services or information and of giving or demanding these commodities. A few of the different roles played by clauses in dialogue are outlined below:

**Clause as 'exchange'**
(interpersonal)

[statement]  *Whale watchers can* distinguish the species of whale.
[question]   *Can whale watchers* distinguish the species of whale?
[command]    *Distinguish* the various species of whale.

As a grammar of textual meaning, the grammar is especially concerned to arrange information in the clause. In English what comes first and what comes last are especially important. The information that comes first is known as Theme; it represents the speaker's point of departure for the clause and often reflects where she or he is coming from. The information that comes last is usually new and represents where the speaker is heading to. Note the different positions of *the Norwegians* and *the explosive harpoons* in the following examples (Theme in italics and New in quotes):

**Clause as 'message'**
(textual)

*The Norwegians* introduced 'explosive harpoons'.
*Explosive harpoons* were introduced 'by the Norwegians'.
*What the Norwegians introduced* was 'explosive harpoons'.

Looking at different types of meaning in the grammar means that clauses have to be analysed in in a number of different ways at the same time. While traditional grammar allowed just one analysis for each clause as outlined in Figure 1, functional grammar looks at the clause from the perspective of each metafunction. It does this to make the analysis meaningful.

To illustrate this, consider the following clause: *By 1500, they were whaling off Greenland*. If we think about this simply as a sequence of classes, then we get an analysis like the following.

| prepositional phrase | nominal group | verbal group | prepositional phrase |
|---|---|---|---|
| By 1500 | they | were whaling | off Greenland |

This analysis says that the clause consists of a prepositional phrase, followed by a nominal group, followed by a group of verbs (a verbal group), followed by another prepositional phrase. Semantically this tells us that the clause is dividing the world up into two circumstances (*by 1500* and *off Greenland*), a participant (*they*) and a process (*were whaling*). This kind of analysis is oriented towards ideational meaning. We can bring this out more clearly by relabelling the parts of the clause for function (what they do) instead of for class (what they are). This analysis, which tells us that 'something was going on, then and there', is presented below:

| Circumstance: location: time | Actor | Process | Circumstance: location: space |
|---|---|---|---|
| By 1500 | they | were whaling | off Greenland |

These two analyses (for class and for ideational functions) tell us what the clause is about; but they don't tell us what it is doing. To find out what the clause is doing, we need to look at it interpersonally as well. As far as interaction is concerned, the most important part of the clause is *they were*, its Subject and Finite (together referred to as the clause's Mood function); the presence or absence of Subject and Finite and their sequence (Subject ^ Finite or Finite ^ Subject) determines the mood of the clause. Since both Subject and Finite are present and the Subject comes before the Finite, we know that grammatically the clause is giving information. Halliday's labelling for this perspective on the clause is outlined below:

| Resi ...... | Mood | | ...................... due | |
|---|---|---|---|---|
| Adjunct | Subject | Finite | Predicator | Adjunct |
| By 1500 | they | were | whaling | off Greenland |

Finally, we need to think about the clause as message — about how it organises its information. Usually in clauses which give information the Subject comes first (with Subject as unmarked Theme). But this clause is different; it begins with an Adjunct (a marked Theme). The reason it does this is that it is part of an historical recount, a genre which is organised around setting in time. So the clause fits itself into this genre by angling through time. The clause finishes with its news — *off Greenland*; this is the information which is new to the reader and could not be predicted from what went before. Halliday's labelling for this aspect of clause structure is as follows:

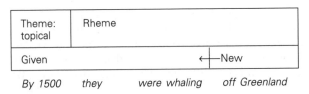

| Theme: topical | Rheme | | |
|---|---|---|---|
| Given | | ←—New | |

| By 1500 | they | were whaling | off Greenland |

We can see that in functional grammar the clause structure is treated as 'polyphonic'. Every English clause is about something, does something, and adapts to its environment. The different ideational, interpersonal and textual analyses we have illustrated here have been designed to show how each of these three types of meaning makes a contribution to grammar. In the next section we will look at how a functional, flexible, text oriented grammar of this kind, which treats language as a resource for meaning, can be used by teachers.

### Making Meaning in the Report Genre

In introducing a functional language model to teachers, we begin with the concept of genre — with the different types of text used in our culture to get things done. We show how genres typically achieve their goals by organising texts in stages. The stages are identified in functional terms — for example, General Classification and description in scientific reports. In the General Classification stage, as the name suggests, the phenomena under focus are classified according to scientific principles. In the Description stage such matters as appearance, location and, if applicable, behaviour are dealt with.

The fact that we can identify stages of a text as having a particular function in its overall organisation is a consequence of the patterning of language choices in each stage. Here we will examine the General Classification stage in a report to show how the grammar makes meaning to construct this stage.

| Title | Bears |
|---|---|
| General Classification | Bears are one type of carnivorous placental mammal. Placental mammals are animals which give birth to live young (rather than laying eggs) and the young at birth are attached to their mothers by a cord. This cord was used to nourish them when they were growing inside their mothers. In this way bears are like people, mice, cattle and whales. Carnivorous mammals are mammals that eat other animals as food and have long sharp eye teeth (canines) which are used for holding and tearing flesh. There are a number of different types of bear: Black bears, Brown bears, Polar bears, Panda bears and some others. Brown bears and Polar bears are described on the following pages. (Christie *et al.*, 1990c, 17) |

Let us look first at the grammatical resources for making ideational meanings in the General Classification stage. Earlier in this chapter, three types of ideational meaning were identified: doing, meaning and being. An analysis of the clauses in this stage of the report reveals several 'being' clauses:

1 Bears *are* one type of carnivorous placental mammal.
2 Placental mammals *are* animals which give birth to live young . . .
3 In this way bears *are* like people, mice, cattle and whales.
4 Carnivorous mammals *are* mammals that eat other animals as food . . .
5 There *are* a number of different types of bear: Black bears, Brown bears. . . .

In the first clause bears are related through *are* to one type of 'carnivorous placental mammal'. They are thus identified as members of a larger group of animals. In the second clause *are* works differently. Here it defines what placental mammals are — 'animals which give birth to live young'. In the fourth clause *are* works in the same way to define 'carnivorous mammals'. In the third clause *are* is used to relate 'bears' to other animals they are like — other mammals, including 'people, mice, cattle and whales'. In the fifth clause the meaning of *are* can be glossed as exists. It is used to present the different types of bears found throughout the world.

Meanings about 'being', in other words, are crucial in building up classifications: in defining, in describing what things are like and in positing the existence of phenomena. These patterns of meaning are crucial for constructing what is in this case a simple scientific classification system and locating bears in this system.

Let us now examine how the meanings about 'being' set up particular kinds of relationship between the animals identified in the general classification. In doing this, we are moving our focus to meanings established between items in different clauses. These relations are known as lexical relations. Here is the simple taxonomy built up by the lexical relations and 'being' clauses in the General Classification:

Figure 3.  *Taxonomy of Animals Constructed in General Classification*

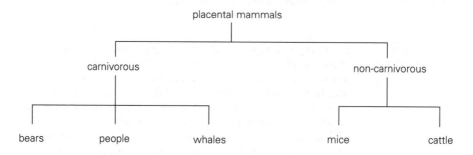

The choice of Theme is a choice for textual meaning in the clause. This choice orders elements in the clause in such a way that they play a role in developing the text — its pattern of development as it unfolds from clause to clause. The pattern of choices for Theme in the General Classification is to do with bears and the species they belong to. Setting aside conjunctions, the Themes are as follows (Themes in italics):

*Bears* are one type of carnivorous placental mammal. *Placental mammals* are animals which give birth to live young (rather than laying eggs) and *the young at birth* are attached to their mothers by a cord. *This cord* was used to nourish them when *they* were growing inside their mothers. In this way *bears* are like people, mice, cattle and whales. *Carnivorous mammals* are mammals that eat other animals as food and have long sharp eye teeth (canines) which are used for holding and tearing flesh. *There* are a number of different types of bear: Black bears, Brown bears, Polar bears, Panda bears and some others are described on the following pages. (Christie *et al.*, 1990c, 17)

Note that Textual Themes like *and* are being passed over here, where the focus is on what Halliday calls Topical Themes — Themes which build experiential meaning. Also *In this way* has been interpreted as a conjunction of manner here (like *thus*), leaving *bears* as the Topical Theme. Notice that the animals that function as Theme (compare, *bears, placental mammals, the young at birth, bears, carnivorous mammals, Brown bears* and *Polar bears*) are referred to generically. This is another example of how particular language choices make the meanings of the report genre, which deals with whole classes of animals, plants, machines and so on. In this respect reports are different from narratives which deal with individuals.

There is another part of the grammar which needs to be looked at closely in considering how meaning is built up in the General Classification stage of reports. This deals with the participants in the text — the animals, plants, machines that are its focus. This part of the grammar names these participants and gives information about them and constructs the participants as nominal groups. However, for a discussion of work on nominal group structure in infants school, see Rothery (1989b).

Once again, the way meaning is built up in nominal groups is described in functional terms. Let's look first at the nominal group *bears*, which is Theme in the first clause. We can identify the function of the words *bears* as Thing. This is the function label we give to central participant in the nominal group. We can represent the analysis as follows:

| bears |
| --- |
| Thing |

Nominal groups have a potential for building up meaning which extends well beyond this Thing function. Consider the group *this cord*. The function of *this* is Deictic (or less technically, Pointer). It selects or points out whatever functions as thing in the nominal group. This group can be analysed as follows:

| this | cord |
| --- | --- |
| Deictic | Thing |

The function label 'Deictic' is the one used by systemic linguists, but 'Pointer' might be a preferable term for use with school students (linguists will be familiar with the technical term 'deixis', from the Greek; for school students terms derived from Latin or Anglo-Saxon usually prove more semantically transparent). Teachers who wish to use the grammar with students can make their own decision about which label they will use. Throughout this section on the nominal group, alternative names will be introduced for some of Halliday's function labels.

To introduce the full potential for nominal group meanings, we shall examine two groups that are not part of the Bears report. The first is as follows:

those two old stone cottages with wrought iron balconies

*Cottages* is Thing in the above group; and there is information about cottages which both precedes and follows it. The first word in the group, *those*, has the function of Deictic (or Pointer); the second word, *two*, has the function Numerative, which can be simplified to Number (this simplification makes it transparent that cardinal numerals like *one*, *two*, *three* and so on, fulfil this function — what perhaps becomes less obvious is that the same function is filled by quantity words like *many*, *much*, *lots of*, *several* and so on — this tension shows the ultimate advantage of the more abstract, less transparent terms). The next word *old* gives a quality of the cottages. Its function label is Epithet or Short Describer (the significance of *short* will become apparent below). The function of *stone* is to subclassify the type of cottage. It is stone, rather than brick or wood. The function of *stone* in the group is that of Classifier. We can distinguish the function Classifier from that of Epithet by the following grammatical 'test': we can intensify the function Epithet by saying things like *very old*, *rather old* and so on; but we do not speak in English of a *very stone cottage*. Another test involves comparative and superlative meanings, which only apply to Epithets; thus we find *the older cottages* and *the oldest cottages* but not *the stoner cottages* or *the stonest cottage*. But we do find *the stoniest path*, in which *stoniest* is the superlative form of the epithet *stoney*.

The analysis presented so far can be represented as follows.

| the | two | old | stone | cottages |
|-----|-----|-----|-------|----------|
| Deictic [Pointer] | Numerative [Number] | Epithet [Short Describer] | Classifier | Thing |

Additional information about cottages follows the Thing: they are cottages *with wrought iron balconies*. The function of this stretch of language is Qualifier, which can also be labelled as Long Describer. The qualifier gives more information about the cottages which serves to identify them more precisely. So the complete analysis is an follows:

| the | two | old | stone | cottages | with wrought iron balconies |
|-----|-----|-----|-------|----------|-----------------------------|
| Deictic [Pointer] | Numerative [Number] | Epithet [Short Describer] | Classifier | Thing | Qualifier [Long Describer] |

This example shows a great deal of the potential for meaning embodied in nominal group structure. It enables a considerable build up of information about the participant being written or spoken about. Making use of the meaning potential in this structure is an important strategy for classifying and describing whatever is being written about in the report.

Let us now examine a nominal group from a report about koalas — the second nominal group in *A koala is a stub-tailed arboreal marsupial with large furry ears, black leathery nose and long strong claws:*

| a | stub-tailed | arboreal | marsupial | with large furry ears, black leathery nose and long strong claws |
|---|---|---|---|---|
| Deictic | Epithet | Classifier | Thing | Qualifier |

Information about the appearance of the koala and its parts is built up through the nominal group structure in a very compact way. The structure places the koala as a member of the group of animals known biologically as marsupials, as well as describing its appearance. If we look more closely at the Qualifier, we can see that there are nominal groups within it. They are: *large furry ears, black leathery nose* and *long straight claws*. These can be analysed in turn as follows:

| large | furry | ears |
|---|---|---|
| Epithet | Epithet | Thing |

| black | leathery | nose |
|---|---|---|
| Epithet | Epithet | Thing |

| long | straight | claws |
|---|---|---|
| Epithet | Epithet | Thing |

These nominal groups are said to be embedded within the Qualifier — embedded because they are nominal groups functioning as part of another nominal group. They also illustrate that the function Epithet can be repeated in nominal group structure.

The sentence from which these nominal groups were taken comes from a report by a primary school student who is able to exploit the potential of nominal group structure to give a lot of information about koalas. Some young writers would handle this information in a number of sentences, more like the following:

A koala is an arboreal marsupial. It has a stub-tail. The koala has large furry ears and a black leathery nose. It also has strong claws.

This rewriting of the information in the nominal group shows how the functions of the nominal group structure provide a more economical way for building up meaning.

If we return to the General Classification of bears, we can examine the structure of some of the nominal groups to see how they build up meanings of classification. The first example is from the opening sentence: *Bears are one type of carnivorous placental mammal.* This being clause identifies bears as *one type of carnivorous placental mammal.* The Deictic and Thing of this group, *one* and *type* respectively, show that bears are being identified with respect to their classification — in a biologist's terms with respect to the relevant taxonomy of living things.

*Figure 4.   Extension of Taxonomy Underpinning Classification in the Bears Report*

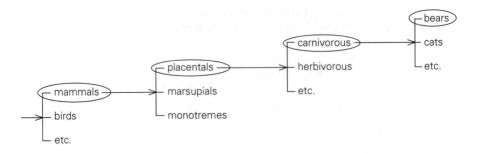

Embedded in its qualifier is the nominal group *carnivorous placental mammal*, with the functions Classifier and Thing:

| carnivorous | placental | mammal |
|-------------|-----------|--------|
| Classifier | Classifier | Thing |

These functions allow the identification to home in on the precise location of bears in this order of things. The parts of the biological taxonomy at issue here are outlined in Figure 4, an extension of Figure 3 (this time with the more general classes to the left of the diagram instead of on top). Classification is pursued in subsequent sentences, for example: *Placental mammals are animals which give birth to live young. . . .* Once again the nominal group structure is used to build up the scientific classification of bears. The first group in this sentence focuses on the relevant part of the taxonomy:

| placental | mammals |
|-----------|---------|
| Classifier | Thing |

This group is related through the verb *are* to another, *animals which give birth to live young . . .* (to simplify the discussion, the remainder of this nominal group qualifier, the clause *rather than laying eggs*, will be passed over here). It has the following structure:

| animals | which give birth to live young |
|---------|-------------------------------|
| Thing | Qualifier |

The Qualifier in this group is a clause. Within this clause is a further nominal group, *live young*, with the structure:

| live | young |
|------|-------|
| Classifier | Thing |

The nominal groups dealt with to this point occur in the first two sentences of the general classification of the bears report. In these few groups the choice of classifier stands out, and this is to be expected in the stage of the report which deals with classification.

In this section we have looked at just a few aspects of how using a functional grammar enables us to understand how meaning is built up in a text. Although we have only considered part of the General Classification stage, we have seen that identifying this stage of the report depends on a patterning of meanings built up through a complex interaction of language choices. This kind of analysis enables us to see how the stages of texts are constructed to function in particular ways.

Being able to look at texts in this way is important in teaching students to write different genres. Knowing the stages of the genre and being able to identify them is an important first step. But ultimately teachers need to know as much as possible about how meaning is built up through language in the different stages of the genre. Teachers need to be able to point out characteristic uses of language in a text of a particular genre as we have done with the report genre. Knowledge of how language is used to mean in different genres is particularly important when it comes to giving students positive assistance with their writing. For example, if students are writing a number of sentences to classify and describe an animal, we can demonstrate how the functions of the nominal group structure enable a much more competent build up of information. To take up a constructive and guiding role of this kind, the teacher needs to know how grammar makes meaning in a text.

### Grammar at Work

In this chapter we have briefly considered the advantages for teachers and students of a functional grammar as opposed to a traditional or formal one. We have offered a brief demonstration of some of the ways in which functional grammar can be used to show how meaning is constructed in text. The choice, in other words, is not between grammar and no grammar, as the debate is often publicly voiced. Rather the choice depends, as it should, on the consumer — on what schools want grammar to do.

We will close with a shopping list of parameters:

Is the grammar functional, formal or traditional?
Is the grammar flexible — is it adaptable to varied needs?
Is the grammar based on the notion of resource or rule?
Is the grammar focused on meaning or syntax?
Is the grammar oriented to text or to sentence?

Contemporary curriculum is rather clear, if less than explicit, about the kind of grammar to be consumed.

*Chapter 7*

# Curriculum Genres: Planning for Effective Teaching

*Frances Christie*

*In examining the issue of planning for effective teaching, Frances Christie's point of departure is the fact that teaching is a goal driven, social activity, a fact best encapsulated in the practice of drawing up teaching programs and writing lesson plans. This, Christie argues, is a basis for another use for the concept of genre in educational settings. She defines genre as a staged, goal driven, purposive activity; in this sense, the notion of genre can be used, not only to describe language, but also to describe the teaching process. This latter use of the concept Christie terms 'curriculum genre'.*

*Just as the general project of genre literacy is to make explicit the way language works to make meaning through different genres, so teaching should be a deliberate activity in which the teacher has an explicit understanding of how teaching and learning are structured through language. To illustrate how curriculum genres work, Christie distinguishes two registers: a pedagogical register which gives structure and purpose to the particular teaching/ learning activity and a content register which refers to the field of experience of that activity. The most critical point of learning in a curriculum genre, Christie argues, is when pedagogical and content registers converge.*

*She illustrates her argument about the workings of curriculum genre with three examples: a morning news session, a relatively unsuccessful writing lesson about the uniforms worn by various workers, and a more successful writing lesson about veterinarians. These examples illustrate the fact that curriculum genres are inevitably staged. Without an explicit understanding of the way in which pedagogical and content registers need to converge in the learning experiences of every student, and without an explicit understanding of the way students learn though language in classroom discourse, teachers are not able to do their job as effectively as they might. This returns Christie's argument to its starting point. Effective curriculum planning is essential in the successful realisation of curriculum genres.*

## The Social Construction of Classroom Experience

The practice of keeping lesson records is an acknowledgment of the fact that teaching-learning activities are intended to be goal driven. Even in the first years of their initial training, student teachers are required to develop and keep careful lesson plans. Once graduated, they are again normally required to keep various records of their teaching programs, though the nature of these varies from place to place. In the Australian context at least, one record is intended to set out the planned overview of a teaching-learning program, while another constitutes an account of how this was taught, indicating any variations on the original plan. Overall, the various lesson records are justified on the grounds that teachers should have goals in their teaching, and that they should show evidence of having identified and worked towards these with their students.

How much and in what ways, then, do teachers typically think about their classroom activities as goal driven? How are the goals determined? How are the goals recognised, once achieved? How many teachers are really conscious of the particular social processes in which they engage with their students in order to achieve the goals? How many teachers are aware that the social processes in which they participate with their students in the pursuit of various goals are structured in distinctive ways, making them instances of particular genres? How many are aware that the teaching-learning activities of schools are really curriculum genres: staged, goal driven, purposive activities, in which students are initiated into ways of working, thinking and dealing with experience valued in an English-speaking culture? Finally, how many teachers are aware of the central role that language plays in structuring the social experiences that make up a curriculum genre?

Like most other groups of people, teachers are not accustomed to thinking about the things they do as social processes, nor do they spend a lot of time thinking about how their language builds these processes. For the most part, teachers get on with the business of living, moving from one task to another, dealing with students, relating to colleagues and to parents, and so on. Thus the ways they structure experience often remain 'invisible', operating at some unconscious level, and hence not subject to close scrutiny or control. Yet teaching should be a deliberate act. The more teachers can be aware of the ways their teaching practices and their students' learning are structured in language, the better they will be in a position to direct and guide their students as they learn.

The social institution of schooling is a remarkable one in many senses. Its most remarkable feature, compared with the many other social institutions in which people operate, is that schooling characteristically deals with fields of experience drawn from outside the school, and it initiates the students into some understanding of these. This in itself accounts for the characteristic pedagogical discourses that are a feature of schooling, as Bernstein (1986) has argued. It accounts, too, for the particular roles and relationships taken up by students and teachers. Students stand in a relationship of apprenticeship to their teachers on the one hand, while teachers operate with some degree of expertise towards their students on the other hand, guiding them into new ways of working. As I shall seek to demonstrate below, the pedagogical discourses found in educational institutions thus show evidence of the operation of two registers. One of these, which is a first order register, I shall call the pedagogical register, because it is primarily to do with the pedagogical goals of a curriculum genre. The second register, which is a second order register, I shall call the content register, because it is to do with the 'content' dealt with in the pursuit of the pedagogical goals. Thus the first order or pedagogical register structures and gives purpose to the teaching-learning activity so that the students can proceed to dealing with the 'content'. The choices made in language build the two registers in different ways to create the overall schematic structure of the curriculum genre. With the exception of one curriculum genre known to me, to be discussed below, an instance of a curriculum genre will be a successful one when the two registers converge for a sustained period of time, for it will be then that genuine learning about how to perform some pedagogically valued task will occur.

Incidentally, the choice of the word 'content' is not perhaps the most appropriate, because it conjures up some sense of a 'package' of information that is passed on in some non-problematic way. In truth, the various skills, information and ways of working with experience that form the basis of what is taught about in schools are always generated in social activities which are varied, changing and hence problematic. Provided we bear this general point in mind, the term 'content' will suffice, since no very adequate alternative is available.

In this chapter I describe briefly the ways in which at least two curriculum genres operate in the years of early childhood schooling. Using a functional grammar (Halliday, 1985a) I want to demonstrate the ways in which knowledge and experience are built up in these genres and the kinds of values that appear to attach to such knowledge and experience. In particular I want to show how a great deal of early literacy is rehearsed in such genres, albeit in rather unconscious ways. Indeed, if teachers had a more conscious control of a functional grammar themselves, they would be much more aware of the manner in which patterns of both oral language and literacy are established in the curriculum genres in question. Possessed of such knowledge, they would be able the more effectively to direct the various teaching-learning activities intended to promote development in both oral language and literacy. To develop these arguments, it will be necessary to say a little more about the nature of the two registers already alluded to, and about their importance in education generally.

### First and Second Order Registers in Education

Two registers operate in any instance of a curriculum genre. This is brought about by the fact that teaching-learning activities in schools characteristically take fields of experience from outside the school and teach about these to their students. Natural scientists, social scientists, mathematicians, writers of literature, for example, operate in a variety of different social contexts in the wider community, and they engage in a great range of corresponding activities. Their insights, skills and ways of going about dealing with problems are taken and relocated in the social contexts of schooling, and these form the 'content' of the natural science, social science, mathematics and English literary programs, both in primary and secondary schools.

Of course, schools never deal with the various kinds of contents in the same ways as do the people who engage in constructing those contents in the adult world outside school. That is because schools exist to initiate the young into some understanding of the fields of experience found in the adult world outside school. Hence, while the language used in teaching students to construct the knowledge of a natural or social science, for example, is related to that used in the adult world of natural or social scientists, it takes its characteristics as well from the fact that the students are learners. As such, they are coming to terms with dealing with experience in what are new ways for them. When students learn new ways of dealing with experience, their commonsense knowledge about the world is transformed and they adopt uncommonsense perspectives of various kinds. For example, all young children in the early years of primary schooling are aware that animals have babies, and that the babies grow into adults: this is commonsense knowledge, acquired from observation of family and community. But an important aspect of uncommonsense knowledge is learning about the nature of the life cycles of different animals, and becoming aware of the similarities and differences, for example, among the life cycles of frogs and butterflies, human beings, dogs and cats. Such knowledge is often taught to students in the primary school years. It is also often taught in the secondary school biology program, where it is considered in greater detail. Capacity to deal with it in greater detail is a condition of the greater maturity of secondary students, and this is in part an effect of the earlier knowledge gained about life cycles in the primary school. The processes of initiation into new ways of knowing are thus cumulative, and in principle never ending, as students transform their earlier forms of understanding into new forms.

Any instance of a curriculum genre starts by bringing to the fore the pedagogical register, and this is why it is a first order register. Consider, for example, the kinds of openings a teacher in early childhood may use as she initiates the teaching-learning activity for an instance of the morning news genre:

*Teacher*:  Good morning everyone.
*Chorus*:  Good morning Mrs P.
*Teacher*:  Let's sing our good morning song.
  [*They all sing together*]
*Chorus*:  Good morning good morning
  And how do you do?
  Good morning, good morning
  And a happy day to you.
  Good morning to you
  Good morning to you
  We're all in our places
  With bright shiny faces
  And this is the way
  To start a new day.
*Teacher*:  That's good thank you.
  Okay it's newstime? News? Who's got some news?

Or consider, by contrast, the opening of an instance of the writing planning genre:

*Teacher*:  Now I want you to sit around me in a big circle so you can all see what we're going to talk about.
  [*The children all move into a horseshoe shaped group around her. As she begins to talk, she spreads out on the floor before her a navy uniform, with silver buttons, and white stripes on the arms. It is accompanied by a peaked cap, and it is in fact a uniform of the naval police.*]
  Right, this week we've had two different uniforms that we've written a report about. We had a visitor and we looked at what she wore.

*Child:*    The crossing lady.
*Teacher:*  Yes that's right. Yesterday we didn't have a person and we just
            talked about it. Who remembers?
*Child:*    A policeman's uniform.

In both cases the teacher is focusing upon, or foregrounding, aspects of the children's behaviour. In the former, the singing of the song reminds the children of the need to be polite in greeting the teacher and each other by saying 'good morning', while the final lines of the song remind the children of how to behave acceptably for the start of the new school day: 'We're all in our places/ with bright shiny faces/ and this is the way/ to start a new day.' Once this is done, the teacher seeks to identify a person to take up the morning news giving role. One of the pedagogical purposes of the morning news genre is that children learn patterns of behaviour acceptable for school learning generally. Sometimes in the opening of the morning news genre teachers make overt reference to the need to have 'good manners' or to 'listen when other people talk'. Of course, teachers will often make reference to 'good manners' in other types of curriculum genres, but this tends to be when some breakdown in desired patterns of behaviour has occurred. The need for good manners, however, is often foregrounded as an aspect of the pedagogical register in the morning news genre. That is because one of its primary pedagogical purposes is that children learn to become well mannered, and to listen quietly as others talk.

In the opening to the instance of the writing planning genre (which was initiated after an instance of the morning news genre), the teacher identifies the kind of behaviour required for this lesson: 'Now I want you to sit around me in a big circle so you can all see what we're going to talk about.' She goes on to reconstruct something of what has been done in earlier lessons: 'this week we've had two different uniforms that we've written a report about. We had a visitor and we looked at what she wore.' This is part of operationalising activity for this lesson and beginning to prepare the children for an eventual writing task. Shortly, the second order or 'content' register will be foregrounded, as the children are moved on to discuss the 'content' which will constitute the basis for the writing.

As already noted, curriculum genres are like other genres in that they are staged and purposive. The stages within a curriculum genre are of great importance, because the movement through their particular sequenced pattern is a necessary part of achieving the goals of the genre. As we shall see below, the movement to each new stage of a curriculum genre is marked in the discourse because it is at these points that the pedagogical register is foregrounded. Once the new stage has thus been identified and directions pointed for that new stage, the lesson proceeds to further engagement with the content register. However, as I shall demonstrate below, the pattern by which this happens does change, partly depending upon the type of curriculum genre involved, and partly upon where in the overall sequence of stages the particular stage in question falls. Thus, for example, in the case of an instance of the writing planning genre, the object is that the students learn to write about a particular content field. The pedagogical register is concerned primarily with teaching about how to write, while the content register concerns the content for writing. In a successful instance of this genre, the two registers should converge in at least one substantial stage of the genre, as the teacher involves the students in discussing and planning how to write about that content. In practice, as I shall argue later, the two converge very briefly indeed in typical instances of the writing planning genre, so that important information concerning how to use language to control some written text is quite often not taught.

At first, however, I propose to look in more detail at an instance of the morning news genre. First, it is of interest because its overall structure differs quite markedly from that of the writing planning genre, and an awareness of this contributes to our general sense that there are a number of types of curriculum genre typically found in schools, not all of them as yet described. Second, it is of interest because, while it does have two registers operating, these are of a different character from those found in other types of curriculum genres. Third, it is of interest because it provides evidence of a rehearsal of language for school learning, including language for literacy.

### The Morning News Genre

The morning news genre is an unusual one, compared with all other curriculum genres, because its content fields, while certainly drawn from outside school experiences, are selected from the children's experiences. That is to say, the subjects about which children tell their news, or sometimes the objects about which they talk to their peers, are drawn from personal activities. In this the morning news genre is in marked contrast with other genres, where even if the teacher does spend time negotiating aspects of the content, the primary responsibility for its choice remains hers. It is the fact that in morning news the children choose the contents which explains why the two registers don't converge in the morning news genre in ways which compare with other curriculum genres such as the writing planning genre.

The morning news genre is one of the familiar curriculum genres of the early school years, where a great deal is learned about what constitutes acceptable behaviour in schools, as already noted above. The particular linguistic capacity that seems to be most important in a morning news genre is the capacity to use language for the representation of experience. Representation of experience is by no means the only function for which language is used, but it is important for school learning, for use in both the oral and the written modes.

Writing of very young children, Halliday (1973, 9–21) has proposed that there is a range of functions for which children learn their mother tongue. These include what he terms the 'instrumental function', to do with using language to get things done, and a closely related function, that of the 'regulatory', to do with influencing the behaviour of others. A third function Halliday identifies is the 'interactional', to do with using language to interrelate with others, while a fourth is the 'personal', having to do with use of language for expression of sense of self. A fifth function is the 'heuristic' one, involving use of language to ask questions about experience, and a sixth is the 'imaginative' function, where this refers to using language for imaginative play. The seventh function for using language Halliday proposes is the 'representational', involving using language for 'communicating about something (or for) expressing propositions' (Halliday, 1973, 16). It comes into play in particular for representing experience in the recall of events and reconstructing these for the benefit of people not present when the events occurred. Capacity to use language to represent or narrate about experience,

Halliday (1978b) suggests, is a difficult one, for it is a significant intellectual challenge to learn that language can be used to represent experience to others. The representational function develops much later than the other functions, and from the point of view of young children it is a less important function than the others. That is because in the important processes of interacting with parents, siblings and community members in the early years of life, what matters most is the achievement of the very immediate goals of seeking goods and services, of establishing relationships with others, or of eliciting information or advice of various kinds about the world.

As very young children learn to use language to serve these various functions, so too they eventually master the lexicogrammar of their mother tongue, and indeed in all children (apart from the most severely intellectually disabled) this is well established before they commence schooling, aged five or six. Nonetheless, at the point of entry to the school, many young children are still learning much about the processes of representing experience. A great deal of experience of guided intervention, or scaffolding, on the part of adults is involved in assisting children to recognise that language can be used to represent experience, as Painter (1986) has demonstrated with respect to her own child, Hal. Consider the following text, collected by Painter (1986, 24):

> [*Hal has eaten his meal with F. Later M. arrives home*]
> M: What did you have for tea?
> H: [*silence*]
> M: What did you have for tea, darling?
> H: Tea.
> M: Yes, what did you have for tea?
> H: [*silence*]
> M: Did you have an egg?
> H: Egg.
> M: And some toast?
> H: [*silence*]

A few months later, Painter (1986, 39) collected the following exchange:

> M: Tell Daddy where you went today.
> F: What did you do today?
> H: Feed the birdies.
> F: Where did you go?
> H: [*silence*]
> M: Did you go to the park?
> H: No.
> F: Where did you go?
> H: On the beach.
> F: Did you go in the sea?
> H: Yes, wash handies in the water.

Here the parents scaffold appropriate language for the child, and in at least three senses they are 'teaching' or at least communicating to their child some significant information about what representation of experience involves. In the first sense they are modelling some of the language that can be used to reconstruct experience: this involves mastery of aspects of the lexicogrammar of the mother tongue. Second, they are establishing the awareness that language can be used to recreate experience, and they are thus encouraging the view that such recreation is useful: this involves development of an ability to deal with experience in a new way. Third, they are guiding the child into making choices about the fields of experience that might be deemed appropriate to recreate: hence children are taught that some experiences are valued over others, because they are deemed more praiseworthy, or more enjoyable, or more significant in some way than others. In this way some ideological awareness is established in children concerning those fields of personal experience that are valued by adults, particularly for the purposes of recreation of these fields.

These are all important understandings, primarily because they assist young children to operate more effectively in their world. The capacity to use language to represent experience is of particular importance for school learning. We must conclude that many of the activities associated with the early years of schooling are designed, often not very consciously, to assist children to develop their capacities to use language to represent experience. Hence the institution of morning news, although as we shall see later, there is reason to question whether this is the best way to develop capacities to represent experience.

Expressed at the simplest level, the overall pattern or schematic structure of a morning news genre involves the following elements or phases:

| | |
|---|---|
| Lesson initiation | where the teacher gets the activity going |
| Morning news nomination | where a child is nominated to take the morn-ing news giving role |
| Morning news greeting | where the selected child exchanges greetings with the rest of the group |
| Morning news giving | where the child actually tells his or her news |
| Morning news finish | where the activity of giving the news is brought to a conclusion |
| Morning news closure | where the whole morning news genre is brought to a close, preparatory to going on to some other curriculum genre |

A number of the elements are recursive, because within any one instance of the morning news genre there will be several examples of different children taking up the morning news giving role.

I have already cited an example of the opening lesson initiation stage of a morning news genre, noting that at this point the pedagogical register is foregrounded, for the teacher is operationalising activities:

*Teacher*: Good morning everyone.
*Chorus*: Good morning Mrs P.
*Teacher*: Let's sing our good morning song.
[*They all sing together*]
*Chorus*: Good morning good morning
And how do you do?

> Good morning, good morning
> And a happy day to you.
> Good morning to you
> Good morning to you
> We're all in our places
> With bright shiny faces
> And this is the way
> To start a new day.
>
> *Teacher:* That's good thank you.
> Okay it's newstime. News? Who's got some news?

Once the good morning song is over, the teacher uses a continuative ('okay') to signal to the children that they are to move to a new phase of activity. Continuatives characteristically appear in teacher talk in all curriculum genres as an aspect of the pedagogical register, and while they do sometimes appear in the 'body' of a given stage of the genre, they are much more frequent in the opening. They are not a feature of children's talk incidentally — at least not in the data from which this chapter is drawn (Christie, 1989b) — although it is clear that children are quite capable of using them. The explanation for this is that their use helps to define the teacher's role as authority figure, responsible for the overall pedagogical goals of the genre. It is she who determines the directions the classroom discourse will take, and one way she signals this is in her use of continuatives at selected points in the overall curriculum genre.

Apart from the use of the continuative, the teacher uses one attributive process (Halliday, 1985a), so-called because it establishes something of the character of the teaching-learning event about to take place. It thus helps to build a sense of what is going on:

> it's newstime,

and so the activity gets under way.

In the morning news nomination, the teacher calls for and then nominates a child:

> News? Who's got some news?
> Now let's hear from you Joseph.

There is never much variation in this stage of the morning news genre, although some teachers allow the children to nominate who is to go after them in taking up the morning news giving role. It is a measure of how important this stage of the genre is to note that if any child attempted to move to the authoritative position at the front of the group without being nominated to do so, he or she would receive a sharp reproof. The pedagogical register is thus very much in evidence here, for it is control of the children's behaviour towards the achievement of pedagogical goals that is at issue.

The morning news greeting is not necessarily required by all teachers, but it is nonetheless reasonably common. It never varies, and its principal purpose is to remind the children of the obligation to show 'good manners' in addressing the teacher and each other:

*Joseph:*    Good morning Mrs P, good morning girls and boys.
*Chorus:*    Good morning Joseph.

The morning news giving stage is, as one might expect, the stage with the most variation, and more than one type of genre can be embedded within this stage. Whatever the genre selected, the associated content field is always drawn from the child's own experience, for it is at this point that the second order or content register comes into play:

*Joseph:*    There's a horse next door and it always jumps over the fence.
*Teacher:*    Gosh, so what do you do?
*Joseph:*    Chase it home again.

Joseph uses an existential process (Halliday, 1985a) to construct a proposition about his experience:

there's a horse next door.

An existential process is so-called because it brings some phenomenon into existence, so that, potentially at least, people can then build further statements about it. This is exactly what Joseph does, for, having established the presence of a horse next door, he proceeds to use a material process to build an aspect of its behaviour:

it always *jumps* over the fence.

The teacher takes a role in furthering the discourse ('gosh, so what do you do?'), and this enables Joseph to offer his last statement, using another material process:

*chase* it home again.

The teacher makes clear that this concludes Joseph's morning news giving stage, for she institutes the morning news finish, signalling a return to the pedagogical register, so that Joseph understands he is to sit down:

*Teacher:*    Well thank you Joseph.

A new phase of morning news giving is then instituted, again by the teacher:

Now your turn Mandy,

and the recursive pattern proceeds.

The final stage of the lesson, the lesson closure, comes when the teacher determines that it is time to move to a new curriculum genre. Just as in the lesson initiation, she uses an attributive process, this time to mark the closure of activities:

That's all we'll have time for today.

Our examination of what Joseph has achieved in his morning news giving stage has revealed that he was indeed reconstructing personal experience (and hence a second order register) for the benefit of a group of people not aware of that experience, and drawing upon the linguistic resources at his command to do so. Two matters are of pedagogical interest. The first is that not all children enjoy success in such activities as morning news giving. The other is that there would seem to be a relationship between what is rehearsed linguistically in morning news and what is it young children write.

Joseph enjoyed reasonable success in taking the morning news giving role, yet there were other children in his class who, over three years of close study, made remarkably little progress. A number regularly volunteered to take the morning news giving role, and they tended to shout the exchange of greetings, clearly feeling comfortable with this, after which they often retreated into silence. On such occasions, teacher promptings would normally generate whispered one-word answers before the children were asked to return to their places. Other children still expressed little interest in taking up the morning news giving role, so that on occasion their teachers thought they had little of interest to say. Given the commonplace nature of the experiences selected and normally approved as newsworthy and hence of interest, the latter judgment is clearly not a justified one.

There are at least two possible explanations for the fact that children do not perform equally well in the morning news giving role. The first we have already referred to: Halliday has argued that the capacity to use language to represent or narrate about experience is a difficult one, and that it develops later in some children than in others. If Halliday is right about this, then teachers need to be alert to the need to assist children to learn to represent experience. The conventional morning news genre may well not be the best genre with which to do this. The other explanation is to do with the kinds of meanings encoded in such activities as morning news, and with the relative significance accorded these as a consequence of social class and background. Teachers tend to favour particular kinds of fields of personal experiences in morning news activities. The result is that even though, as noted earlier, the children select the personal fields of experience of which they talk, an important ideology actually operates determining that choice. Celebratory experiences, such as the birth of a new baby or the acquisition of a new possession, or funny experiences such as having a horse that often escapes, are particularly valued and rewarded with teacher approval. Children most disposed by prior life and language-learning opportunity to construct fields of personal experiences of these sorts are likely to be advantaged when they participate in morning news giving activities.

Hasan (1987, 1989) and Williams (1990, 1991) have both provided important evidence for the general proposition that children perform differently in the early years of schooling, depending upon social class. Neither has examined morning news activities. However, Williams (1991) in particular, investigating the 'relationships between home practices in mothers' reading to children and teachers' practices in the first two months of formal schooling', provides support for the general claim that children of different social class groups interpret and respond to teachers' talk in different ways. Using Hasan's (1989) method for grouping families, he concludes that children from families where the family breadwinner is of the 'higher-autonomy professions' are disposed to interpret and respond to teacher questions with greater understanding than children whose major family breadwinner is of a 'lower autonomy profession'.

Some years ago, working with the Aboriginal children at Traeger Park primary school, Alice Springs, Gray (1985) developed a language program which focused upon identifying the language abilities the children needed to be successful at school learning, and making these directly available in a great deal of carefully developed teaching. The children spoke Aboriginal English and it served the children well for the purposes they had in their own communities, as Walker (1981) had demonstrated. However, they needed to learn to use English for the purposes of school learning, and, given the significant cultural differences between Aboriginal and European ways of dealing with experience, this meant learning to handle experience in entirely new ways. A great deal of modelling of ways of using language in the oral mode for the representation of experience was always a feature of the Traeger Park program. Teacher modelling of appropriate linguistic patterns, as well as guided student rehearsal of ways of constructing aspects of such experience, was always a feature of the program. Sometimes this involved retelling familiar narratives that had been read to the children, while on other occasions it involved rehearsing the oral patterns by which people in selected roles negotiated joint understandings. In both types of activities teacher intervention to assist the children is essential. What is critical for such processes of modelling and guided repetition of linguistic patterns to occur is a great deal of sharing of the experiences on the part of the teacher and students. Gray (1990b) has recently discussed the critical issue of shared experience, around which teacher and students can together practise representation of experience.

Given that the principal justification of the morning news genre is that it allows children to select their own fields of experience for discussion, it will be clear that since the teacher has not been party to these fields, she is not able to enter into any joint construction or modelling of language with children experiencing difficulties. Thus the morning news genre, while certainly enjoyed by many children, does appear to benefit those children who are already advantaged. That is to say, it appears to benefit those whose prior life experience has caused them to learn how to select personal fields of the kind normally approved for morning news giving, and to select the appropriate language with which to reconstruct these fields.

To turn to the issue of the rehearsal of literacy in the morning news genre, many early childhood teachers involve their students in writing from fields of personal experience, and hence the texts rehearsed orally in the one curriculum genre often find expression in another, as the following early texts (spelling corrected) produced by Joseph and others in his class indicate:

Kevin likes jumping.
I went swimming with Mark.
We got a new video.

These are rudimentary versions of the observation genres discussed by Martin and Rothery (1980, 1981) in examining children's early writing development, and explored in some detail by Plum (1988) examining spoken discourse in the adult world.

Thus far this discussion has demonstrated, first, that the morning news genre is a curriculum genre, and that it has two registers, the pedagogical register to do with teacher structuring of the activity, and the content register to do with the actual morning news giving role. Second, it has established that ways of representing experience are rehearsed within morning news, although it would seem that the institution of morning news primarily rewards children already able to use language for such representation. Finally, it has established that patterns of early literacy are rehearsed in such curriculum genres, although this is not necessarily recognised to be the case. A more explicit sense on the part of teachers of the ways in which children learn to represent experience, whether in the oral or the written mode, would enable them more effectively to scaffold, negotiate and jointly construct texts with their students.

## The Writing Planning Genre

The schematic structure of an instance of the writing planning genre must have at least three obligatory stages, although several optional stages can also be found. The obligatory stages are all that will concern us here: the task orientation, the task specification, and the task. In the task orientation the teacher indicates the general purpose of the teaching-learning activity, and he or she (normally a woman in the junior primary school) moves the children on to talk of the content register about which they are to write. A brief convergence of the two registers occurs at the start of this stage, when the pedagogical register is prominent although the content register finds some expression. Then the teacher quickly moves into the 'body' of the task orientation, and the children explore aspects of the content register about which they are to write. The task orientation is normally the longest stage in the overall structure of the curriculum genre, and this is because teachers tend to devote most of their teaching activity to discussing the content.

Some sense of the content having been established, the object of the task specification stage is to define the actual task for writing. The two registers converge here as well, as there is talk about how to write about the content. However, the talk is often of a very general kind, so that the linguistic features of the genre the children are to write tend to remain not well developed in the talk. In the sample text to be examined below, a degree of advice about the writing task is offered, although its effect is not altogether helpful. In practice, since there is generally not much sustained talk about the task of writing in the task specification, the result is that the children are left to deduce what they can from the general context, much as they do in the morning news genre. Little explicit advice to do with the overall organisation of the genre for writing is made available.

The final stage of the writing planning genre is always the shortest, for it is in the task stage that the children are operationalised to write. In the early childhood classrooms I investigated, this meant that the children got up from the floor to return to their places. A change to the physical disposition of students very commonly marks the closure of one curriculum genre and the start of another. The example of a writing planning genre reproduced here had as its second order or content register a concern with the uniforms worn by people in different occupational groups. In fact, the uniforms used were worn by the parents of class members, although one was that of the husband of the teacher involved. The three uniforms examined were those of a naval policeman, a train driver and a nurse aide, sometimes also referred to as a nurse. The lesson constituted one in the integrated curriculum of the junior primary school, although the particular content register selected belonged most directly to the social science element of that curriculum. The choice of the content field in itself has some problems, and these are worthy of comment.

There is a very close relationship between the genres we write and the content fields about which we write. In other words, the connection between content fields and the genres we select to write about them is not an arbitrary one. A genre is always selected because it serves some social purpose we have with respect to the content field about which we write. Reports, for example, are selected in particular in the social and natural sciences, and they are used to build factual information about aspects of the world. Capacity to write a good report is dependent in part upon control of the schematic structure of the genre, but it is equally dependent upon control of the content field, so that the finished genre is a text of some substance. The processes of exploration of content fields for writing should normally take several lessons, as students become familiar with the information with which they can fashion the target genre. Accounts of desirable ways to build a strong sense of content fields as well as of the elements of a genre are given in the *Language a Resource for Meaning* series (Christie *et al.*, 1990a–j, 1992a–e).

As the opening of the text here makes clear, previous lessons have involved some discussion of the content field, although one is not left with a sense of cumulative growth established in the children. I would suggest this is because the study of uniforms is not in itself a fertile content field for study. The occupations of being a naval policeman, a train driver and a nurse aide would constitute rewarding fields to examine, very consistent with the general aims of social science programs. Furthermore, if these were dealt with, then the discussion of the uniforms worn by people within these occupations would constitute a small but useful aspect of the overall treatment of these fields. As it is, well intended though the teacher's directions may be, the discussion of the writing task within the task specification examined here does not develop capacities to write a coherent genre about a substantial field. A more explicit sense of the nature of different fields and their value, as well as of the relationship of these to particular genres, would equip the teacher to develop writing abilities in rewarding ways.

Only extracts from the text will be provided here. A row of dots indicates that portion of the text is removed. Some commentary on the text will be provided to demonstrate how a functional grammar can be used to unpack the nature and significance of the meanings being made in the text.

| **Task Orientation** | **Commentary** |
|---|---|
| *Teacher:*     **Now**, I want you to sit around me in a big circle so you <u>can</u> all <u>see</u> what we're <u>going to talk</u> about. [*The children all move into a horseshoe shaped group. As Teacher begins to talk, she spreads out before her a navy uniform with silver buttons,* | The pedagogical register is foregrounded as the teacher gets the activity going. She uses a cluster of continuatives (e.g., 'Now' in boldface) to point the children forward. She also uses a series of processes (underlined) to do with the children's behaviour, some of them mental (e.g., 'can see'), others behavioural (e.g., 'have written'), |

and white stripes on the arm. It is accompanied by a peaked cap, and it is in fact a uniform of the naval police.] **Right** this week we've had two different uniforms that we've written a report about. We had a visitor and we looked at what she wore.

Child: The crossing lady.

Teacher: **Yes** that's right. Yesterday we didn't have a person and we just talked about it. Who remembers?

Child: A policeman's uniform. [*There are several calls and a general movement among the children, as they are clearly interested.*]

Teacher: **Well** today I brought some special clothes in. Who knows who might wear them? Helen? [*No answer*]

David: A sailor.

Teacher: Today I've brought an old policeman's uniform. It's very dusty. It's a naval policeman's uniform.

Joseph: Was it your husband's?

Teacher: Yes. See, it's got big silver buttons, and this is where a big badge is worn, but there isn't a badge on it now, because it's been taken off.

Joseph: You wouldn't be allowed to go on a ship like that. [*He points to the absence of the badge*] Does it have those colours like yesterday?

Geoffrey: No . . . and it hasn't got that sort of elastic around the neck

others possessive (e.g., 'didn't have'), because she aims to direct the children's behaviour. The teacher talks more than the children in this opening part.

The principal participants referred to are the class members ('we') because it is their behaviour that is being made prominent. Prior learning experiences are alluded to, when aspects of the content register are constructed in such items as 'two different uniforms' and 'the crossing lady'.

The use of the continuative 'well' here helps signal a move to a new aspect of the content register — 'some special clothes'. From here on, it is the content register that is prominent. The principal participants referred to are now the uniform and/or its parts. Processes build features of the uniform, and are: attributive (e.g., 'it's a naval policeman's uniform'), or possessive (e.g., 'it's got big silver buttons'), or existential (e.g., 'there isn't a badge on it'). Occasionally a material process builds an aspect of what people can or can't do with the uniform (e.g., 'you wouldn't be allowed to go').

The children talk rather more than in the opening of the element, as they help construct aspects of the content register, hence exploring the content for eventual writing.

| | | |
|---|---|---|
| *Second child*: | You <u>look</u> like a train driver. | The teacher makes less use of continuatives because the opening is over and the content register is prominent. |
| *Teacher*: | [*She points to part of the sleeve*] what'<u>s</u> this written here? | |
| *Mandy*: | It's <u>got</u> buttons on the side of the hat. [*Great excitement*] | |
| *Teacher*: | **Now** [*turning to Jodie*] Jodie seems to have brought a uniform . . . no two uniforms. That's a good girl. Bring me that one first, Jodie. [*Jodie brings out a uniform of a train driver*] | The continuative 'now' signals a move to a new aspect of the content register, as a class member introduces two uniforms. Processes are: identifying ('that one's my dad's'), possessive ('it has a jacket'), attributive ('that's a special train uniform'), and sometimes material, e.g., ('takes you all over Australia'). |
| *Jodie*: | That one'<u>s</u> my dad's. | |
| *Teacher*: | See. It'<u>s</u> a V Line uniform from the train. | |
| *Jodie*: | It <u>has</u> a jacket. He <u>has</u> a blue overall and he <u>has</u> green pants and a jumper and a coat. That'<u>s</u> a special train uniform. | |
| *Joseph*: | <u>Takes</u> you all over Australia. | |
| *Teacher*: | There's a little badge. | |
| *Teacher*: | **Well** that's very good, Jodie. **Now** let's see the other uniform you've brought. <u>Is</u> that your mum's? | Two continuatives signal a move to a new aspect of the content register. Process types are again attributive (e.g., 'it's a nurse's aide uniform', or 'is your mum a nurse's aide?'), or material (e.g., 'where do you get a nurse's aide?'). |
| *Jodie*: | Yes. | |
| *Teacher*: | It'<u>s</u> a nurse's aide uniform. <u>Is</u> your mum a nurse's aide? | |
| *Jodie*: | Yes. | |
| *Teacher*: | Where <u>do</u> you get nurse's aides, Stacey? [<u>*No answer*</u>] Who knows? | |
| *Teacher*: | **Well, now**, on Monday and Tuesday we'<u>ve been writing</u> reports on different poeple's uniforms. **Now** today you <u>can choose</u> what you're <u>going to report</u> on. [*Here she turns to the board and writes in a list:* | The teacher indicates the opening of the new element of structure in several ways and once again the pedagogical register, to do with the pedagogical goals of the lesson, is foregrounded. Thus, she uses a cluster of continuatives ('well'), pointing directions; she identifies the class members again as main |

'Policeman'; 'Train driver'; 'Nurse'.] **Now** every single day when we've written a report we've answered three questions about what the person wears. [*Here she writes on the board 'What does a — wear?'*] The first question says 'What does a — wear?' And your answer begins. . . .?

*Elizabeth:* A uniform.

*Teacher:* **No**, it doesn't begin that way. That's not a sentence. Stacey?

*Stacey:* 'A nurse wears a uniform' [*Here T. writes on the board beneath the question: 'A nurse wears a uniform'*]

*Teacher:* **Yes**, that's right. That's a sentence.

*Teacher:* **Now** here's the second question: 'What does the uniform look like?' [*She writes this on the board*] **Now** on Monday and Tuesday we drew the uniforms.

*David:* We drew the uniforms [*overlaps Mrs P.*]

*Teacher:* **Yes**, David has been listening carefully. You can take the band off and hold the hat up. [*She motions to David, who stands up, comes to the front and picks up the peaked cap from the naval policeman's uniform.*] David is holding up the cap so you can see what it looks like if you want to draw it.

*Teacher:* Good, **now** here's the third question: 'Why do these people wear the uniform? [*She writes this on the board as she speaks.*]

participants ('we'); she uses processes which are to do with *the children's* behaviour, and what they are to do. These are mainly behavioural ('we've written a report'), but some are mental ('you can choose'). An occasional one is to do with the people who use the uniforms ('what the person wears').

At this point the two registers converge, as there is talk of 'how to write' (the pedagogical register) 'about the uniforms' (the content register). Some of the language, as in the case of the first question the teacher poses, is quite explicitly to do with writing (e.g., 'What does a — wear? And your answer begins. . . .?'), where an attempt to scaffold takes place. But this is not helpful, because, since its grammar is that of a spoken question, it invites a spoken answer ('a uniform'), rather than one drawing upon the grammar of the written mode. A second question intended to guide writing tends to dispose the children to draw, rather than to write, so that again, despite the apparent intention, little help in scaffolding an effective writing activity is provided. Material processes explicitly identify previous drawing activity ('we drew the uniforms'). The discourse moves back to further talk about the content register, so that there is no further explicit talk of the writing task in respect to the second question.

Another continuative ('now') indicates a move to a new question intended to guide writing, and an attributive process is used to help introduce it ('here's the third

|  |  |
|---|---|
| | Why do all these different people wear uniforms? What are the reasons? That's what you're going to have to write here. |
| *Joel:* | They're all the same. [*He means the reasons in each case are the same.*] |
| *Teacher:* | They're not all the same. You tell me why these people wear their uniforms, Jodie. [*This is a different girl called Jodie from the child who brought the nurse's aide's uniform. She does not answer the question.*] |
| *Teacher:* | Oh come on now, think about Jodie's mum who's the nurse's aide. If she didn't wear a uniform, would we know she was a nurse? |
| *Chorus:* | No. |
| *Teacher:* | Well what does she wear it for? |
| *Stacey:* | So we know who she is. |
| *Teacher:* | Yes and what else? What sorts of jobs does she have to do round the hospital? Does she have to clean the place? |
| *Teacher:* | **Now**, let's look at these questions. There are three questions, aren't there? See, they're numbered 1 to 3 on the board. When you write your answers to them are you going to write the numbers 1, 2 and 3? |
| *Chorus:* | No. |
| *Teacher:* | No, you're not. You just answer the questions. In the newspaper if you're reading something you don't see questions and numbers. Now your |

question'). An identifying process ('that's what you're going to have to write here') helps establish what is to be done as a writing task.

The talk soon turns once again to aspects of the content register. For example, processes are mainly material (e.g., 'why these people wear these uniforms'), but also mental ('think about Jodie's mum . . .), some are identifying ('Jodie's mum who's the nurse' aide'). There is no explicit language to do with the writing task.

A teacher continuative signals another move forward. An existential process is used to help bring together the information intended to guide writing ('there are three questions').

More behavioural processes identify behaviours for the children (you write your answers . . .; you're reading'; 'you're going to write') questions. An identifying process helps establish an aspect of the heading <u>could be</u> 'Nurse's Uniform', or 'Policeman's Uniform', or 'Traindriver's Uniform'. And your answers to the first question <u>are</u> all going to be the same. A nurse's uniform looks like this. [*She holds it up*] And you're going to write 'A nurse <u>wears</u> a uniform because . . .' and you give your reasons. Or you can say 'A train driver wears a uniform because. . . .' whatever your reasons are. Or you'<u>ll write</u> 'A policeman wears a uniform because . . .' and you'll say why. Stacey, spell 'because'.

*Stacey*: B- e -c -a- u- s- e.

*Teacher*: Right. Do I want to see anyone putting 'becos'? [*Writes this on the board*]

*Chorus*: No.

*Teacher*: If you're not sure, turn back to yesterday. Why do these people wear a uniform? A train driver wears a uniform because we know who he is. You can choose which uniform you like but don't forget there's a few pieces in them.

*Teacher*: **All right** now everybody start writing. And you <u>can do</u> a picture of the uniform <u>you choose</u> after you'<u>ve written</u> about it. [*The children get up off the floor and move back to their desks and start writing.*]

writing task ('your heading could be "Nurse's Uniform" . . .'). In these and other processes like them, the two registers converge, going to be the same is not even then, particularly directive of writing activity.

Explicit advice with respect to spelling of a word is provided.

A continuative signals the opening of the last element of structure. The pedagogical register is foregrounded in all the process choices ('start writing', 'can do', 'choose' and 'you've written'). The time for talk is over: hence the children take no active part in constructing the talk, and the content register finds very little expression in the language the teacher uses.

This commentary has served to indicate how the choices made in the language operate to build the meanings made in the text. In the task orientation the teacher initiates the task for writing, at which point the pedagogical register is foregrounded, and as she subsequently foregrounds the content register, so she involves the children in some discussion of the content about which they are to write. In the task specification the teacher again begins by foregrounding the pedagogical register, and subsequently some convergence of the two registers is effected, as she involves the children in talk about how to write on the content, albeit of a rather limited kind. Finally, in the task element the children are directed to commence their work. In this short discussion of what the commentary has revealed, I shall comment briefly on both the nature of the language used with respect to the content field and the language used to scaffold the task for writing.

I noted above that there is a very close relationship between the genres we write and the content fields about which we write. The relationship between the two is not arbitrary, and the genres we select are chosen because they serve important social purposes. The content field chosen for this lesson, I suggested, did not provide a substantial basis for the writing of any genre. The content field certainly has the real merit that it relates to the children's commonsense experience of the world, but it has the disadvantage that it does not permit development of new or uncommonsense understandings about that world. Discussion of the occupations of the people whose uniforms were displayed would have provided the capacity to build uncommonsense knowledge: the uniforms themselves do not provide enough. Consider the language used for dealing with the content field. A proportion of the process types used are material, and they build the activities engaged in by those who wear the uniforms, as in:

> you wouldn't be allowed to go on a ship like that
> (it) takes you all over Australia.

Most of the processes used are either attributive or possessive, and they build description of the uniforms, as the above commentary has already indicated. Attributive processes include:

> you look like a train driver
> it's a naval policeman's uniform
> it's a V Line uniform from the train
> that's a special train uniform
> it's a nurse's aid uniform,

while the possessive processes include:

> it's got big silver buttons
> it hasn't got that sort of elastic around the neck
> it has a jacket
> he has green pants and a jumper and a coat

There are also a few identifying processes, as in:

> that one's my dad's.

All these processes have a part to play in building the content field, although it is noticeable that none helps build any technical language. One measure of whether a content field of some substance is being constructed will be the presence of a technical language. A report about kangaroos, for example, would build its technical language, among other ways, through use of attributive processes, such as:

the kangaroo is a marsupial animal

One helpful way teachers can assess the significance of the content fields they select for teaching purposes will be through considering the kinds of technical language they involve. Assisting even quite young children to move from their commonsense understanding of the world towards some uncommonsense understandings is an important function of schooling, and development of control of a technical language will be a measure of control of such uncommonsense knowledge. Well intended though the choice of the content field was in this text, it is difficult to see that the children's exploration of it does lead to the development of uncommonsense knowledge.

With respect to the language used to scaffold the writing tasks, it will be apparent once more that the teacher's intention is good, as she does provide her three questions in order to direct the children's writing. But the grammar of the questions does not provide an appropriate scaffolding, as the above commentary made clear. Without a more adequate grasp of how language works, of the kind that only a functional grammar can provide, a teacher will always be disadvantaged in attempting to assist children learning to write. The three questions provided, as noted above, are questions of speech rather than of writing:

what does a — (i.e. naval policeman, train driver, nurse's aide) wear?
what does the uniform look like?
why do these people wear uniforms?

and the written texts they provoked demonstrate their limitations. Mandy, for example, (producing a picture of a policeman) remembered the teacher's advice to write a full sentence, so she did provide one in response to the first question, but she forgot with respect to the third question, which clearly disposed her to write as she did:

A policeman wears a uniform. A policeman wears a uniform that looks like this. So you no [know] what he is and what his job is.

Stacey wrote the following accompanied by a series of pictures, revealing that her answer to the third question also provoked her to write an incomplete sentence:

A nurse wears a uniform because she is a nurse. Because it is ese ease [easy] to wash every day.

A more complete text, consistent with what the teacher had asked for, was written by Jodie:

A train driver wears a uniform. A train driver uniform looks like this [pictures accompanying]. The train driver wears a uniform so you know that he is a train driver.

This has the merit that it stands as a coherent text, accompanying the information also contained in the pictures. Nonetheless, a consideration of Jodie's piece causes me to return to my observations concerning the relationship of genre and field. No substantial field is available to the child with which to write here, as I have noted. Equally, however, no very clear genre is apparent either.

The latter observation is not in itself a criticism of the teacher. Rather, it is a comment on the difficulties any teacher has in developing a writing lesson, unless he or she has an explicit sense of the manner in which language works to build both significant content fields about which to write and genres for writing about those fields. By way of suggesting what teachers can do when they have such a more explicit sense of how language works, I turn now to an example of a reasonably successful piece of writing from a group of children of the same age as those in the classroom text I have been examining.

### Generating a Successful Example of a Written Genre

Working with a class of young children, an early childhood teacher developed a major thematic unit of lessons on various occupations, including those of teachers, nurses, doctors and veterinarians. She chose these because she judged them to be examples of so-called 'caring professionals' of the kind the children could be expected to have encountered in their own lives. In this sense, the content field was a good choice because it built upon the children's own commonsense knowledge of the world. Equally, however, it permitted the building of much uncommonsense knowledge of the kind schooling is intended to provide.

After an initial lesson in which the general interest in the occupations was established, she proceeded to develop subsequent lessons which focused on the different occupations in some detail. An important part of building a knowledge of the content field in each case involved researching what could be discovered about each occupation, and here extensive use was made of the school library and its various books about the occupations. Selecting, reading and discussing the books took several lessons, for the teacher aimed to establish various uncommonsense understandings about the occupations before she involved the children in writing about them. For the most part, when the writing activities were commenced, the teacher jointly constructed a number of written genres with the children, as they were very young.

After several lessons in which medical doctors had been examined and written about, the teacher directed the children towards examination of veterinarians. One aspect of focusing upon the vet's functions and responsibilities was to compare and contrast these with those of the medical doctor. Eventually, after reading and discussing several books, the teacher and students jointly wrote the following report, having first discussed its various stages and their functions:

The Vet

The vet looks after all sorts of animals, including pets and wild animals like those in the zoo, circus and farm animals.

The vet makes sick animals better by giving them medicine, injections or pills. Sometimes he has to put them to sleep and operate on them. If the animals are too sick he gives them a needle which puts them to sleep and they die.

The vet wears a clean, white coat and when he operates he wears rubber gloves and boots and a mask over his face.

A vet uses the same sorts of things as a doctor. He has a stethoscope, an electric razor to shave the animals' fur, and X-ray machine to see whether the animals have broken any bones. He uses scissors and must wash them in very hot water to kill the germs. He uses tweezers too, and a needle and thread to make stitches.

The teacher and children planned that each paragraph should mark a new stage or element of schematic structure. Thus the first stage offers a generalisation, of a kind which classifies the occupation of being a vet, hence marking it out as different from other occupations. This is built through some important linguistic choices. First, an opening topical theme ('the vet') serves to mark the topic of the first element of the genre. Second, there are two process choices of importance: the vet 'looks after' animals 'including' the various ones listed. The first of these, a material process, tells us what the vet does, while the second, an identifying process, helps to establish the animals with which he deals. Thus is provided crucially important information about what a vet does. The subsequent elements all build description of different aspects of the vet's behaviour, in the first case to do with treatment of animals, in the second case to do with what the vet wears and in the final case to do with the implements used by the vet.

Each element of description is built differently, although it is notable that the same topical theme as appeared in the opening generalisation (with one small variation in the use of 'a' rather than 'the' in the last case) reappears as part of opening each of the subsequent elements:

*The vet* makes sick animals better . . .
*The vet* wears a clean white coat . . .
*A vet* uses the same sorts of things. . . .

It is a very characteristic feature of report genres to have the phenomenon being reported on reappear in topical theme position throughout the text. This is one of the main means by which such a text is carried forward. Ability to produce such topical theme choices in this patterned way needs to be modelled by the teacher. (Contrast the kinds of questions used by the teacher above in the classroom text, and it will be clear that these do not help children select the appropriate topical theme choices to develop a sustained report genre.)

In the second element of structure, to do with description of treatment of animals, the first process is attributive, telling how animals are when vets look after them ('the vet makes animals better'). One other process is attributive, also building description ('if the animals are too sick'), while the remaining ones are material, building what the vet does, such as 'he has to put them to sleep', or 'he gives them a needle'.

The third element of structure, dealing with description of the vet's clothes, is built through use of three material process ('wear' used twice and 'he operates'). Placed within the overall structure of this report genre, it is notable that such descriptive information about the clothing a vet wears is relevant to building up the content field about the occupation here. This makes an interesting contrast with the earlier text discussed in the classroom, where the clothing associated with occupations became the major focus of attention, and where, as we saw, this offered a rather 'thin' content for discussion or for writing.

To turn to the last element of structure, dealing with the implements associated with a vet, the process types are mainly material, and one of them ('use') is actually employed three times. Other examples include 'to shave' or 'wash'. One possessive process tells us that 'the vet has a stethoscope'. In the main, however, the process types here build what the vet does with the various implements.

In general, as this short analysis has served to demonstrate, the language has been used confidently to build the various stages of schematic structure, and hence to serve the overall function of reporting on the responsibilities of the occupational group known as veterinarians. It is noteworthy, in addition, that in the process of making the linguistic choices a number of other associated choices have also been made, helping to build a specialist language to do with the practices of vets. Consider, for example, the ways in which the following items, relevant to the field of being a vet, have been used throughout the text: 'medicine', 'injections', 'stethoscope', 'electric razor', 'X-ray machine', 'scissors', 'germs', 'tweezers', 'needle and thread' and 'stitches'. The twin demands of researching the field and of writing such a genre about the field required that the children learn to handle quite an elaborate specialist language.

It was considerably to the teacher's credit that she had guided the children into making intelligent and well controlled use of language both for the overall building of the various stages of schematic structure and for the satisfactory use of the relevant specialist language within that genre. She was enabled to do so, it should be stated, because she was one of the growing number of teachers who work with a strong sense of a functional grammar of the English language, enabling her to direct and focus their own curriculum planning, and hence to direct the language learning activities in which their students engage.

## Conclusion

I began this chapter by referring to the time-honoured manner in which student teachers and teachers alike are asked both to plan lessons and to keep records of their plans. The practice of keeping such plans, I stated, was evidence that teachers are encouraged to see their teaching activities as purposive. I suggested, however, that a great deal of curriculum planning was not necessarily informed by the particular insights gained by viewing lessons as instances of curriculum genres:

staged, purposive activities, realised in language. That is because, I suggested, as in so many other activities realised in language, the role of language in teaching and learning is often only partially understood. In fact, what children in schools are enabled to do in using language is very much a condition of what they have been enabled to learn to do. The latter observation may seem self-evident, but like so many other statements about language, it is not particularly well understood, nor are its implications for teaching practice always made clear. There is a very intimate relationship between the ways children use language to structure experience and the kinds of linguistic patterns their life experiences have taught them to use. In differing ways, the analyses of both the instance of the morning news genre and the writing planning genre have demonstrated a close relationship between what the children involved did in language and the linguistic demands of the curriculum genre involved in each case.

Where teachers have a sense of the manner in which meanings are actually constructed in language, of a kind that a functional grammar can afford, they are enabled to focus their teaching activities in a manner which will allow children to become effective learners of oral language and literacy. Thus the analysis of the written report on veterinarians, and the account of how this was generated, served to suggest both why this was a successful example of a written report for the early primary school, and also something of the kinds of curriculum planning decisions teachers might well make in order to become truly effective teachers.

*Chapter 8*

# Genre in Practice

*Mike Callaghan, Peter Knapp and Greg Noble*

*In this chapter Callaghan, Knapp and Noble discuss genre literacy in practice by detailing their experience while working on the Language and Social Power Project — one of the most important sites where genre as a theory of language was translated into genre literacy as an approach to teaching writing in schools. During this project, carried out for the Disadvantaged Schools Program (DSP) in the Metropolitan East Region (in Sydney) of the New South Wales Department of School Education, Callaghan, as a curriculum consultant seconded to the DSP from his position as a secondary school teacher, was a critical person in introducing genre literacy to the DSP. Peter Knapp later joined the DSP and together Callaghan and Knapp coordinated the production of the pathbreaking 'Language and Social Power' materials. The context in which this project took place is explained in the Bibliographical Essay which concludes this book.*

*Callaghan, Knapp and Noble begin with an outline of the teaching-learning curriculum cycle, which has already been touched on in the Introduction to this book. This was the first attempt to translate genre theory into a pedagogical practice. An example of the way the cycle worked in practice is then given, in the form of a lesson on the greenhouse effect. This is followed by a critical review of some of the difficulties they encountered while trialling this approach.*

*Callaghan, Knapp and Noble go on to suggest an alternative approach to genre which they feel overcomes some of the perceived difficulties in the curriculum cycle. This approach builds on the work of Gunther Kress in the area of social semiotics. As already discussed in the Introduction, this view of genres gives most weight to the position as social processes, rather than concentrate on them as textual products. Finally, this view of genre is further exemplified through a case study of a lesson on packaging.*

### Introduction

In this chapter we deal with some of the issues surrounding two quite different approaches to teaching practice based on genre theory. The first was pioneered by the Metropolitan East Disadvantaged Schools Program's Language and Social Power Project and since has become known as the curriculum cycle or the 'wheel'. The second approach is a response to the problems encountered with the 'wheel' model — particularly as experienced in high schools — and reflects another view of genre theory.

The different approaches to teaching-learning proposed here, of course, share some common beliefs. First, they attempt to deal with some of the limitations of Piagetian-based notions of language development. The argument is not so much against Piaget's ideas of cognitive and language development but that interpretations of these ideas have resulted in what could be termed passive pedagogies — teachers are encouraged to wait for the learning to develop; intervention is seen as unnatural; and subsequently interventionist teaching strategies have been viewed with a great deal of suspicion. Structure and grammar, if not seen as dangerous, are at the very least treated with utmost caution. In contrast to traditional grammar, with its emphasis on the rote learning of fixed rules, genre theory stresses the social context and communicative role of language. In contrast to the 'process' learning model (where language is seen to be learnt naturally, almost by osmosis, given the right experience), genre theory emphasises the social structures that in turn structure language use. Genre theory transfers this idea to the teaching of language. Both these insights — the social purpose of language and the structured nature of language learning — have led to the formulation of the different teaching-learning approaches which embody a view of how language can be taught both effectively and efficiently in the classroom.

This chapter is divided into four parts. First, we present an outline of the curriculum cycle as it was originally developed by Martin and Rothery. Second, we work through a particular sequence of lessons which were used to translate the cycle into a practical teaching strategy and trialled through the Language and Social Power Project for the Metropolitan East Region Disadvantaged Schools Program (DSP) and the LERN Project (a project carried out by the Literacy and Education Research Network for the Studies Directorate of the NSW Department of School Education) in a number of primary and secondary schools. Third, we offer a critique of this teaching-learning model, looking at the problems observed during its translation into classroom practice; and fourth, we propose a new working model that attempts to overcome some of these problems. It must be stressed, however, that genre theory is not a 'finished' approach but is developing all the time. For this reason, it is only by engaging in re-evaluation that we can identify problems and begin to offer solutions. This chapter must be read as part of this spirit of development and enquiry.

## The Curriculum Cycle or 'Wheel'

Despite the apparent natural progression of a child's language acquisition, this model assumes that, at the very least, there is an equal input from the social in this process. Adults play a crucial role in providing language models for children, in helping to teach language through asking questions, restating phrases and so on. It is a social, interactive process, such that language development is best described as active construction, not passive acquisition. The role of the adult in offering models, and guiding in the construction of texts with children, has been taken by genre theorists to be the pattern through which language learning can be achieved in schools.

The Martin/Rothery curriculum cycle attempts to engage students in an awareness of the social purposes, text structure and language features in a range of identified text types or genres. Paralleling the insights into early language development, the cycle involves phases of modelling, joint negotiation and independent construction. The rationale for this pedagogy is based upon studies of parent-child language interactions, which show that rather than language acquisition being a 'natural' process of osmosis, it is really highly interventionist. When we think about the proportion of teachers who are also parents, it is difficult to understand how it could ever have been thought to be otherwise. Parents, of course, have an enormous advantage over teachers in terms of teaching language — that is the factor of time. Teachers have only a small fraction of the time for individual language interaction that parents have. For this reason, teaching strategies in the classroom must be far more explicit and efficient than what happens in the home environment.

It was always the intention that the cycle be a guide to developing a sequence of lessons rather than a fixed procedure. This enables entry into the cycle at any point, depending largely on the language competence of the students in relation to the language activity being taught. This requires that teachers be clear about the reasons they are in any one stage at any particular time. It also requires that teachers be precise with their students with both the stage and outcomes of each classroom activity. In other words, we would argue that teachers do not have the luxury of sufficient time to be able to give vague directions such as 'go and write a story about such and such' and then sit back and see what happens. The more clearly defined each language activity, the more specific each of the learning outcomes for the activity can be. Because writing is such an important part of the education process, it simply cannot be left to 'hit and miss' strategies. One of the fundamental aims of this curriculum cycle, therefore, was to specify what some of the stages in an effective and efficient writing program might be, and beyond this, how they might be managed with large and small groups of students.

The first stage of the curriculum cycle is 'modelling'. A key insight of genre theory is that language occurs in a social context and that it is structured according to the purposes it serves in a particular context and according to the social relations entailed by that activity. This is important because the notion of genre is sometimes misrecognised as a basis for arbitrary impositions on childhood creativity. It is not linguists or teachers, however, but the social context which 'imposes' certain requirements. Therefore, it is necessary for students to understand the context of a given interaction in order to understand the purpose of a genre. The context, therefore, can be specific to either an educational setting or subject (such as the scientific ways of describing animals, for example), or a wider social activity (such as newspaper articles, procedures for recipes, discussions among friends). Social context is one possible starting point when teaching students a new genre. A number of model texts can be used to draw out the significant features of the genre: those things which make a report a report, or a discussion a discussion and not a procedure. In the modelling stage, the social purpose, text structure and language features of the genre are investigated.

At the second stage of the curriculum cycle, 'joint negotiation' of a text, students (usually as a class or group) begin writing in generic text types. This involves a period of preparation with the close guidance of the teacher, who provides support and 'scaffolding'. During the process of preparation, students gather and organise the information to be used in writing a text. This may involve a number of individual and group activities such as research and discussion. Teachers necessarily use those activities best suited to the demands of the students and the genre.

The teacher then acts as a scribe for the class and helps turn student ideas into an approximation of the genre. This joint negotiation of a text will depend largely on the level of competence of the students given the degree of technical language and knowledge of the field. The concept of 'approximation', therefore, is essential to the cycle because of the aim of students having increasing control over the genre and its language features. In other words, the degree of approximation will depend on the familiarity of the genre and the language development of students. As students become more confident and familiar with the genre, there will be less need for teacher assistance and negotiation. This phase also helps link spoken and written language. This is achieved by the teacher acting as the scribe and moving through each of the generic stages with the students and negotiating with the students the appropriate information for the given stage. The teacher's role is to take the students' spoken language and, through careful negotiation, transform the speech into writing. At this point it is useful for teachers to review progress made before proceeding to independent construction. If the class did not handle the stage well, it would be worthwhile to return to the modelling phase and examine further model texts and then engage in more joint construction.

'Independent construction' of a text by students, the third stage in the curriculum cycle, involves a number of steps: from preparation through drafting, conferencing, editing and evaluating; to the creative manipulation of the genre and its possible uses. Without the previous stages, expectations that students can write will only be met by those students with substantial language resources already at hand. For students with limited control over written language, explicit guidance in understanding purpose, schematic structure and the language features of a genre is needed before they can launch into independent construction. Because these issues have been covered in earlier stages, students and teachers will have a shared language and knowledge with which to discuss the problems encountered in independent construction. It is also useful in this stage for teachers to implement activities which aim to expand field or content knowledge and knowledge of language features or grammar. It is important for teachers to evaluate the success of each step and stage, but it is particularly important to set up procedures during independent construction to assess students' control of the genre and the success of the whole learning cycle, in order to indicate where the class needs to move next.

A worthwhile final step is to have students explore the possibilities of the genre by working creatively within and beyond it. This is important not only because creativity is in itself a useful and necessary part of learning, but because it allows students to see how aspects of a genre, and their modification, affect the process of communication.

Of course, the curriculum cycle is not a fixed, lock-step procedure. It allows teachers room to move with the space to develop activities and enter the cycle in a way that best meets students' needs. It is possible to return to any stage where necessary and to spend as much time as is needed on each step. For example, it is possible to construct a number of texts jointly before initiating independent construction, or to return to the modelling phase at frequent intervals, or to have students work in small groups jointly constructing texts before writing on their own.

## The Curriculum Cycle in Practice

The following series of lessons based on this cycle was designed for a Year 8 science class. The class was completing a unit on the greenhouse effect, which provided the basis for work on the genre of explanation.

The aims of this unit were for students:

to develop an understanding of the greenhouse effect — its causes, consequences and possible solutions;

to develop an understanding of ozone layer depletion;

to develop an understanding of the interdependence of plants, animals and the environment;

to develop an understanding of the role of science in the decision-making process regarding the greenhouse effect;

to develop an understanding of the role they can play in the decision-making process about the environment;

to develop an understanding of the way scientists use language to explain natural phenomena; and, finally,

to demonstrate an understanding of the social purpose, generic structure and linguistic features of the explanation genre by writing an explanation in small groups.

*Session 1: Modelling the Social Purpose of the Explanation Genre*

The teacher introduced the unit by outlining the goals listed above. The following topics were set and it was explained that the students were to establish small groups and at the end of the unit each group would have to produce a text on their chosen topic as part of their assessment.

Topics offered:

Explain how a gardener's greenhouse works.

Explain how a hydroelectric power station generates electricity.

Explain how a coal fired power station generates electricity.

Explain how a nuclear power station generates electricity.

Explain how plants contribute to the greenhouse effect.

Explain the process of photosynthesis.

Explain how people contribute to the greenhouse effect.

Explain what happens when people breathe.

Explain what happens to life in the ocean when its temperature rises.

Explain what happens to the climate when the atmosphere warms up.

Explain how the coastline will be affected if the earth warms up.

Explain how recycling helps reduce the greenhouse effect.

The teacher led a class discussion based on the students' commonsense understandings of the greenhouse effect — its causes and effects and whether it was a reality or simply a media 'beat-up'. They also discussed what could be done to control the greenhouse effect; on a personal level and indeed if it was the responsibility of individuals at all or rather the responsibility of large corporations and governments as perhaps they were most responsible for causing the global warming.

From the points the teacher recorded during the discussion, an assessment of the students' level of understanding of the greenhouse effect was made. The lesson concluded with the class deciding to hold a role play to explore the issues from a range of perspectives. The students were to research the topic by collecting newspaper clippings and watching the news to gather information on greenhouse and global warming.

### *Session 2: Modelling the Text*

This lesson was devoted to a follow-up of the previous lesson with the class group pooling the data they had collected and establishing a data bank. By way of summary, the teacher introduced the concept of scientific language to explain natural phenomena. She briefly talked about the explanation genre and how it was commonly used in science. She then read the following text as a model, pointing out that it was an example of the explanation genre.

The Greenhouse Effect

Heat energy from the Sun warms the Earth. As this energy reaches the Earth's atmosphere, most of it is reflected back to space, a small amount is absorbed, while the rest reaches the Earth. Some of this heat energy is absorbed to warm up its surface and the rest is reflected back into the atmosphere.

When the heat is reflected back from the Earth's surface a lot of this energy is absorbed by the gases in the atmosphere. This helps keep the planet warm.

The Earth's atmosphere acts like a blanket of insulation allowing sunlight through to heat the Earth, while trapping the warmth that radiates back to space. In this way the atmosphere works like a greenhouse — except a greenhouse uses glass or perspex instead of gas — and that is why it is called the greenhouse effect.

The greenhouse gases in the atmosphere help maintain the right temperature on Earth to sustain life. When too many of these gases are present in the atmosphere, too much heat energy is trapped, causing the Earth's temperature to rise. Air pollution produces an increase in the quantity of the greenhouse gases in the atmosphere which causes the earth to overheat.

### *Session 3: Building Up Field Knowledge*

This session was a double period practical lesson where the class used several aquaria to build model greenhouses in which to conduct experiments taking temperature readings both inside and outside the greenhouses. They then conducted a simple experiment to demonstrate that during photosynthesis plants give off water vapour and carbon dioxide.

### Session 4: Writing Up Students' Experiments

In this lesson the students wrote up their experiments. The teacher had previously taught the students how to write a lab report and so she had only to provide the following scaffold:

Aim: Write a short sentence to show what we were trying to find out in the experiment. Start with the word To. . . .

Method: Write the steps you followed in the experiment. Begin each step with the action word that tells the reader what to do and remember to write it in the present tense. Don't forget to number the steps.

Result: Write and tell the reader what happened. In here you can include a table of figures to show the results and then write a sentence summarising the results.

Conclusion: Write down some general statements to show what you discovered by doing the experiment.

### Session 5: Modelling the Generic Structure

This lesson began with the teacher revising the concept of social context — that is, when people write, they do so with a particular purpose and audience in mind and this influences the structure of the language used. She explained how the purpose shapes the overall text by revising the concept of beginning, middle and end structure. Using an annotated copy of the greenhouse text, she pointed out the generic structure of the explanation. She then asked the following questions:

Why would someone write this?

What occupation do you think would require a person to write this type of writing?

Where is the reader told what this text is about?

Where is the reader told what happens to the Sun's energy when it reaches the Earth's atmosphere?

What part of the text tells the reader what happens to the Sun's heat energy once it is reflected back from the Earth's surface?

Who can read out the words that tell the reader the actions that are going on?

Can you see how these words divide the text up into the steps of the Greenhouse Effect? Who can tell us what these steps are?

Are there any other words that tell the reader that the process is moving from one stage to another?

The teacher explained the concept of an implication sequence. She showed how in some processes one action leads to another and so on till a final state or stage is reached. She then told the students that this type of sequence is characteristic of scientific explanations. This was exemplified with reference to a number of processes, and the following general principle was used to reinforce the point. An implication sequence can be expressed as: if step 1, then step 2; if steps 1 and 2, then step 3; if steps 1, 2 and 3, then step 4; and so on. The class then matched this principle to the processes involved in global warming and was asked to outline the various steps involved. The class was then given a number of texts. In small groups, they had to decide which were explanations and which were not, justifying their choices with reference to the purpose of the text and any other criteria they felt were relevant.

*Session 6: More Analysis of the Explanation Genre*

In this session students completed a stencil using the information provided in the greenhouse text. The lesson was designed to reinforce the generic structure of the explanation genre.

Greenhouse Effect

Heat energy travels from sun
Reaches Earth's atmosphere

| | | |
|---|---|---|
| Reflected | Absorbed | Passes through |
| Absorbed by | Reflected back | |
| Earth's surface | into atmosphere | |

Absorbed by greenhouse gases and warms atmosphere

*Session 7: Building Up More Field Knowledge*

The students studied diagrams of the carbon and nutrient cycles to develop their understanding of the greenhouse effect. They were given a table to complete for homework.

Causes of Greenhouse Effect

Gases released by

Grazing animals
Burning of fossil fuels
Decomposing organic material
Air conditioners and refrigerators
Forest fires
Foam plastics
Thermal power stations
Breathing
Chlorinated swimming pools
Population increase
CFC propellants

*Session 8: Preparation for the Joint Construction*

This session began with the teacher explaining that the class was to research information about the ozone layer depletion for the purpose of writing a text about it. The class was divided into groups to research different aspects of this issue. The teacher then conducted a lesson on skim reading and note taking. She focused on the function of:

a table of contents;
an index;
chapter headings and subheadings;
topic sentences and paragraphing; and
diagrams and tables.

The class then went to the library with a series of questions to answer.

*Session 9: More Field Knowledge*

During this session the class continued their research in the school library.

*Session 10: Towards a Joint Construction*

The teacher used this session to collate the information the students had gathered. She then led the class in planning the stages of the text they were going to write. They decided on the following stages:

What is ozone?
What is the ozone layer?
Who discovered the hole in the ozone layer?
What is causing ozone layer depletion?
What are the effects of ozone layer depletion?
How does ozone layer depletion contribute to the greenhouse effect?
How are people trying to repair the damage to the ozone layer?

The teacher and class then decided which information would fit under each heading.

*Session 11: The Joint Construction of an Explanation*

During this lesson the teacher acted as scribe and the class and teacher jointly wrote their text about ozone layer depletion.

*Session 12: More Work on Field*

This lesson was devoted to research in the library where the students searched for information for their independent topics.

### Session 13: Deconstructing Explanations

The teacher used this session to focus on some of the grammatical features of the explanation genre. She began by talking about different types of words. Using the text that the class had jointly written, she drew attention to the process words, explaining that the actual scientific process is realised through these words in explanations. The class did some cooperative cloze exercises using a number of explanations to focus on the process types. Here the students were able to see how some of the process words signalled that the genre was moving to another stage.

### Session 14: More Work on Field

This session was a double period practical lesson and the class performed a number of experiments to examine a number of questions:

What will happen to the oceans if the Earth warms?
What will happen to the climate if the atmosphere warms?
What will happen to plants if there is an increase in carbon dioxide and the atmosphere warms up?
How does plant life in the oceans influence the greenhouse effect?

These experiments were performed in small groups and at the end of the session those groups which had obtained results explained their experiments to the rest of the class and shared their results. The others simply explained what their experiments were designed to discover.

### Session 15: The Experiment Results

The students used this session to write up the results of their experiments and those who did not obtain results in the last session reported on the results of their experiments.

### Session 16: More Modelling

In this session the teacher modelled the function of conjunction in explanations as further preparation for the students to write their own texts.

### Session 17: Individual Construction

In this session the students were given time to write their own explanation in groups and the teacher provided assistance to individual groups.

### Session 18: Reflecting on the Social Purpose of the Genre

The final session of this unit was devoted to critically analysing the field and the genre. The teacher led a class discussion where the students discussed the following issues:

What is the evidence to suggest that the globe is actually warming? Is this evidence sufficient or are certain scientists and lobby groups using limited local variations in climate to argue a case for their own political ends?

Is the fact that Sydney's climate has undergone some extremes over the last three years sufficient evidence to support the notion of a greenhouse effect?

Is the explanation genre a suitable way to explain natural phenomena or would it be better to adopt another genre — for example, a narrative similar to the traditional aboriginal dreamtime stories?

Does the way the explanation genre presents information give the scientific knowledge more credence than it deserves?

## Reviewing the Curriculum Cycle: A Critique

Despite a number of minor problems of organisation and detail, this sequence of lessons proved to be successful and worthwhile. However, we can use this unit to highlight some of the broader problems sometimes raised in the genre approach and its attendant teaching-learning cycle — problems which need to be addressed to ensure the ongoing development of this approach and its usefulness and practicality in the classroom. These problems range from the limitations of the conceptual model to the practical issues of turning good ideas into good practice.

The first and most general problem is the conceptualisation of the curriculum genre as a cycle. This has been recognised by many people who have worked with genre for some time, and some have been trying to move towards a conceptualisation of the model in terms of a helix — a three-dimensional spiral. There is some concern, however, that while a three-dimensional spiral may be theoretically pleasing, its complexity might be of little benefit to teachers, who basically want a simple, workable model. Within the one genre, students can work through the sequence of the curriculum genre a number of times to gain ever greater control of the genre, to explore increasingly complex language features, and to explore increasingly complex field issues or more sophisticated content. We see some evidence of this in the unit on the greenhouse effect, where passing reference to 'present tense', 'topic sentences' and 'beginning, middle and end structure' points to previous work. The degrees of complexity within singular genres and their requisite language features, however, may not be sufficient to cover all the knowledge demands of the unit content. In other words, in the above unit is a pedagogy that attempts to funnel all the relevant content through the explanation text type really the best one?

This raises an important issue in relation to the product or text type orientation of genre being promoted in this teaching-learning cycle. This unit appears to to be focused on the production of the text type or genre of explanation on the one hand, and the coverage of a diverse amount of content on the other. Unfortunately, the unit at times seems almost to be at cross-purposes as the content in places tends to work against the genre and vice versa. In many ways this particular unit is typical (in the complexity of content) of many junior secondary curriculum areas. As teachers are expected to cover an enormous amount of content, it would seem, therefore, that what is required is a teaching-learning model that will, at the very least, not make this task any harder.

The question is whether a product-based orientation to genre is the most productive way to go in covering the complexity of the content. If we were to shift our orientation to genre away from product, would the concept of genre still work? Besides these issues of genre and content, there are other issues of pedagogy that concern us with this particular model. The curriculum cycle borrows heavily from insights into early child development. It is best seen as a crucial sequence of stages which embody aspects of the learning process, but without filling in the detail of how learning actually occurs in the classroom. In this sense it is a 'behaviourist' model, centred on a series of activities. It lacks any specificity in the cognitive dimension. In saying this, we are not attempting to make a dichotomy of behaviour and cognition. However, a basically behavioural model of language teaching-learning such as this needs to make explicit connections between, for example, the level of language abstraction being taught on the one hand, and the cognitive development of the students on the other. Beyond this it needs to make explicit to teachers the connections between the language-based behaviours of the 'staged' activities and the cognitive processes involved in the students making the language their own.

This is not simply a theoretical issue: it is expressed most fundamentally by those teachers who say they understand what the cycle means but are not quite sure how to translate it into a series of lessons. The outline for the unit on the greenhouse effect, for example, structures individual lessons in an often glib way. The teacher had to help the class 'to develop an understanding of the role of science in the decision-making process regarding the greenhouse effect', or 'The students studied diagrams of the carbon and nutrient cycles to develop their understanding of the greenhouse effect', or even 'The class then went to the library with a series of questions to answer', does not give a practical directive. As most teachers will know, such directions do not constitute a clear outline of how the lesson is to operate. Similarly, a list of questions, as in sessions 5, 10 and 18, does not represent a lesson plan. As usual, the task of turning useful insights into useful lessons is left to the teacher — rather unfairly, given the demands on teachers who may have no language training in any case.

Classroom practice and curriculum work best when informed by a clearly defined pedagogy. Such a pedagogy could involve a structured sequence of input, analysis, generalisation and reflection, progressing from the particular to the general, the concrete to the abstract, and back again. The Social Literacy Project has worked with this sequencing in relation to developing a concept-based social science program (Kalantzis and Cope, 1988). It allows the progressive grasp of complex concepts on the basis of more specific and simpler concepts, not in a lock-step fashion but founded on the insight that conceptual and linguistic development is cumulative. It also has the aim of making sense of a complex social world. Both these themes — social context and development as cumulative — are shared by the genre approach.

The cycle also appears to make some simplistic assumptions about language learning. While there is a quite correct assumption that children learn to speak through interaction with, and intervention by, adult carers, this assumption has been quite unproblematically transferred to the joint negotiation stage of the model where the teacher is instructed to shift students' language from speech to writing. The problem here is that speech and writing are quite different and separate modes, and writing is not speech transcribed. Students are simply being told that we speak one way but write another and then the teacher writes it down for the students. This is not a pedagogy, it is a demonstration to students in how to write correctly. Texts from whole classes of students who 'independently produced' their texts after having participated in the practice of 'teacher scribing' often show a monotonous similarity to their 'individual' writing. In other words this practice of 'teacher scribing' has the potential of being a very efficient model of 'reproduction' pedagogy.

As a large part of the 'wheel' approach has been derived from early work carried out in a middle-class school with the majority of students from English-speaking backgrounds, it is not surprising that the joint negotiation teaching strategy proved succesful. The students' family and school backgrounds provided an environment where negotiated learning was the norm. This strategy, however, did not directly translate into the classrooms of working-class and NESB students where genre-based approaches were being implemented. In these classrooms many of the students come from backgrounds where learning and meaning are not necessarily a matter for negotiation.

Another problem, this time identified by teachers after trialling the LERN Project, was the seeming lack of distinction between concrete and abstract knowledge. Early writers were learning to write the report genre, but rather than starting with descriptions of their concrete world of experience, they were starting with the abstract world of science and, for example, writing reports on abstract/scientific classes of things. The following quote from one of the teachers from the LERN Project explains further ramifications of this problem. Her Year 5 class, after successfully writing a report on whales, attempted to transcribe those language skills onto an abstraction of that knowledge.

> But then when I went a bit further and we did Whaling, it just blew out because 'what's the Classification of whaling?' They just went on to do something completely different. To see if they could deliver a whole lot of information, we went right into the background of whaling. But you couldn't use the Classification of appearance, behaviour, etc. in the same way as with whales: it just doesn't fit. So it's a limited framework I think. They kept saying 'what's the appearance of whaling?' (Macken *et al.*, 1989d, 52)

The difficulty here is that students were now attempting to write a report on the process of killing whales for various types of industrial and human consumption. Here all of the processes (or verbs) of the human activity of killing whales are transformed into a thing (or noun) called whaling. This teacher was able to point out a key issue in the language/knowledge problem that had previously been completely overlooked, and it is this issue that typifies our problem with genre as text-type or product.

For these reasons, although remaining convinced that many aspects of the genre-based approach were indeed valuable and useful for teachers, we believe that more work is required for it to fulfil its promise. Briefly, the problems can be defined as the following questions:

Is a product-based orientation to genre productive from a pedagogical perspective?
Is the 'curriculum genre' a pedagogy or a flexible set of teaching instructions?

Is the joint negotiation stage (teacher scribing) good teaching practice?

What is the relationship of knowledge/grammar/text?

Is the pedagogical aim to reproduce genres or to understand and control the above relationship of knowledge/grammar/text?

Finally, how can the process of reading/writing be explicitly connected to achieve the above aim?

## A New Model for Teaching-Learning Experiences

As a result of the above problems, we devised a model that attempted to address some of the key questions. The first to be addressed were the concerns with a product-based orientation to genre; here we changed the orientation from product to process — that is, genres as social processes (see Figure 1).

We have seen how a genre-based approach to language is a social account of language use. Genres are the ways that we get particular things done through language — the ways we exchange information and knowledge and interact socially. All cultures engage in language exchange but have particular ways or forms for performing each exchange. Genres are a useful way of categorising the social processes that are realised through the use of language. From a teaching-learning perspective, therefore, it is productive to work with genre as a process that leads to a product or text type. Genres reflect the relative stability of the ways that we socially interact. As a result of this, the text types that are necessary for students to learn can be identified as report, exposition, explanation, debate and so on.

The approach to genre being suggested in this new model broadens the application of the commonly used concept of genre. For example, in film and media studies it is used to categorise text types by their conventional characteristics (soap opera, horror, science fiction and the like). Similarly, in literature studies genres represent conventional text types (for example, romance, short story, novella and biography). It also argues for a more flexible concept that views genre not as an end product, but as the process that produces text types — a dynamic interaction of social participants and appropriate generic resources. This approach enables the teaching-learning of language to be a dynamic social process that encourages the development of creative and independent writers. Rather than thinking of genres as things to be replicated, such as reports, procedures and discussions, they become processes to be thought through, for example, describing, explaining and arguing.

This distinction is important because teaching genres as processes rather than products enables the genres to be applicable to all text types written by students from infants to senior secondary school. That is, the generic features (grammar and structure) of the genre of describing, for example, remain consistent for all writers, from the experiential-based descriptions of early writers to the scientific descriptions of senior secondary students. This enables a developmental approach to teaching where writers are building on and developing from what they already know about each of the genres. Teaching aspects of genres, such as structure and grammar, becomes more a part of the process of writers realising the generic purpose of their texts, rather than being fragmented and 'rule-governed'. This enables the teaching of grammar to be a basic part of teaching programs for early writers onwards. While text types can be relatively simple and straightforward in

Figure 1.   A Model for a Process-based Orientation to Genre

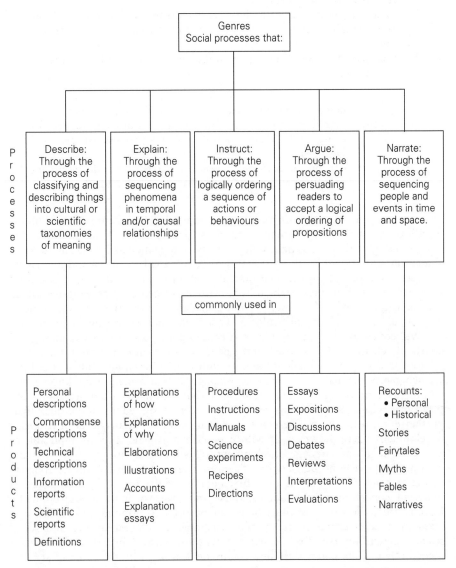

primary school, in secondary school students are expected to produce 'multigeneric' texts.

For example, consider the following three Higher School Certificate questions and notice the genres students are being asked to use in each of the questions.

1   Why does the government protect Australian industries from overseas competition? What methods are used to provide this protection? What

is the likely impact on the economy of a reduction in protection for Australia's manufacturing industries?

2   What is economic growth? How is it measured? How can Australia achieve higher rates of economic growth? What are the costs and benefits of economic growth?

3   What part does weathering play in the development of landforms? In your answer

   (i)    define the terms chemical and physical weathering;
   (ii)   describe ONE example of the process of chemical weathering and ONE example of the process of physical weathering;
   (iii)  explain the part weathering has played in the development of TWO landforms in an area you have studied.

The first two questions, from an economics paper, have the genres 'buried' in the wording. A considerable amount of work is required to read the questions and understand what they are asking. Question 1 is asking students to explain, describe and argue. Question 2 is asking students to define, explain, argue and discuss. In contrast, the geography question is quite upfront in asking for the required genres. Provided that students understand how to write in the genres of defining/describing and explaining, and, of course, provided that they know the relevant content, they should not have any difficulty understanding and answering the question.

Moreover, as the types of genres in contemporary society are expanding and constantly changing due, in part, to the proliferation of information technologies, schools need to prepare students to deal with this by teaching students the basic written genres that have developed to exchange such information and knowledge. Competence at this level will establish a foundation for later flexibility and creativity. Consequently, this model has been designed to allow just that. Furthermore, it has been designed for teaching students at any level of language development. Here, however, it will be described in general terms applicable to a range of levels of language development. This model exemplifies the 'text and grammar' approach through a range of genres. The model moves from the concrete to the abstract. Describing is used first because of the way it uses language to represent concretely what students know and observe in their environments. Beyond this, the genre of describing can be used to arrange knowledge into taxonomies as a characteristic of the disciplines of natural science and social science. Describing could be classed as a genre of learning in terms of its fundamental role in all teaching-learning. The model finishes with the genre of arguing to deal with the discursive demands of disciplines in the social sciences.

The first stage of this model introduces genres that concretely represent what students have experienced or observed — genres that define and describe their world. Stage two involves generalising the concrete as the model moves from empirical observation to generalised abstract knowledge. It does this because by moving from generalised knowledge to experience, students are forced to redefine experience into dominant cultural paradigms at the expense of their own knowledge. The model sets out to teach grammar through writing, so this element is introduced at this stage. In this model, while this involves recognition that students have competence in many spoken genres, it does not imply that moving from speech to writing is a simple matter of the teacher intervening at the transcription stage. Students learn the grammar of writing through understanding the way that their own writing works. Exercises such as asking students to write simple, short, well defined writing tasks, for example, 'describe the appearance of what you see', and then comparing and contrasting the different approaches to this task, are particularly useful here. Students can also be given the grammatical names and functions of the language they have used for this task.

Stage three involves the introduction of reading models. The purpose here is to deconstruct the materials in relation to purpose, structure, message, grammar; and to link this to what has already been covered in the previous writing activities. Learning to read generally depends on the commonsense of teachers to use a range of strategies where needed and the ability of students to 'pick it up'. The model suggests using strategies to cover the middle ground between 'reading' and comprehension, for example, choosing texts that are generically 'simple' or using the text as an object that can be pulled apart and examined. It is recommended that the teacher does several readings, each time examining different aspects such as purpose (why is the text written like this?), message (what is the text about?), structure (are different parts of the text doing different jobs?), and grammar (what type of language is being used to do each job?).

Stage four introduces experiential-based research. By this time it is hoped that students will have begun to make connections between their generalisations of the concrete and the abstract concepts involved. Exercises must be devised to give them first-hand knowledge — for example, a teacher could collaborate with the librarian to conduct a research lesson in the library; have students work in pairs or groups; assist students by providing research sheets scaffolded to accommodate the generic structure; and/or show how to collect relevant information in point form (the format of the research sheets will assist in this task).

Stage five introduces a writing/editing dimension. At first students will be asked to write their texts stage by stage. For example, if they are to be writing a description, they would first be asked to write a topic classification, then asked to compare and contrast different approaches to this task. For example, they could build on the grammatical names and functions of the language they have used for the task and, using their knowledge of genre and grammar, they could be asked to rebuild or edit what they have written. Their essays at this point should show whether their writing is approaching a critical developmental stage — whether or not it is moving from the concrete world of action into the abstract world of knowledge; moving from the temporally sequenced world of action recounts to the cause and effect world of rational argument; and moving from the commonsense world of concrete phenomena to the abstract world of objectified knowledge.

To build on this, a series of teaching-learning strategies must be designed to help students, both as enquirers into particular disciplines and as literate participants in that particular world of knowledge. From such a perspective, an explicit knowledge of grammar is a highly effective and efficient teaching-learning strategy. By an analysis of their own texts, students are taught about grammar and its functions. Students can then be asked to rewrite their texts in the light of what has been learnt. The following model for teaching-learning experiences, while not sufficiently developed to be called a pedagogy, does try to address some of the pedagogical issues raised above (see Figure 2).

*Figure 2. A Model of Teaching-Learning Experiences*

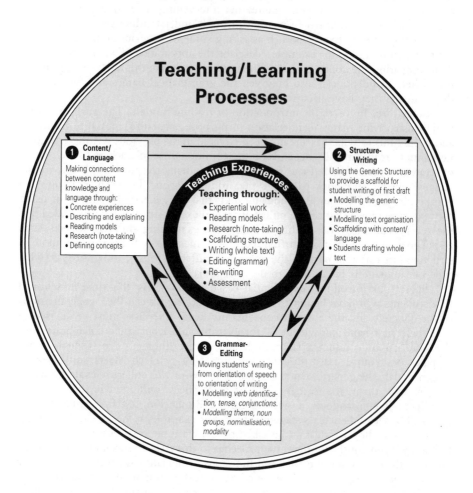

## Trialling Another Model of Teaching-Learning Experiences

One of the main outcomes proposed for this unit was to give students an understanding of the economic and environmental issues related to the role and function of packaging in the market place. To reach this final outcome, students moved from dealing with concrete examples of packages and associated language activities, to confront the abstract concept of packaging along with the abstract language of the discourse of economics. The unit was planned to be multigeneric, dealing with the genres of describing, explaining and arguing. In particular, it was decided that students would be involved in extensive language activities relating the discursive and disciplinary practices of economics through the grammatical and generic resources required at each stage of the unit. In its structure the completed unit progressed through five definite stages.

*Stage 1: Concrete Materials*

Students were asked to bring in examples of packaging. They had to:

> decide on ways of classifying and describing different types of packages: for example, what it is made of (composition); what it is used for (function); whether it is reusable and whether it can be reprocessed;
> consider ways of organising information that classifies and describes; and
> analyse the genre of describing: for example, what type of package (classification); what possible functions and uses; the composition; and the appearance (names, labels, warnings, instructions and so on).

As students were being introduced to a 'genre and grammar' approach for the first time, they needed to have the generic and grammatical features of the genre of describing explained to them. They needed to know the way that language operates at this concrete level before moving on to the abstract concept of packaging.

*Stage 2: Generalising the Concrete*

Activities were now introduced to enable students to organise packages into groups of packages: for example, packages made from paper products, plastic products, glass products, etc. The class was asked to:

> list groups of packages that come into these categories;
> list groups of packages according to their uses and functions;
> see if there are any connections between the composition of packages and their functions and uses;
> list groups of packages according to their recyclability;
> see if there are any connections between package composition and recyclability.

By now the students should have had a database for generalising about packages and the above categories of composition, functions and uses, and recyclability. Students were now asked to write classifications for different groups of packages. This could be a group activity, where different groups look at different groups of packages. Once this had been done, they were asked to write each one on the board. Alternately, each group could have been asked to write their classification on an overhead transparency, to save time. Each classification was then compared and contrasted. Students were asked to look for relational verbs (such as 'is' and 'are'); generic rather than individual names or nouns (such as paper, glass, food, drink, etc.); technical names or terms; and nominalisations (such as noun forms of verbs — production, consumption, etc.). This was then thrown into class discussion to decide:

> how relational verbs are essential for classification;
> how technical names and terms are more precise and efficient when classifying phenomena;
> how generic names and nominalisations are abstractions of concrete objects and activities.

### Stage 3: Reading Models

Students were shown overheads, and photocopies were distributed of a variety of written information relating to packaging. Suitable reading models, however, were not readily available so handouts consisted of a 'cut and paste' process of relevant material. Using a board or overhead transparency of some of the reading materials, the class began some joint reading strategies. The purpose was to deconstruct the materials in relation to purpose, structure, message, grammar; and to link this to what had already been covered in the previous writing activities. Students were then asked to use the handout material to see if they could add to the information they had categorised on groups of packages.

### Stage 4: Experiential-based Research

By this time it was hoped that students should have begun to make connections between the packages they know and use in their everyday lives and some of the social and environmental issues involved in the phenomenon of packaging. To help them gain first-hand knowledge, an excursion was organised to the manufacturers of two types of packaging: paper and glass. In preparation for this, the class brainstormed the questions and issues that they would be investigating at each plant:

> What is the proportion of recycled materials used in the manufacture?
> How much energy is used in the manufacture process?
> How much pollution is created in the manufacture?
> What proportion of the packaging produced is reusable?
> What proportion of the packaging produced is recycled?

Students were then asked to make up their own research sheets to use on the excursion.

### Stage 5: Writing — Editing

At this stage in the unit students were given an essay topic: 'Packaging is an unnecessary burden on the environment. Discuss.' Most of the class had already had experience writing this type of essay and were quite clear about the purpose of a discussion-type essay. They were also quite clear about the way such an essay is structured to achieve such a purpose. Below is a typical example of the quality of the essays produced:

> The statement 'Packaging is an unnecessary burden on the environment', can be argued in many ways. Packaging has a major impact on our environment even if we don't know it while people think otherwise.
>
> Packaging is essential in preserving, protecting and transporting products. If there were no packaging we could not buy any food without getting

messy and the food could go off easily. People today are also making their packages environmentally friendly in ways such as making refill packets for plastic bottles so it wont take up so much space. We are also trying to preserve our resources by making recycled paper, glass, and metal packages. Packaging can also attract buyers by advertising on the packet and giving helpful information.

On the other hand, packaging can have many disadvantages. To start, packaging takes up a lot of landfill in tips, rubbish dumps and just careless littering. Things such as plastic are not easily disposed of. Packaging can also harm the wildlife in particular areas. When the packages are dumped animals may swallow or get trapped in them.

Some of the resources used to make packaging are not renewable. Things like wood, sand and other materials are running out. Overpackaging also has a major contribution in taking up space.

Packing toothpaste in a tube and then in a box is a waste. Products are also unnecessarily packed a lot of these things can be avoided.

I believe packaging is needed but can be reduced in some ways.

The essays demonstrated that the students' writing was approaching a critical developmental stage:

> moving from the concrete world of action into the abstract world of commerce and economics,
> moving from the temporally sequenced world of action recounts to the cause and effect world of rational argument,
> moving from the commonsense world of concrete phenomena to the abstract world of objectified knowledge.

To build on this, the following teaching-learning strategies were designed to help students, both as enquirers into the particular discipline of knowledge defined as commerce, and as literate participants in that particular world of knowledge. From such a perspective, an explicit knowledge of grammar is a highly effective and efficient teaching-learning strategy. The students in this class had what could be described as a poor to non-existent knowledge of grammar which required a 'back to basics' approach starting with simple sentence and clause structure, verb and conjunction identification and simple nominalisation. Students were taught to identify the function and purpose of the above categories through their own writing. Specifically, the class dealt with stages of the above essay to understand and recognise how the grammatical categories realised the textual purpose of each stage.

To exemplify how this was done, we will look at one paragraph of the essay labelled 'arguments for'.

Packaging is essential in *preserving, protecting and transporting* products. If there *were* no packaging we *could not buy* any food without *getting messy* and the food *could go off* easily. People today *are* also *making* their packages environmentally friendly in ways such as *making* refill packets for plastic bottles so it *wont take up* so much space. *We are* also *trying to preserve* our resources by *making* recycled paper, glass, and metal packages. Packaging *can* also *attract* buyers by *advertising* on the packet and *giving* helpful information.

Students were taught about verbs and their functions in sentences and clauses. With the above paragraph on the board (or an overhead transparency could have been used), the class first identified all of the verbs (in italics). Once the class became confident about identifying verbs, the teacher then began to classify them according to their function. She used three classifications or verb types: action, mental, relational. Action verbs were described as those verbs that represented actions or activities going on 'out there' or exterior. Mental verbs were described as actions or activities going on 'in there' or inside human bodies or interior (thinking, feeling, communicating). Finally, relational verbs were described as verbs that define, describe or identify (often the verbs 'to be' or 'to have').

The whole class then classified the identified verbs into these three categories, and the resultant activity produced a great deal of animated discussion and argument. Students were asked to identify and classify the verbs in the first paragraph of the 'arguments for' in their own texts for homework. It was suggested that they draw up a grid to help organise this information.

| Action | Mental | Relational |
|---|---|---|
| preserving<br>protecting<br>transporting<br>could not buy<br>getting messy<br>could go off<br>making<br>making<br>wont take up | | is<br>were |

The arrangement of verbs in the above grid was typical of the whole class's texts — that is, there was a predominance of action verbs. This proved a useful exercise because it demonstrated to the students the extent to which their texts had an action orientation. In the work done with reading models it had been pointed out that economists do not write about the world of commerce as action oriented events but rather as one set of objects or abstractions in relation with another set of objects or relations.

A simple strategy for teaching how grammar deals with this reorientation was an exercise in nominalisation. Starting with the lists of action verbs used in their texts, the class looked at different ways of changing the actions into things. For homework students were asked to try and change their own list of action verbs into nouns.

| Action verbs | Nouns |
|---|---|
| preserving | preservation |
| protecting | protection |
| transporting | transportation |
| could (not) buy | purchase |
| getting messy | mess |
| could go off | spoilage |
| making | production |
| won't take up | use |

Students were then asked to rewrite their paragraphs substituting, where possible, the nominalisations of the action verbs. The following represents the student's rewrite of the above paragraph.

Argument 1: Against

Packaging is essential for the preservation, protection and transportation of products. Without packaging the purchase of food would be difficult resulting in waste and spoilage. Today manufacturers are producing environmentally friendly packages such as refill packets for plastic bottles which use less space in landfills.

Another aspect of the grammar of writing dealt with in this unit was conjunctions. A typical feature of spoken language is the repeated use of temporal and additional conjunctions ('and', 'then'). These conjunctions were a feature of most of the writing produced by the class. Similar exercises to the 'verb identification' exercise described above were carried out by the class. In this case students identified conjunctions and then categorised them as temporal, additional, causal, comparative, exemplifying. In the rewritten paragraph above, there is now a predominance of causal conjunctions, which would be expected in this type of written text.

This approach to teaching writing is different from the 'wheel' in significant ways. It is multigeneric; that is, it moves through a series of genres in order to cover the content knowledge. In other words, the aim here is not just to teach the class to produce a generic text type. Rather, it aims to use language to help teach the abstraction of the content knowledge and the skills of generalising and synthesising and hypothesising. The approach, therefore, seeks to avoid the problem of making text types seem formulaic by focusing instead on the relationship of knowledge/text/grammar. Rather than the teacher scribing for the students, the students learn through their own writing. Editing skills are taught through a knowledge of the basic grammar of written language. In other words, genre is shifted from being an end-product to being an integral part of the teaching-learning process.

We believe it is absolutely essential that teaching grammar must be a fundamental part of an effective genre-based approach to reading and writing. Without grammar, we will not be able to deal with the language issues which are so much a part of the concrete-abstract knowledge continuum. Grammar also enables us to break out of the reductiveness of the genre as end-product problem. Finally, it gives both teachers and students a way of talking about and dealing with language as an object that can be manipulated and changed to do particular things both in communication and expressing and organising knowledge.

*Chapter 9*

# Assessment: A Foundation for Effective Learning in the School Context

*Mary Macken and Diana Slade*

*Chapter 9 addresses the question of how writing is evaluated in school. As Macken and Slade argue, this is not simply a question that comes at the tail end of our educational discussions. As schools are coming under increasing public and political scrutiny, testing is more frequently being presented as an important instrument for accountability. In some very important ways, the issue of testing is driving current educational discussions. As progressivist curriculum does not have a very convincing response in this area, there is a danger that we will be drawn back in the direction of standardised tests.*

*In order to put the issues of assessment into the broader context of curriculum debates, Macken and Slade draw on the models of traditional and progressivist pedagogies introduced by Cope and Kalantzis in Chapter 2. If we are destined to return to the former model, we are most likely to see a revival of antiquated tests. If progressivism manages to hold its ground, however, in the area of student assessment we are more likely to experience the benevolent inertia of a 'just let them write' attitude.*

*Instead of these two inadequate approaches, Macken and Slade suggest teachers need an assessment metalanguage that is linguistically principled and rigorous. This metalanguage has to be one that invokes explicit criteria for evaluating language performance. This is precisely what they attempt to exemplify in the rest of the chapter.*

*Building on the notion of genre introduced by Martin and Rothery in Chapters 5 and 6, Macken and Slade differentiate genre (the 'why' of a text in its cultural context) and three contributing elements of register: field (the 'what' of a text), tenor (the 'who' of a text) and mode (the 'how' of a text). They use these concepts to delineate the key grammatical features of two genres: report and narrative. Their grammatical analysis shows the way in which some sample student texts are more successful than others.*

## Introduction: The Current Situation

Progressivism — still the dominant paradigm in education at this time — is under attack. Calls for across-the-board, standardised, external assessment measures are again surfacing. Educators in the United Kingdom, key parts of the United States and in Australia are increasingly faced with calls for a move 'back to basics' — especially when it comes to 'the three Rs'. Many calling for this move maintain that progressive education has failed its 'consumers', especially those most disadvantaged by reason of ethnicity, language, class or gender.

The pressure to make curriculum and assessment more explicit, content-substantive and goal-directed is reflected in the kind and number of reports surfacing about education at a national level. In Britain, for example, the Kingman Report on the 'Teaching of the English Language' addressed itself specifically to the need for mastery of speaking, writing, listening and reading through 'an explicit knowledge of the structure of the English language' (Kingman, 1988, 3). At the same time the Black Report on 'Assessment and Testing' called for a systematic approach to assessment via the application of 'attainment targets' for all students from the ages of five to eleven (Black, 1987). Since then, the Department of Education and Science has ensured that these 'attainment targets' be fleshed out in full for each subject.

In Australia, despite a history of resistance by state governments to centralised control of education, all education departments are now being asked to contribute to the formation of a national curriculum and assessment program. Against the background of the 1991 Finn Report the introduction of 'assessment levels' against which student progress will be monitored seems somewhat tame. Furthermore, this 'system-wide' development cannot be reduced by an historical 'sleight of hand' to the political incursion into education of 'Thatcherism' or the 'New Right'. It includes not only people who might be seen to have a vested interest in traditional curriculum, but also ordinary members of the 'community' who strongly believe their children need conventional academic skills and accreditation to succeed in the world outside the classroom. Both at national and local levels, there are increasing pressures on schools and education systems to produce indications of students' performance — ones that will satisfy community demands to know what students are achieving throughout their school years. These concerns are constantly exacerbated by media stories about 'falling standards of literacy'.

Even among teachers there is growing recognition that lack of explicitness in school-based curriculum documents is causing problems in producing satisfactory assessment procedures — procedures that would be accurate in terms of state standards and, at the same time, give a true picture of their students' achievements. Current informal assessment advice offers teachers a 'grab bag' of procedures such as observations of students' behaviours, checklists of skills to watch for like 'invented spelling' or 'connecting ideas' or 'choosing topics' and keeping anecdotal records about writing folders. None of the procedures is able to demonstrate student achievement clearly in terms which relate to those of students in other classrooms. We believe that progressivism has left teachers with a disabling legacy when it comes to assessment and that this 'vacuum' has negatively facilitated the imposition of external, standardised tests which are incompatible both with the classroom experiences of the vast majority of teachers and their students and with the goals of the wider curriculum.

In Australia, for example, the worst fears of the progressive teachers are being realised. In 1989 the newly elected Liberal Government called for a battery of 'Basic Skills Tests' in New South Wales, the heartland of progressivism and its offshoot — process writing. It argued, rather convincingly, that the government had very little information to go on about what students were achieving as a result of their years of primary and secondary schooling. They therefore introduced compulsory, external testing for students in Years 3 and 6. These tests are based on item-response theory but have much in common with traditional standardised tests. They are summative assessment procedures that deliver 'objective' quantitative measurements of students' achievement to the sponsors of state education. In fact, in the tests of 'Aspects of Literacy', the students produce very little language at all. The tests are mostly 'multiple choice' so there is guaranteed marker reliability; they are easy to mark, and economical. However, they have all the pitfalls of standardised testing: they are psychometrically sound, in that they are based on a sophisticated measurement, but the conception of language they embody is very narrow. Because of the very nature of the quantitative measurement, when it comes to literacy, what is being assessed is essentially trivial. In other words, what is easy to test and practical in terms of giving a clear message to the government gives only a narrow indication of what the learner can or cannot do.

In this chapter we argue that teachers need access to an assessment metalanguage which is linguistically principled and rigorous but which is, at the same time, sensitive to variations in learning contexts and individual differences. Furthermore, this assessment framework has to be integrated with the goals of the subject curricula and the processes of learning by which students reach these. Our approach offers educators a way of deconstructing the learning demands across the curriculum from a semiotic point of view (that is, from the point of view of the meanings which students are expected to build up in the process of learning a particular subject or discipline).

As part of this argument, we outline a set of criteria against which a language assessment framework can be evaluated. We review some different approaches to writing assessment currently operating in schools: the traditional approaches to language assessment and the progressivist approaches. Neither of these approaches enables the development of a linguistically informed and educationally responsible assessment program in schools. Our central argument is that the crux of the matter with both positions is the conception of language underlying each of these positions.

In the next section we propose an alternative approach to assessment which is based on the functional model of 'language in use' developed by Michael Halliday initially and applied to educational contexts by many of the contributors to this volume. Then we show how the model can be utilised for purposes of literacy assessment in two genres: scientific report and narrative. Here the focus is on writing collected from one primary school, although we have applied the framework to language assessment in both secondary and tertiary educational contexts. The approach outlined here was trialled in a number of classrooms in NSW as part of teachers' work on 'genre-based' approaches to teaching writing. Finally, we return to the problem of developing a framework for assessment which provides a 'foundation for effective learning'.

## Principles for an Effective Approach to Assessment

Assessment is an important strategy for promoting language learning in school. However, if it is to provide an effective foundation for learning, there are certain criteria on which it must stand and against which different assessment procedures can be evaluated: we believe that an effective language assessment program must be linguistically principled, explicit, criterion-referenced, and must inform different types of assessment, including diagnostic, formative and summative assessment. We will deal with each of these principles in turn.

Assessment should be a linguistically principled procedure. It is a commonplace practice in documents about literacy to stress the importance of fostering learning of the macroskills — speaking, listening, reading and writing — in all subjects. But a major omission in many curriculum documents is information about how these macroskills differ and what language development in the oral and written modes entails. Learning to write, for example, unlike learning to speak, is a highly conscious process: it requires that children begin to exploit the potential of language in new and often unfamiliar ways. For learners from non-English-speaking backgrounds or from backgrounds where written language does not have the same salience as it does in school, the 'challenge of school literacy' can turn into another experience of exclusion. The teachers of these learners need access to a systematically organised metalanguage for understanding, assessing and promoting their abilities in both the spoken and the written modes. Furthermore, this same metalanguage should enable educators to deconstruct the communicative requirements of particular disciplines, especially those to do with reading and writing. This latter aspect of language variation is especially relevant to teachers in the secondary and tertiary sectors of education.

Explicitness about language is another important foundation for ensuring that all learners can participate in school education. This involves more than simply spelling out the necessary skills relevant to successful completion of a task. It involves fostering common perceptions about the meanings and purposes of any formal learning situation established in the classroom. It is in this respect that a 'shared metalanguage' promises to make connections with learners' different starting points when it comes to schooling and literacy. It also promises to offer all of them opportunities for access to the discourses of the dominant culture. Gaining control of the written mode is essential to learning in all subject areas. As such, reading and writing are the concern of all teachers, although different text types will feature more in some subjects than in others. Gaining confidence with information-processing skills — like using a microfiche, a computer, a library catalogue, an index, a glossary, etc. — is not something that happens exclusively within the domain of any one subject either. They form part of the 'essential curriculum'. An adequate model of assessment will have to take account of language skills which are specific to particular subjects or disciplines and those which are generic to formal education in the late twentieth century. Such a metalanguage will be required to function at microlevels of particular tasks in particular subjects (for example, a description of the criteria relevant to a writing task in industrial arts) and at macrolevels across wide spans of school learning (for example, a description of the writing demands of junior secondary science or geography).

This second principle relates closely to the third: linking achievement to specific criteria in different assessment tasks. Learners can only take control over their learning if they understand what it is asking of them. Being 'up front' about the criteria for success in any task enables those who are not 'naturally good' at it to take some responsibility for improving in it. From the point of view of linking the assessment process to the outcomes intended in the curriculum, the criteria relevant to students' achievement should be related clearly to the goals for learning as they are expressed in official syllabus documents. The assessment process should enable teachers to chart students' progress towards these goals and articulate the nature of this progress. With respect to promoting language development over time, the same principles should inform all phases of teaching-learning — the planning, the reflecting and the assessing phases. This means linking assessment to the whole learning process — not just tacking it on as an afterthought but ensuring that it informs teachers' planning of a unit of work.

Assessment should be both diagnostic and formative as well as summative. Shared criteria based on a sound knowledge of language and its varieties will enable teachers to reflect on the strengths and to diagnose weaknesses in the texts produced by their students. Furthermore, if the language model is contextually sensitive along a number of dimensions, it is possible to acknowledge both strengths and weaknesses in the one student text. It is possible when reading a piece of writing, for example, to see that a student may have learned a great deal about the operations of a machine but may not be confident about writing a procedure for its use. Knowledge of the goals for learning and how students' language approximate these enables teachers to acknowledge students' positive achievements and to plan the appropriate next steps in their learning.

In short, in planning learning experiences for their students, teachers need to know where they're going and why, how far students have come and what this progress means in terms of their positive achievements and future needs. These criteria form the basis for promoting learning in the school environment. Against this background we turn now to a consideration of assessment as it is practised in schools at the present time.

## Two Positions on Language Assessment in the School Context

Educators, with an interest in writing assessment, can visit any number of schools and find a confusing array of approaches to assessment. Indeed, it is our experience that the scenarios outlined for pedagogy in Chapter 2 reflect different assessment practices. A visit to any school in Australia can confront observers with assessment practices which range from benevolent inertia — 'Just let them write' — to quite antiquated literacy tests handed out each year to assess basic 'reading ages' or 'grammatical abilities' — 'We need to know what standard they're at!'

This same trend can be observed in secondary and tertiary institutions. Students in junior secondary school move from a situation where teachers refuse to give 'across-the-year tests' — usually on the grounds that these will discriminate against the weaker students — to the imposition of onerous final exams such as the Higher School Certificate in New South Wales. These varied practices can be broadly linked to two different positions on language assessment still operating in the current educational environment: the traditional and the progressivist. We will examine each of these in the light of the assessment framework we have proposed.

The traditional curriculum, as discussed in Chapter 2, consisted of centrally prescribed syllabuses, and ended with a factual examination or test. In English literature, however, assessment took the form of, for example, free essays and, in language classes, students were assessed on the basis of their skills at translation, composition and sentence completion. One obvious advantage was that both the teachers and the students knew exactly what was expected of them, and in most cases assessment directly followed the content of the curriculum and so could be argued to have high content validity (Davies, 1969; Palmer and Bachman, 1981).

As it is practised in contemporary classrooms, ratings are norm-referenced — especially in English literature. That is, students are marked relative to each other, and the mark provided is not set against explicit criteria: it involves an informed, but intuitive grade given by the teacher/assessor. So, the students are often left with no real understanding as to why they have failed or done well, and given no explicit guidelines about how they can improve their writing. In traditional methods of assessment, because the assessment procedure is essentially subjective, the reliability is low. Reliability is the criterion that the test should give the same results every time it is used (within a short period) on the same subject, regardless of who is giving and marking it. Where the marks are awarded on intuitive grounds, it is extremely difficult to give clear guidelines to examinees about why they received a particular grade. We argue that these summative procedures fail students where they need most assistance — in understanding what it is that they are required to do and how they can improve their efforts to succeed.

Nevertheless, this form of assessment is still common in schools today — and the final year external exam still performs a powerful selecting and dividing role. How students perform in the end of school exams affects career chances. Yet these exams provide marks that are not necessarily meaningful beyond branding students as comparative successes or failures. Furthermore, the assessment implicates the curriculum — especially in the final years of secondary schooling. In other words, the major purpose of the curriculum is to prepare students for the final exam. As the progressive educationalists rightly point out, traditional approaches to assessment are obsessed with 'product' at the expense of 'process'. Processes of learning are far more difficult to assess than products like test papers or essays. Traditional approaches to assessment sever the link between processes of learning and learning outcomes.

Furthermore, it can be argued that traditional forms of assessment advantage middle-class Anglo-Saxon children of English-speaking background, who are more familiar with the linguistic demands of educational knowledge and who are socialised early into understanding school as a sorting system where formal credentials are necessary for success. It is they who are able to 'read' the hidden instructions in exams and to transform an apparently open question or instruction — 'Write in any form you like' — into its covert command — 'Write a well formed narrative.'

The progressive education movement — or that version of it allied with postmodernist thinking — came about in the 1960s as a reaction against traditional curriculum. By the late 1970s it had emerged, if curriculum materials and espoused teaching practice are to be believed, as the dominant paradigm in school education. Progressivist education initiated a move towards a school-based curriculum — which prioritised the notion of relevance to students' interests and needs. In contrast to traditional curriculum, teachers became concerned with identifying the skills and processes their students brought to their actual use of language. They focused on learning processes as opposed to learned content, on developing a 'relevant curriculum' as opposed to a 'core curriculum', and on the meaning intentions of the learner rather than on the formal correctness of his/her language use. Not surprisingly, this leads to the celebration of non-judgmental, informal assessment procedures.

But these features are not our primary worry with progressivist education as it is currently practised in schools. It is their 'decontextualised' notion of learning processes that has most negatively influenced the assessment of language learning. Progressivists argue that as educators they are not there to hand down the only true interpretation of the world (a fixed content), but to help their students develop processes for questioning their world, making up their own minds and acting according to their own freely formed consciousness. Particular importance is attached to such things as 'capacity to reason', 'to solve problems' and 'to think critically'. These are seen as socially useful skills, important not only in schools but for successful participation in the community. Educational institutions, then, have a responsibility to develop these kinds of mental abilities and capacities in the students. Munby (1978) places a similar emphasis on the teaching of 'mental' skills and abilities to adult ESL learners and provides an inventory of microskills from which to teach. This inventory includes such skills as 'expressing the communicative value of sentences and utterances', 'identifying the main point or important information in a piece of discourse' and 'extracting salient points to summarise' (Munby, 1978, 127–129).

Apart from the difficulty of clearly defining and then isolating such skills for teaching and testing, the major issue is that context or knowledge is seen as something that may be divorced from considerations of the language processes in which content comes into being. Furthermore, there is a general view that these skills are more important than the content or information, because, it is argued, these are generalisable skills and cut across 'contents' and so are much more useful to teach. Knowledge is thought of as a kind of product, and the skills and abilities are thought of in process terms. Once mental processes are developed, it is argued, students can master different products.

This dualising tendency in Western thinking — separating process from product, meaning from linguistic discourse and language from knowledge — has affected other disciplines. As Christie (1986) has pointed out, it is also a misconception that prevails in twentieth century educational psychology: that language has no more than a neutral role to play in relation to thought and to content; that language is there to serve ideas; and that the ideas have an independent existence. However, both language process (that is, skills) and language product (that is, knowledge) are two aspects of the same phenomenon. Language is both a process and a product, and to view it meaningfully as text, one needs to take both perspectives. In other words, to learn content is to learn language; it is to learn how to recognise and manipulate the discourse of different disciplines, and to learn how to address issues and solve problems in a way which is characteristic of a particular subject. In fact, success or failure at school is closely tied to the student's ability to construct discourses appropriate to different disciplines.

A more rigorous form of 'process assessment' involves the design of criteria against which the learner's progress can be judged. This is a very important and necessary step in language assessment. One of the central problems of criterion-referenced assessment is how you actually define the criteria against which language performance is to be judged so as to avoid poorly specified and vague terminology. The process often becomes very subjective, with the teacher having 'a hunch' at the level of the student. Essentially, the problem is that as long as these 'skills' are considered to be separate from the language in which they are encoded, they will continue to be vague. How can you test, for example, 'the ability to reason', or 'ability to scan a test' without clearly describing the way these processes are encoded in various language patterns characteristic of different disciplines?

Both traditional and progressivist approaches to assessment sever the links between processes of learning and the discourses which give these processes meaning. Traditional pedagogies fetishised canonical texts and received bodies of knowledge. They tested for knowledge of these fixed contents. They elided concern for the processual aspect of learning. Progressivist pedagogies have sought to operate with a 'contentless curriculum' — celebrating individual differences while excluding most students from the powerful discourses necessary for success in the wider socio-cultural environment.

The 'back to basics' movement is able to exploit these contradictory agendas operating in school curriculum. 'Basic skills' tests are large-scale, external summative, assessment procedures that are reliable and objective and intended to assess 'knowledge' ('product' oriented). But teachers utilise ongoing informal assessment techniques which are unreliable, subjective and intended to assess 'skills' ('process' oriented). So there is an inevitable conflict created between the needs of the sponsors of education and the participants in it, where the participants are interested in the process, and the sponsors are interested in outcomes.

In conclusion, then, we are arguing that there are two central issues. The major issue is to do with the view of language that underpins assessment procedures. This is gone into in more detail in the next section. The central argument, however, is that explicit criteria need to be designed against which a student's language performance can be evaluated. But for these criteria to be explicit and as objective as possible, they must be based on a model of language that incorporates both process and content. From the linguistic point of view, this means being able to demonstrate the relationship of instances of language use and the potential of the language system from which the learner makes choices for meaning. We also need to make use of the mutually informing relationship between texts and the contexts in which they occur.

The second and equally important issue is to do with the need for the development of a well articulated curriculum that explicitly deals with the language demands of each discipline. If testing is to have educational legitimacy, either as a way of setting goals and monitoring development, or by introducing the possibility of improving standards, then it can only succeed on the basis of a broadly implemented literacy (or other) curriculum. Without a well articulated curriculum, the introduction of testing will simply lead to the entrenchment of the current widespread inequities. Table 1 summarises the different positions characterised above.

## The Language Model Underpinning the Proposed Approach to Assessment

Sooner or later when teachers talk to their students about writing, they are going to have to talk about language. Linguistics is the formal and scientific study of language — of both the language system as a whole and instances of its use. It is a body of knowledge which teachers should be free to make use of in their professional capacity as language educators. Systemic functional linguistics offers

Table 1. Three Positions on Language Assessment in the School Context

| Descriptors | | Position 1 (traditional) | Position 2: (progressive) | Position 3: (explicit/functional) |
|---|---|---|---|---|
| view of language | [i] | product | process | product/process |
| | [ii] | narrow view of language (e.g., formal aspects and prescriptive grammar) | broad area of language (e.g., communicative strategies, 'enabling skills', no grammar) | contextualised view of language (e.g., a functional grammar of system and instance; text in context) |
| rating | | norm-referenced | criterion-referenced (skills and processes) | criterion-referenced (contextually and linguistically informed) |
| focus | | performing in final tests | learning skills and processes | exploiting the potential of language as a means of learning |
| type of assessment | | summative | diagnostic (generalised) | diagnostic and formative (language specific) |

teachers an approach to the study of language as people really use it, that is, as it varies according to dialect and register. It also offers them a grammar in which words, phrases and clauses are described in terms of their contribution to the creation of text. This grammar is directly related to the spoken and written texts created by students and can be used to help them reflect on what their texts are 'doing'.

As outlined in Chapter 6, this functional approach to linguistics differs fundamentally from traditional and other formal grammars. The linguistic criteria we are dealing with in our students' writing take us beyond the formal aspects of surface conventions and notions of 'correctness' in language use. Although we acknowledge that the formal aspects of punctuation, paragraphing and spelling do have a place in the presentation of a text, tidying up the surface features of a text does not help a writer to restructure his or her writing so that it makes meanings appropriate to the overall purpose and context. What systemic functional linguistics offers educators is a systematic way of relating matters of purpose and audience to language itself.

What does it mean to say that a particular piece of writing can be evaluated against a background knowledge of the purpose and context of a text? If we consider context as the environment of a text, there are four aspects of the environment which are especially relevant to the interpretation and production of a text. We can treat genre (as an aspect of the context of culture) and look briefly at the three aspects of register (the meanings typically associated with particular contexts of situation): the field, the tenor and the mode of a text. Although these categories have been dealt with elsewhere in the book, we revisit them here and consider them from the point of view of assessing writing.

Text types or genres are shaped according to the purposes of their users. The repetition and predictability of most social occasions serve to stabilise and even to standardise the texts people use in dealing with each other and with their experience. These socially constructed text types reveal in their overall structure (their stages) and language choices the purposes of their users. These social processes can be as mundane as buying stamps, ordering a takeaway meal, or making a complaint about soiled goods, and as specialised as writing an environmental impact statement, giving a quote on car repair or having afternoon tea with the Minister of Education. Whether familiar or specialised, these genres are utilised in predictable ways and, from the point of view of participating in the culture, usually need to be learnt. Genre is the 'why' of a text.

The written genres relevant to formal schooling also need to be learnt — and taught. Some of the key written genres in different subject areas like science, social science, English and history include reports, narratives, explanations, procedures and argumentative genres like expositions and discussions. The typical structure of two of these key genres reveals the differences in their social purpose. The stages of a scientific report run: {general classification ^ description of distinctive features}, while that of a simple narrative can be written as: orientation^{complication ^ evaluation} ^ resolution ^ (reorientation or coda).

This notation is one means by which linguists express what appear to be the obligatory and optional features of genres. The caret sign ^ means that the stage to the left precedes the one to the right. The brace { } indicates that the stages within are recursive, and the stages within the brackets ( ) are optional features of the genre. Each stage in the genre, for example, general classification, is given a functional label which attempts to represent its meaning — what it 'does' in semantic terms — such as sorting phenomena into biological classes. Of course, people innovate on the basic sequence of obligatory stages and often play in imaginative ways with the optional stages of all genres. For example, in the narrative above, the coda and the reorientation stage are often used to round off the story or to point out the moral implication of the event sequence. As we shall see, students who are able to exploit the potential of these optional stages of the genre are often rewarded for imagination by their teachers.

There are three other contextual factors that determine the meanings of a text. Register is a term developed within systemic functional linguistics to refer to configurations of meaning associated with the field, tenor and mode of a discourse. These three dimensions of the context are linked to three kinds of meaning within a text — which are referred to as the three metafunctions — ideational, interpersonal and textual respectively. It is the hook-up between three aspects of the context of situation and three general kinds of meaning which a text makes that enables linguists to move in a predictive way between text and context. Each text then can be seen as a polyphonic construct — harmonising three kinds of meaning in response to three functional pressures in the semiotic environment. And it is the category of genre which integrates and combines the meanings in ways allowable within a culture. The semiotic environment can be represented in terms of dimensions. We will look briefly at these three dimensions as they have a bearing on the approach to assessment exemplified in the next section.

Texts vary along a field dimension. The field is concerned with social activity — what is going on, in terms of some overall social institution. Field, in other words, is the 'what' of a text. Because the number of activities people engage in is enormous, texts show great variation along the field dimension. This is also true of the material students have to deal with in their different subjects at school. Most generally, the fields of science, industrial arts, literature and art organise activity sequences (people, places and things and what they do) very differently. Teachers of these 'content area' subjects tend to focus on this dimension of meaning when they read students' writing. That is, they assess students' written texts for the knowledge of the field that they reveal.

Texts vary along the tenor dimension. This dimension is influenced by the relationships of those taking part in a speech or writing event — the addressor and addressee(s). Tenor is the 'who' of a text. Different genres involve establishing and assuming different relationships between interlocutors. Some genres — like telephone conversations between friends or anecdotes — assume a far closer relationship than those like government reports or 'safety first' procedures. When it comes to written texts, tenor involves a consideration of something like 'reading position'. The kind of reader assumed in a narrative is different from that assumed in a scientific report. Successful texts show awareness of this as well as the ability to exploit it.

Texts vary according to whether they are spoken or written. Mode is the 'how' of a text. In the written mode, students are learning to develop texts which are more 'context independent' than spoken texts. With written language, the writer has to build up the relevant context for interpretation of the text for the reader. This calls for greater explicitness on the part of the student/writer — a skill which involves imagining the needs of a reader who is not already familiar with the 'world' projected in the text.

Some of the language skills which relate to control of the written mode involve learning to use sentences which integrate different clause types: exploit first position in the clause (theme) appropriately; be more discriminating about when and how to use conjunctions (for example, not to use a string of conjunctions like 'and then', 'then' and so on); refer correctly and consistently to the relevant participants in a text, using appropriate pronouns or synonyms; and use vocabulary relevant to the field which the text is constructing.

In short, these four contextual dimensions — genre, field, tenor, mode — serve as a matrix by which texts can be both understood and evaluated. The genre dimension requires that we consider the text as a whole — as serving an identifiable purpose. And the genres are named in such a way as to imply something of their overall social purpose. For example, reports give information about something; recounts tell about what happened; procedures show a novice how to do something. The register dimensions help to tie the text into the situation in which it occurs, and this is considered not as a material setting but as a semiotic environment. The matrix allows us to relate student texts to others in the same genre, about the same field, assuming a similar tenor and exploiting the resources of the grammar in similar ways. It also allows us to contrast texts along the same dimensions. But, above all, it allows us to make connections with texts as they are deployed in the community outside the classroom. Teachers can assist their students to read and write for 'real purposes' and to understand the language requirements for doing so. We turn now to a consideration of how a linguistically principled approach to assessment can work in practice.

## Using the Functional Approach in Two Genres: Scientific Report and Narrative

Developing a linguistically principled approach to assessing student achievement is not a challenge most teachers face in their day-to-day classroom lives, but, as we have noted, this situation is changing. Calls for greater accountability by educational stakeholders are forcing teachers into an 'assessment corner'. Against this background, the following 'assessment scenario' is not difficult for an upper primary school teacher to imagine:

> Someone outside your classroom — like a regional director — has asked you to participate in an exercise in which you show how you assess your students' writing. You are to choose written texts in two genres (one factual and one non-factual) from your students and then to provide detailed descriptions of how you:
>
> 1) rank and grade their texts in each writing task;
> 2) provide information about the criteria against which you assessed the texts in each task;
> 3) diagnose specific weaknesses as well as acknowledge strengths in these pieces of writing;
> 4) formulate suggestions about how to improve future written work in similar tasks.

> Imagine further that this director has asked you to meet with other teachers in your region to look at other samples of writing from students in a similar age/grade range. As a second step in this process, you are asked to evaluate the achievements of your students against a background knowledge of what other students are doing. You and these other teachers are to develop criteria against which the writing for each task can be assessed.

In this section we will take three sample texts in two genres — narrative and scientific report — and show how teachers faced with such demands could assess students' writing in a linguistically principled way. The three texts in each genre are graded and ranked from A to C, representing the top, the middling and the lowest range of achievement for writing in each genre in one particular class. The criteria are based on the categories of genre, field, tenor and mode. The criteria by which each text is assessed will vary according to context, but in a predictable way. The generic demands of scientific report writing are very different from those of narrative; the experience of the 'possible world' of fairytales contrasts with knowledge the 'biological facts'; and so on. We turn first to the narratives collected from a Year 5 classroom in a Sydney primary school.

The ten-year-olds in this class had been working on a unit on fairytales. Over about six weeks they had been introduced to the social function and the generic structure of a prototypical narrative. They had learned, for example, that narratives introduce the reader to a 'possible world' in which individual characters experience a 'problem' of some kind which they have to face and overcome. The students read a number of fairytales and discussed their appeal and qualities with the teacher over a sequence of lessons. After their initial work on the narrative, the students prepared jointly to construct their own class text. As part of this, they agreed on and wrote up a storyline — a sequence of events for each stage of the fairy tale. Some of the class also developed 'character profiles' for the major characters. Small groups then wrote the text with the help of the teacher — each group contributing to a different stage of the narrative. Some of the students experimented with literary devices like the use of foreshadowing in the orientation stage of the narrative and building up the 'interpersonal meanings' of the text through exclamatives, rhetorical questions, attitudinal epithets and mental process clauses.

In short, the students spent quite a lot of time considering the structure of narrative, the kinds of characters and events possible in the world of the fairytale, and some of them had even begun to explore the possibilities for interpersonal meanings in their contributions to the class narrative. When it came to writing their own fairytales, therefore, they had a basic knowledge of the criteria against which these would be assessed. The following pieces of writing (1A, 1B and 1C) were given by students to their teacher at the end of their work on this unit. The framework by which the texts can be assessed is presented with examples from text 1A.

Text 1A: The Dragon's Tooth

Many years ago when the world was full of magic there lived a princess who was more beautiful than you can imagine. One day she was walking through the woods smelling wild flowers and listening to the animals and birds, when suddenly a witch jumped out in front of her and screamed 'Aha !' The witch pull(ed) a tube containing some green liquid out of her pocket and drank it, then instantly turned into a beautiful lady looking just like the princess. The witch dropped a piece of paper and the princess picked it up, it read:

The Cure
'The princess Agather must kill a dragon and pull out its tooth to regain her beauty (without help or weapons).'

Agather wondered what it meant by 'regain her beauty'. Presently she came across a shining clear lake! She couldn't help going over to the lake and just letting her hands glide through the water. As she leant over to pick up a lily, Agather looked at her reflection she saw the face of a witch. She frantically ran around weeping and imagining herself as an old spinster.

Presently she came across a cave with the words 'Beware A Dragon' written above it. It reminded her of the instructions on the paper. Agather walked in bravely, looking around cautiously, when she came to a halt. There in front of her was some stairs and below that — low and behold was the dragon!!!

She grabbed a stick for protection. The dragon turned its gigantic head, breathing fire, the princess held the stick out for protection and closed her eyes, when she opened them again and realised the top of the branch had caught alight. She worked up some courage, and with a running jump aimed for the dragons back. Agather was usually a frisky sporty girl but had put on a lot of weight when the witch changed her. She didn't jump far enough and landed with a bump but was too frightened to feel a thing. She ran stumbling over her own feet. Luckily as Agather ran she didn't drop the stick and the flame didn't go out. Agather clambered up the dragon's tail, burning him as she went. Just as she got to the top the dragon jolted and she slipped off. She burnt the dragon to death!!! Agather pulled out a tooth and the blood oozed out of the dragon's mouth. The princess sank down into the hard soil.

Just as the dragon gave his last wail a knight passed by and went into the cave. He found the princess beautiful again, exhausted holding the tooth. The knight carried both the princess and the tooth back to the castle. When they got there the princess had miraculously recovered and screamed 'Never again'. The princess had a pimple on her nose because she used a weapon but the knight and princess married and lived happily ever after.

> by Nicole

Text 1B: The Tree That Grew Money

Long long ago there lived a girl called Cindy who was very poor. Cindy wanted to find the tree that grew money. One day she went to the princess and asked her if she could go to find the tree that grew money. The princess said yes and gave her the equipment. The princess also said that if she didn't come back after a week someone will come to look for her.

After three months of travelling Cindy went to the wise old lion and said 'Where can I find the tree that grows money?' The wise old lion said 'The tree is near a village called Sedan.' So off Cindy went. After many days of walking Cindy arrived at the tree. She collected all the money and put it in her bag. While she was walking she fell in a enormous hole in the road. When she reached the bottom of the hole a gigantic spider came towards her. Cindy tried to get away but she couldn't. The spider got hold of her and then threw her in the web.

Back at the palace the princess had sent for one of the knights to save Cindy. The knight was travelling for a day when suddenly he saw the enormous hole in the road. He stopped and listened carefully. He heard someone crying. The knight got out a rope and tied it to a tree. Then he threw it down the hole and he started to climb it. When he reached the bottom of it he saw Cindy and the giant spider. The knight got a huge stick and he hit the spider on the head. Then the knight climbed the web and took Cindy off. When they got back to [the] Palace the princess was happy to see Cindy. Cindy showed the princess the money and then she lived happily ever after.

> by Adela

Text 1C: The Magical Land Of. . . .

Far, far away in another universe far from our own is a land full of happiness and gold but in this land lives the great evil witch.

To this land arrives a boy named John who found out what this evil witch had done to all the gold in the land. The witch had turned all of the gold in the land. John found out where the lair of the witch, which is the dark side of the land. John left for his long journey ahead.

After many days of travelling through dense bushland he finally met the witch face to face. The witch with her powerful spells and illusions disappeared, John armed only with a lead sword swung his sword heavily where the witch was before and his sword turned to gold. And they lived happily ever after.

by Brett

Of course, the readers would not respond to these narratives in terms of separate compartments or dimensions. But they do value some texts more positively than others. The categories of genre and register represent an attempt to understand what it is that informs intuitions about a text being 'good' or 'poor'. So what can we learn about narrative by considering development along these dimensions?

With regard to the overall structure of the text, students need to understand the purpose (or telos) of the genre. Fairytales, for example, project an imaginary world in which certain characters (usually stereotypical ones like 'Red Riding Hood' or 'Rapunzel') are faced with an experience which they regard as problematic in some way and which they have to resolve. The events of the narrative are given their significance through evaluative meanings. Successful narratives have a telos. They give the reader a sense that they are moving via different textual manoeuvres towards some end point: the resolution of some conflict in the experience of an individual or individuals. In this respect, then, novice writers can benefit from an overarching generic structure when writing their first narratives: The notation [orientation^ {complication . evaluation} ^ resolution ^ (re-Orientation or coda)] offers developing writers a useful synoptic perspective on narrative.

Along the tenor dimension students are learning to explore subjectivity as it can be projected in a narrative. The writer learns to take up a fictionalised persona — interested less in overt expressions of his or her personal feelings and attitudes and more in the management of the reader's responses. Interpersonal meanings of this kind require that the writer exploit resources like the following: reporting and quoting the speech of imagined characters, revealing their thinking in mental processes ('wondered', 'imagining', reminded), commenting on events ('bravely', 'cautiously', 'luckily') and creating a sense of the characters' responses and motives (via epithets like 'an *old* spinster' and '*frisky, sporty* girl'). In more sophisticated narratives, students begin to experiment with devices like imagery, rhetorical questions, repetition, and exclamatives in building suspense, atmosphere and characterisation. This is very visible in the evaluation stages — where the writer halts the sequence of events in order to evaluate their significance for the character(s).

Along the field dimension, students are learning to build up the reality of a possible world: sequencing events properly and exploiting them in ways appropriate to the genre — so that there is not too much or too little detail. For

example, the texts are not about 'girls' in general but about one particular girl —
a princess called 'Agather'. The physical events are also specified — usually in
'doing', or material processes. In sophisticated narratives, students learn to specify
events more precisely; they learn to use words like 'grabbed' instead of 'got' or
'clambered' instead of 'climbed'. Making more discriminating and evocative word
choices (especially of the thinking and doing processes) is part of becoming a real
writer of fiction. It is also very important in constructing the physical reality of
this 'possible world' that the relevant circumstances are built up clearly. This is
often achieved through the use of prepositional phrases ('through the woods', 'out
of her pocket', 'through the water') or adverbials ('suddenly', 'instantly', 'frantically'). The reader needs enough information about the circumstances of the
characters in this 'possible world' to participate in it as an observer/reader.

The choice of written mode involves the student in learning to create a 'context-independent text'. The written text itself has to do more of the 'work' in
helping the reader to create a context for the events of the narrative. The use of
the sentence and appropriate punctuation is important here. The experienced student
will be able to combine different types of clauses and even to embed one inside
the other when necessary. S/he will also need to link clauses and sentences in
different ways and to be increasingly discriminating about when to use explicit
conjunctions like 'when', 'but', 'until' and others. Controlling the textual resources
of the language also means learning to use theme (first position in the clause) in
appropriate ways — usually signalling changes in the temporal sequence of events.
Finally, the narrator has to make the text cohesive: with respect to identifying
participants, for instance, to assist the reader to recover referents by phoric ties
of one kind or another (e.g., 'A princess', 'she', 'The princess Agather', 'an old
spinster', 'she', 'a frisky sporty girl').

We can look at each narrative text again from both the diagnostic and the
formative point of view, showing how teachers can move from understanding the
strengths and weaknesses of students' written texts to strategies for improving
them. It is in this respect that a functional model of language has most to offer
teachers and students. Focusing on four dimensions of a task (in this case its
contextual dimensions) takes teachers beyond a narrowly formal perspective on
the language demands of a task. It takes into account the functional pressures on
the writer and therefore points to strategies for working with him or her in future
efforts. Where the criteria are known by both teacher and students, future work
on the genre and the register proceeds on the basis of shared understandings about
learning goals. The students are 'in on the act' as far as future development is
concerned, and other teachers can dialogue in the same metalanguage about texts
in the same genre — with a reasonable expectation that they mean the same thing.

We will return now to the three narrative texts and evaluate them from the
point of view of genre and register. Text 1A is in the highest range of achievement for this class in narrative writing. The writer's control of the genre, her
exploration of the possibilities of the narrative 'tenor' and her confidence with
written language in general make it a superior piece from the point of view of a
modern fairytale. In terms of the genre, Nicole has manipulated both the orien-
tation^ complication ^ resolution sequence very competently and plays with
evaluative meanings in interesting ways. Note, for example, the way she foreshadows the events to come as Agather wonders at the meaning of 'regain her
beauty' early in the text.

With respect to the tenor, the writer is beginning to experiment with the subjectivity of the characters rather than simply expressing her personal responses. A large part of the entertainment of this fairytale comes from its feminist treatment of the heroine. Agather, unlike most fairytale heroines, is human: she has a 'weight problem' and achieves her goals through somewhat contradictory means: 'Just as she got to the top, the dragon's tail jolted and she slipped off. She burnt the dragon to death!!!' On top of this, Agather is far more active on her own behalf than most fairytale heroines. In terms of the subjective world of the characters, Nicole is experimenting with the possibilities of tenor in this narrative — making use of devices like imagery (for example, 'the world was full of magic'; 'imagining herself as an old spinster'), exclamatives ('Lo and behold there was the dragon!') and even humour (for example, 'The princess had a pimple on her nose because she used a weapon') in building atmosphere, suspense and character. Of course, Nicole is not able to do away with the generic constraints entirely: Agather eventually faints from exhaustion and is rescued (rather unconvincingly) by a passing knight.

In relation to the field projected by the text, the writer has constructed a plausible sequence of events for a fairytale. Although Agather's problem is resolved rather arbitrarily by the abrupt arrival of the hero/knight, Nicole has, nevertheless, given enough information about the participants and their 'goings on' to establish a believable — albeit fairytale — world for the reader. The relevant circumstances of the participants and their doings are made explicit. Note also the development of vocabulary evident in discriminating lexical choices — especially in the area of processes: 'screamed', 'grabbed', 'clambered' and 'sank down'. The text also shows consistent control of the tense patterns appropriate to a fairytale: 'was', 'was walking', 'screamed', 'pulled').

The text is well handled in terms of the written mode, although her use of sentence punctuation could be improved. Nicole is a competent writer; this is evidenced by her control of the sentence and her use of varied sentence beginnings (or to express this linguistically, themes). These are sensitive to the overall development of the narrative: pushing forward the event sequence especially at points where the narrative stages change: for example, orientation: 'Many years ago . . .'; complication: 'One day . . .'. Note the use of a range of cohesive devices (conjunctions, both reference and ellipsis) which she uses to combine clauses and link ideas. For example, '*Agather* was usually *a frisky, sporty girl* but had put on a lot of weight when the witch. . . .'

In terms of formative assessment, the teacher should be well pleased with Nicole's development in writing narratives. However, she could be encouraged to take more risks with the tenor of the narrative persona — perhaps experimenting with more feminist versions of the fairytale narrative. This would give her an increased range of options in exploiting the subversive potential of the genre. So, instead of lapsing into a clichéd ending where the heroine faints and is rescued by the hero, the writer could look at more active ways by which the heroine could resolve her own future.

Text 1B, on the other hand, is in the middle range of achievement for narrative writing. The student understands and utilises narrative structure competently and the activity/event sequence is easily recoverable from the text. In terms of the genre, Adela constructs a fairytale narrative in which a heroine, Cindy, is presented with a problem which she must solve. She resolves the complication of the 'deep hole and the giant spider' through the agency of a travelling knight. He rescues her from the hole, kills the spider and they carry the money back to the palace and live 'happily ever after'. The absence of any significant evaluative meanings, however, leaves the narrative rather flat.

With respect to the tenor, the text is unremarkable. The subjectivity of the characters is left undeveloped. We learn little of the characters' motives or needs, and there is no attempt to build suspense or atmosphere. Consequently, there are very few mental processes, attitudinal epithets, comment adjuncts, rhetorical questions or exclamatives in the text. The writer has been content to write a narrative event sequence with no evidence of interest in the interpersonal world of the characters or its meaning for the reader.

Along the field dimension, the writer presents a 'possible world' in which specific participants, such as Cindy, the wise old lion, a spider, act on the world and on each other. The treatment of the activity sequence is believable and coherent; that is, it is possible to understand what goes on and to follow the sequence of events. There is little effort to elaborate the physical details of the world, however, and so the reader comes to the end of the tale with a 'So what ?' response.

In terms of mode, Adela has a reasonable degree of control of written language. She is able to integrate and embed a range of clause types within the sentence, for example, | | 'One day she went to the princess | | and asked her | | if she could go to the tree [[ that grew money]] | |'). Like the writer of Text 1A, she uses varied and interesting sentence beginnings. The themes for each new paragraph herald a change in the temporal setting which helps to push the narrative forward (Paragraph 1 'Long long ago'; Paragraph 2 'After three months of travelling'; Paragraph 3 'Back at the palace').

In terms of formative assessment, Adela needs to look more closely at other narratives and to identify what it is she responds to in stories she likes. When preparing to write her next narrative, it would be helpful to think about (even research) the world she wants to create. When it comes to writing the text, she can focus more carefully on her characters' motives and responses and this will help her to build up the evaluative meanings in her narrative. The teacher could ask Adela to think about the effect she wants to have on the reader as s/he reads her next narrative. Control of the written mode itself is not a major consideration for this writer: developing a more active interest in narrative itself is far more important when it comes to future work.

Finally, Text 1C is in the lowest range of achievement for this class in narrative writing. Although very evocative of a world of fantasy or legend, the narrative as a whole is incomplete and unresolved. It is much shorter than the other texts presented by this class. This contributes to the impression of a very 'slapdash' effort. In terms of the genre, there is a minimal orientation ^ complication ^ resolution structure established. We learn that an evil witch has done something to all the gold in a far away land. John arrives and travels to the witch's lair and faces the witch. Somehow the witch disappears as John swings his sword and it is turned to gold and they live 'happily ever after'. The student, Brett, may be trying to 'spoof' the fairytale genre. But this text does not show any evidence of sustained control over the event sequence and the genre. The reader is left with a sense of a very incomplete narrative.

With respect to the tenor, an atmosphere of a legendary world is established through 'high intensity' expressions (for example, 'Far far away in another universe far from our own'; 'the great evil witch'; 'the lair of the witch which is the dark side of the land'). But the writer does not exploit this potential in any sustained way. Brett has made little effort to differentiate the subjective world of the characters — John and the witch. There is no consistent development of the characters' motives and consequently no development of interpersonal meanings via dialogue, questions, exclamatives or mental process clauses.

In relation to the field, the narrative is a set of activity sequences involving a quest to destroy a great evil witch and to restore the 'happiness and gold' of this far away land. The events are temporally sequenced but are unmotivated. The reader has no idea why they occur as they do. Furthermore, with respect to the actual circumstances of the quest, there are many unanswered questions: for example, into what does the witch turn all the gold? How does John kill the witch? Why does his sword turn into gold? Why, after all this effort, does he 'live happily ever after' with the witch? The reader cannot enter into the 'possible world' of the story because the writer has not been able/willing to build up a sense of its material reality. The shifts from present to past tense only add to this problem.

The text is only moderately well handled in terms of the written mode. Brett makes some interesting theme choices (for example, 'Far, far away in another universe far from our own'; 'but in this land'; 'To this land'; 'The witch'). Nevertheless, his control of the sentence is uneasy; for example, 'The witch had turned all of the gold in the land' [into what?]; 'John found out where the lair of the witch' [was?]. Logical relations between events are not well established. Note the relative absence of conjunctions apart from 'and'. Overall, the text does not hang together very well.

In terms of formative assessment, the teacher has a major challenge on his/her hands. Brett obviously has some command of written language. But either this particular writing task has left him cold or he resists writing more generally. The teacher could focus his attention on any one of the variables: genre, tenor, field or mode. In terms of genre, Brett and the teacher could talk about whether the text makes a 'good story'; about whether an evaluative stage could be introduced; or about how he could construct an orientation stage which 'situates' the events of the narrative more clearly. In terms of tenor, Brett and the teacher could explore ways of building on the atmospheric feeling of the text by using devices like exclamatives, dialogue, descriptive epithets, mental process clauses and so on. Regarding field, the physical reality of the 'possible world' could be better developed. They could talk about what information about the participants, processes and circumstances needs to supplied in the text so that the reader can understand the sequence of events. In regard to mode, Brett needs encouragement with his writing in general. Opportunities to read other students' stories and to display his own work in the class or school library may make him more inclined to take more care with his final draft and to write more extended texts in the future.

Table 1 sets out the linguistic criteria used for assessing these Year 5 narratives. The examples have been drawn from Text 1A.

Let us turn now to the scientific report genre and consider how the same framework can be used to assess scientific reports in a classroom context. Once again the following information reports were not produced out of the blue. The same students were working on a biology unit — in particular, on the classification of animals. They were asked to take one major class within the animal kingdom,

Table 1.   *Assessing Year 5 Narratives Using Linguistic Criteria*

---

**Purpose: Entertaining, Amusing, or Reflecting on Experience**

Generic
staging: Orientation ∧ Complication ∧ Evaluation ∧ Resolution

Orientation: *A beautiful princess wanders in the woods*
Complication: *Agather meets a witch and learns she has to kill a dragon to regain her beauty*
Evaluation: *Agather wonders about the note's meaning*
Complication: *Agather encounters the dragon*
Resolution: *Agather kills dragon and is found by a knight*
Re-orientation (optional): *They marry and live happily ever after.*

**Tenor: Control of Subjectivity in the Narrative World**

Interpersonal
meanings: Focus on and control of the subjective world of the characters; their needs, motives, emotional responses

Via reported and quoted speech; mental processes; attitudinal epithets, comment adjuncts
Use of imagery and metaphor: *the world was full of magic; imagining herself as an old spinster*
Rhetorical questions: *Could this be happening?*
Repetition
Exclamative: *Lo and behold there was the dragon!!; She burnt the dragon to death!*
''(builds atmosphere, suspense and characterisation

**Field: Constructing a Possible World via Event Sequence**

Experiential
meanings: Sequencing events properly and exploiting them appropriately for purposes of the genre

Specific, individualised participants: *The Princess Agather; a frisky sporty girl*
Inclusion of relevant circumstantial information: *through the woods; in front of her; out of her pocket*
Discriminating word choices, especially of processes: *screamed; grabbed; clambered; sank down*
Consistent use of past tense: *was; was walking; jumped; screamed; pulled*
Use of language that extends, enhances and elaborates on information and an increasing range of linking words and ellipsis to combine clauses and link sentences (clause complex): *Agather was usually a frisky, sporty girl <u>but</u> had put on a lot of weight <u>when</u> the witch changed her*

**Mode: Creating a Context for the Reader via Text**

Textual
resources: Presentation as text

Interesting and varied use of first position in the clause (theme): *Many years ago; A princess; when suddenly a witch; Just as the dragon*
Integrating clauses within the sentence; appropriate punctuation
Control of reference: *A princess'; she, The princess Agather; a frisky sporty girl*

---

*Source*: Macken *et al.* (1989c).

such as birds, mammals, reptiles, or fish, and to do a detailed study of different species within the class. As part of this work, they concentrated on the biological characteristics by which the animals are classified: the features they share with others in the same class and which distinguish them as a particular species.

The class spent many weeks focusing on the scientific report as a genre — with its specific social function and distinctive generic structure. It should be noted here that they were working with a narrower understanding of the term 'report'. It is the name given to the factual texts which children write about phenomena of any kind and, since early days of genre writing research, reports have had a distinctive generic structure. It can be expressed in the notation: [general classification ^ description of distinctive features].

The students learnt to identify the stages of the biological reports they were reading — whether those of the encyclopaedia entries on different animals, or in the class model text they constructed about dolphins. As the teacher stressed, the students spent many weeks immersing themselves in the field. They were becoming familiar with content-area reading and with the impersonal tenor of most scientific writing. Use of modelling and joint construction activities meant that the less confident writers were able to draw on the writing experiences supported by the teacher. Thus they were well equipped to handle the task that they were given at the end of this work. Following a writing exercise during which they wrote a report about one creature, their teacher asked them to write a scientific report comparing and contrasting this with another one from the same class.

The following texts (2A, 2B and 2C) represent the top, middle and lower range of achievement in the class's final texts respectively. The framework by which they can be assessed is presented with examples from text 2A.

Text 2A: The Californian Condor and the Albatross

1. Introduction

In all truthfulness the Californian Condor and the Albatross are not convincingly similar. But they are alike in all essential characteristics. The Condor and the Albatross are extremely large birds with massive wingspans. The main difference is the Condor is a land bird whereas the Albatross is a sea bird. The other difference is that the Californian Condor is rare and the Albatross common. But I have written a comparison report on these two marvellous birds.

2. Tearing, scratching and impaling dead bodies

The Condor's prey is totally unlike its seaborn brother, the Albatross. The Condor's foods are mainly old dead bodies, but it can eat sheep, cows, goats, horses and coyotes. The Condor's talons are especially designed for picking up its prey at speed, whereas the Albatross' feet are for swimming and speed breakage.

The Condor's colour scheme is mainly black with white underlining the wings and a beautiful reddish neck. The Condor mainly lives in caves on high mountains and cliffs. Sometimes smaller birds (such as Vultures, Bald Eagle and smaller birds) will share the nest with the Condor. The Condor usually lives in twos and fours.

### 3. The Californian Condor

The Californian Condor is the largest land bird in the world, whereas the albatross is the largest sea bird in the world and also the largest bird. The Condor is a very rare bird that lives in California only but the Albatross lives in most oceans and seas. The Condor has a wingspan of 2.4 to 2.9 metres and in this respect is larger than the albatross, its sea descendant of 2 metres. The Condor has a very distinct beak which is quite long and mainly yellow. The beak is hooked and sharp unlike the Albatross's which is long and straight for plucking fish and scraps whilst moving. It is unlike the Condors for the Condor lays one to two eggs per year. The Condor stays with its mother until six years of age when it is ready to breed.

In early 1980, 30 Californian Condors were left but now they are totally protected by natural reserves and if this continues they should survive.

### 4. The Albatross

The Albatross is an extremely large sea bird related to the Condor, Vulture, Sea Eagle and Arctic Duck.

The Albatross has a wingspan of 11 feet (3.5m) compared with 10 feet for the Condor. This makes it the largest bird in the world. The Albatross weighs 15 to 25 kg making it 10kg heavier than the Condor which is a big difference. The Albatross is 2m long making it in this respect smaller than the Condor by 20cm. The Albatross lives mainly in the South Atlantic, North Pacific and Indian Ocean. The Albatross comes to land to breed only these places are mainly uninhabited Polar islands.

### 5. Eggs

The Albatross lays one egg (spotted), it will sit on it for 70–85 days before hatching. The Condor's egg colour is black and soot-grey. The baby Albatross has a very fluffy down. The Albatross lays one to two eggs per year and the baby Albatross will stay with its mother until two years of age.

### 6.

The Albatross will follow ships for hundreds of kilometres picking up scraps and garbage dropped off the ship.

Albatross Species include: Royal Albatross, short tailed, black browed, Red foot and black tailed which came from the Atlantic, Pacific, Indian, Mediterranean, Tasman and Japan Seas and Oceans and the most common, the wandering Albatross, comes from all of these except the Sea of Japan.

The Albatross is now entirely protected and will undoubtedly last for many years to come.

by Frank

Text 2B: Comparison of tiger and lion

The tiger cat and the lion both belong to the cat family. Tiger cat's length is 1.2 metres and the lion is 3 metres long. The tiger cat's colour is brown and white with spotted fur. The lion usually has golden or reddish-brown fur. The tiger cat's fur is much lighter than the lion, and the lion is darker.

Tiger cats usually eat what domestic cats eat although the lion doesn't. The lion can eat much larger animals. It can fit an animal as large as a horse in its jaw and eats lots of meat. The tiger cat and the lion live far away from each other. The tiger cat lives in the East and South East of Tasmania, whereas the lion is found in Africa and India.

The tiger cat's roar is not as loud as the lion's, but is still loud. The lion's roar is the most terrifying sound in nature. Even though they both belong to the same cat family, they are extremely different in most ways.
        by Ismini

Text 2C: Comparison of the red bellied black snake and the death adder

The red bellied black snake and the death adder are both poisonous.

The red bellied black snake and the death adder are both found in New Guinea and Australia.

The red bellied is longer than the death adder. They both have a thin tail. They are both brown in colour. The death adder has very bad effects on people. The death adder comes easily disturbed. The death adder has a very narrow tail.

The red bellied and death adder can both kill people and animals. The death adder can attack small creatures. The death adder has darker bands on the back. They can make their tail curve they can both wriggle.

The red bellied black snake hisses and pretends to strike at people. Other animals like this are crocodiles and the alligators.
        Geoffrey

What each writer has achieved in this exercise can also be described in terms of the linguistic criteria relevant to genre and register. Development in handling scientific report writing involves learning to control language features relevant to the following four dimensions.

With regard to the overall structure of the text, students need to understand the purpose of the genre. In this case the purpose of reports of this kind is to give information about whole classes of phenomena — their distinctive features and behaviours. The structure of the genre reflects its distinctive purpose: classifying and describing.

Along the tenor dimension, students are learning to explore more objective ways of treating their experience of the natural world. In linguistic terms, this means learning to make generic participants the subject of the discourse (for example, 'the Californian Condor', 'the albatross' 'they', 'the Condor') rather than their personal feelings and attitudes. Scientists prefer to grade and measure phenomena rather than respond to it in subjective or idiosyncratic ways (for example, 'a wingspan of 2.4 to 2.9 metres'; 'weighs 12 to 14 kg'). Overt expressions of attitude are inappropriate in scientific writing.

Along the field dimension, the texts should demonstrate the ability to classify and describe phenomena. The student is learning to interpret phenomena in new ways. This often means using technical terms. For example, 'The Condor and the Albatross are extremely large birds with massive *wingspans.*' Control of the field is indicated by the use of language which extends, enhances and elaborates on the information (for example, | | 'a large sea bird' | | = 'related to the Condor Vulture Sea Eagle and Arctic Duck.' | | and | | 'The Condor's talons are especially designed' | | × 'for swimming and speed breakage.' | |). Furthermore, reports about the way things are feature the universal present tense. Students should be able to handle this tense consistently through their writing (for example, 'has' or 'They have').

The choice of written mode involves the student in learning to create a 'context-independent text': one by which a reader is able to rely on the language alone to construe the context. Once again, the use of the sentence and appropriate punctuation is important here. The experienced student will be able to combine different types of clauses and even to embed one inside the other when necessary. An example here is 'The main difference is the Condor is a landbird// whereas the Albatross is a sea bird.'). Writers make use of an increasing range of linking words and ellipsis to combine clauses and link sentences, such as 'The *other difference* is that the Californian Condor is rare *and* the Albatross is common.' They will also be aware of the need to make the text cohesive and so will refer correctly and consistently to the people, places and things once they are introduced rather than assuming these participants are self-evident to a reader who doesn't share the experience recreated in the text. For example, 'The Californian Condor and the Albatross', 'they' and 'large birds').

We will return now to the three report texts and evaluate them from the point of genre and register, making suggestions about the implications for diagnostic and formative assessment.

Text 2A is in the highest range of achievement for report writing in this class. Its length, the organisation of information under headings, the depth of field knowledge and the cohesiveness of the text all contribute to making it a superior achievement. In terms of genre, note the sophistication of the general classification stage. Both the Californian condor and the albatross are described as similar in 'essential characteristics' in the fact that both 'are extremely large birds with massive wingspans.' The most important 'difference' is that 'one is a land' and the other 'is a sea bird'. Frank has taxonomised the birds in terms of essential similarities and differences. In other words, he has grasped in writing the fact that science is interested more in 'essential characteristics' than in observable ones.

When it comes to tenor, predictably enough for scientific writing, the generic participants are the subject of study: groupings of phenomena like condors or albatrosses. As an incumbent biological student, Frank focuses on grading and measurement — of wingspan length, width, number of days hatching the egg and so on. He employs these measurements to explore the relevant contrasts between the two birds, for example, 'The Albatross has a wingspan of 11 feet (3.5m) compared with 10 feet for the Condor. This makes it the largest bird in the world.' The writer largely avoids any overt attitudinal comments on the birds. The text thus takes up the appropriate tenor for scientific reporting.

The text is particularly successful with respect to construction of the field. The function of particular features of the birds' appearance is elaborated in far greater detail here than in the other sample texts (e.g., 'The Condor's talons are especially designed for picking up its prey at high speed, whereas the Albatross's feet are for swimming and speed breakage). The information about each bird is related to issues like adaptation to the environment and survival.

In terms of the written mode, the report is relatively successful, although the writer does tend to repeat the name of the main participant (bird) too often, especially in the second half. He needs help with using cohesive ties like pronouns or synonyms more effectively to refer to the subject. The contrastive focus of the text is evidenced in the wide variety of compare and contrast conjunctions across the text as a whole.

The writer is making use of nominalisations for reasoning as well as conjunctions in the following: 'But they are alike in all *essential characteristics*.' or 'The *main difference* is . . . whereas the Albatross is. . . .' In nominalised reasoning, logical relations are expressed as nouns or verbs, in this case as nouns. It enables the writer to organise information in abstract ways, for example, in terms of 'essential characteristics' or 'main differences'. This is important for essay writing in later years of schooling. The writer, however, needs more practice with using topic-focused headings.

Text 2B is a reasonably successful piece of report writing by a student in this class. In terms of genre, Ismini shows the ability to compare and contrast two members of the cat family in relation to their appearance and habits. In terms of tenor, the generic participants, such as 'the lion', 'the tiger', 'the tiger's fur', 'tiger cats' and so on, are the subject of the discourse. Also the appearance of the two creatures is compared in terms of measurement such as their length, or their grading — 'reddish-brown fur' or 'much lighter than'. This move away from personal responses or bald assertions about phenomena into grading and measurement is a development in her report writing towards greater economy and accuracy of scientific description, although handled awkwardly here.

In terms of field, Ismini shows an understanding of the characteristics which distinguish the two members of the cat family, but these differences are explored in commonsense terms, for example, 'the . . . length', 'the colour'. She attempts to exemplify statements via exaggerated assertions like the following: 'Tiger cats eat what domestic cats eat although the lion doesn't' and 'the lion can eat much larger animals. It can fit an animal as large as a horse in its jaw and eat lots of meat.' This is rather like the commonsense observations by youngsters about the feats of animals like lions or tigers. A more economical way to represent the differences between the animals in scientific writing would be to describe both cats as 'carnivorous' but having a different 'diet' of such and such. The writer also needs to specify that the particular species she is referring to is the 'Tasmanian tiger cat'. This is unclear until the end of the report.

With respect to the written mode, the writer has written a reasonably coherent text. She has control of a much wider range of clause types than the writer of Text 2C. There is a corresponding diversity of conjunctive relations linking clauses which compare and contrast the two creatures, for example, 'The tiger cat lives in the East and South East of Tasmania *whereas* the lion is found in Africa and India'; 'the tiger cat's roar is not as loud as the lion's *but* is still loud'.

Text 2C is not a particularly successful piece of report writing for a Year 5 student. In terms of genre, Geoffrey has not shown where the two snakes belong in the classificatory schemas of biology. The two species of snake are poisonous, but the writer doesn't indicate why both are classified as snakes. Biology would taxonomise them as 'venomous' rather than 'poisonous' snakes. The report, as a whole, is a list of generic statements about what the two creatures have in common. But there is little attempt by the writer to organise the statements in any order of priority. In terms of tenor, the writer is focusing on generic participants, though the repetition of 'red bellied black snake' and 'death adder' becomes rather tiresome after a while. In situations like this, students need help with exploiting the pronoun system to refer to previously mentioned participants. The writer's presence intrudes in comments like 'the death adder has very bad effects on people' or [the] 'can both kill people and animals'.

The text does not reveal a great deal of field knowledge about snakes. The writer appears to be relying on observation of pictures of snakes and commonsense information about snakes, such as 'The red bellied black snake hisses and pretends to strike at people. Other animals like this are crocodiles and the alligators.' The writer is falling back on previous, rather sensationalised, accounts of snakes and crocodiles to fill out the report. With respect to the written mode, the sentences are simply piled up and appear to come out of the blue. This is because they are mostly loosely coordinated, single-clause sentences and because the writer has made little attempt to connect one clause with another via conjunctions or exemplification.

In terms of formative assessment, Geoffrey needs help with organising information under headings and making use of the scaffolding provided by general classification. The writer also needs to do some more research into the field and perhaps create a matrix which organises details related to snakes' appearance, behaviour (eating, breeding, habitat and so on). A comparison of the two snakes along these dimensions would be much better organised and lead to a more successful report.

Table 2 sets out the linguistic criteria used to assess these Year 5 scientific reports. The examples have been taken from Text 2A.

Finally, we take a synoptic look at these four contextual dimensions to show that they can illuminate the assessment process for many different writing tasks. Each aspect of the context can be transformed into a 'probe' and can be used to assess learners' development. We would argue that the probes will work for any text which is self-contextualising. It is these texts which students find hardest to write.

| | |
|---|---|
| Genre | Does the text reveal a clear sense of purpose? |
| | Is it well organised into stages? |
| Tenor | Does the text construct a consistent reading position for the reader? |
| | How well does the writer exploit the interpersonal resources of the grammar in this task? |
| Field | Does the text project a coherent 'possible world'? |
| | How well does the writer exploit the ideational resources of the grammar in this task? |
| Mode | Is the text cohesive? |
| | How well does the writer exploit the textual resources of the grammar in this task? |

*Table 2. Assessing Year 5 Scientific Report Writing Using Linguistic Criteria*

---

**Purpose: Classifying and Describing Phenomena**

Generic
staging: General Classification ∧ Description

**Tenor: Growth of Objectivity in Report Writing**

Interpersonal
resources: Interaction between interlocutors — child to (unknown) readers as expert

> Non-interactant subjects; generic participants (rather than interactants: *I; you*; impersonal *we*; as subject: *The Condor; the albatross.*
> Non-attitudinal; rather than expression of personal feelings and attitudes
> Non-modalised, untagged declarative: *The condor and the albatross are extremely large birds* rather than *I think the condor is a large bird; a condor is a large bird, isn't it?, is a condor a large bird?*

**Field: Moving from Commonsense to Technical Knowledge**

Ideational
resources: Representation of experience

> Information selected from the field — classifying, grading, measuring and describing phenomena: *A dolphin is a mammal that can swim; fifteen years; a bit of hair*
> Clause (Transitivity) — relational: *dolphins have flippers, dolphins are mammals*; material: *they use their flippers, they bump their mothers*
> Lexis or use of technical terms where relevant, building up lexical taxonomies: *with massive wingspans; the condor's talons*
> Use of language which extends, enhances and elaborates on the information (clause complex): *The condor's talons are especially designed for picking up its prey at speed, whereas the albatross's feet are for swimming and speed breakage*; conditions on processes; linking processes: *whereas the albatross's feet*
> Verbal and nominal groups — Generalised events (time) and Participants (reference): *The Condor and the Albatross*; ['the class of'] *are* ['always'] *extremely large birds*; consistent use of present tense when phenomena exist in an ongoing way: *is; lives*

**Mode: Creating a Context for the Reader via Text**

Textual
resources: Presentation as text

> Constructing its own context. Reference inside rather than outside text: *Condor; it; They*
> Integrating clauses within the sentence and appropriate punctuation: *The condor's foods are mainly old dead bodies, but it can eat sheep, cows, goats, horses and coyotes*
> Monologic — topical themes; progression through these: *The Condor; They; The Californian Condor*

---

*Source*: Adapted from Matthiessen *et al.* (in press).

## The Potential of the Approach

In summary, this model of context is a helpful tool for teachers in planning and assessing their students' writing for a number of reasons. First, it enables them to predict systematically the likely linguistic features of the writing their students will produce. It spells out the criteria for successful negotiation of a writing task. Second, it helps them to formalise their intuitive judgments of different students' written products, and to substantiate their claims about one text being better or worse than another. Third, it makes the demands of particular writing tasks, as well as the criteria against which they will be evaluated, clear. It also provides both teachers and students with a language for reflecting on the texts they encounter and produce. Fourth, it enables the goals of students' writing to be linked with the learning objectives in different subjects across the curriculum.

System functional linguistics has been utilised in many language assessment sites. Here we have focused on literacy and on writing in particular, and we have drawn our examples from a primary classroom. But any social process which involves language as a critical component can be analysed in terms of genre, field, tenor and mode. Our concern has been that these categories be made available to educators and deployed in such a way that both teachers and students can benefit. A linguistically informed approach to literacy assessment offers teachers and students a metalanguage (a linguistic technology) for entering into productive dialogue with one another and for reflecting on the communicative requirements of written tasks.

# Bibliographical Essay: Developing the Theory and Practice of Genre-based Literacy

*Bill Cope, Mary Kalantzis, Gunther Kress and Jim Martin; compiled by Lorraine Murphy*

### Evolution of a Theory

As an introduction to the world of genre-based literacy teaching, this book has so far provided a detailed account of both the technicalities and the philosophy of genre theory. It is now time to integrate this into an historical and bibliographical setting, sketching how genre theory and the genre school developed and siting the bibliographical references in terms of this evolution.

It was Michael Halliday, founding Professor of Linguistics at the University of Sydney from late 1975, who was to provide the catalyst for the development of genre theory. His theory of systemic functional linguistics, which he later set out in *An Introduction to Functional Grammar* (Halliday, 1985a), introduced the theme of 'learning language, learning through language, learning about language'. Halliday's idea was to bring together linguists and educators to forge educational linguistics into a transdisciplinary, rather than simply an interdisciplinary, field. He believed that a special cooperation between systemic linguists and educators was necessary to achieve truly revolutionary ends. Linguists must begin working with teachers and teachers in turn would begin to see linguistics as a practical, rather than an esoteric tool which they could use in their everyday work. In other words, experts would start to examine the same problems from different points of view. The resulting crossfertilisation was soon to create a revolution which stretched far beyond the confines of applied linguistics.

In 1978, when J.R. Martin planned his functional varieties course for the MA Applied Linguistics program at the University of Sydney, he made his first tentative reworking of his colleagues, Halliday and Hasan's work, using Michael Gregory's field, mode, personal tenor and functional tenor model (Martin, 1991b). During the course the idea of starting a research project using systemic functional linguistics to analyse writing produced in schools was discussed by Martin and two of his students, Joan Rothery and Frances Christie. The following year at the first Language in Education workshop (another Halliday initiative), Martin and Rothery, who remained at the University of Sydney, organised their first workshops on writing and began to work together. Frances Christie meanwhile, first as Director of the Language Development Project in Canberra and then as a lecturer in education at Deakin University, began to pursue her own research along similar lines.

From 1980 Martin and Rothery were examining samples of student writing which had been collected over the years. They identified key types, analysed their field, mode and personal and functional tenor, and worked on the realisation of these contextual variables in discourse semantics and lexicogrammar. From this time, genre theory began developing in Sydney. Rothery theorised that if purpose was made a controlling register variable, this would access the overall function of text and coordinate the way in which field, mode and personal tenor choices combine. Functional tenor was stratified with respect to field, mode and personal tenor in their early work. From the start this, however, created a problem. Tenor now existed on two levels. So, influenced by Hasan's work on generalised text structure, functional tenor was renamed as genre, leaving personal tenor as tenor, and giving rise to the stratified model of register and genre that continues to underpin the work of Martin and Rothery. In effect, as this brief instance shows, the theory developed from the process of analysing and classifying texts — theory and practice moving together, not one informing the other.

In Adelaide, Gunther Kress first became interested in questions of genre while he was Dean of the School of Communication and Cultural Studies at the Murray Park College of Advanced Education. Here part of his work involved working directly with primary school teachers and it was this set of experiences which motivated him to write about the process of acquiring literacy. In fact, it was to be Kress's book, *Learning to Write* (Kress, 1982), which would first introduce the concept of genre to an international audience. Kress's interest in literacy questions and his involvement with teachers and their experiences went back a long way. In 1974, while he was a lecturer in linguistics at the University of East Anglia, he had been approached by representatives of Keswick Hall College of Education at Norwich to help set up a fourth year strand in language and education. His input into this project even at this early date had a distinctive touch for he was already interested in the concept of a critical sociolinguistics, and during the years he worked in England, first at the University of Kent and then at the University of East Anglia, he had been working towards developing a critical theory of language. The product of this research, *Language as Ideology* (written in collaboration with Robert Hodge), was the first comprehensive account of the theory of language which was later to be known as critical discourse analysis (Kress and Hodge, 1979).

Kress and Hodge felt that linguistics needed to become at once a socially responsive and a responsible discipline. Linguistics, as it stood in the late 1970s, they felt, simply could not provide a satisfactory theory of language. Much of its knowledge, while remaining relevant enough, had inherent problems of organisation which made it impossible to use unmodified, as a starting point. The way knowledge is organised, they believed, crucially affects how it can be used, and what it can or cannot do. As a trailblazer for early critical discourse analysis, Kress and Hodge's book was to set its theory of how grammar carries social meaning within a broadly based program for the study of language and social meaning. As was separately the case with Martin, Rothery and Christie, Kress's theory of grammar was inspired by practice, which at the same time was refracted by the form of the evolving theory. Remaining central to the book's project, however, were two defining features: a concern with power as the condition of social life, and the need for a theory of language which incorporates this as a major premise.

Kress and Hodge's ideas had stemmed from the work of such diverse writers as Chomsky, Bernstein, Hymes, Labov, Althusser, Foucault and Marcuse, set in a broadly Hallidayan framework. Their aim in 1979 was to insert potential points of contact with what was then an inchoate and emerging set of discourses, giving the theory an open set of possible uses. Critical sociolinguistics, while not existing as a coherent force, they felt, was already well and truly adumbrated. For example, Blom and Gumperz (1972) had implied questions about a social structure marked by differences of access and by differences of power when they had asked questions about code-switching. Labov (1972b), by asking questions about the differential uses of microlevel phonetic features, had also pointed to the existence of a class-segmented society as well as the different social histories of their speakers, and their consequent differential standing in the language community.

When Kress left England for Australia in late 1978, he again began working directly with primary school teachers. The ideas behind *Learning to Write* incorporated that set of experiences into his earlier Kent and East Anglia work. Kress's first personal contact with Martin and Rothery at the University of Sydney came when he sent Martin the typescript of *Learning to Write* and asked for comments. Martin was very enthusiastic and reciprocated by sending Kress a copy of the first Martin/Rothery *Working Papers*. Martin had already read *Language as Ideology* (Kress and Hodge, 1979), a book which inspired Martin's first attempts to model the interaction between ideology and genre (Martin, 1985, 1989, 1986c). In 1983 the link between Martin, Rothery and Kress could only deepen after Kress moved to Sydney and a position as Dean in the Faculty of Humanities and Social Sciences at the then New South Wales Institute of Technology, Sydney and became a regular participant in the linguistics seminars at the University of Sydney.

By this date Martin and Rothery's research was progressing rapidly as they systematically analysed, in terms of their developing genre theory, writing produced at infant as well as primary level, from both traditional and process writing classrooms. Cate Poynton had joined them as ethnographer on a project dedicated to an examination of process writing results, allowing them to analyse an increased database. Most of these texts, they found, were quite short and limited to just a few major genres — labelling, observation/comments, reports, recounts and narratives — with observations and recounts predominating. Martin (1984) and Rothery (1989a) provide a useful introduction to this work. The texts also lacked development even within the story genres; were highly gendered in nature; and appeared practically irrelevant to the needs of the community or secondary school. That this was the result of an unsatisfactory pedagogy was backed up by Frances Christie's research at Deakin University, where she was working on applying genre theory to the study of classroom interaction (Christie, 1984, 1986, 1987a–b). The need to develop a theoretically distinctive pedagogy to address this situation was becoming obvious, although it was to take a few more years of research and trialling before the curriculum cycle was satisfactorily established (Callaghan and Rothery, 1988).

In 1985 Rothery began to work closely with a Year 2 and a Year 3/4/5 (composite class) teacher to develop a pedagogy which would draw on a language-based theory of learning. Working with teachers who were interested in experimenting with other genres, however, in some ways made the task more difficult

(Rothery, 1986, 1989b). Texts became longer, and Martin and Rothery found themselves developing new categories for the range of factual writing produced (Martin, 1985). Meanwhile, Christie's research, indicating that the way teachers prepared children for writing then became the main influence on what they wrote, disproved some of Martin and Rothery's earlier hypotheses about the development of writing. Christie (1984) and Rothery (1986) demonstrated that context was a far more important factor than linguistic maturity in terms of the development of writing. To facilitate their research, they developed an 'intruder', as opposed to simply an 'observer', role as educational linguists.

Martin and Rothery were also interested in studying the role of learning about language in literacy teaching. They believed that learning to write was different from learning to talk in terms of consciousness. From their work arose analyses of text in context — including deconstructions at the level of genre (text structure), discourse semantics and grammar. It was not until later, however, that they began work on deconstructing field and mode. In 1985 Rothery worked with teachers introducing the generic structure of genres and analysing foregrounded aspects of their grammar — for example, the grammar of nominal groups in reports. At the same time they experimented with a pedagogy in which teachers adopted an authoritative negotiating role — as opposed to what Halliday has called 'benevolent inertia'. The results, they believed, were encouraging.

By 1986 the genre school had grown considerably and researchers were now turning to studies of writing in secondary schools. Research teams began working intensively on scientific writing, first in science and geography and only later in the disciplines of mathematics, history and the social sciences (Macken and Rothery, 1991a–b). Initially the main source of inspiration was Halliday's work on the development of scientific English (Halliday, 1988), although this was expanded and developed as the research gathered momentum (Halliday, 1990, in press; Halliday and Martin, 1993). Researchers were particularly concerned with the role of technicality in building up uncommonsense interpretations of reality, and the complementary ways in which technicality was established in the report and explanation genres. To do this, the interpretation of the explanation genre needed to be refined, and researchers were thinking in terms of constructing a distinction between explanations in the 'natural' sciences such as geography, biology, geology, meteorology, and explanations relying more on the 'hard' science of physics. Textbooks were subjected to genre analysis as these were the main models used by students for their writing (Eggins, Wignell and Martin, 1987; Wignell, Martin and Eggins, 1987; Wignell, 1988; Martin, Wignell, Eggins and Rothery, 1988; Shea, 1988; Martin, 1990b; McNamara, 1989).

These new discipline-specific literacy contexts made it essential to develop models of field and mode. In relation to field, genre theorists tried to unpack the notion of technicality and what it means to move from common to uncommonsense. With mode, focus was on abstraction — studying the ways in which ideational metaphor is mobilised to differentiate 'spoken' from 'written' text. Working individually, Louise Ravelli and Janet Jones both began important work developing the theory of grammatical metaphor and mobilising it in such a way that it could be used to measure the degree of abstraction in text. Genre writers also began experimenting with pedagogies to guide students into technical and abstract discourse in secondary school. These, it was argued, would have to be field- rather than genre-based, unlike the interventions in primary school.

By now there were genre researchers in the Learning Assistance Centre at the University of Sydney and the Institute of Languages at New South Wales University becoming involved in research. During 1990 Peter Wignell concentrated in particular on the discourse of sociology at a tertiary level. Social science, he found, involves a blending of science and humanities oriented discourse styles. Social science essays, he argued, were more than just technical; they were often extremely abstract as well. For example, in an economics essay the degree of abstraction is partly reflected in the number of nouns in the text which refer not to people, places and things but to processes: inflation, demand, push, increase, supply, intervention and so on. Extensive nominalisation of this kind he isolated as one feature that economics essays shared with writing in history or literary criticism, resulting in a very condensed form of argumentation. Further research into the texture of abstract humanities style writing also became focused on the ways in which nominalisations are used to organise information — making predictions about what will come and summing up what has been presented (Martin, 1986c, 1991d, 1992, in press a, b). Martin draws on this work in making a number of suggestions for theorising the structure of what he calls 'macro-genres'. His concern was to move beyond 'staging', to consider prosodic and periodic structure at the level of genre (Cranny-Francis and Martin, 1992).

This was also a period of intensive investigation into 'story' writing, leading to a significant reappraisal of the role of interpersonal meaning across a range of narrative-type genres. Both Rothery and Plum distinguished a number of story genres — including recount, anecdote, exemplum, fable and narrative — and drew attention to the ways in which interpersonal meaning is criterial in distinguishing the different types (Rothery, 1990; Plum, 1988). Following from this, J.R. Martin began reconsidering the significance of prosodic (interpersonal) and periodic (textual) patterning at the level of genre, where a particulate focus had been generally adopted and Rothery started working on the problem of story writing in secondary school, drawing on this work. Genre work also became interested in the lower levels of description — for example, adapting the model of conversational structure to the needs of classroom discourse analysis; refining the theory of grammatical metaphor; exploring grading across a range of interpersonal resources; and introducing more delicacy for relational processes.

All this activity generated the need for further research. In particular, there was a vital need for researchers to work on assessment, especially of story writing in junior secondary school, and for ongoing in-service in this area for secondary English teachers (Macken and Rothery, 1991a–b). The question of interpersonal meaning and the ways in which it can be deployed to construct different types of writer-reader relationship presented as another area needing analysis. It was felt that this was critical in any literacy program for, while varieties of tenor are very important in narrative writing, these may be dysfunctional elsewhere. For example, a geography text which assumes a personal relationship with its reader would distract from the necessary scientific positioning. Interpersonal meaning, it was argued, was also an important variable when it came to the interpretation of curriculum genres, since one of the major challenges for teachers implementing a literacy program drawing on a functional language model is to assume an authoritative position where appropriate, without becoming authoritarian. Martin and Rothery (in press) and Poynton (1985, 1990b) laid the foundations for interpersonally oriented analyses of this kind.

Halliday's continuing work on differences between spoken and written language provided another avenue of research (Halliday, 1979b, 1985b, 1987a). Work was directed towards investigating just how similar were the processes of learning to talk and learning to write (Hammond, 1990, 1991). Hammond concluded that 'a more conscious, deliberate and analytic effort is involved in learning to read and write than in learning to speak' (Hammond, 1990, 51), while Painter (1986) and Gray (1987) explored some of the pedagogical implications of this research. Brian Gray's work on 'concentrated language encounters' with Aboriginal children at Traeger Park school in Alice Springs moved genre research into new areas. Gray, with a background in reading and psychology, had been strongly influenced by Bruner and Vygotsky. His ideas on the kind of guiding role teachers could play in literacy programs proved a useful adjunct to Michael Halliday and Clare Painter's work on child language development. A particular concern was the nature of the teacher-student interaction that most effectively scaffolds entry to various genres, and 'natural' language learning (Painter, 1986; Gray, 1987, 1990b).

Another important initiative in the area of genre research was taken up by feminists. Cate Poynton began examining the social consequences of the kinds of writing undertaken by boys and girls in infants and primary schools, drawing on her ethnographic studies from 1983 (Poynton, 1985, 34–40). White (1986, 1990), Gilbert (1990), Gilbert and Rowe (1989) and Gilbert and Taylor (1991) have all pursued the issues of gender, literacy and social power. Cranny-Francis's deconstructions of semiotic subversion in feminist fiction provide a good example of some of the work in this field (Cranny-Francis, 1990a–e, 1992; Cranny-Francis and Martin, 1992, in press). Another frontier was workplace literacy. Martin (1986a) had already reported on his experiences working with the CSIRO, Australia's key government funded industrial and scientific research organisation. During 1990 Helen Joyce completed an important study of workplace literacy in the context of award restructuring, and from that date two very large research projects, funded by the NSW Education and Training Foundation, were developed with Mary Kalantzis directing the Centre for Workplace Communication and Culture at the University of Technology in Sydney, and the Metropolitan East DSP undertaking Write It Right — an on-the-job training program for secondary school teachers with special reference to school and workplace literacy. David Rose, David McInnes and Henrike Korner completed an intensive study of literacy demands in the science industry (Rose, McInnes and Korner, 1992).

Although Kress continued to work as part of this growing group of researchers, he argued against what he saw as the too narrow limits of genre research in the Martin/Rothery school and their move towards an authoritative concept of teacher-student relations. His basic commitment to the social ideals of genre theory, however, continued to bind him to the movement both in theory and in practice. His belief that a critical theory of language needed to present a fuller picture than concentration on textual form could give, however, was to widen the gap between the direction of his ideas and that in which Martin and Rothery were heading. Influenced by Bernstein and Bourdieu, Kress argued that textual form was just one form of cultural capital. For this reason he believed that to emphasise genre was unwise. Instead, he argued, genre should just be given equal weight with all the other aspects of a critical theory: such as the distinctions between speech and writing; the organisation of discourse; the development of the sentence as a textually determined unit; the importance of form as a signal of meaning; and the role of both the speaking and reading subject in a critical theory.

Kress's academic move from research in applied linguistics to research in the field of communication and cultural studies reflected his theoretical move from linguistics towards broader interests. Of course, the genre movement has profited from such diversification. For example, Kress and Van Leeuven's work has provided a framework for analysing visual semiosis, such as the figures, tables, diagrams, photographs and drawings which often accompany language in young children's writing and much discipline-specific secondary discourse (Kress and Van Leeuven, 1990). The study of communication in structures of power; of reading as an active process; and the idea that each and every text involves multiple authorship; Kress found as inescapable in cultural or media studies as it was alien to the current thinking of linguistics. The production of the filmic text, with its highly complex authorship and production process, was to become for Kress the guiding metaphor in his later research, as was the contested reading which is exemplified by the image of the BUGAUP rewriting of billboards, which he introduced in *Social Semiotics* (Hodge and Kress, 1988). Cultural and media studies also reinforced Kress's conviction that as language was not the only form of com-munication — or even the major form — so concentration on written texts was problematic. However, although Kress moved away from linguistics to engage other disciplines — with Theo Van Leeuven in music and Terry Threadgold in performance, for example — he is still interested in the concept of writing and is currently working on a book, *Writing as Social Practice*.

By the late 1980s, therefore, what had begun from the germ of an idea generated in the Halliday-influenced Linguistics Department of the University of Sydney had developed into a school of thought which was seriously questioning not only linguistics but pedagogy itself. There were genre school researchers now working at Deakin University; in the Education Faculties at the Universities of Sydney, New South Wales and Wollongong; in the Learning Assistance Centre at the University of Sydney; in the Institute of Languages at the University of New South Wales; at the National Centre for English Language Teaching Research at Macquarie University; in the Language and Literacy Unit, Faculty of Humanities, the University of Technology in Sydney; in the Adult Migrant Education Service; and in the Centre for Multicultural Studies at the University of Wollongong. It was the symbiotic relationship that had always existed between theory and practice in the genre school that was now moving the body of theory out of the research establishments and into the classroom to an ever-widening extent.

### Genre in Action

From the start genre theorists had been concerned with equitable outcomes, so dis-courses of generation, gender, ethnicity and class had been a constant preoccupation, and the liberal humanist discourse underlying progressivism was always being carefully deconstructed to test its assumptions. As a result of this work, reservations about progressivist pedagogy tended to become stronger rather than weaker. It was quite obvious that the 'invisible education' (Bernstein, 1975) the progressive curriculum promoted was marginalising working-class, migrant, Aboriginal and other disadvantaged children. And Australian academics and educators, as fervent educational innovators, were leading the world in the acceptance of the progressivist curriculum.

The years of research behind genre theory by the late 1980s had been cumulatively groundbreaking, but the genre school did not yet have the acceptance of the centres of power in Australian education — quite the contrary, in fact. Systemic functional linguistics, let alone its genre school offshoot, was given no input into syllabus planning, which remained squarely in the hands of the process writers. Nor was there any reason that the genre school expected to be handed such a brief. Genre research, though extensively worked out in a dialogue with practice, was still in real terms an untried body of theory, no more, no less, and as such was considered marginal and of little importance as a lobby group. This was the case until Martin's paper at the Australian Reading Association's annual conference in Perth in 1986 sparked a major conflict between the process and genre schools. When Martin introduced the notion of genre, reviewed Clare Painter's important critique of process writing pedagogy (Painter, 1986), reported on Rothery's work with a Year 2 class in 1985 (Rothery, 1989a–b), and gave a critique of the individualistic free enterprise discourse used by Graves to promote his concept of ownership, much of what he said found an audience prepared to listen.

One of those inspired by Martin's paper was Mike Callaghan, the literacy consultant with the Disadvantaged Schools Program (DSP) in Sydney's Metropolitan East Region of the New South Wales Department of School Education. Callaghan, who was very aware that many teachers opposed process writing for very good reasons, decided that the as yet obscure theoretical approach that the genre theorists were putting forward was worth a trial. The resulting Language and Social Power Project, a co-research project of the Metropolitan East DSP and the Linguistics Department of the University of Sydney, was a highly innovative program. The project was designed to test whether a genre-based literacy program would, or could, improve the written outcomes of students. Callaghan wanted to explore the possibilities of genre in action; he wanted to see what would happen if theory could be brought to bear on practice in a wide-ranging project.

The DSP, for various reasons, was an unlikely vehicle for such an experiment. It had been established almost two decades before with the idea that through curriculum reform working-class, Aboriginal and non-English-speaking-background students could be helped to achieve equality in educational outcomes. But it had a strictly progressivist view as to how to achieve this goal. While it was generally agreed that students needed to acquire competence in the basic skills, it was felt that the DSP should not be 'primarily concerned with reading, writing and arithmetic' because these were 'not so much basic skills as basic social screening measures'. Many felt that the prime concern should be 'with making school a happier and more stimulating experience for children and a more welcoming place for their parents. . . .' Most important of all were 'the skills of understanding and respecting the poor. Basically, the program uses public funds to demonstrate public respect, offering friendship and a little help in a way acceptable to the poor. The rich and powerful need that friendship too' (Blackburn and Waters, 1978).

The Language and Social Power Project, therefore, was a radical step for the DSP, which had been a pioneer in the 'process writing' movement in Australia.

Prior to this experiment DSP programs had always been slanted towards personal growth and development as its compensatory logic was geared at enhancing students' self-esteem. In terms of literacy, this had been translated into an emphasis on process writing, and in practice this meant a concentration on narrative writing at the expense of the factual writing most needed by both students and the community. While process writing appeared quite efficient at getting students to write, it proved to be unable to help them develop as writers in terms of language development. And, contrary to the theory, students did not necessarily develop into writers simply on their own motivation. For this requires active and explicit teaching to explain the structures and grammar of written language. The Language and Social Power Project, motivated by this growing evidence that all was not well with current literacy programs, was designed specifically to redress these problems. By 1987 these insights were by no means only held by a few intellectuals and theorists. While the process approach seemed to fit quite comfortably into the 'happy schools' philosophy, many teachers were finding themselves, in despair, becoming actively opposed to it, feeling that it was simply not working. Furthermore, teachers were rejecting school-based curriculum as unrealistic and unproductive.

The teachers were not the only ones decidedly disillusioned with progressive teaching methods. Parents from all backgrounds were becoming increasingly anxious about the hidden assumptions and agendas in progressivist teaching. They were unable to comprehend what it was that their children were supposed to be learning, and the gradual removal of textbooks and homework was alienating them even further. Even the periodic reports on their children's progress seemed to have become incomprehensible as a measure of achievement as these were couched in the relativistic language of process-based curricula. Commonsense told many in the community that it was time to get 'back to basics', stop all this nonsense and return to what now seemed to be a more satisfactory past with its traditional curriculum. It was into this troubled context that the Literacy and Education Research Network (LERN), with ideas backed up by what was rapidly becoming a major trialling program, intervened.

At the time the Department of School Education was in the final stages of preparing a new curriculum document called *Writing K-12*, a curriculum strategy designed to institutionalise process writing and effectively dispense with the traditional curriculum with its formal grammar, rules of punctuation and spelling lists. LERN's founding members, Mike Callaghan, Bill Cope, Anne Cranny-Francis, Mary Kalantzis, Peter Knapp, Gunther Kress, Mary Macken, Robyn Mamouney, Jim Martin, Joan Rothery and Diana Slade, were determined not to let this happen without some form of debate about alternatives. That they succeeded is a tribute to the fact that they were not the only people in the community who were unhappy about institutionalizing the process curriculum with all its faults as well as its progressions. Teachers and parents alike actively welcomed another route forward rather than accept an ignominious retreat to the past.

In 1987, of course, such levels of community support was still very much in the future. While the issues being raised by LERN at the *Writing K-12* launch could not be easily answered or brushed aside, group members knew they needed to strengthen their foothold in the school system itself, if they were to refine their concepts and demonstrate their validity. This genre-based approach might, on the surface at least, appear to be the antithesis of liberal education practice, but in real terms it was soon to prove itself a revolutionary step forward. It might be unashamedly explicit, and appear to leave nothing to chance. It might not appear to embody liberal educational psychology and progressivist pedagogy. But it did not align itself with the reactionary 'back to basics' movement. More importantly, it soon gained the support, not just of teachers who had consistently rejected the progressivism of the process methods, but also of those who had been struggling for a long time to make this process-based pedagogy actually work.

Stepping back from its explicitness, its authoritativeness, its texts and sequences, the teachers involved in the Language and Social Power Project were discovering that genre theory was a progression in the true sense of the word. Moreover, it was easily recognisable as a literacy program which embraced the issues of equity and empowerment — the cornerstones of progressivist and process-based pedagogies — although it approached these from a radically different direction. Teachers discovered that the genre-based approach did not want simply to dismantle all the progressivists' language and educational theory, or all the teaching methodologies which had preceded it. Instead, it sought to build on progressivism's insights, while learning from its mistakes. By showing teachers that there was a social purpose in writing, and developing their skills and knowledge through extensive in-servicing, especially prepared materials and in-class support, this approach gave teachers a practical route out of their educational dilemma.

The largely exploratory genre-based approach adopted by the Metropolitan East DSP was, in keeping with genre theory's insistence on the inevitable link between theory and practice, a trialling ground for theoretical and pedagogical processes in more ways than one. Mike Callaghan and the teachers of Years 5–8 who agreed to take part in the first trial used as their focus the factual genres that Martin and Rothery had identified in earlier research (Martin and Rothery, 1986). These were text types categorised as reports, expositions, discussions, recounts, explanations and procedures. The trial took a typically linguistic approach with each text type being broken into its structural features — the schematic stages — and each of these stages being examined for their typical grammatical features (Callaghan and Rothery, 1988). For example, an explanation was described first by its function:

> Factual text used to explain the processes involved in the evolution of natural phenomena. Explanations are used to account for why things are as they are. Explanations are more about processes than things. In the school curriculum, explanations are often found in Science and Social Studies.

Then by its generic (schematic) structure:

> A general statement to position the reader then sequenced explanation of why/how something occurs (usually a set of logical steps in the process).

And, finally, by its language features:

> Focus on Generic, non-human participants.
> Use of simple present tense.

Use of temporal and causal conjunctive relations.
Use of mainly material (action) processes, some passives used to get
theme right.

As the project progressed, data of this kind were translated into classroom practice
using a pedagogical model, especially developed by project members (Callaghan
and Rothery, 1988). From 1988, when a second major trialling project — the
LERN Project — joined the Language and Social Power Project, there was increasing scope for crossfertilisation and development. The result was to become
the curriculum genre or teaching-learning cycle (Callaghan and Rothery, 1988,
39), which produced a major breakthrough in pedagogical terms.

Building on what was already being learned in the Language and Social Power
Project, the LERN Project of 1988–1989 was undertaken for, and funded by, the
Studies Directorate of the NSW Department of School Education, a testimony to
the fact that genre literacy had finally become recognised as a force in educational
debates. This important breakthrough was signalled by the appointment of Mary
Macken to the Directorate of Studies in 1988. The LERN Project, which brought
together experts from the Centre for Multicultural Studies at the University of
Wollongong (Kalantzis and Cope), the Linguistics Department of the University
of Sydney (J.R. Martin and Joan Rothery) and the Faculty of Humanities and
Social Sciences in the University of Technology, Sydney (Gunther Kress), specifically involved the development of genre-based curriculum materials to support
the *Writing K-12* syllabus (Macken *et al.*, 1989a–d).

Christie had long been developing course materials in her BEd and MEd
programs at Deakin University — work which was later to be commercially
published (Christie, 1989c; Christie *et al.*, 1990a–j, 1992a–e) — but in 1988 the fact
that the Studies Directorate had requested genre theorists to produce curriculum
materials was an important step forward. The resulting curriculum documents,
four books specifically designed for primary schools, introduced teachers to
concepts of register, genre, grammar and discourse, and presented strategies for
evaluation. Once again the project proceeded via an action research model. Under
the guidance of the project consultants, Mary Macken worked with teachers and
students generating sample student writings; devising strategies for language
learning in the areas delineated in the emerging documents; drafting and trialling
the curriculum documents; and, finally, completing the documents in accessible
form for general dissemination. Using the books, teachers were at last able to
access a truly alternate, genre-based rather than process writing-based approach
to the *Writing K-12* syllabus. Book 1 presented teachers with an introduction to
genre-based writing concepts by explaining the rudiments of genre theory; outlining the teaching-learning cycle; indicating the division between story and factual
genres; presenting examples of the different genres and explaining their use; and
linking these to learning in specific areas of the curriculum (Macken *et al.*, 1989a).

Book 2 dealt in depth with scientific report writing, providing a teaching unit
which embodied practical examples of how to approach the three stages of the
curriculum cycle for the purpose of both teaching and learning the report genre.
To this end the teacher information pages were amplified by student activity
pages, and a concluding resource section dealt with assessment and the language
of reports, to ensure the material could be integrated in the classroom into a
meaningful whole (Macken *et al.*, 1989b). Book 3, using the same formula as the

previous book, turned its attention to the story genres (narrative, news story, exemplum, anecdote and recount), once more combining theory, examples and activities to put story writing for the first time into a fully cultural context (Macken *et al.*, 1989c). Book 4 drew all this together, introducing the key linguistic concepts as well as detailing the trialling experiences generated by the LERN Project itself (Macken *et al.*, 1989d).

The success of both the LERN and Language and Social Power Projects reinforced the conviction of LERN members that genre theory should become the basis of a successful, truly equitable literacy program. In addition to the four books produced in the LERN Project, there was now a growing number of books explaining the various genres and outlining genre theory in increasingly practical terms (Kalantzis and Wignell, 1988; Christie, 1989c; New South Wales Department of School Education, 1989a–b, 1990, 1991; Christie *et al.*, 1990a–j, 1992a–e). All that remained was for a major independent report to present proof.

The opportunity presented itself in 1990 when the DSP commissioned the National Centre for English Language Teaching and Research, Macquarie University (NCELTR) to evaluate the Language and Social Power Project's effectiveness (Walsh *et al.*, 1990). This was not simply to be a test of its ability to improve children's writing. As the emphasis of the program had been on a whole school effect, the report by definition had to be more wide-ranging than this. It was also to be an evaluation of its effect on the teachers' pedagogy, on the teachers' knowledge of the social function of language, and in the final analysis of the teachers' capability to assess the effectiveness of students' writing. Finally, the DSP asked the NCELTR to identify the most beneficial elements of the program and to isolate any areas requiring particular amendment.

The evaluation followed two lines of enquiry: the first through a survey of teachers who had participated in the in-service training course offered to schools, and the second through text analyses and assessment of samples of student writing from both participating and non-participating schools (by way of a control). Student texts were organised into the macro (genre) categories of narrative and factual. The writing was then assessed on the basis of the criteria set out in Hammond (1983) that 'the essence of good writing lies essentially in the overall structure of a text, its development and cohesion and whether or not it is written in language appropriate for its intended purpose and audience' (Walsh *et al.*, 1990, 17). The texts needed to show 'a schematic structure appropriate for the genre of the text', 'explicit identification of topic and development of the topic' and 'appropriate use of reference' (Walsh *et al.*, 1990, 17).

The report concluded that the program had generated an 'overwhelmingly positive response from participating teachers' who in general had praised the in-services and the in-class support of the demonstration lessons as well as the back-up materials, both printed and audiovisual. In general, teachers found genre-based literacy to be 'relevant' and 'useful' (Walsh *et al.*, 1990, 51); most had 'accepted the pedagogy' and used the curriculum cycle, although some did this by adapting it 'to suit their own specific needs' (Walsh *et al.*, 1990, 28), thus making the impact on methodology and pedagogy perhaps less than intended (Walsh *et al.*, 1990, 37). Many teachers praised the project because they found 'it enabled them to give the children clear direction in how/what/why to write' and had resulted in 'a changed attitude of the children to writing tasks' (Walsh *et al.*, 1990, 13). As one teacher responded:

I concentrated on Report Writing and Notetaking and in this short time they are looking at things in a more mature way and they are looking at writing as a different medium than before. I'm not suggesting that they're brilliant but I certainly see an improvement and they are looking more carefully at tasks they approach. I mean the changes in their attitudes toward writing and their knowledge of what to put down on paper. Before they just didn't know how to write and what I've shown them is how — they've never been taught. (Walsh *et al.*, 1990, 13)

Others felt that it had 'challenged' them as teachers 'to think about language development and articulate their views, many for the first time' (Walsh *et al.*, 1990, 28). In other words, the project helped both students and teachers to achieve better results.

The teachers who were surveyed perceived improvements in their students' writing in terms of their ability to organise, structure and sequence ideas in written texts. Teachers felt that they were able to give clearer guidance to their students and that the students were clearer about the purpose and development of texts that they were writing as a result of this guidance. (Walsh *et al.*, 1990, 52)

As the project had also stressed that literacy must mean language-across-the-curriculum, not writing as a separate subject area, this was another area that the report examined. It was found that the great majority of teachers who participated in the trialling exercise agreed that for them as primary school teachers, teaching literacy was their most important task. In the words of one teacher: 'I'm completely phasing out the half hour writing lesson every day and I'm slotting it [writing] into every subject area, because genre writing lends itself to every subject area. It's important that the children understand that writing isn't just writing but that it extends across the curriculum' (Walsh *et al.*, 1990, 39).

In terms of the evaluation of students' text, the report found important differences between participating ('package') and non-participating ('non-package') schools. 'Across all years there were considerably more factual texts being written in package schools. Fewer factual texts and more personal response texts were being written in non-package schools.' While in terms of text quality 'all students in all schools had high success rates with personal response texts', it was found that students from participating schools 'had a higher success rate with factual texts.' This was interpreted as giving 'a clear indication of the impact of the package on students' writing.' The report concluded that 'not only are students' from package schools writing a broad range of factual texts, but generally they are writing them successfully' (Walsh *et al.*, 1990, 52–53). Year 2 students in participating schools produced texts which were found to include such genres as procedures, expositions and descriptions, while their counterparts in non-participating schools produced no examples of factual texts at all.

Overall, from the Year 2 data it would appear that children in Package schools are writing a broad range of genres. They are achieving a quite good overall success rate with all categories of texts although their success rate with factual texts is considerably higher (86%) than for the other categories (52% and 57%). Children in non-Package schools are almost exclusively writing personal response texts. They are writing these well, but when they attempt to write narratives they have greater difficulty with structure and development of topic than their 'Package' counterparts. They are writing no factual texts. (Walsh *et al.*, 1990, 23)

In Year 6 students in non-participating schools were found to have produced a 'small proportion of factual texts' (21%) overall, and of these 'their range was quite narrow, consisting of note taking, reports from "Behind the News" and lists of rules.' In general, these showed 'difficulties with schematic structure', and the majority were also personal response texts. In comparison, the Year 6 students from the participating schools produced a large proportion of factual texts (66%), followed by narratives at 28%, and personal response texts at only 6% (Walsh *et al.*, 1990, 26). Year 6 students from both participating and non-participating schools, however, were found to produce a reasonable rate of successful texts.

The report also discerned major differences in teacher attitude between the participating and non-participating schools. 'Also of note is that the teachers in non-package schools considered all personal response texts to be factual type texts. . . . Factual writing . . . was relegated to a minor position in the curriculum. If personal response texts are grouped separately, then data from two of the non-package schools contained less than 10% of factual text types' (Walsh *et al.*, 1990, 16). Yet the report was also able to identify key areas in which the project needed refinement. While the model of in-service was considered 'an effective one' and 'the objectives of the DSP Package are largely being met', it was concluded that more work still needed to be done in this area. Teachers were found to be able to identify specific genres, such as recounts, reports, procedures, explanations and discussion, and confidently identify their schematic structures, but they showed a less competent understanding of each genre's distinctive language features — a more difficult proposition. It was likewise found that many teachers had only 'an implicit rather than an explicit awareness of the social functions of language' (Walsh *et al.*, 1990, 40), and in general many were not making 'a strong connection between the analysis of genres and assessment of students' writing' (Walsh *et al.*, 1990, 44). In its closing paragraph the report concluded that: 'Provided appropriate human and material resources continue to be allocated to the Package, there would seem to be no reason why the initial gains described in this evaluation cannot be built on and extended in the future' (Walsh *et al.*, 1990, 44).

It is a testimony to the overall coherence of the genre school that these two major trialling experiments were such a success. While both projects had developed the Martin/Rothery model for the purposes of cohesion, they also sought to interpret and synthesise the various theories of genre into a practical, useful approach for teachers to work with in classrooms. Nevertheless, the pedagogical and theoretical divisions within the school were becoming increasingly obvious to those involved. As discussed earlier, Kress's reservations about the pedagogical and theoretical direction the Martin/Rothery camp was taking, while not hindering cooperation within the genre school itself, were certainly leading his research into different directions. Similarly, although Kalantzis and Cope remained enthusiastic supporters of the Language and Social Power and LERN Projects, they continued to argue against using the Martin/Rothery curriculum cycle as a model. As their own work producing the Social Literacy materials had long told them, such modelling can too easily be converted into a prescription, with assessment rewarding work in terms of the ability to copy a fixed generic structure.

Behind the scenes Kalantzis and Cope argued that it was necessary to move beyond strict categorisations of the generic, to make the learning of different genres not a matter of duplication of a standard form but mastery of a tool which encourages development and change (even disruption), rather than simply reproduction. They argued, nevertheless, that there was a real need for curriculum scaffolding. If students were to develop a metalanguage with the linguistic-cognitive skills for generalisation and abstraction, in their view, only an authoritative (but not authoritarian) teacher role could carry the framed microstructures and macrostructures necessary for the task.

In their Social Literacy Project — an extensive program of action research in social studies teaching — Kalantzis and Cope (1989a) had already developed a framework which bridged the gap between the traditional emphasis on teaching academic skills through expert guidance and the progressivist enquiry pedagogy with its emphasis on complex social issues and its ability to incorporate areas of local relevance. The structured and explicit approach to learning they developed operates at two main levels: a microlevel where the teaching-learning strategy is carried over a lesson or series of lessons, and a macrolevel where the learning of social concepts is structured over a year or a number of years. It also develops a new role for textbooks — carefully planned material, developed by experts with a knowledge not just of field but of genre. Only texts such as this, they believe, will be able to develop the linguistic-cognitive skills of generalisation and abstraction, while giving the opportunity to master language at a sophisticated level.

The Years 5–8 component of the Social Literacy Project had initially received financial support from the Centre for Multicultural Studies at the University of Wollongong, the Multicultural Education Coordinating Committee of New South Wales, the Catholic Education Office, Sydney, and the Projects of National Significance Scheme of the Commonwealth Schools Commission. By the end of 1987 tens of thousands of copies of final versions of the Social Literacy textbooks had been produced for distribution to Australian schools, with growing international interest in the project, particularly from the UK, USA and Israel. Participating teachers appreciated the success of such an innovative approach in teaching students to comprehend a complex set of social concepts as tools for self and social understanding. They had also found that the concepts were sufficiently general to be relevant for all students, so the materials could form a core curriculum which was usable in any school. This emphasis on concepts also meant that the materials were open to the injection of locally relevant content and examples.

The microstructure in the Social Literacy Program runs: {focus question ^ input ^ critical analysis of input ^ generalisation ^ reapplying theory ^ evaluation}. Focus questions move from what? to how? embodying a linguistic shift from the artificially static world (momentarily frozen for analysis) to encapsulate a dynamic view of the world in action. At times a focus question will move to why? marking a shift by which the key genre becomes an argument. The inputs span a range of genres from reports embodying different viewpoints, to narratives, non-verbal information (tables, maps, graphs, pictures and so on), classifications, lists, explanations, procedures and arguments. Similarly, within a single textbook the main ideas sections will shift from one genre to another — for example, from report to explanation — drawing on already established technical terms or taxonomic relationships as they do so. The analysis and evaluation sections also demonstrate marked genre shifts with exercises embodying a wide range of texts such as classifications, lists, narratives, explanations, reports, arguments, procedures, oral debates and even diary or letter writing.

The focus question establishes the subject of the enquiry and implies the relationship which will be found to exist between the parts and the whole. The inputs establish technical language and indirectly serve to define the field, while the main ideas section reinforces these while also introducing new terms. What's more, the abstractions embodied in the grammatical metaphors are directly traceable to their congruent forms. This line of connection links not only the input data and the main ideas section, but often takes place within the main ideas section itself. Here both forms are carefully juxtaposed within a single piece of text or are put in a grammatical position between the nominalised realisation and the congruent one to facilitate linguistic understanding. As a book (and the series of books) develops, relationships between things become relationships between processes, all of which can be realised linguistically. In this way the materials extend far beyond the limitations of the traditional social science textbook with its reliance on the report genre.

In this way the Social Literacy materials had always possessed a strong, albeit implicit, emphasis on language learning. The Language in Social Education Project in 1987 highlighted this link for the first time and brought the project into a visible relation with the other two major trials of genre research that were taking place. The Language in Social Education Project was a joint action research project between the Centre for Multicultural Studies at the University of Wollongong (Kalantzis and Cope) and the Department of Linguistics at the University of Sydney (J.R. Martin and Peter Wignell), and funded by the Australian Research Grants Scheme. In this project the genres modelled in the Social Literacy materials were linguistically delineated and analysed. At the same time samples of writing were collected from a cross-section of the schools using the materials in Years 7 and 8. These were examined to gauge the degree to which genre goals were being met. The ultimate object was to develop teaching strategies where necessary to assist students to meet the demands of writing in a variety of genres.

Wignell (1988) found there were both similarities and differences between Social Literacy textbooks and traditional textbooks. Both were concerned with creating field, and were 'organised around things and relationship between things'. Similarly, both technicalised and used texts which were 'oriented towards establishing taxonomic relationships among terms' (Wignell, 1988, 16). In other words, he argued, 'the ways that . . . [they] organise the world is much the same.' This being said, he also found significant differences. Whereas the traditional textbook presented its field as 'given' and as 'fact', Social Literacy texts presented field input as raw data upon which the student must work to 'generate technicality'. The field shifted repeatedly between the non-technical and the technical (Wignell, 1988, 18). Implication sequences were established, but these were never presented as 'certainties'. Rather, they were 'conditional' or 'hypothetical', thus generating questions and arguments and stimulating the students' critical faculties. Implication sequences were also used as a means of drawing together things from different fields, for example from earlier sections or earlier books, and this was a feature of the organic integration of the series into a meaningful whole.

In terms of mode, he found the texts moved the student backwards and forwards between abstraction and source or context, and there was a marked integration of mode and field, although those units concerned with the discipline of geography tended, like most geography texts (Eggins, Wignell and Martin, 1987), to be organised primarily around field. Despite the wide range of genres involved, Wignell noted from his examination of students' texts that there was still a narrow range of genres actually being produced — short comprehension type answers, short classifying type exercises, narratives (including recounts and fables), short arguments, reports (mainly individual projects) and a few procedures. Students tended to write more proficiently in the genre to which they received the most overall exposure in their daily lives — that is, the narrative — or those mainly represented in school texts — the report. They wrote with least proficiency in the genres for which they have fewer models — such as the written argument and the procedure.

Part of this, he argued, was a product of the selection process used by the teachers, although he found the lack of explicit modelling information for the specified genres was also a contributory cause. Still, he argued, the greatest problem was teacher adaptation — a problem which was also to limit the effectiveness of results in the Language and Social Power and LERN Projects. For example, Wignell found that 'tasks which involve disruptions to classroom order are hardly ever done.' Moreover, he discovered, teachers still tended to test and assess on the basis of field knowledge. In other words, they still used the texts to achieve traditional aims.

As the concept of a genre-based literacy pedagogy becomes more widely understood, misunderstandings of this type will gradually become less of a problem. Of course, the only way to ensure this is by educating the educators. The Language and Social Power, the LERN, and Social Literacy Projects all shared a common regard for the importance of in-servicing. But teacher education is, of course, a lot more than a matter of in-servicing.

It is far too early to write the definitive history of the genre movement. All that has been sketched here is an interim report — and a brief one at that. But the task the LERN group had set itself back in 1987 — to bring genre research into the front line of the education debate — has been well and truly achieved. In its first five years LERN has managed to meet, and even exceed, all its original objectives — an achievement which has meant wide-reaching implications for the genre school in general. It has actively stimulated public debate not just in schools but in the media as well. It has developed a genre-based literacy curriculum and, in the 'tradition' of genre research models, worked hard to refine these in the light of all that had been learnt to date in the trialling process.

# A Glossary of Terms

*Gunther Kress*

**adverbial group:** the part of a clause realising a circumstance of manner, modifying the process; normally realised by a string of one or more adverbs. For example, *fast, very fast, rather too quickly.*

**argument:** the body of an exposition, presenting the evidence in favour of a thesis.

**arguments against:** part of the body of a discussion presenting arguments against the proposition in the issue stage.

**arguments for:** part of the body of a discussion presenting arguments in favour of the proposition in the issue stage.

**attributive process:** a type of being relational process that describes or classifies (they are not reversible). For example, *Flo is fast/ a fast runner.*

**buried reasoning:** the realisation of logical connections inside instead of between clauses; inside the clause they may appear as verbs, nouns or prepositions instead of the conjunctions that are more typical of spoken language. For example, compare the translations of *because* below:
In speaking:
    Cause as a conjunction (two clauses): *Flo won because she trained hard.*
In writing:
    Cause buried as a process (one clause): *Flo's training led to her win.*
    Cause buried as a noun (one clause): *Flo's training was the reason for her win.*
    Cause buried as a proposition (one clause): *Flo's win was because of her training.*

**circumstance:** the part of the clause which specifies location in time or space, manner, cause, accompaniment, matter or role; circumstances are realised by adverbs or prepositional phrases. For example,

*Ben is in the starting blocks.*
*Flo ran very fast.*
*Ben ran because of steroids.*

*Flo won <u>because of steroids</u>.*
*Ben talked <u>about his problems</u>.*
*Flo came <u>as Dracula</u>.*

**clause:** the unit of grammar which weaves together experiential, interpersonal and textual meaning; it is generally built up around a process (expressed by a verb) alongside one, two or three participants and one or more circumstances.

**clause complex:** a combination of clauses related through parataxis (that is, *and, or* and appositional relations) or hypotaxis (that is, dependency relations of time, cause, manner, condition, purpose); a clause complex is punctuated as a sentence in written English and can be referred to as such in the written mode.

**complication:** the second stage of a narrative in which a problem arises which the hero must overcome.

**content words:** the words which express the lexical meaning of the clause (compare function words). For example: *The <u>medal Flo wanted</u> to <u>win</u> most of all was the <u>gold</u> one.*

**context:** the social and cultural setting in which texts occur; within systemic theory this is sometimes broken down into a number of levels, including ideology, genre and register.

**deixis:** the system realised through articles at the beginning of a nominal group which point forward, backward, within or outside the text; realised by *this, these, those* and *the*; sometimes also used to refer to tense in the verbal group, to pointing adverbs (that is *here, there, now, then*) and to 'pointing' pronouns (that is *I, me, my, you, your, we, our, us*).

**description:** the body of a report; it describes the appearance and functions/ habits/uses of the topic of the report.

**doing process:** a process oriented to action by human or non-human participants; the action processes which have to be undertaken by humans are sometimes referred to as *behavioural* and opposed to material processes which can be initiated by human and non-human actors which are referred to as material. For example:

Behavioural: *The woman <u>laughed</u>.*
Material: *The wind <u>blew</u> open the door.*

**evaluation:** a stage between complication and resolution in which the action is suspended so that the characters or the writer can comment on what is going on; evaluation comments may also be found elsewhere in a narrative.

**experiential:** the type of meaning oriented to field; it constructs the people, places, things, qualities and actions of the social world and the interrelationships among them.

**field:** the register variable focusing on what is going on (the social activity), with subject matter as a special instance when texts are describing rather than being part of these activities.

**formal grammar:** the theory of grammar usually associated with Noam Chomsky and linguists influenced by him, which interprets the structure of the clause and its parts in terms of rules which reflect neurological limitations on the kind of structures that human beings are capable of using to make meaning.

**function words:** the words which express the grammatical meaning of the clause, tying content words together (compare content words). For example, *The medal Flo wanted to win most of all was the gold one.*

**general classification:** the opening stage of a report; it is often an attributive relational clause telling which class the topic of the report belongs to. For example, *The whale is a sea mammal.*

**generic participant:** a participant constructed by the grammar as referring to all members of a class. For example, *sprinters, they in What about sprinters? Do they always take steroids?*

**genre:** a type or kind of text, defined in terms of its social purpose; also the level of context dealing with social purpose.

**grammar:** the name of the level of language that maps experiential, interpersonal and textual meaning onto the structure of the clause and its parts.

**hypotaxis:** the name of the relationship between clauses in a clause complex where one clause is dependent on the other (including reporting indirect speech or thought). For example:

> *Even though grammar makes meaning*
> *meaning is realised through grammar too.*

> *The glossary said*
> *that grammar made meaning*

**identifying process:** a type of being relational process that identifies, equates or defines participants (they are always reversible). For example:

> *That one is Ben/*
> *Ben is that one.*

> *The whale is the largest mammal/*
> *The largest mammal is the whale.*

> *Identifying processes are processes that identify, equate or define participants/*
> *Processes that identify/equate or define participants are identifying processes.*

**interpersonal:** the type of meaning oriented to tenor; it constructs the patterns of dialogue, assessments of probability and obligation and attitudes and evaluations of interlocutors.

**intonation:** the tune of a clause. For example, the difference between rising and falling tone to distinguish statement from question.

**issue:** the opening stage of a discussion, presenting the debatable position to be considered from different points of view.

**lexis:** the name for the more specific lexicogrammatical meanings expressed by words rather than grammatical structures. *See also* nominalised lexis and technical lexis.

**logical connectives:** markers of logical relations of time, cause, comparison and addition between clauses and clause complexes. For example:

Temporal: *Ben had a good start and then broke down.*
Causal: *Flo won because she'd trained hard.*
Comparative: *Ben lost his medal. Flo on the other hand kept hers.*
Additive: *Carl lost the race. In addition he lost his pride.*

**meaning process:** a process oriented to the verbal and mental projection of meaning; meaning processes can be used to quote and report and can be divided into verbal processes (processes of communication) and mental processes (process of perception, affection and cognition). For example:

Verbal: *She said she'd come.*
Mental: *She thought he'd leave.*

**modality:** part of the clause's interpersonal meaning, expressing assessment of probability through modal verbs and adverbs. For example, *Perhaps it might be Ben.*

**mode:** the register variable focusing on how the language relates to its context, such as is the text monologic or dialogic? and is it part of what is going on (for example, the talk during football training)? or constitutive of what is going on (for example, a news story on the weekend's fixtures)?

**modulation:** part of the clause's interpersonal meaning, expressing assessments of obligation and inclination through modal verbs and adjectives. For example, *She must go/ She's able to win/ She's keen to come.*

**mood:** the part of the clause's interpersonal meaning which organises the clause as a piece of dialogue, to function as statement, question, command, offer or exclamation. For example:

Statement (declarative): *Flo has just won.*
Question (interrogative): *Has Flo just won? or Who won?*
Command (imperative): *Win.*

Offer (interrogative): <u>*Shall I win then ?*</u>
Exclamation (exclamative): <u>*How easily she won!*</u>

**nominal group:** the part of the clause realising participants or the nominal part of the prepositional phrases (following the preposition); normally a string of one or more nouns, adjective, numerals and articles. For example:

*he*
*Ben Johnson*
*that sprinter*
*the three lovely gold medals*

**nominalised lexis:** noun lexis which codes meanings that typically come out as actions, qualities, assessments or logical connections. For example:

Nominalised action: *assessment* (more typically the verb *assess*)
Nominalised quality: *strength* (more typically the adjective *strong*)
Nominalised assessment: *ability* (more typically the modal verb *can*)
Nominalised logical connection: *reason* (more typically the conjunction *because*)

**orientation:** the opening stage of a narrative, introducing the main characters and setting the story in time and place.

**parataxis:** the name of the relationship between clauses in a clause complex where the clauses have equal status (including quoting direct speech or thought). For example:

*Grammar makes meaning*
*and meaning is realised through grammar.*

*The glossary says,*
*'Grammar makes meaning.'*

**participant:** the people, places and things which can be related experientially to a process without preposition. For example:

| *The grammar* | *gave* | *the text* | *its meaning* |
|---|---|---|---|
| participant | process | participant | participant |
| actor | process | recipient | goal |

*See also* generic participant and specific participant.

**process:** the verbal part of a clause which constructs social reality experientially in terms of doing, meaning or relationships among participants and circumstances. *See also* attributive process, doing process, identifying process, meaning process, relational process.

**process and product:** these represent static and dynamic perspectives (respectively) on the nature of text: seen as process, text is interpreted as unfolding in real time with choices at one point influencing those to come; seen as product, on the other hand, text is interpreted as an object with a part/whole structure reflecting what has been accomplished overall in the context at hand.

**quoted clauses:** clauses projected directly by a mental or verbal process. For example:

> *She asked, 'When are you coming?'*
> *She wondered, 'When is he coming?'*

**reference:** the semantic system realised through articles, pronouns and proper names which tracks and identifies participants throughout a text; typically, the system introduces participants indefinitely (presenting reference) and refers to them definitely once they've been introduced (presuming reference). For example:

> *Presenting: Once upon a time there was a little girl . . .*
> *Presuming: and she was walking to her grandma's house*

**register:** the level of context comprising field, mode and tenor.

**relational process:** a process oriented to types of relationship between participants; these can be divided into being and having processes. For example:

> Being: *The cat is contented/ a mammal/ on the mat.*
> Having: *The cat has whiskers/ kittens.*

**reported clauses:** clauses projected indirectly by a mental or verbal process. For example:

> *She wrote she'd visit*
> *She feared he'd visit*

**resolution:** the stage of a narrative following the complication in which the hero resolves the problem arising in the complication.

**schematic structure:** the distinctive beginning-middle-end structure of a genre, that is, the stages accomplishing a genre's social purpose. The stages may be either obligatory (always present) or optional (present only under certain conditions).

**semantics:** the name of the level of language underlying and more abstract than grammar.

**sentence:** in systemic theory this is the name of a unit of writing, and corresponds to the unit 'clause complex' in spoken language.

**specific participant:** a participant constructed by the grammar as having a specific identifiable referent in the context. For example, *Flo, she, that man over there* in *Flo, she's talking to that man over there.*

**subject:** the part of the clause that inverts with part of the verb to form a question. For example:

>  Statement: *Flo's test was okay.*
>  Question: *Was Flo's test okay?*

**systemic functional grammar:** the theory of grammar developed by M.A.K. Halliday and his colleagues which interprets the structure of the clause with respect to the meanings it makes in text (which is by definition always situated in context).

**taxonomy:** an organisation of people, places or things in classes and subclasses; also sometimes used for their organisation into parts and wholes.

**technical lexis:** lexis that is defined through identifying clauses to build up specific fields; technical lexis goes beyond commonsense understanding to build alternative pictures of the world (for example, all of the lexis being explained in this glossary is technical lexis).

**tenor:** the register variable focusing on interpersonal relationships: status relations, degrees of familiarity and attitudes.

**tense:** the setting in time of the clause from the point of view of the speaker at the time the clause is spoken; the basic choices in English are past, present or future. For example:

>  Past: *Ben won last year.: Oh did he?*
>  Present: *Ben is winning now.: Oh is he?*
>  Future: *Flo will win in Rome.: Oh will she?*

**text:** a unit of meaning which is coherent and appropriate for its context.

**textual:** the type of meaning oriented to mode; it constructs relationships between parts of a text and between that text and the context in which it is situated.

**theme:** in English, the clause parts up to and including the subject, which organise part of the clause's textual meaning. For example, *But unfortunately the test proved positive.*

**thesis:** the opening stage of an exposition, presenting the position to be argued for.

**transitivity:** the system constructing experiential meaning in the clause; it builds relationships among participants, processes and circumstances. For example:

| *Grammar* | *makes* | *meaning* | *in context* |
|---|---|---|---|
| participant | process | participant | circumstance |
| actor | process | goal | circumstance: location |

**verbal group:** the part of the clause realising the process; normally a string of one or more verbs. For example:

*left*
*will be leaving*
*had been trying to get started*

**voice:** the experiential clause system which allows different participants to be realised as subject; the active voice is more common, but the passive voice is used when participants that normally follow the process function better as theme or as subject. For example:

*Active: The coach gave Ben the steroids in the West Indies.*
*Passive: Ben was given the steroids in the West Indies. or The steroids were given to Ben in the West Indies.*

# Bibliography

ANDREWS, R. (ed.) (1989) *Narrative and Argument*, Open University Press, Milton Keynes.

ANG, LEN (1985) *Watching Dallas: Soap Opera and the Melodramatic Imagination*, Methuen, London and New York.

ARONOWITZ, STANLEY and GIROUX, HENRY (1988) 'Schooling, Culture, and Literacy in the Age of Broken Dreams: A Review of Bloom and Hirsch,' *Harvard Educational Review*, 58, 2, 172–94.

ARONOWITZ, STANLEY and GIROUX, HENRY (1991) *Postmodern Education: Politics, Culture and Social Criticism*, University of Minnesota Press, Minneapolis.

ASHCROFT, BILL, GRIFFITHS, GARETH and TIFFIN, HELEN (eds) (1989) *The Empire Writes Back: Theory and Practice in Post-Colonial Literatures*, Methuen, London.

BAKHTIN, M.M. (1968) *Rabelais and His World*, MIT Press, Cambridge, Mass.

BAKHTIN, M.M. (1981) *The Dialogic Imagination: Four Essays*, University of Texas Press, Austin.

BAKHTIN, M.M. (1984) *Problems of Dostoyevsky's Poetics*, Manchester University Press, Manchester.

BAKHTIN, M.M. (1986) *Speech Genres and Other Late Essays*, University of Texas Press, Austin.

BENNETT, WILLIAM (1984) *To Reclaim a Legacy: A Report on the Humanities in Higher Education*, National Endowment for the Humanities, Washington D.C.

BERNSTEIN, BASIL (1971) *Class, Codes and Control, Volume 1: Theoretical Studies towards a Sociology of Language*, Routledge and Kegan Paul, London.

BERNSTEIN, BASIL (1973) *Class, Codes and Control, Volume 2: Applied Studies towards a Sociology of Language*, Routledge and Kegan Paul, London.

BERNSTEIN, BASIL (1975) *Class, Codes and Control Volume 3: Towards a Theory of Educational Transmissions*, Routledge and Kegan Paul, London.

BERNSTEIN, BASIL (1986) 'On Pedagogic Discourse', in J. RICHARDSON (ed.), *Handbook of Theory and Research in the Sociology of Education*, pp. 205–39, Greenwood Press, New York.

BERNSTEIN, BASIL (1990) *The Structuring of Pedagogic Discourse*, Routledge and Kegan Paul, London.

BIELAK, A.T. (1989a) 'Introduction', in A.T. BIELAK (ed.), *Innovative Fisheries Management Initiatives*, Canadian Wildlife Federation, Ottawa.

BIELAK, A.T. (1989b) 'Program Chairman's Synthesis,' in A.T. BIELAK (ed.), *Innovative Fisheries Management Initiatives*, Canadian Wildlife Federation, Ottawa.

BIELAK, A.T. (ed.) (1989c) *Innovative Fisheries Management Initiatives*, Canadian Wildlife Federation, Ottawa.

BLACK, P.J. (1987) *National Curriculum Task Group on Assessment and Testing: A Report*, Department of Education and Science and the Welsh Office, HMSO, London.

BLACKBURN, J. and WATERS, D. (1978) *Basic Skills: Two Views: A Commonwealth Schools Commission Discussion Paper*, Australian Government Publishing Service, Canberra.

BLOM, J.P. and GUMPERZ, JOHN J. (1972) 'Social Meaning in Linguistic Structures: Code Switching in Norway,' in JOHN J. GUMPERZ and DELL HYMES (eds), *Directions in Sociolinguistics: The Ethnography of Communication*, pp. 407–34, Holt, Rinehart and Winston, New York.

BLOOM, ALLAN (1987) *The Closing of the American Mind: How Higher Education Has Failed Democracy and Impoverished the Souls of Today's Students*, Simon and Schuster, New York.

BOOMER, GARTH (1982) *Negotiating the Curriculum*, Ashton, Sydney.

BOWERS, C.A. (1987) *Elements of a Post-Liberal Theory of Education*, Teachers College Press, New York.

BRADLEY, MARION ZIMMER (1978) *The Shattered Chain*, Arrow, London.

BROWN, MARY ELLEN (ed.) (1990) *Television and Women's Culture: The Politics of the Popular*, Currency Press, Sydney.

BRUNER, JEROME (1960) *The Process of Education*, Harvard University Press, Cambridge, Mass. (reprinted 1977).

BUTT, D. (1989) *Living with English: Some Resources on the Smaller Scale*, Literacy Technologies, Sydney.

CAINE, BARBARA, GROSZ, E.A. and DE LEPERVANCHE, MARIE (eds) (1988) *Crossing Boundaries: Feminisms and the Critique of Knowledges*, Allen and Unwin, Sydney.

CALLAGHAN, MICHAEL and ROTHERY, JOAN (1988) *Teaching Factual Writing: A Genre-based Approach*, Metropolitan East Disadvantaged Schools Program, Sydney.

CARTER, ANGELA (1979) *The Bloody Chamber and Other Stories*, Victor Gollancz, London.

CASTLES, STEPHEN, COPE, BILL, KALANTZIS, MARY and MORRISSEY, MICHAEL (1990) *Mistaken Identity: Multiculturalism and the Demise of Nationalism in Australia*, Pluto Press, Sydney and London.

CAZDEN, COURTNEY B. (1988) *Classroom Discourse: The Language of Teaching and Learning*, Heinemann, Portsmouth, N.H.

CERTAU, MICHEL DE (1984) *The Practice of Everyday Life*, University of California Press, Berkeley.

CHARNAS, SUZY MCKEE (1980) *The Vampire Tapestry*, Granada, London.

CHOMSKY, NOAM A. (1965) *Aspects of the Theory of Syntax*, MIT Press, Cambridge, Mass.

CHRISTIE, FRANCES (1976) The Teaching of English in Elementary Schools in New South Wales 1848–1900: An Enquiry into Social Conditions and Pedagogical Theories Determining the Teaching of English, MEd thesis, University of Sydney.

CHRISTIE, FRANCES (1981) The 'Received Tradition' of English Language Study in Schools: The Decline of Rhetoric and the Corruption of Grammar, MA thesis, University of Sydney.

CHRISTIE, FRANCES (1984) 'Young Children's Writing Development: The Relationship of Written Genres to Curriculum Genres,' in B. BARTLETT and J. CARR (eds), pp. 41–69, *Language in Education Conference: A Report of Proceedings*, Brisbane CAE, Mt Gravatt Campus.

CHRISTIE, FRANCES (1986) 'Setting the Context: Language in Education', Paper presented at a conference on ESL in Mainstream Education, Canberra.

CHRISTIE, FRANCES (1987a) 'The Morning News Genre: Using a Functional Grammar to Illuminate Educational Issues,' *Australian Review of Applied Linguistics*, 10, 2.

CHRISTIE, FRANCES (1987b) 'Young Children's Writing: From Spoken to Written Genre,' *Language in Education,* 1, 1, 3–13.

CHRISTIE, FRANCES (1989a) 'Language Development in Education,' in RAQAIYA HASAN and J.R. MARTIN (eds), *Language Development: Learning Language, Learning Culture,* Ablex, Norwood, N.J.

CHRISTIE, FRANCES (1989b) Curriculum Genres in Early Childhood Education: A Case Study in Writing Development, PhD thesis, University of Sydney.

CHRISTIE, FRANCES (ed.) (1989c) *Writing in Schools: B.Ed. Course Reader,* Deakin University Press, Geelong.

CHRISTIE, FRANCES (1990a) 'The Changing Face of Literacy,' in FRANCES CHRISTIE (ed.), *Literacy for a Changing World,* pp. 1–25, Australian Council for Educational Research, Melbourne.

CHRISTIE, FRANCES (1990b) 'The Morning News Genre,' *Language and Education,* 4, 3, 161–79.

CHRISTIE, FRANCES, GRAY, BRIAN, GRAY, PAM, MACKEN, MARY, MARTIN, J.R. and ROTHERY, JOAN (1990a) *Language: A Resource for Meaning. Exploring Reports about Reptiles: Student Book (Level 1),* Harcourt Brace Jovanovich, Sydney.

CHRISTIE, FRANCES, GRAY, BRIAN, GRAY, PAM, MACKEN, MARY, MARTIN, J.R. and ROTHERY, JOAN (1990b) *Language: A Resource for Meaning. Language: A Resource for Meaning. Exploring Reports about Machines: Student Book (Level 2),* Harcourt Brace Jovanovich, Sydney.

CHRISTIE, FRANCES, GRAY, BRIAN, GRAY, PAM, MACKEN, MARY, MARTIN, J.R. and ROTHERY, JOAN (1990c) *Language: A Resource for Meaning. Exploring Reports about Bears: Student Book (Level 3),* Harcourt Brace Jovanovich, Sydney.

CHRISTIE, FRANCES, GRAY, BRIAN, GRAY, PAM, MACKEN, MARY, MARTIN, J.R. and ROTHERY, JOAN (1990d) *Language: A Resource for Meaning. Exploring Reports about Countries: Student Book (Level 4),* Harcourt Brace Jovanovich, Sydney.

CHRISTIE, FRANCES, GRAY, BRIAN, GRAY, PAM, MACKEN, MARY, MARTIN, J.R. and ROTHERY, JOAN (1990e) *Language: A Resource for Meaning. Exploring Reports: Teachers Book (Levels 1–4),* Harcourt Brace Jovanovich, Sydney.

CHRISTIE, FRANCES, GRAY, BRIAN, GRAY, PAM, MACKEN, MARY, MARTIN, J.R. and ROTHERY, JOAN (1990f) *Language: A Resource for Meaning. Exploring Procedures about Magic: Student Book (Level 1),* Harcourt Brace Jovanovich, Sydney.

CHRISTIE, FRANCES, GRAY, BRIAN, GRAY, PAM, MACKEN, MARY, MARTIN, J.R. and ROTHERY, JOAN (1990g) *Language: A Resource for Meaning. Exploring Procedures about Cooking: Student Book (Level 2),* Harcourt Brace Jovanovich, Sydney.

CHRISTIE, FRANCES, GRAY, BRIAN, GRAY, PAM, MACKEN, MARY, MARTIN, J.R. and ROTHERY, JOAN (1990h) *Language: A Resource for Meaning. Exploring Procedures about Paper Making: Student Book (Level 3),* Harcourt Brace Jovanovich, Sydney.

CHRISTIE, FRANCES, GRAY, BRIAN, GRAY, PAM, MACKEN, MARY, MARTIN, J.R. and ROTHERY, JOAN (1990i) *Language: A Resource for Meaning. Exploring Procedures about Experiments: Student Book (Level 4),* Harcourt Brace Jovanovich, Sydney.

CHRISTIE, FRANCES, GRAY, BRIAN, GRAY, PAM, MACKEN, MARY, MARTIN, J.R. and ROTHERY, JOAN (1990j) *Language: A Resource for Meaning. Exploring Procedures: Teachers' Book (Levels 1–4),* Harcourt Brace Jovanovich, Sydney.

CHRISTIE, FRANCES, GRAY, BRIAN, GRAY, PAM, MACKEN, MARY, MARTIN, J.R. and ROTHERY, JOAN (1992a) *Language: A Resource for Meaning. Exploring Explanations about Natural Disasters (Level 1),* Harcourt Brace Jovanovich, Sydney.

CHRISTIE, FRANCES, GRAY, BRIAN, GRAY, PAM, MACKEN, MARY, MARTIN, J.R. and ROTHERY, JOAN (1992b) *Language: A Resource for Meaning. Exploring Explanations about Life Cycles (Level 2),* Harcourt Brace Jovanovich, Sydney.

CHRISTIE, FRANCES, GRAY, BRIAN, GRAY, PAM, MACKEN, MARY, MARTIN, J.R. and ROTHERY, JOAN (1992c) *Language: A Resource for Meaning. Exploring Explanations about Electricity (Level 3),* Harcourt Brace Jovanovich, Sydney.

CHRISTIE, FRANCES, GRAY, BRIAN, GRAY, PAM, MACKEN, MARY, MARTIN, J.R. and ROTHERY, JOAN (1992d) *Language: A Resource for Meaning. Exploring Explanations about Astronomy (Level 4)*, Harcourt Brace Jovanovich, Sydney.

CHRISTIE, FRANCES, GRAY, BRIAN, GRAY, PAM, MACKEN, MARY, MARTIN, J.R. and ROTHERY, JOAN (1992e) *Language: A Resource for Meaning: Exploring Explanations: Teachers' Book (Levels 1–4)*, Harcourt Brace Jovanovich, Sydney.

CHRISTIE, FRANCES, MARTIN, J.R. and ROTHERY, JOAN (1989) 'Genres Make Meaning: Another Reply to Sawyer and Watson', *English in Australia*, 90, 43–59.

COLLERSON, J. (ed.) (1988) *Writing for Life*, Primary English Teaching Association, Sydney.

COLLINS, JAMES and MICHAELS, SARAH (1986) 'Speaking and Writing: Discourse Strategies and the Acquisition of Literacy', in JENNY COOK-GUMPERZ (ed.), *The Social Construction of Literacy*, Cambridge University Press, Cambridge.

COOK-GUMPERZ, JENNY (1986) 'Literacy and Schooling: An Unchanging Equation?' in JENNY COOK-GUMPERZ (ed.), *The Social Construction of Literacy*, pp. 16–44, Cambridge University Press, Cambridge.

COPE, BILL (1986) 'Traditional versus Progressivist Pedagogy', *Social Literacy Monograph No. 11*, Common Ground, Sydney.

COPE, BILL (1987) 'Racism, Popular Culture and Australian Identity in Transition: A Case Study of Change in School Textbooks Since 1945,' in RADHA, RASMUSSEN and ANDREW MARKUS, *Prejudice in the Public Arena: Racism*, pp. 73–92, Centre for Migrant and Intercultural Studies, Monash University, Melbourne, 1987.

COPE, BILL (1987) Losing the Australian Way: The Rise of Multiculturalism and the Crisis of National Identity. A Study of Changing Popular Conceptions of Australian History and the Construction of New Cultural Identities through Schooling, PhD thesis, Macquarie University.

COPE, BILL (1990) 'Facing the Challenge of "Back to Basics": An Historical Perspective', *Curriculum Perspectives*, 10, 2, 20–33.

COPE, BILL (ed.) (1991) *Working with Genre: Papers from the 1989 LERN Conference, University of Technology, Sydney, 25–26 November 1989*, Common Ground, Sydney.

COPE, BILL and KALANTZIS, MARY (1985) 'Pedagogy after Progressivism', *Education Links*, 27, December 1985.

COPE, BILL and KALANTZIS, MARY (1990) 'Cultural Differences and Self-Esteem: Alternative Curriculum Approaches,' in JANE KENWAY and SUE WILLIS (eds), *Hearts and Minds: Self-Esteem and the Schooling of Girls*, Falmer Press, London.

COPE, BILL and KALANTZIS, MARY (1992) 'Contradictions in the Canon: Nationalism and the Cultural Literacy Debate,' *Discourse*, 12, 2, 85–115.

CRANNY-FRANCIS, ANNE (1988a) 'The Moving Image: Film and Television,' in G.R. KRESS (ed.), *Communication and Culture: An Introduction*, pp. 155–180, New South Wales University Press, Sydney.

CRANNY-FRANCIS, ANNE (1988b) 'Gender and Genre: Feminist Rewritings of Detective Fiction,' *Women's Studies International Forum*, 11, 1, 69–84.

CRANNY-FRANCIS, ANNE (1988c) 'Out among the Stars in a Red Shift: Women and Science Fiction,' *Australian Feminist Studies*, 6, 71–86.

CRANNY-FRANCIS, ANNE (1989a) '"Nineteen Eighty-Four in 1984" in 1989: Raymond Williams and George Orwell,' *Southern Review*, 22, 2, 152–62.

CRANNY-FRANCIS, ANNE (1989b) 'Gender and Genre: Breaking the Boundaries,' *Education Australia*, 7, 19–20.

CRANNY-FRANCIS, ANNE (1990a) *Feminist Fiction: Feminist Uses of Generic Fiction*, Polity Press, Cambridge.

CRANNY-FRANCIS, ANNE (1990b) 'Feminist Futures: A Generic Study,' in ANNETTE KUHN (ed.), *Alien Zone: Critical Theory and Contemporary Science Fiction Cinema*, pp. 219–27, Verso, London.

CRANNY-FRANCIS, ANNE (1990c) 'De-fanging the Vampire: S.M. Charnas' "The Vampire Tapestry" as Subversive Horror Fiction,' in BRIAN DOCHERTY (ed.), *American Horror Fiction*, pp. 155–75, Macmillan, London.

CRANNY-FRANCIS, ANNE (1990d) 'Man-made Monsters: The Dystopian Feminist Science Fiction of Suzy McKee Charnas,' in R.J. ELLIS and RHYS GARNETT (eds), *Science Fiction Roots and Branches: Contemporary Critical Approaches*, pp. 183–206, Macmillan, London.

CRANNY-FRANCIS, ANNE (1990e) 'Science Fiction: Myths of Gender and Their Deconstruction,' in *Myth and Ideology: Unit D Surviving Myths*, pp. 65–98, Deakin University Press, Geelong.

CRANNY-FRANCIS, ANNE (1991a) 'Batman: Hollywood and the Postmodern,' *Social Semiotics*, 1, 1.

CRANNY-FRANCIS, ANNE (1991b) 'The Education of Desire: Utopian Fiction and Feminist Fantasy,' in K. FILMER (ed.), *The Victorian Fantasists: Essays on Culture, Society and Belief in the Mythopoeic Fiction of the Victorian Age*, Macmillan, London.

CRANNY-FRANCIS, ANNE (1991c) 'The Value of Genre in English Literature Teaching,' in FRANCES CHRISTIE (ed.), *Teaching Literacy: A Project of National Significance on the Preservice Preparation of Teachers for Teaching English Literacy. Volume 2: Papers*.

CRANNY-FRANCIS, ANNE (1992) *Engendered Fiction*, New South Wales University Press, Sydney.

CRANNY-FRANCIS, ANNE and GILLARD, PATRICIA PALMER (1990) 'Soap Opera as Gender Training: Teenage Girls and TV,' in TERRY THREADGOLD and ANNE CRANNY-FRANCIS (eds), *Feminine/Masculine and Representation*, pp. 171–89, Allen and Unwin, Sydney.

CRANNY-FRANCIS, ANNE and MARTIN, J.R. (1992) 'Contratextuality: The Poetics of Subversion,' in FRANCES CHRISTIE (ed.), *Social Processes in Education: Proceedings of the First Australian Systemic Network Conference, Deakin University, January 1990*, Centre for Studies of Language in Education, Northern Territory University, Darwin.

CRANNY-FRANCIS, ANNE and MARTIN, J.R. (in press) 'In/visible Education: Gender, Class and Pedagogy in *The Dead Poets Society* and *Educating Rita*,' Paper presented at the Australian Systemic Linguistics Conference, Brisbane, January 1991.

CRANNY-FRANCIS, ANNE, LEE, A., MCCORMACK, R. and MARTIN, J.R. (1992) 'Danger — Shark: Assessment and Evaluation of a Student Text,' in FRANCES CHRISTIE (ed.), *Social Processes in Education: Proceedings of the First Australian Systemic Network Conference, Deakin University, January 1990*, Centre for Studies of Language in Education, Northern Territory University, Darwin.

CREED, BARBARA (1984) 'The Women's Romance as Sexual Fantasy: Mills and Boon,' in Women and Labour Publications Collective (eds), *All Her Labours: TWO Embroidering the Framework*, Hale and Iremonger, Sydney.

CUBAN, LARRY (1984) *How Teachers Taught: Constancy and Change in American Classrooms, 1890–1980*, Longman, New York.

DAVIES, A. (ed.) (1969) *Language Testing Symposium*, Oxford University Press.

DAY, MARELE (1988) *The Life and Crimes of Harry Lavender*, Allen and Unwin, Sydney.

DAY, MARELE (1990) *The Case of the Chinese Boxes*, Allen and Unwin, Sydney.

DE LAURETIS, TERESA (1987) *Technologies of Gender: Essays on Theory, Film and Fiction*, Indiana University Press, Bloomington and Indianapolis.

DELPIT, LISA D. (1988) 'The Silenced Dialogue: Power and Pedagogy in Educating Other People's Children,' *Harvard Educational Review*, 58, 3, 280–98.

DEPARTMENT OF EDUCATION AND SCIENCE (1988) *English for Ages 5 to 11*, HMSO, London.

DEREWIANKA, BEVERLEY (1990) *Exploring How Text Works*, Primary English Teaching Association, Sydney.

DEWEY, JOHN (1900a) *The School and Society*, University of Chicago Press, Chicago (reprinted 1956).

DEWEY, JOHN (1900b) *The Child and the Curriculum*, University of Chicago Press, Chicago (reprinted 1956).

DEWEY, JOHN (1916) *Democracy and Education*, The Free Press, New York (reprinted 1966).

DEWEY, JOHN (1938) *Experience and Education*, Macmillan, New York (reprinted 1956).

DEWEY, JOHN and DEWEY, EVELYN (1915) *Schools of Tomorrow*, E.P. Dutton and Company, New York.

DORMAN, SONYA (1978) 'The Child Dreams,' in PAMELA SARGENT (ed.), *Women of Wonder: Science-fiction Stories by Women about Women*, p. 55, Penguin, Harmondsworth.

D'SOUZA, DINESH (1991) *Illiberal Education: The Politics of Race and Sex on Campus*, The Free Press, New York.

DU PLESSIS, RACHEL BLAU (1985) *Writing beyond the Ending: Narrative Strategies of Twentieth-Century Women Writers*, Indiana University Press, Bloomington and Indianapolis.

EGGINS, SUZANNE, WIGNELL, PETER and J.R. MARTIN (1987/1993) *The Discourse of History: Distancing the Recoverable Past. Working Papers in Linguistics 5: Writing Project. Report 1987*, pp. 66–116, Department of Linguistics, University of Sydney; republished in M. GHADESSY (ed.) (1993) *Register Analysis: Theory into Practice*, London, Pinter.

ELIOT, GEORGE (1965) *Middlemarch*, Ed. W.J. Harvey, Penguin, Harmondsworth.

ELLSWORTH, ELIZABETH (1989) 'Why Doesn't This Feel Empowering? Working through the Repressive Myths of Critical Pedagogy,' *Harvard Educational Review*, 59, 3, 297–324.

FIRTH, J.R. (1957) *Papers in Linguistics, 1934–1951*, Oxford University Press, London.

FREIRE, PAULO and MACEDO, DONALDO (1987) *Literacy: Reading the Word and the World*, Bergin and Garvey, South Hadley, Mass.

FRIES, P.H. (1983) 'On the Status of Theme in English: Arguments from Discourse,' in J.S. PETOFI and E. SOZER (eds), *Micro and Macro Connexity of Texts*, pp. 116–52, Helmut Buske Verlag, Hamburg (originally published in *Forum Linguisticum* (1981) 6, 1, 1–38).

GATENS, MOIRA (1983) 'A Critique of the Sex/Gender Distinction,' in JUDITH ALLEN and PAUL PATTON (eds), *Beyond Marxism? Interventions after Marx*, pp. 143–60, Intervention Publications, Sydney.

GATENS, MOIRA (1986) 'Feminism, Philosophy and Riddles Without Answers,' in CAROLE PATEMAN and ELIZABETH GROSZ (eds), *Feminist Challenges: Social and Political Theory*, pp. 13–29, Allen and Unwin, Sydney.

GATENS, MOIRA (1988) 'Towards a Feminist Philosophy of the Body,' in BARBARA CAINE, E.A. GROSZ and MARIE DE LEPERVANCHE (eds), *Crossing Boundaries: Feminism and the Critique of Knowledge*, pp. 59–70, Allen and Unwin, Sydney.

GATENS, MOIRA (1989) 'Woman and Her Double(s): Sex, Gender and Ethics,' *Australian Feminist Studies*, 10, 33–47.

GIBLETT, R. and O'CARROLL, J. (eds) (1990) *Discipline — Dialogue — Difference: Proceedings of the Language in Education Conference, Murdoch University, December 1989*, 4D Duration Publications, School of Humanities, Murdoch University, Perth.

GILBERT, PAM (1989a) *Gender, Literacy and the Classroom*, Australian Reading Association, Carlton.

GILBERT, PAM (1989b) 'Stoning the Romance: Girls as Resistant Readers and Writers,' in FRANCES CHRISTIE (ed.), *Writing in Schools: B.Ed. Course Reader*, pp. 73–80, Deakin University Press, Geelong.

GILBERT, PAM (1989c) *Writing, Schooling and Deconstruction*, Routledge and Kegan Paul, London.

GILBERT, PAM (1990) 'Authorising Disadvantage: Authorship and Creativity in the Language Classroom,' in FRANCES CHRISTIE *et al.*, *Language: A Resource for Meaning*, Harcourt Brace Jovanovich, Sydney.

GILBERT, PAM and LUKE, ALAN (1992) 'Australian Discourses on Literacy,' *Discourse*, 12, 2, 82–111.

GILBERT, PAM and ROWE, K. (1989) *Gender, Literacy and the Classroom*, Australian Reading Association, Melbourne.

GILBERT, PAM and TAYLOR, SANDRA (1991) *Fashioning the Feminine: Girls, Popular Culture and Schooling*, Allen and Unwin, Sydney.

GIROUX, HENRY A. (1988) *Schooling and the Struggle for Public Life: Critical Pedagogy in the Modern Age*, University of Minnesota Press, Minneapolis.

GLEASON, H.A., JR (1965) *Linguistics and English Grammar*, Holt, Rinehart and Winston, New York.

GOODMAN, Ken (1986) *What's Whole in Whole Language?*, Heinemann, Portsmouth, N.H.

GRAFF, HARVEY (1987) *The Legacies of Literacy: Continuities and Contradictions in Western Culture and Society*, Indiana University Press, Bloomington and Indianapolis.

GRAFTON, SUE (1986) *'B' Is for Burglar*, Bantam, Toronto.

GRAFTON, SUE (1987a) *'A' Is for Alibi*, Bantam, Toronto.

GRAFTON, SUE (1987b) *'C' Is for Corpse*, Bantam, Toronto.

GRAFTON, SUE (1988) *'D' Is for Deadbeat*, Bantam, Toronto.

GRAFTON, SUE (1989) *'E' Is for Evidence*, Bantam, Toronto.

GRAFTON, SUE (1991a) *'F' Is for Fugitive*, Pan, London.

GRAFTON, SUE (1991b) *'G' Is for Gumshoe*, Pan, London.

GRAVES, DONALD M. (1983) *Writing: Teachers and Children at Work*, Heinemann Educational Books, Exeter, N.H.

GRAY, BRIAN (1985) 'Helping Children Become Language Learners in the Classroom,' Paper given at the Annual Conference of the Meanjin Reading Council, Brisbane, May 1983, in MICHAEL CHRISTIE (ed.), *Aboriginal Perspectives on Experience and Learning: The Role of Language in Aboriginal Education*, pp. 87–104, Deakin University Press, Geelong.

GRAY, BRIAN (1986) 'Aboriginal Education: Some Implications of Genre for Literacy Development', in CLARE PAINTER and MARTIN, J.R. (eds), *Writing to Mean: Teaching Genres across the Curriculum*, pp. 188–208, Applied Linguistics Association of Australia (Occasional Papers 9).

GRAY, BRIAN (1987) 'How Natural Is "Natural" Language Teaching? Employing Wholistic Methodology in the Classroom,' *Australian Journal of Early Childhood*, 12, 4, 105–39.

GRAY, BRIAN (1990a) 'Natural Language Learning in Aboriginal Classrooms: Reflections on Teaching and Learning,' in C. WALTON and W. EGGINGTON (eds), *Language: Maintenance, Power and Education in Australian Aboriginal Contexts*, pp. 105–39, Northern Territory University Press, Darwin.

GRAY, BRIAN (1990b) 'Successful Negotiation in the Classroom: A Social Process', Paper given at the Annual Australian Reading Association Conference, Canberra, July 1990.

GUMPERZ, JOHN J. (1986) 'Interactional Linguistics and the Study of Schooling,' in JENNY COOK-GUMPERZ (ed.), *The Social Construction of Literacy*, pp. 45–68, Cambridge University Press.

HALLIDAY, M.A.K. (1964) 'Syntax and the Consumer,' in C.I.J.M. STUART (ed.), *Report on the Fifteenth Annual (First International) Round Table Meeting on Linguistics and Language Study* (Monograph Series in Language and Linguistics 17), pp. 11–24, Georgetown University Press, Washington, D.C. (reprinted in part in M.A.K. HALLIDAY and J.R. MARTIN (eds), (1981) *Readings in Systemic Linguistics*, pp. 21–8, Batsford, London).

HALLIDAY, M.A.K. (1971) 'Linguistic Function and Literary Style: An Enquiry into the

Language of William Golding's The Inheritors,' in S. CHATMAN (ed.), *Literary Style: A Symposium*, Oxford University Press, New York.

HALLIDAY, M.A.K. (1973) 'Relevant Models of Language,' in *Explorations in the Functions of Language* (Series: Explorations in Language Study), Edward Arnold, London.

HALLIDAY, M.A.K. (1978a) *Language as Social Semiotic: The Social Interpretation of Language and Meaning*, Edward Arnold, London.

HALLIDAY, M.A.K. (1978b) 'Meaning and the Construction of Reality in Early Childhood,' in HERBERT L. PICK JR. and ELLIOT SALTZMAN (eds), *Modes of Perceiving and Processing Information* (volume based on conferences sponsored by the Committee on Cognitive Research of the Social Science Research Council), pp. 67–96, Lawrence Erlbaum Associates, N.J.

HALLIDAY, M.A.K. (1979a) 'A Grammar for Schools?' in M.A.K. HALLIDAY (ed.), *Working Conference on Language in Education: Report to Participants*, pp. 184–6, Sydney University Extension Programme, Sydney.

HALLIDAY, M.A.K. (1979b) 'Differences between Spoken and Written Language: Some Implications for Literacy Teaching,' in G. PAGE, J. ELKINS and B. O'CONNOR (eds), *Communication through Reading: Proceedings of the Fourth Australian Reading Conference*, Vol. 2, pp. 37–52, Australian Reading Association, Adelaide.

HALLIDAY, M.A.K. (1984) 'Linguistics in the University: The Question of Social Accountability,' in J.E. COPELAND (ed.), *New Directions in Linguistics and Semiotics*, pp. 51–67, Rice University, Houston.

HALLIDAY, M.A.K. (1985a) *An Introduction to Functional Grammar*, Edward Arnold, London.

HALLIDAY, M.A.K. (1985b) *Spoken and Written Language*, Deakin University Press, Geelong (republished by Oxford University Press, 1989).

HALLIDAY, M.A.K. (1985c) 'Systemic Background,' in J.D. BENSON and W.S. GREAVES (eds), *Systemic Perspectives on Discourse Vol. 1: Selected Theoretical Papers from the 9th International Systemic Workshop*, pp. 1–15, Ablex, Norwood, N.J.

HALLIDAY, M.A.K. (1987a) 'Spoken and Written Modes of Meaning,' in R. HOROWITZ and S.J. SAMUELS (eds), *Comprehending Oral and Written Language*, pp. 55–82, Academic Press, New York.

HALLIDAY, M.A.K. (1987b) 'Language and the Order of Nature,' in N. FABB, D. ATTRIDGE, A. DURANT and C. MACCABE (eds), *The Linguistics of Writing: Arguments between Language and Literature*, pp. 135–54, Manchester University Press.

HALLIDAY, M.A.K. (1988) 'On the Language of Physical Science,' in M. GHADESSY (ed.), *Registers of Written English: Situational Factors and Linguistic Features*, pp. 162–78, Pinter, London.

HALLIDAY, M.A.K. (1990) 'Some Grammatical Problems in Scientific English,' *Australian Review of Applied Linguistics*, S:6, 13–37.

HALLIDAY, M.A.K. (in press) *Language and Learning: Linguistic Aspects of Education and Scientific Knowledge*, Singapore University Press.

HALLIDAY, M.A.K. and HASAN, RUQAIYA (1976) *Cohesion in English*, Longman, London.

HALLIDAY, M.A.K. and HASAN, RUQAIYA (1985) *Language, Context and Text: Aspects of Language in a Social Semiotic Perspective*, Deakin University Press, Geelong.

HALLIDAY, M.A.K. and MARTIN, J.R. (1993) *Writing Science: Literacy and Discursive Power*, Falmer Press, London.

HAMBLY, BARBARA (1986) *Dragonsbane*, Unwin, London.

HAMMOND, JENNIFER (1983) *An Examination of the Effect on Children's Writing of the Use of Different Language/Reading Schemes*, Centre for Studies in Literacy, University of Wollongong.

HAMMOND, JENNIFER (1986) 'The Effect of Modelling Reports and Narratives on the Writing of Year 2 Children from Non-English Speaking Backgrounds,' *Australian Review of Applied Linguistics*, 9, 2, 75–93.

HAMMOND, JENNIFER (1987) 'An Overview of the Genre-based Approach to the Teaching of Writing in Australia', *Australian Review of Applied Linguistics*, 10, 2, 163–81.

HAMMOND, JENNIFER (1990) 'Is Learning to Read and Write the Same as Learning to Speak?' in FRANCES CHRISTIE (ed.), *Literacy for a Changing World*, pp. 26–53, Australian Council for Educational Research, Melbourne.

HAMMOND, JENNIFER (1991) 'Oral and Written Language in the Educational Context,' in J. GIBBONS, M.A.K. HALLIDAY and H. NICHOLAS (eds), *Selected Proceedings of the 8th World Congress of Applied Linguistics*, Benjamins, Amsterdam.

HARVEY, D. (1989) *The Condition of Post-Modernity: An Enquiry into the Origins of Cultural Change*, Blackwell, Oxford.

HASAN, RUQAIYA (1973) 'Code, Register and Social Dialect,' in BASIL BERNSTEIN (ed.), *Class, Codes and Control, Volume 2: Applied Studies towards a Sociology of Language*, pp. 253–92, Routledge and Kegan Paul, London.

HASAN, RUQAIYA (1978) 'Text in the Systemic Functional Model,' in W. DRESSLER (ed.), *Current Trends in Text Linguistics*, pp. 230–46, Walter de Gruyter, Berlin.

HASAN, RUQAIYA (1985) 'The Structure of a Text,' in M.A.K. HALLIDAY and RUQAIYA HASAN, *Language, Context, and Text: Aspects of Language in a Social-semiotic Perspective*, Deakin University Press, Geelong.

HASAN, RUQAIYA (1987) 'Reading Picture Reading: Invisible Instruction at Home and in School,' Paper given at the 13th Australian Reading Association Conference, Sydney, 11–14 July 1987.

HASAN, RUQAIYA (1989) 'Semantic Variation and Sociolinguistics,' *Australian Journal of Linguistics*, 9, 2, 221–75.

HASAN, RUQAIYA (1992) 'The Conception of Context in Text,' Mimeo, Macquarie University, Sydney.

HIRSCH, E.D. (1988) *What Every American Needs to Know*, Vintage Books, New York.

HIRSCH, E.D. (1989) *A First Dictionary of Cultural Literacy: What Our Children Need to Know*, Houghton Mifflin, Boston, Mass.

HIRSCH, E.D., KETT, JOSEPH F. and TREFFIL, JAMES (1988) *The Dictionary of Cultural Literacy: What Every American Needs to Know*, Houghton Mifflin, Boston, Mass.

HODGE, ROBERT and KRESS, G.R. (1988) *Social Semiotics*, Priority Press, London.

HUDDLESTON, R.D. (1989) *English Grammar in School Textbooks: Towards a Consistent Linguistic Alternative*, Applied Linguistics Association of Australia (Occasional Papers 11).

JAMESON, FREDRIC (1981) *The Political Unconscious: Narrative as a Socially Symbolic Act*, Methuen, London.

KALANTZIS, MARY (1986) 'Community Languages: Politics or Pedagogy?' *Australian Review of Applied Linguistics*, Series S, No. 2, pp. 168–79.

KALANTZIS, MARY (1988a) 'Aspirations, Participation and Outcomes: From Research to a Curriculum Project for Reform,' in V. FOSTER (ed.), *Including Girls: Curriculum Perspectives on the Education of Girls*, pp. 37–46, Curriculum Development Centre, Canberra.

KALANTZIS, MARY (1988b) 'The Cultural Deconstruction of Racism: Education and Multiculturalism', in MARIE DE LEPERVANCHE and GILLIAN BOTTOMLEY (eds), *The Cultural Construction of Race*, pp. 90–8, Sydney.

KALANTZIS, MARY (1989) 'Ethnicity Meets Class Meets Gender in Australia,' in SOPHIE WATSON (ed.), *Australian Feminist Interventions*, pp. 39–59, Verso, London.

KALANTZIS, MARY and COPE, BILL (1981) *Just Spaghetti and Polka? An Introduction to Australian Multicultural Education*, Multicultural Education Coordinating Committee of NSW, Sydney.

KALANTZIS, MARY and COPE, BILL (1984) 'Multiculturalism and Education Policy,' in GILLIAN BOTTOMLEY and MARIE DE LEPERVANCHE (eds), *Class, Gender and Ethnicity in Australia*, pp. 82–97, Allen and Unwin, Sydney.

KALANTZIS, MARY and COPE, BILL (1987) 'Gender Differences and Cultural Differences: Towards an Inclusive Curriculum,' *Curriculum Perspectives*, 7, 1, 64–8.

KALANTZIS, MARY and COPE, BILL (1988a) *The Fundamentals of Literacy: A Critique of Process Writing and the New South Wales Writing K-12 Syllabus*, Common Ground, Sydney.

KALANTZIS, MARY and COPE, BILL (1988b) 'Why We Need Multicultural Education: A Review of the "Ethnic Disadvantage" Debate', *Journal of Intercultural Studies*, 9, 1, 39–57.

KALANTZIS, MARY and COPE, BILL (1989a) *An Overview: Teaching/Learning Social Literacy*, Common Ground, Sydney.

KALANTZIS, MARY and COPE, BILL (1989b) 'Pluralism and Equitability: Multicultural Curriculum Strategies for Schools,' *Curriculum and Teaching*, 4, 1.

KALANTZIS, MARY and COPE, BILL (1990) 'Literacy in the Social Sciences,' in FRANCES CHRISTIE (ed.), *Literacy for a Changing World*, pp. 118–42, Australian Council for Educational Research, Melbourne.

KALANTZIS, MARY and KRESS, GUNTHER (1989) 'Going Soft on the Basics', *Education Australia*, 5, 17.

KALANTZIS, MARY and WIGNELL, PETER (1988) *Explain, Argue, Discuss: Writing for Essays and Exams*, Common Ground, Sydney.

KALANTZIS, MARY, COPE, BILL and GURNEY, ROBYN (1991) *A Study of Parent Participation in DSP Schools*, Disadvantaged Schools' Program, Metropolitan East Region, NSW Department of Education, Sydney.

KALANTZIS, MARY, COPE, BILL and HUGHES, CHRIS (1984) 'Making Curriculum in Australia,' in D. SIMKIN (ed.), *Curriculum Development in Action*, pp. 159–78, Tressell Publications, Brighton.

KALANTZIS, MARY, COPE, BILL and HUGHES, CHRIS (1985) 'Pluralism and Social Reform: A Review of Multiculturalism in Australian Education,' *Thesis Eleven*, 10, 11, 195–215.

KALANTZIS, MARY, COPE, BILL and HUGHES, CHRIS (1989) 'The Ideology of Multiculturalism', in FAZAL RIZVI (ed.), *Migration, Ethnicity and Multiculturalism: Making Policy for a Polyethnic Society*, pp. 146–50, Deakin University Press, Geelong.

KALANTZIS, MARY, COPE, BILL and NOBLE, GREG (1991) *The Economics of Multicultural Education*, Working Papers on Multiculturalism, Office of Multicultural Affairs, Department of the Prime Minister and Cabinet, Canberra.

KALANTZIS, MARY, COPE, BILL, NOBLE, GREG and POYNTING, SCOTT (1989) *Cultures of Schooling: Pedagogies for Cultural Difference and Social Access*, Australian Advisory Committee on Languages and Multicultural Education, Canberra.

KALANTZIS, MARY, COPE, BILL and SLADE, DIANA (1989) *Minority Languages and Dominant Culture: Issues of Education, Assessment and Social Equity*, Falmer Press, London.

KALANTZIS, MARY, COPE, BILL and WIGNELL, PETER (1992) *The Language of Social Studies: Using Texts of Society and Culture in the Primary School*, Macmillan, Sydney.

KALANTZIS, MARY, SLADE, DIANA and COPE, BILL (1990) 'Minority Languages and Mainstream Culture: Problems of Equity and Assessment,' in JOHN H.A.L. DE JONG and DOUGLAS STEVENSON (eds), *Individualising the Assessment of Language Abilities*, pp. 196–213, Multilingual Matters, Clevedon, England and Philadelphia, Pa.

KEATS, JOHN (1950) 'Ode to a Nightingale,' in WILLIAM FROST (ed.), *Romantic and Victorian Poetry*, Prentice-Hall, Englewood Cliffs, N.J.

KINGMAN, JOHN (1988) *Report of the Committee of Inquiry into the Teaching of the English Language*, Department of Education and Science, HMSO, London.

KNAPP, PETER and KRESS, G.R. (1992) *Genre and Grammar*, Thomas Nelson, Melbourne.

KRESS, G.R. (1982) *Learning to Write*, Routledge and Kegan Paul, London.

KRESS, G.R. (1984) 'Things Children Read and Things Children Write,' in LEN UNSWORTH (ed.), *Proceedings of the Fifth Macarthur Reading/Language Symposium*, MIHE, Sydney.

KRESS, G.R. (1985) *Linguistic Processes in Sociocultural Practice*, Deakin University Press, Geelong.

KRESS, G.R. (1986a) 'Interrelations of Reading and Writing,' in A. WILKINSON (ed.), *The Writing of Writing*, Open University Press, Stony Stratford.

KRESS, G.R. (1986b) 'Language in the Media: The Construction of the Domains of Public and Private,' *Media, Culture and Society*, 8, 4, 395–419.

KRESS, G.R. (1986c) 'Reading, Writing and Power,' in CLARE PAINTER and J.R. MARTIN (eds), *Writing to Learn*, Applied Linguistics Association of Australia, Linguistics Association of Australia, Occasional Papers 9, Melbourne.

KRESS, G.R. (1986d) 'Curriculum Areas and Forms of Writing: Learning What Writing Is Really About,' in R.D. WALSHE and P. and D. JENSEN (eds), *Writing and Learning in Australia*, Oxford University Press, Melbourne.

KRESS, G.R. (1987) 'Genre in a Social Theory of Language,' in IAN REID (ed.), *The Place of Genre in Learning*, Deakin University Press, Geelong.

KRESS, G.R. (ed.) (1988) *Communication and Culture: An Introduction*, New South Wales University Press, Sydney.

KRESS, G.R. (1989a) 'Learning by Reading: Potential Possibilities and Problems,' *LERN Monograph 1*, Common Ground, Sydney.

KRESS, G.R. (1989b) 'Texture as Meaning,' in R. ANDREWS (ed.), *Narrative and Argument*, pp. 9–21, Open University Press, Milton Keynes.

KRESS, G.R. (1990) 'Critical Discourse Analysis,' in W. GRABE (ed.), *Annual Review of Applied Linguistics, Vol. 11*, Cambridge University Press, New York.

KRESS, G.R. (1991) 'The Social Production of Language: History and Structures of Domination,' in P. FRIES and M. GREGORY (eds), *Discourse in Society*, Ablex Publishing, Norwood, N.J.

KRESS, G.R. (1992a) 'English and the Production of a Culture of Innovation: The Case of the LINC Materials,' *English and Media Magazine*, 26, Winter.

KRESS, G.R. (1992b) 'Genre in a Social Theory of Language,' *English in Education*, June edition.

KRESS, G.R. (1992c) *Learning to Write*, rev. ed., Routledge and Kegan Paul, London.

KRESS, G.R. (1992d) 'Participation and Difference: The Role of Language in Producing a Culture of Innovation.' *Discourse*, 12, 2, 82–111.

KRESS, G.R. and HODGE, ROBERT (1979) *Language as Ideology*, Routledge and Kegan Paul, London.

KRESS, G.R. and THREADGOLD, TERRY (1988) 'Towards a Social Theory of Genre,' *Southern Review*, 21, 3, 215–43.

KRESS, G.R. and VAN LEEUVEN, THEO (1990) *Reading Images*, Deakin University Press, Geelong.

KRESS, G.R. and VAN LEEUVEN, THEO (1992) 'Structures of Visual Representation,' *Journal of Literary Semantics*, Winter.

KRESS, G.R., FOWLER, R., HODGE, ROBERT and TREW, T. (1979) *Language and Control*, Routledge and Kegan Paul, London.

LABOV, WILLIAM (1972a) *Language in the Inner City: Studies in the Black English Vernacular*, University of Pennsylvania Press, Philadelphia.

LABOV, WILLIAM (1972b) 'On the Mechanism of Linguistic Change,' in JOHN J. GUMPERZ and DELL HYMES (eds), *Directions in Sociolinguistics: The Ethnography of Communication*, pp. 512–38, Holt, Rinehart and Winston, New York.

LAKOFF, ROBIN TOLMACH (1982) 'Some of My Favorite Writers Are Literate: The Mingling of Oral and Literate Strategies in Written Communication,' in DEBORAH TANNEN (ed.), *Spoken and Written Language: Exploring Orality and Literacy*, pp. 239–60, Ablex Publishing, Norwood, N.J.

LEE, A. and GREEN, B. (1990) 'Staging the Differences: On School Literacy and the Socially-Critical Curriculum,' in R. GIBLETT and J. O'CARROLL (eds), *Discipline — Dialogue — Difference: Proceedings of the Language in Education Conference, Murdoch University, December 1989*, pp. 225–61, 4D Duration Publications, School of Humanities, Murdoch University.

LEE, TANITH (1983) *Red as Blood, Or Tales from the Sisters Grimmer*, Daw, New York.

LEFANU, SARAH (1988) *In the Chinks of the World Machine: Feminism and Science Fiction*, Women's Press, London.

LEGUIN, URSULA K. (1979) *The Language of the Night: Essays on Fantasy and Science Fiction*, Perigee, New York.

LEGUIN, URSULA K. (1980) *The Word for World Is Forest*, Granada, London.

LEGUIN, URSULA K. (1981) *The Left Hand of Darkness*, Futura, London.

LÉVI-STRAUSS, CLAUDE (1966) *The Savage Mind*, University of Chicago Press.

LIEBERMAN, MARCIA (1986) 'Some Day My Prince Will Come: Female Acculturation through the Fairy Tale,' in JACK ZIPES (ed.), *Don't Bet on the Prince: Contemporary Feminist Fairy Tales in North America and England*, pp. 185–200, Gower, Aldershot.

LUKE, ALLEN and GILBERT, PAM (1993) *Literacy in Contexts: Australian Perspectives and Issues*, Allen and Unwin, Sydney.

LURIA, A.R. (1976) *Cognitive Development: Its Cultural and Social Foundations*, Harvard University Press, Cambridge, Mass.

LURIA, A.R. (1981) *Language and Cognition*, Wiley, New York.

LYNN, ELIZABETH (1981) *The Northern Girl*, Berkley, New York.

MACKAY, ALEXANDER (1869) *Facts and Dates*, William Blackwood, Edinburgh.

MACKEN, MARY (1990) 'Language across the Curriculum: A Systematic Approach,' Unpublished paper, Disadvantaged Schools' Program, Metropolitan East Region, NSW Department of Education, Sydney.

MACKEN, MARY and ROTHERY, JOAN (1991a) *Developing Critical Literacy through Systemic Functional Linguistics: A Model for Literacy in Subject Learning*, Disadvantaged Schools' Program, Metropolitan East Region, NSW Department of Education, Sydney.

MACKEN, MARY and ROTHERY, JOAN (1991b) *Developing Critical Literacy through Systemic Functional Linguistics: An Analysis of the Writing Task in a Year 10 Reference Test*, Disadvantaged Schools' Program, Metropolitan East Region, NSW Department of Education, Sydney.

MACKEN, MARY, KALANTZIS, MARY, KRESS, GUNTHER, MARTIN, J.R., COPE, BILL and ROTHERY, JOAN (1989a) *A Genre-Based Approach to Teaching Writing, Years 3–6, Book 1: Introduction*, Directorate of Studies, NSW Department of Education, in association with the Literacy and Education Research Network, Sydney.

MACKEN, MARY, KALANTZIS, MARY, KRESS, GUNTHER, MARTIN, J.R., COPE, BILL and ROTHERY, JOAN (1989b) *A Genre-Based Approach to Teaching Writing, Years 3–6, Book 2: Factual Writing: A Teaching Unit Based on Reports about Sea Mammals*, Directorate of Studies, NSW Department of Education, in association with the Literacy and Education Research Network, Sydney.

MACKEN, MARY, KALANTZIS, MARY, KRESS, GUNTHER, MARTIN, J.R., COPE, BILL and ROTHERY, JOAN (1989c) *A Genre-Based Approach to Teaching Writing, Years 3–6, Book 3. Writing Stories: A Teaching Unit Based on Narratives about Fairy Tales*, Directorate of Studies, NSW Department of Education, in association with the Literacy and Education Research Network, Sydney.

MACKEN, MARY, KALANTZIS, MARY, KRESS, GUNTHER, MARTIN, J.R., COPE, BILL and ROTHERY, JOAN (1989d) *A Genre-Based Approach to Teaching Writing, Years 3–6, Book 4. The Theory and Practice of Genre-Based Writing*, Directorate of Studies, NSW Department of Education, in association with the Literacy and Education Research Network, Sydney.

MCLAREN, PETER L. (1988) 'Culture or Canon? Critical Pedagogy and the Politics of Literacy,' *Harvard Educational Review*, 58, 2, 213–34.

McLaren, Peter L. (1989) *Life in Schools: An Introduction to Critical Pedagogy in the Foundations of Education*, Longman, New York.

McNamara, J. (1989) 'The Writing in Science and History Project: The Research Questions and Implications for Teachers,' in Frances Christie (ed.), *Writing in Schools: Reader*, pp. 24–35, Deakin University Press, Geelong.

Mamouney, Robyn (1990) *Assessing Writing: Assessing Scientific Reports*, Disadvantaged Schools' Program, Metropolitan East Region, NSW Department of Education, Sydney.

Martin, J.R. (1984) 'Types of Writing in Infants and Primary School,' in Len Unsworth (ed.), *Reading, Writing, Spelling: Proceedings of the Fifth Macarthur Reading/Language Symposium*, pp. 34–55, Macarthur Institute of Higher Education, Sydney.

Martin, J.R. (1985) *Factual Writing: Exploring and Challenging Social Reality*, Deakin University Press, Geelong (republished by Oxford University Press, 1989).

Martin, J.R. (1986a) 'Grammaticalising Ecology: The Politics of Baby Seals and Kangaroos,' in Terry Threadgold, E.A. Grosz, G.R. Kress and M.A.K. Halliday (eds), *Language, Semiotics, Ideology*, pp. 225–68, Sydney Association for Studies in Society and Culture (Sydney Studies in Society and Culture 3), Sydney.

Martin, J.R. (1986b) Intervening in the Process of Writing Development,' in Clare Painter and J.R. Martin (eds), *Writing to Mean: Teaching Genres across the Curriculum*, Applied Linguistics Association of Australia, Occasional Papers 9, 11–43.

Martin, J.R. (1986c) 'Prewriting: Oral Models for Written Text,' in R.D. Walshe, P. March and D. Jensen (eds), *Writing and Learning in Australia*, pp. 138–42, Dellasta Books, Melbourne (unabridged version published in *Prospect: The Journal of the Adult Migrant Education Program*, 3, 1 (1987): 75–90).

Martin, J.R. (1987) *Writing Project Report No. 5*, Department of Linguistics, University of Sydney.

Martin, J.R. (1989) 'Technicality and Abstraction: Language for the Creation of Specialised Texts,' in Frances Christie (ed.), *Writing in Schools: Reader*, pp. 36–44, Deakin University Press, Geelong.

Martin, J.R. (1990a) 'Language and Control: Fighting with Words', in C. Walton and W. Eggington (eds), *Language: Maintenance, Power and Education in Australian Aboriginal Contexts*, pp. 12–43, Northern Territory University Press, Darwin.

Martin, J.R. (1990b) 'Literacy in Science: Learning How to Handle Text as Technology,' in Frances Christie (ed.), *Literacy for a Changing World*, pp. 70–117, Australian Council for Educational Research, Melbourne.

Martin, J.R. (1991a) 'Critical Literacy: The Role of a Functional Model of Language', *Australian Journal of Reading*, 14, 2, 117–32.

Martin, J.R. (1991b) *English Text: System and Structure*, Benjamins, Amsterdam.

Martin, J.R. (1991c) 'Intrinsic Functionality: Implications for Contextual Theory', *Social Semiotics*, 1, 1, 99–162.

Martin, J.R. (1991d) 'Nominalisation in Science and Humanities: Distilling Knowledge and Scaffolding Text,' in Eija Ventola (ed.), *Recent Systemic and Other Functional Views on Language*, pp. 307–38, Mouton de Gruyter, Amsterdam.

Martin, J.R. (1992) 'Theme, Method of Development and Existentiality: The Price of Reply', *Occasional Papers in Systemic Linguistics*, 6.

Martin, J.R. (1993) *English Text*, Benjamins, Amsterdam.

Martin, J.R. (in press a) 'Macro-genres: How Do Texts Get Bigger Than a Page?' in Beverley Derewianka and W. Winser (eds), *Language in Education Workshop Papers, December 1990*, University of Wollongong.

Martin, J.R. (in press b) 'Life as a Noun: Arresting the Universe in Science and Humanities,' in M.A.K. Halliday and J.R. Martin, *Writing Science: Literacy as Discursive Power*, Falmer Press, London.

Martin, J.R. and Christie, Frances (1984) *Language Register and Genre in Children's Writing*, Deakin University Press, Geelong.

MARTIN, J.R. and MATTHIESSEN, C.M.I.M. (1990) 'Systemic Typology and Topology,' in FRANCES CHRISTIE (ed.), *Social Processes in Education: Proceedings of the First Australian Systemic Network Conference*, Deakin University, January 1990, Centre for Studies of Language in Education, Northern Territory University, Darwin.

MARTIN, J.R. and ROTHERY, JOAN (1980) *Writing Project Report Number 1*, Working Papers in Linguistics, Department of Linguistics, University of Sydney.

MARTIN, J.R. and ROTHERY, JOAN (1981) *Writing Project Report Number 2*, Working Papers in Linguistics, Department of Linguistics, University of Sydney.

MARTIN, J.R. and ROTHERY, J.R. (1986) *Writing Project Report No. 4*, Department of Linguistics, University of Sydney.

MARTIN, J.R. and ROTHERY, JOAN (1991) *Literacy for a Lifetime — Teachers' Notes*, Film Australia, Sydney.

MARTIN, J.R. and ROTHERY, JOAN (in press) 'Classification and Framing: Double Dealing in Pedagogic Discourse', Paper presented at the the Post-World Reading Congress Symposium on Language in Learning, Brisbane, July 1988.

MARTIN, J.R., CHRISTIE, FRANCES and ROTHERY, JOAN (1987) 'Social Processes in Education: A Reply to Sawyer and Watson (and others),' in I. REID (ed.), *The Place of Genre in Learning: Current Debates*, pp. 46–57. Typereader Publications 1, Geelong (reprinted in *The Teaching of English: Journal of the English Teachers' Association of New South Wales*, 53 (1987): 3–22).

MARTIN, J.R., WIGNELL, PETER, EGGINS, SUZANNE and ROTHERY, JOAN (1988) 'Secret English: Discourse Technology in a Junior Secondary School', in THEO VAN LEEUVEN and L. GEROT (eds), *Language and Socialisation: Home and School*, pp. 143–73, Report of the 1986 Working Conference on Language in Education, School of English and Linguistics, Macquarie University, Sydney.

MARTIN, W.R (1989) 'Innovative Fisheries Management: International Whaling,' in A.T. BIELAK (ed.), *Innovative Fisheries Management Initiatives*, pp. 1–4, Canadian Wildlife Federation, Ottawa.

MATTHIESSEN, C.M.I.M. (1990) *Lexicogrammatical Cartography: English Systems*, Department of Linguistics, University of Sydney.

MATTHIESSEN, C.M.I.M., SLADE, DIANA and MACKEN, MARY (1992) 'Language in Context: A New Model for Evaluating Student Writing,' *Language in Education* (in press).

MAYER, JOHN S. (1990) *Uncommon Sense: Theoretical Practice in Language Education*, Heinemann, Portsmouth, N.H.

MODLESKI, TANIA (1984) *Loving with a Vengeance: Mass-Produced Fantasies for Women*, Methuen, New York and London.

MODLESKI, TANIA (1986) 'Feminism and the Power of Interpretation: Some Critical Readings,' in TERESA DE LAURETIS (ed.), *Feminist Studies/Critical Studies*, pp. 121–38, Indiana University Press, Bloomington and Indianapolis.

MOFFETT, JAMES (1968a) *A Student-Centered Language Arts Curriculum, Grades K-6: A Handbook for Teachers*, Houghton Mifflin, Boston, Mass.

MOFFETT, JAMES (1968b) *Teaching the Universe of Discourse*, Houghton Mifflin, Boston, Mass.

MOI, TORIL (1985) *Sexual/Textual Politics: Feminist Literary Theory*, Methuen, London and New York.

MORRIS, MEAGHAN (1988) *The Pirate's Fiancée: Feminism, Reading, Postmodernism*, Verso, London and New York.

MUNBY, J. (1978) *Communicative Syllabus Design*, Cambridge University Press.

MURRAY, DONALD M. (1982) *Learning by Teaching: Selected Articles on Writing and Teaching*, Boynton/Cook, Montclair, N.J.

MYERS, G. (1990) *Writing Biology*, University of Wisconsin Press, Madison.

NEW SOUTH WALES DEPARTMENT OF SCHOOL EDUCATION (1987) *Writing K-12*, NSW Department of Education, Sydney.

New South Wales Department of School Education (1989a) *The Discussion Genre*, Disadvantaged Schools' Program, Metropolitan East Region, NSW Department of Education, Sydney.

New South Wales Department of School Education (1989b) *The Report Genre*, Disadvantaged Schools' Program, Metropolitan East Region, NSW Department of Education, Sydney.

New South Wales Department of School Education (1990) *Assessing Writing: Scientific Reports*, Disadvantaged Schools' Program, Metropolitan East Region, NSW Department of Education, Sydney.

New South Wales Department of School Education (1991) *The Recount Genre*, Disadvantaged Schools' Program, Metropolitan East Region, NSW Department of Education, Sydney.

Ong, Walter J. (1982) *Orality and Literacy: The Technologizing of the Word*, Methuen, London.

Ong, Walter J. (1983) *Ramus, Method and the Decay of Dialogue*, Harvard University Press, Cambridge Mass.

Painter, Clare (1986) 'The Role of Interaction in Learning to Speak and Learning to Write,' in Clare Painter and J.R. Martin (eds), *Writing to Mean: Teaching Genres across the Curriculum*, pp. 62–97, Applied Linguistics Association of Australia, Occasional Papers 9.

Painter, Clare and Martin, J.R. (eds) (1986) *Writing to Mean: Teaching Genres across the Curriculum*, Applied Linguistics Association of Australia, Occasional Papers 9.

Palmer, A.S. and Bachman, C.F. (1981) 'Basic Exams in Test Validation,' in J.C. Alderson and A. Hughes (eds), *Issues in Language Testing*, ELT Documents, British Council, London.

Paretsky, Sara (1985a) *Deadlock*, Ballantine, New York.

Paretsky, Sara (1985b) *Killing Orders*, Penguin, Harmondsworth.

Paretsky, Sara (1987) *Indemnity Only*, Penguin, Harmondsworth.

Paretsky, Sara (1988a) *Bitter Medicine*, Penguin, Harmondsworth.

Paretsky, Sara (1988b) *Blood Shot*, Dell, New York (also known as *Toxic Shock*).

Paretsky, Sara (1990) *Burn Marks*, Chatto and Windus, London.

Pateman, Carole and Gross, Elizabeth (eds) (1986) *Feminist Challenges: Social and Political Theory*, Allen and Unwin, Sydney.

Piercy, Marge (1979) *Woman on the Edge of Time*, Women's Press, London.

Plum, Guenter (1988) Text and Contextual Conditioning in Spoken English, PhD thesis, University of Sydney.

Poynton, Cate (1985) *Language and Gender: Making the Difference*, Deakin University Press, Geelong (republished Oxford University Press, 1989).

Poynton, Cate (1990a) Address and the Semiotics of Social Relations: A Systemic-functional Account of Address Forms and Practices in Australian English, PhD thesis, Department of Linguistics, University of Sydney.

Poynton, Cate (1990b) 'The Privileging of Representation and the Marginalising of the Interpersonal: A Metaphor (and More) for Contemporary Gender Relations,' in Terry Threadgold and Anne Cranny-Francis (eds), *Feminine/Masculine and Representation*, pp. 231–55, Allen and Unwin, Sydney.

Radford, A. (1981) *Transformational Syntax: A Student's Guide to Chomsky's Extended Standard Theory*, Cambridge University Press.

Radway, Janice A. (1984) *Reading the Romance: Women, Patriarchy, and Popular Culture*, Chapel Hill, London.

Radway, Janice A. (ed.) (1986) *The Progress of Romance: The Politics of Popular Fiction*, Routledge and Kegan Paul, London.

Ravitch, Diane and Finn, Chester (1988) *What Do Our 17 Year-Olds Know?* Harper and Row, New York.

REID, I. (ed.) (1987) *The Place of Genre in Learning: Current Debates*, Centre for Studies in Literary Education, Deakin University Press, Geelong.

RIGG, PAT and KAZEMEK, FRANCIS E. (1985) '23 Million Illiterates? By Whose Definition?' *Journal of Reading*.

ROSE, DAVID, MCINNES, DAVID and KORNER, HENRIKE (1992) *Literacy in Industry Research Project: Stage 1 — Scientific Literacy*, Disadvantaged Schools Program, Metropolitan East Region, NSW Department of Education, Sydney.

ROTHERY, JOAN (1986) 'Teaching Genre in the Primary School: A Genre-based Approach to the Development of Writing Abilities', *Writing Project — Report 1986*, Working Papers in Linguistics 4, pp. 3–62, Department of Linguistics, University of Sydney.

ROTHERY, JOAN (1989a) 'Exploring the Written Mode and the Range of Factual Genres', in FRANCES CHRISTIE (ed.), *Writing in Schools: Study Guide*, pp. 49–90, Deakin University Press, Geelong.

ROTHERY, JOAN (1989b) 'Learning about Language,' in RUQAIYA HASAN and J.R. MARTIN (eds), *Language Development: Learning Language, Learning Culture*, pp. 199–256, Ablex Publishing, Norwood, N.J.

ROTHERY, JOAN (1990) Story Writing in Primary School: Assessing Narrative Type Genres, PhD thesis, Department of Linguistics, University of Sydney.

RUSS, JOANNA (1973) 'Somebody's Trying to Kill Me and I Think It's My Husband: The Modern Gothic,' *Journal of Popular Culture*, 6, 4, 666–91.

RUSS, JOANNA (1984) *How to Suppress Women's Writing*, Women's Press, London.

RUSS, JOANNA (1985) *The Female Man*, Women's Press, London.

SARGENT, PAMELA (1978) 'Introduction: Women in Science Fiction,' in PAMELA SARGENT (ed.), *Women of Wonder: Science-Fiction Stories by Women about Women*, pp. 11–51, Penguin, Harmondsworth.

SCRIBNER, SYLVIA and COLE, MICHAEL (1981) *The Psychology of Literacy*, Harvard University Press, Cambridge, Mass.

SHEA, N. (1988) The Language of Junior Secondary Science Textbooks, BA Hons thesis, Department of Linguistics, University of Sydney.

SHOWALTER, ELAINE (ed.) (1986) *The New Feminist Criticism: Essays on Women, Literature, and Theory*, Virago, London.

STEEDMAN, CAROLYN (1986) *Landscape for a Good Woman: A Story of Two Lives*, Virago, London.

SWALES, JOHN M. (1990) *Genre Analysis: English in Academic and Research Settings*, Cambridge University Press.

SWAN, WILLIAM D. (1844) *The Grammar School Reader; Consisting of Selections in Prose and Poetry, with Exercises in Articulation; Designed to Follow the Primary School Reader, Part Third*, Improved Edition, Thomas, Cowperthwait and Co., Philadelphia.

TANNEN, DEBORAH (1982) 'The Oral/Literate Continuum in Discourse,' in DEBORAH TANNEN (ed.), *Spoken and Written Language: Exploring Orality and Literacy*, pp. 1–16, Ablex Publishing, Norwood, N.J.

THIBAULT, PAUL (1989) 'Genres, Social Action and Pedagogy: Towards a Critical Social Semiotic Account', *Southern Review*, 22, 3, 338–62.

THREADGOLD, TERRY (1988) 'The Genre Debate', *Southern Review*, 21, 3, 315–30.

THREADGOLD, TERRY (1989) 'Talking about Genre: Ideologies and Incompatible Discourses,' *Cultural Studies*, 3, 1, 101–27.

THREADGOLD, TERRY and ANNE CRANNY-FRANCIS (1990) *Feminine/Masculine and Representation*, Allen and Unwin, Sydney.

THURSTON, CAROL (1987) *The Romance Revolution: Erotic Novels for Women and the Quest for a New Sexual Identity*, University of Illinois Press, Urbana and Chicago.

TIPTREE, JAMES, JR (1975) *Warm Worlds and Otherwise*, Ballantine, New York.

TIPTREE, JAMES, JR (1976) 'Houston, Houston, Do You Read?' in SUSAN ANDERSON and VONDA MCINTYRE (eds), *Aurora: Beyond Equality*, Fawcett, New York.

TIPTREE, JAMES, JR (1981) *Out of the Everywhere, and Other Extraordinary Visions*, Ballantine, New York.

TODOROV, TZEVETAN (1984) *Mikhail Bakhtin: The Dialogical Principle*, Manchester University Press.

VENTOLA, EIJA (1987) *The Structure of Social Interaction: A Systemic Approach to the Semiotics of Service Encounters*, Francis Pinter, London.

VOIRST, JUDITH (1976) '. . . And Then the Prince Knelt Down and Tried to Put the Glass Slipper on Cinderella's Foot,' in JACK ZIPES (ed.), *Don't Bet on the Prince: Contemporary Feminist Fairy Tales in North America and England*, Gower, Aldershot.

VONNEGUT, KURT, JR (1976) *Wampeters Foma and Granfalloons*, Panther, London.

VYGOTSKY, L.S. (1962) *Thought and Language*, MIT Press, Cambridge, Mass.

VYGOTSKY, L.S. (1978) *Mind in Society: The Development of Higher Psychological Processes*, Harvard University Press, Cambridge, Mass.

WALKER, R.F. (1981) *Report on the English Spoken by Aboriginal Entrants to Traeger Park School*, Curriculum Development Centre, Occasional Paper 11, Canberra.

WALKERDINE, VALERIE (1989) *Counting Girls Out*, Virago, London.

WALKERDINE, VALERIE and LUCY, HELEN (1989) *Democracy in the Kitchen: Regulating Mothers and Socialising Daughters*, Virago, London.

WALSH, JOHN, HAMMOND, JENNIFER, BRINDLEY, GEOFF and NUNAN, DAVID (1990) *Metropolitan East Disadvantaged Schools Program: Factual Writing Project Evaluation*, National Centre for English Language Teaching and Research, Macquarie University, Sydney.

WHITE, J. (1986) 'The Writing on the Wall: The Beginning or End of a Girl's Career?' *Women's Studies International Forum*, 9, 5, 561–74 (republished in F. CHRISTIE (ed.), *Writing in Schools: Reader*, pp. 61–72, Deakin University Press, Geelong).

WHITE, J. (1990) 'On Literacy and Gender,' in FRANCES CHRISTIE (ed.), *Literacy for a Changing World*, pp. 143–66, Australian Council for Educational Research, Melbourne.

WIGNELL, PETER (1988) The *Language of Social Literacy: A Linguistic Analysis of the Materials in Action in Years 7 and 8*, Common Ground, Sydney.

WIGNELL, PETER, MARTIN, J.R. and EGGINS, SUZANNE (1987) 'The Discourse of Geography, Ordering and Explaining the Experiential World,' *Working Papers in Linguistics No. 5*, Linguistics Department, University of Sydney (republished in *Linguistics and Education*, 1, 4 (1990): 359–92).

WILLIAMS, G. (1990) 'Variation in Home Reading Contexts', Paper given at the 16th Conference of the Australian Reading Association, Canberra, July 1991.

WILLIAMS, G. (1991) 'Framing literacy', Paper given at the Second Australian Systemic Linguistics Conference, University of Brisbane, January 1991.

WILLIS, PAUL E. (1977) *Learning to Labour: How Working Class Kids Get Working Class Jobs*, Gower, London.

WORDSWORTH, WILLIAM (1950) 'I Wandered Lonely as a Cloud . . .', in WILLIAM FROST (ed.), *Romantic and Victorian Poetry*, Prentice-Hall, Englewood Cliffs, N.J.

ZIPES, JACK (1979) *Breaking the Magic Spell: Radical Theories of Folk and Fairy Tales*, Heinemann, London.

ZIPES, JACK (1983) *The Trials and Tribulations of Little Red Riding Hood: Versions of the Tale in Sociocultural Context*, Heinemann, London.

ZIPES, JACK (1986) *Don't Bet on the Prince: Contemporary Feminist Fairy Tales in North America and England*, Gower, Aldershot.

# Notes on Contributors

**Mike Callaghan**, a founder member of LERN, first became involved in genre research while working as the literacy consultant with the Disadvantaged Schools Program for the New South Wales Department of School Education. He coordinated, co-wrote and trialled the Language and Social Power Project — the project which first introduced a genre-based literacy program in Australian schools. As co-author (with Joan Rothery) of *Teaching Factual Writing: A Genre-based Approach*, he helped develop the teaching-learning strategy now known as the curriculum cycle, to translate genre theory into a workable pedagogy.

**Frances Christie** is Foundation Professor of Education and Director of the Centre for Studies of Language in Education at the Northern Territory University, Darwin. She has well established interests in the study of language in education, and has researched the development of both oral language and of literacy in classrooms. Some years ago she worked at the Commonwealth Curriculum Development Centre, Canberra, where she had a major responsibility for the national Language Development Project. In 1990–91 she was awarded a grant from the Commonwealth Department of Employment, Education and Training to undertake a Project of National Significance to investigate the preservice preparation of teachers to teach English literacy. Together with the research team she created, Frances Christie produced the report, *Teaching English Literacy: A Project of National Significance on the Preservice Preparation of Teachers to Teach English Literacy.*

**Bill Cope** first became involved in the areas of literacy and pedagogy as Project Officer for the Social Literacy Project in 1979. Since then he has published widely in the fields of literacy education, communication and culture. A founding member of the Literacy in Education Research Network (LERN), the editor of the LERN conference papers, and a consultant for the LERN Project, he has actively worked towards introducing the ideas of genre theory to a widening audience. He is currently Senior Research Fellow at the Centre for Workplace Communication and Culture at the University of Technology, Sydney, and managing editor of *Education Australia.*

**Anne Cranny-Francis** is Senior Lecturer in Cultural Studies at the University of Wollongong and co-editor of the journal, *Social Semiotics.* She has published widely in the areas of feminist and critical theory, popular fiction and film, contemporary feminist writing, and nineteenth century literature. Her latest book, *Engendered Fiction*, is a study of the many ways in which gender issues influence textual production and reception. As a founder member of LERN, she was involved in introducing genre research to a national audience. She is currently writing a monograph on popular culture for Frances Christie's Deakin series, and a monograph on textual realisations of the contemporary theoretical work on 'the body'.

**Mary Kalantzis** is Director of the Centre for Workplace Communication and Culture at the University of Technology, Sydney, which has been set up to provide both research and counsel in the areas of cross-cultural communication and managing cultural diversity in the workplace. She is currently a Member of the Australia Council's Multicultural Advisory Committee and its Community Cultural Development Committee, as well as being the founding editor of *Education Australia* and advisory editor for the *Australian Journal of Education*. As a founder member of the LERN group and as coordinator and writer with the Social Literacy Project since 1979, she has an extensive expertise in the area of literacy pedagogy.

**Peter Knapp** is an independent researcher, writer, film and video maker. A founding member of the LERN group, he was also involved in writing and trialling the Language and Social Power Project for the Disadvantaged Schools Program. He is currently working on a book with Gunther Kress and producing a teacher training package on literacy and learning across the curriculum in the junior secondary school for the New South Wales Department of School Education.

**Gunther Kress**, who is Professor of Education at the Institute of Education, University of London, has written widely on questions of literacy from the standpoint of a social theory of language, in the broad framework of critical discourse analysis and social semiotics. As a founding member of the LERN group, and as co-author (with Robert Hodge) of *Learning to Write*, he has been actively involved in introducing genre theory to an international audience. He is currently working on a book with Peter Knapp, *Genre and Grammar*, to be published by Thomas Nelson. More recently he has become interested in questions of visual communication, and in the increasing prominence of visual forms of communication.

**Mary Macken** first worked as an English teacher in Sydney's inner-city secondary schools in 1979. She specialised in teaching students from non-English-speaking backgrounds and became increasingly aware of the invisibility of language in pedagogies operating at that time. Her later work with Aboriginal students in remote areas of the Northern Territory led to an interest in educational linguistics and its applications to curriculum development. In 1988 she began developing genre-based materials for primary teachers in collaboration with LERN and has since continued this work in secondary education. She is currently working on a doctorate about critical literacy for secondary students.

**J.R. Martin** is Associate Professor of Linguistics at the University of Sydney. A founder member of LERN, he has long been involved in genre research; his research interests include systemic theory, functional grammar, discourse analysis, register, genre and ideology, focusing on English and Tagalog, with special reference to the interdisciplinary fields of educational linguistics and social semiotics. He is currently a consultant with the Disadvantaged Schools' Program's Write It Right Project and has been widely involved in developing a genre-based literacy pedagogy.

**Lorraine Murphy** has worked with Bill Cope and Mary Kalantzis as a researcher and writer on the Social Literacy Project since 1980. She is currently working for the Centre for Workplace Communication and Culture as a researcher and subeditor.

**Joan Rothery**, a founder member of LERN, is currently working on the Disadvantaged Schools' Program's Write It Right Project. Her main research interest is to develop a genre-based literacy pedagogy and to this end she has worked on both the Language and Social Power Project and the LERN Project.

**Diana Slade**, as Associate Director of the Centre for Workplace Communication and Culture, is currently involved in developing language and literacy research and training projects in industry. She has had extensive previous experience in the designing and teaching of adult programs, and teaching English language and communication skills to people from non-English speaking backgrounds. As a founding member of LERN, and as a lecturer in the Department of Linguistics at the University of Sydney from 1985 to 1989, she has been involved in the development of genre research for a number of years. She is currently working on a doctorate on teaching casual conversation at the University of Sydney.

# Index